Through the Year with George MacDonald

366 Daily Readings
Rolland Hein, Editor

Through The Year With George MacDonald:
366 Daily Readings

Copyright © 2012 Rolland Hein

Winged Lion Press
Hamden, CT

All rights reserved. Except in the case of quotations embodied in critical articles or reviews, no part of this book may be reproduced or transmitted in any form or by any means, electronic or mechanical, including photocopying, recording, or by any information storage or retrieval system, without written permission of the publisher.
For information, contact Winged Lion Press www.WingedLionPress.com

Winged Lion Press titles may be purchased for business or promotional use or special sales.

10-9-8-7-6-5-4-3-2-1

WINGED LION PRESS

ISBN-13 978-1-935688-02-0

"Traveler, what lies over the hill?"

"My child, a valley green lies there,
  Lovely with trees, and sky;
And a tiny brook that says, 'Take care,
  Or I'll drown you by and by!'

"Is it far away?"– "I do not know:
  You must fix your eyes thereon,
And travel, travel through thunder and snow,
  Till the weary way is gone."

"But, oh! I have not told you the best,
  I have not told you the end;
If you want to escape, away in the west
  You will see a stair ascend,

"Built of all colors of lovely stones,
  A stair up into the sky
Where no one is weary, and no one moans,
  Or wishes to be laid by."

"Is the stair right up? is it very steep?"
  "Too steep for you to climb;
You must lie at the foot of the glorious heap
  And patient wait your time."

"Pilgrims from near and from distant lands
  Will step on you lying there;
But a wayfaring man with wounded hands
  Will carry you up the stair."

– George MacDonald

ACKNOWLEDGEMENTS

I would like to express appreciation to Douglas Gresham, for kindly writing a Foreword; to Barbara Amell, whose tireless research uncovered the sermon "The Unexpected Guest"; to Todd Kelsey for his encouragement and his work with computer logistics; to Marjorie Lamp Mead and Monika Hilder for their commendations; to Robert Trexler for his careful handling of design and formatting; to Chris Mitchell and the staff at the Wade Center for providing a home and support for my ongoing lecture series on C. S. Lewis, George MacDonald, Charles Williams, and other authors; and to my many students who have reinforced my sense of the worth of MacDonald's writings. The poem on the previous page is my cutting of George MacDonald's much longer poem, "Tell Me."

CONTENTS

Foreword	Douglas Gresham
Introduction	Rolland Hein
Daily Readings	January through December
Appendix 1	Titles of Daily Readings by Month
Appendix 2	Alphabetical List of Scripture Selections
Appendix 3	Supporting Scripture Passages by Month
	About the Author
	Other Books of Interest

This caricature by Frederick Waddy appeared in "Once a Week" magazine apropo of George MacDonald's editorship (1869-1872) of "Good Works for the Young."

FOREWORD

George MacDonald's writings have fascinated me ever since my stepfather (C.S. Lewis) introduced me to them in the early 1950s. Possibly one of the greatest writers of instructional fiction of all time, MacDonald's works are often overlooked in today's strange world of superficial immediacy, despite the huge influence this Scottish author had on the culture of his own time and the years that followed it. We need his wisdom and the beauty of his words now more than ever before.

At the very least, I hope this book will whet your appetite for MacDonald's amazingly beautiful stories and perhaps even stimulate a deep longing to read more of his work. The list of George MacDonald's friends and acquaintances reads almost like a "Who's Who" of the literary luminaries of the 19th century. The list of 20th century writers he has influenced includes many of the greatest, my stepfather among them. Jack (C.S. Lewis) wrote that he had never written anything that was not strongly influenced by MacDonald, adding that reading his book *Phantastes*, "baptised my imagination".

MacDonald writes from a depth of wisdom and of joy that is rare among men and is only found in perhaps one man in each century. Short selected daily readings from the work of this astonishingly loving author must be one of the very best ways to begin each day. If we spend our first few minutes of the day with George MacDonald, we will find love, joy, comfort, excitement, beauty and delight.

Most importantly, we will find ourselves, for that is what MacDonald's works show us best. In reading MacDonald at length, we discover who we are and are enabled to compare that which we find with whom we wish to be and whom we ought to be, making realisations which allow us to correct our lives and to begin to attain our deepest longings.

There have been many books of daily readings from many writers, but I can think of none that I would prefer than those of C.S. Lewis or George MacDonald. For anyone who respects C.S. Lewis' works, we must pay an equal tribute to George MacDonald, for he was the forerunner and tutor of Jack as he himself openly and gladly admitted.

Douglas Gresham

INTRODUCTION

The fuller thought of this godly nineteenth century Scotsman is only slightly known to many who have become fascinated with his fairy tales, or who have seen statements as to how highly influential he was both in precipitating C. S. Lewis's conversion and also in shaping his Christian thought. The purpose of this collection is first to provide a handy tool for furthering knowledge of his thinking and his character, and, second, to offer a devotional calendar for people who may desire a guide for daily meditation.

George MacDonald wrote in his novel *The Marquis of Lossie*: "Life and religion are one, or neither is anything. . . . Religion is no way of life, no show of life, no observance of any sort . . . . It is life essential. The man to whom virtue is but the ornament of character, something over and above, not essential to it, is not yet a man." One cannot read far in his writings without realizing how thoroughly he held this conviction. He had a disdain for any abstract theological thought that was not integrally related to the everyday dimensions of life. The omnipresent Spirit of God works relentlessly, if needs be through suffering and adversity, to perfect the image of Christ in everyone, though the task require eons of time for its fulfillment.

A profound student of Scripture with a careful knowledge of the Greek text, MacDonald from an early age became enamored of the person of Christ as the gospels present him. He saw in the intimacy of Christ's relation with the Father and in the range of Christ's attitudes toward life the model for each individual's success in this lifetime and for their eternal joy in the life to come. Any life consumed simply with the quest for satisfaction of its self-centered ambitions and sensual desires results in the diminishment of one's very being here, and the unspeakable agonies of unsatiated desires in the next, as the soul must face the full consequences of its moral turpitude.

MacDonald's thinking was shaped in the main by several elements. First, losing his mother as a child of eight, he developed a close relationship with his stern but loving father, a godly man who undertook to be both father and mother to his children, instilling within them both a love for the stories of the Bible and the rich tradition of Celtic and Gaelic fairy lore. This model father impressed upon his son the beauty of ideal fatherhood that affected all of MacDonald's future thinking. Second, his religious upbringing was shaped by the tenets of an abstract and atrophied Calvinist theology, from which as a mature thinker he retained what was biblically sound and vehemently rejected all that he felt offered insult to the nature of God and to humanity. All people are created by, and in the image of, the God of love, and God will do his best for each one. Third, as an aspiring student at King's College, Aberdeen, he encountered the writing of then rather recent German poets and authors of fantasy, writers who fired his fertile imagination and gave him a vision of the ideal life as a quest for fullness of being. Fourth, during his years of seminary training he was deeply affected by the theological lectures of A. J. Scott, who later became president of Owens College, Manchester. Fifth, the character and deportment of F. D. Maurice, vicar of the Chapel of St. Peter's in London where the MacDonald's worshiped, was to MacDonald the highest embodiment of the Christian ideal.

His creative efforts are at their best in his fairy tales, his fantasies for youth, and his fantasies for adults. *The Golden Key, The Light Princess,* and *The Carasoyn* illustrate well the first category; *The Princess and the Goblin, The Princess and Curdie,* and *At the Back of the North Wind* the second; and *Phantastes and Lilith* the third. Because these texts, fine as they are, do not lend themselves well to the approach of this anthology, only a handful of selections are taken from them.

His novels compose the great proportion of his creative work, and excerpts from several are here included. Immensely popular in his own day, his stories compare well with such contemporary efforts as George Eliot's *Scenes from Clerical Life* and *Adam Bede,* or with Anthony Trollope's Barchester novels. Although lapsing occasionally into Gothic conventions, he tells a good story, convincingly portraying commonplace life and human psychology. This collection includes several of his running commentaries on character and action. They illustrate with what penetrating insights he understood the spiritual psychology of different character types, and how astutely he applied Christian thought to everyday situations.

The largest number of selections here presented are chosen from his expository efforts: the three volumes of *Unspoken Sermons, The Hope of the Gospel,* and *Miracles.* It is principally in them that the reader encounters his provocative handling of spiritual truths, enabling one to see the consistency and depth of his thought, and the pattern of the whole. The Scripture passages listed at the conclusion of each selection are intended to suggest how thoroughly MacDonald's thought is in harmony with the spirit of the biblical text.

Rolland Hein

BECOMING TEN TIMES A MAN   JANUARY 1

These excerpts are from Henry W. Bellow's paraphrase of a sermon George MacDonald gave in New York at the Church of all Souls on May 11, 1873.

We are here in this world isolated and displaced, having come we know not whence and going we know not whither. We did not place ourselves here and were not consulted about our existence. Besides, we are full of the inheritance of transmitted unruly appetites and bad passions. Yet we have also a sense of truth and goodness that makes us pant for an excellence we find ourselves unable to attain. We look about for help, and find only other souls and lives spotted and stained like our own. . . .

Now, long ago there came a man into the world who, in the most solemn and searching way, declared that he understood the whole situation and had found the key to the whole problem of human existence. We have the tradition and record of his words and life. But, alas! He lived nearly two thousand years ago, and men dispute the authority and authenticity of the books that record His life and words, and nothing can be demonstrated as to their genuineness any more than God's existence can be proved. But he said: "If any man shall do his will he shall know of the doctrine." And thousands, nay, millions, have accepted this invitation, and from moral and spiritual sympathy trusted His words, and have gone to Him as he appears in the New Testament, and have found everything he said to be true, so far as to discover that active and thorough obedience to His precepts has brought them into right relations with themselves, with each other and with God. . . .

Let a man, then stir himself up to know Christ, and God through Christ. Nobody can do this work but him. All the pulpits and creeds and churches cannot help him if he does not help himself. It is only by the exercise of his own spiritual faculties, the strain of his own *will* that he can achieve emancipation and put himself into harmonious relations with Christ and God. When a man says "I will" he becomes ten times a man. He changes from an impulse into a free chooser of a divine way. And once in the right way, once in the obedience and right with God through it, all things in the soul and in the universe tend to right themselves—the jargon tends to significant speech, the discord to music, life into order and harmony. . .

"George MacDonald in the Pulpit,"
Spoken Sermons, Barbara Amell, ed.
Matt. 11:25-30

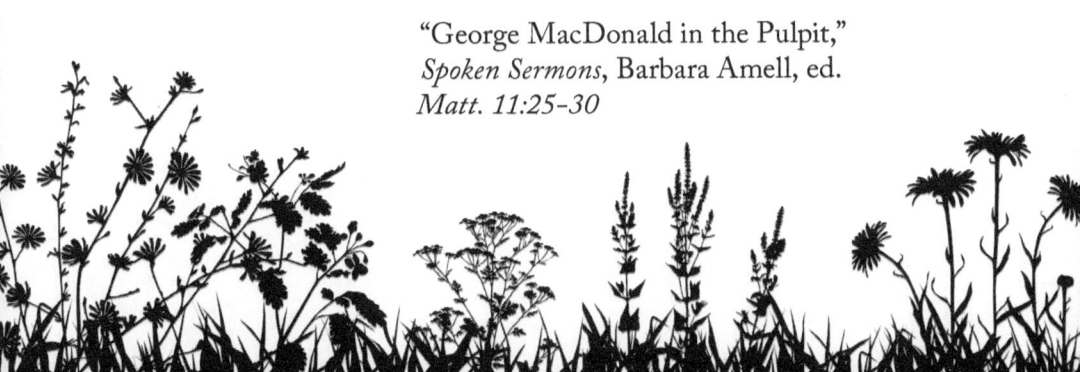

January 2 — The Offer Is Ours

This is an excerpt from a speech delivered in the Union Park Congregational Church in Chicago on Sunday evening, April 13, 1873. MacDonald's text was Rev. 3:20: "Listen! I am standing at the door, knocking; if you hear my voice and open the door, I will come in to you and eat with you, and you with me."

Friends, I have done as many of you have done. I have pored upon and pondered this old tale, and every year I live the conviction keeps gathering that here is the life of the world. The mists and the fog recede from before me. I know what it is to question. I know what it is to be troubled. But it seems to me more and more, that there, in the very heart of this Man, did lie, and still lies, the secret—a secret which is there to be revealed, for God must know secrets. His whose effort since that Man existed has been to unfold and reveal the energy of His nature which comes out in the revelation He wants us to know. And I say in the Man Jesus Christ is the revelation of the mystery. He has lived and died and loved, and has left the story behind Him of His three-and-thirty years. Some times we are tempted to long for more; and when we come to hear some little glimmer of a legend about Him, we grasp eagerly after it, as if, perhaps, here might be some little additional tale about Him that would add to the wealth of our knowledge, now small, but rich as it is.

But friends, if we knew the whole story, if we had every moment of His life mapped out for us, if we knew every single hour in every day he spent on earth, we might have it and be no better for it; yet, every moment we have the offer of the whole self of Him if we will but take it. Is He received up into heaven? Is He sitting with His Father on the throne? Did He arise again on Easter day, as we say, and ascend afterwards, up whence He came? Has He gone from sight? Did He not say, "Behold I am with you always"? And in His vision of His apostle who ought to have known whether it was He or not, for he reclined with his head on His bosom, did He not say, "I am a messenger on earth"? So He speaks always to us, and to every human being, "Behold I stand at the door and knock; if any man hear my voice and open the door I will come in to him, and will sup with him, and he with me."

"The Unexpected Guest," *The Chicago Pulpit*
Rev. 3:14-22

WHAT A SCHEME! JANUARY 3

This is an excerpt from a speech delivered in the Union Park Congregational Church in Chicago on Sunday evening, April 13, 1873. MacDonald's text was Rev. 3:20: "Listen! I am standing at the door, knocking; if you hear my voice and open the door, I will come in to you and eat with you, and you with me."

The friend says, "I have come to sup with you." And he whose voice the disciples heard as they went to Him, you hear, though it is a stranger, deeper, and a more tender voice still; and he will sit with you and talk with you as if there were not another soul in the universe that wanted Him. How it is you can not tell; but if that be not true, it ought to be true before our hearts can be quiet. But do not wait until He ceases knocking. Let Him in. Let Him in and hearken to Him. What is the best thing in this world? What is the best thing we have got? Jesus, some human heart that can love ours and be honest to it, some heart that loves our heart so well that it would die rather than there should be a blot upon it, or a speck of defilement upon it.

But, for a moment, imagine such a friend as you would like. Imagine the perfection of the ideal of your soul. I do not care, for a moment, how low you are. I know that a creature that God made must imagine an ideal. I say if you are the lowest, and most sensual creature in the world, imagine honestly, what you think your ideal man to be. Then I say to the loftiest of you, dream your highest dream, your highest ideal, your loftiest dream, your most glorious fancy, if you will, of what a friend, a man, a hero, and a perfect human being might be, and he is standing at your door, and knocking to get into your heart, only he is a thousand times grander than it is possible for you to think. He is always knocking and always wanting to get in.

It seems to me, that we are surrounded on all sides by an infinite sea of truth and love, pressing on all sides of us, in order that we might be benefited thereby. It stands to the law of truth that man made like God can not be satisfied with less than God. And at every heart of the poorest man, and the richest man, God is standing knocking and asking to be taken in, that it may be well with them, so that the child of the Divine shall be made glorious by the presence of the Divine, that the child of the Father may become, throughout the world, the sharer of the glory of the Most High. What a scheme of salvation!

"The Unexpected Guest," *The Chicago Pulpit*
Psalms 91:1- 4

January 4   Expecting Great Things

This birthday letter, written on January 4, 1891 from Brodighera, Italy, is to his oldest daughter, Lilia visiting her brother Ronald in America. She dies of tuberculosis the following November.

Dearest Child

I could say so much to you, and yet I am constantly surrounded by a sort of cactus-hedge that seems to make adequate utterance impossible. It is so much easier to write romance, where you cannot easily lie, than to say the commonest things where you may go wrong any moment. Even this is not the kind of way I meant to write to you. It is all wrong. I can only tell you I love you with true heart fervently, and love you far more because you are God's child than because you are mine.

I don't thank you for coming to us, for you could not help it, but the whole universe is "tented" with love, and you hold one of the corners of the great love-canopy for your mother and me. I don't thing I am very ambitious, except the strong desire "to go where I am" be ambition; and I know I take small satisfaction in looking on my past, but I do live expecting great things in the life that is ripening for me and all mine—when we shall all have the universe for our own, and be good merry helpful children in the great house of our father. I think then we shall be able to pass into and through each others very soul's as we please, knowing each other's thought and being, along with our own, and so being *like* God. When we are all just as loving and unselfish as Jesus; when like him, our one thought of delight is that God is, and is what he is; when the fact that a being is just another person from ourselves, is enough to make that being precious—then, darling, you and I and all will have the grand liberty wherewith Christ makes free—opening his hand to send us out like white doves to range the universe.

Have I not shown that the attempt to speak what you mean is the same kind of failure that walking is—a mere, constantly recurring, recovery from falling. . . ? Tell Ronald from me that Novalis says: "This world is not a dream, but it may, and perhaps ought to become one." Anyhow, it will pass—to make way for the world God has hidden in our hearts. Darling, I wish you life eternal. I daresay the birthdays will still be sparks in its glory. May I one day see the mould in God out of which you came.

                                        Your loving Father.

The Beinecke Rare Book and Manuscript Library
Isa. 35:10

Turned Inside Out   January 5

The following excerpts are from MacDonald's extended essay on the imagination, published in 1867. It presents the guiding principles which shape all his creative work.

As the thoughts move in the mind of man, so move the worlds of men and women in the mind of God, and make no confusion there, for there they had their birth, the offspring of his imagination. Man is but a thought of God.

If we now consider the so-called creative faculty in man, we shall find that in no *primary* sense is this faculty creative. Indeed, a man is rather *being thought* than *thinking*, when a new thought arises in his mind. He knew it not till he found it there, therefore he could not even have sent for it. He did not create it, else how could it be the surprise that it was when it arose? He may, indeed, in rare instances foresee that something is coming. . . but that is the utmost relation of consciousness and will he can bear to the dawning idea. Leaving this aside, however, and turning to the *embodiment* or revelation of thought, we shall find that a man no more *creates* the forms by which he would reveal his thoughts, than he creates those thoughts themselves.

For what are the forms by means of which a man may reveal his thoughts? Are they not those of nature? But although he is created in the closest sympathy with these forms, yet even these forms are not born in his mind. What springs there is the perception that this or that form is already an expression of this or that phase of thought or of feeling. For the world around him is an outward figuration of the condition of his mind; an inexhaustible storehouse of forms whence he may choose exponents. . . . the world is—allow us the homely figure—the human being turned inside out. All that moves in the mind is symbolized in Nature. . . .

In very truth, a wise imagination, which is the presence of the spirit of God, is the best guide that man or woman can have; for it is not the things we see the most clearly that influence us the most powerfully; undefined, yet vivid visions of something beyond, something which eye has not seen nor ear heard, have far more influence than any logical sequences whereby the same sequences may be demonstrated to the intellect.

      "The Imagination: Its Function and Its Culture," *Orts*.
      Psalms 33:14-15

January 6 — Heed Those Inside Hands

In the mythopoeic novel The Princess and Curdie
*the great-great-grandmother Princess Irene, who is a symbol for the
Divine Presence, is here preparing Curdie for his mission:*

"Have you ever heard what some philosophers say—that men were all animals once?"

"No, ma'am."

"It is of no consequence. But there is another thing that is of the greatest consequence —this: that all men, if they do not take care, go down the hill to the animal's country; that many men are actually, all their lives, going to the beasts. People knew it once, but it is long since they forgot it."

"I am not surprised to hear it, ma'am, when I think of some of our miners."

"Ah! But you must beware, Curdie, how you say of this man or that man that he is traveling beastward. There are not nearly so many going that way as at first sight you might think. When you met you father on the hill tonight, you stood and spoke together on the same spot. And although one of you was going up and the other coming down, at a little distance no one could have told which was bound in the one direction and which in the other. Just so two people may be at the same spot in manners and behavior, and yet one may be getting better and the other worse, which is just the greatest of all differences that could possibly exist between them."

"But, ma'am, where is the good of knowing that there is such a difference, if you can never know where it is?"

Now, Curdie, you must mind exactly what words I use. . . . I did not say *you can never know.* . . . Since it is always what they *do*, whether in their minds or bodies, that makes men go down to be less than men, that is, beasts, the change always comes first in their hands—and first of all in the inside hands, to which the outside ones are but as gloves."

The Princess and Curdie, Chapter 8
Eph. 3:14-19

The Inside Is the Same All The Time — January 7

*In the mythopoeic novel The Princess and Curdie
the great-great-grandmother Princess Irene, who is a symbol for the
Divine Presence, is here preparing Curdie for his mission:*

"Then would you mind telling me now, ma'am, for I feel very confused about it—are you the Lady of the Silver Moon? . . . And now I see you dark, and clothed in green, and the mother of all the light that dwells in the stones of the earth! And up there they call you Old Mother Wotherwop! And the Princess Irene told me you were her great-great-grandmother! And you spin the spider threads, and take care of a whole people of pigeons; and you are worn to a pale shadow with old age; and are as young as anybody can be, not to be too young; and as strong, I do believe, as I am. . . . I don't know what to make of it."

"I could give you twenty names more to call me, Curdie, and not one of them would be a false one. What does it matter how many names if the person is one? . . . Shapes are only dresses, Curdie, and dresses are only names. That which is inside is the same all the time."

"But then how can all the shapes speak the truth?"

"It would want thousands more to speak the truth, Curdie—and then they could not. But there is a point I must not let you mistake about. It is one thing the shape I choose to put on, and quite another the shape that foolish talk and nursery tale may please to put upon me. Also, it is one thing what you or your father may think about me, and quite another what a foolish of bad man may see in me. For instance, if a thief were to come in here just now, he would think he saw the demon of the mine, all in green flames, come to protect her treasure, and would run like a hunted wild goat. I should be all the same, but his evil eyes would see me as I was not."

The Princess and Curdie, Chapter 7
Psalms 18:20-28

January 8   "Our God is a consuming fire."

Our God is a consuming fire. Heb. 12:29

Nothing is inexorable but love. Love which will yield to prayer is imperfect and poor. It is not love that grants a boon unwillingly; still less is it love that answers a prayer to the wrong and hurt of him who prays. Love is one, and love is changeless.

For love loves unto purity. Love has ever in view the absolute loveliness of that which it beholds. Where loveliness is incomplete, and love cannot love its fill of loving, it spends itself to make more lovely, that it may love more; it strives for perfection, even that itself may be perfected—not in itself, but in the object. . . . Therefore all that is not beautiful in the beloved, all that comes between and is not of love's kind, must be destroyed.

And our God is a consuming fire.

It is the nature of God, so terribly pure that it destroys all that is not pure as fire, which demands like purity in our worship. He will have purity. It is not that the fire will burn us if we do not worship thus; but that the fire will burn us until we worship thus; yea, will go on burning within us after all that is foreign to it has yielded to its force, no longer with pain and consuming, but as the highest consciousness of life, the presence of God. When evil, which alone is consumable, shall have passed away in his fire from the dwellers in the immovable kingdom, the nature of man shall look the nature of God in the face, and his fear shall then be pure; for an eternal, that is a holy fear, must spring from a knowledge of [His] nature, not from a sense of power.

       "The Consuming Fire," *Unspoken Sermons: Series One.*
       Heb. 12:18-29

The Outer Darkness   January 9

Our God is a consuming fire. Heb. 12:29

The man whose deeds are evil, fears the burning. But the burning will not come the less that he fears it or denies it. Escape is hopeless. For Love is inexorable. Our God is a consuming fire. He shall not come out till he has paid the uttermost farthing.

If the man resist the burning of God, the consuming fire of Love, a terrible doom awaits him, and its day will come. He shall be cast into the outer darkness who hates the fire of God. What sick dismay will then seize upon him! For let a man think and care ever so little about God, he does not therefore exist without God. God is here with him, upholding, warming, delighting, teaching him—making life a good thing to him. God gives him himself, though he knows it not. But when God withdraws from a man as far as that can be without the man's ceasing to be; when the man feels himself abandoned, hanging in a ceaseless vertigo of existence upon the verge of the gulf of his being, without support, without refuge, without aim, without end . . . . Imagination cannot mislead us into too much horror of being without God—that one living death . . . .

But at length, O God, wilt thou not cast Death and Hell into the lake of Fire—even into thine own consuming self? Death shall then die everlastingly,

And Hell itself will pass away,
And leave her dolorous mansions to the peering day.

Then indeed wilt thou be all in all. For then our poor brothers and sisters, every one—O God, we trust in thee, the Consuming Fire—shall have been burnt clean and brought home. For it their moans, myriads of ages away, would turn heaven for us into hell—shall a man be more merciful than God? Shall a brother love a brother more than The Father loves a son?—more than The Brother Christ loves his brother? Would he not die yet again to save one brother more?

"The Consuming Fire," *Unspoken Sermons, Series One*
Isa. 45:20-25

January 10 — Our Childlike Inperturbable God

"Whosoever shall receive one of such children in my name, receiveth me; and whosoever shall receive me, receiveth not me, but him that sent me." Mark 9:37

In this, then, is God like the child: that he is simply and altogether our friend, our father—our more than friend, father, and mother—our infinite love-perfect God. Grand and strong beyond all that human imagination can conceive of poet-thinking and kingly action, he is delicate beyond all that human tenderness can conceive of husband or wife, homely beyond all that human heart can conceive of father or mother. He has not two thoughts about us. With him all is simplicity of purpose and meaning and effort and end—namely, that we should be as he is, think the same thoughts, mean the same things, possess the same blessedness. It is so plain that any one may see it, every one ought to see it, every one shall see it. It must be so. He is utterly true and good to us, nor shall anything withstand his will.

For it is his childlikeness that makes him our God and Father. The perfection of his relation to us swallows up all our imperfections, all our defects, all our evils; for our childhood is born of his fatherhood. That man is perfect in faith who can come to God in the utter dearth of his feelings, and his desire, without a glow or an aspiration, with the weight of low thoughts failures, neglects, and wandering forgetfulness, and say to him, "Thou art my refuge, because thou art my home."

Such faith will not lead to presumption. The man who can pray such a prayer will know better than another, that God is not mocked; that he is not a man that he should repent; that tears and entreaties will not work on him to the breach of one of his laws; that for God to give a man because he asked for it that which was not in harmony with his laws of truth and right, would be to damn him—to cast him into the outer darkness. And he knows that out of that prison the childlike, imperturbable God will let no man come till he has paid the uttermost farthing.

"The Child in the Midst," *Unspoken Sermons: Series One*
Mark 9:33-37

AWAY WITH THE MONSTROSITY! JANUARY 11

"Whosoever shall receive one of such children in my name, receiveth me; and whosoever shall receive me, receiveth not me, but him that sent me." Mark 9:37

How terribly, then, have the theologians misrepresented God in the measures of the low and showy, not the lofty and simple humanities! Nearly all of them represent him as a great King on a grand throne, thinking how grand he is, and making it the business of his being and the end of his universe to keep up his glory, wielding the bolts of a Jupiter against them that take his name in vain. They would not allow this, but follow out what they say, and it comes to much of this.

Brothers, have you found our king? There he is, kissing little children and saying they are like God. There he is at table with head of a fisherman lying on his bosom, and somewhat heavy at heart that even he, the beloved disciple, cannot yet understand him well. The simplest peasant who loves his children and his sheep were—no, not a truer, for the other is false, but—a true type of our God beside the monstrosity of a monarch.

The God who is ever uttering himself in the changeful profusions of nature; who takes millions of years to form a soul that shall understand him and be blessed; who never needs to be, and never is, in haste; who welcomes the simplest thought of truth or beauty as the return for seed he has sown upon the old fallows of eternity; who rejoices in the response of a faltering moment to the age-long cry of his wisdom in the streets; the God of music, of painting, of building, the Lord of Hosts, the God of mountains and oceans; whose laws go forth from one unseen point of wisdom, and thither return without an atom of loss; the God of history working in time unto Christianity; this God is the God of little children, and he alone can be perfectly, abandonedly simple and devoted.

"A Child in the Midst," *Unspoken Sermons: Series One.*
Acts 17:22-28

On this day in 1882: MacDonald family as an acting troup present a public performance of Shakespeare's Twelfth Night in Cannes on the French Riviera.

January 12 — What Seems vs What Is

MacDonald wrote many moving letters of condolence, of which this is an example. It was written at Bordighera on this day in 1888 to Susan Scott, daughter of A. J. Scott, a teacher and friend whom MacDonald greatly admired.

My dear Susan,

You will be missing your mother more now than when first she went away! As the days go on and the common look gathers again upon the things round you, and the Kingdom of heaven seems no nearer, we are apt to feel more of a separation. There seems sometimes to be nowhere beyond, because no voice comes back from the beloved. This parting seems so complete at times. Why is all so dumb? Why no personal revelation of the world to which they are gone?

God knows and cares, and uses for us a means of education for our hearts and spirits which we do not ourselves understand. It is not needful that we understand the motive power in the processes that go on within us. It is enough to him who believes it that the Lord *did* rise again, although after that he was hidden from their sight. Yes, I will believe that I shall hold my own in my arms again, their hearts nearer to mine than ever before.

It is a blessed thing to be children and to be parents of children. So God binds us all together. You and I have much to thank God for that we came of such parents. And we shall see them again and our hearts shall rejoice. For what is true of the Lord is true of all his, for they are one with him.

I need not say to you that I owe your father and mother more than I can tell. I looked up to your father more than to any man except my own father, who did not know half so much, but who was worthy of knowing whatever God taught him. We *shall* see them all and love them more and more in all eternity . . . .

Yours affectionately,
George MacDonald

The Beinecke Rare Book and Manuscript Library
Eph. 6:1-4

Our New Name

JANUARY 13

To everyone who conquers I will give . . . a white stone, and on the white stone is written a new name that no one knows except the one who receives it." Rev. 2:17

I say in brief, the giving of the white stone with the new name is the communication of what God thinks about the man to the man. It is the divine judgment, the solemn holy doom of the righteous man, the "Come thou blessed," spoken to the individual.

The true name is one which expresses the character, the nature, the being, the *meaning* of the person who bears it. It is the man's own symbol—his soul's picture, in a word—the sign which belongs to him and to no one else. Who can give a man this, his own name? God alone. For no one but God sees what the man is, or even, seeing what he is, could express in a name-word the sum and harmony of what he sees. To whom is the name given? To him that overcomes. When is it given? When he has overcome. Does God then not know what a man is going to become? As surely as he sees the oak which he put there lying in the heart of the acorn. Why then does he wait till the man has become by overcoming ere he settles what his name shall be? He does not wait; he knows his name from the first. But as—although repentance comes because God pardons—yet the man becomes aware of the pardon only in the repentance; so it is only when the man has become his name that God gives him the stone with the name upon it, for then first can he understand what his name signifies.

God's name for a man must be the expression in a mystical word—a word of that language which all who have overcome understand—of his own idea of the man, that being whom he had in his thought when he began to make the child, and whom he kept in his thought through the long process of creation that went to realize the idea. To tell the name is to seal the success—to say, "In thee also I am well pleased."

"The New Name," *Unspoken Sermons: Series One*
Rev. 2:12-17

On this day in 1902: Louisa MacDonald dies at Casa Corragio, the family home in Bordighera, Italy.

January 14 — Ambition vs Aspiration

To everyone who conquers I will give . . . a white stone, and on the white stone is written a new name that no one knows except the one who receives it." Rev. 2:17

"But is there not the worst of all dangers involved in such teaching—the danger of spiritual pride?" If there be, are we to refuse the spirit for fear of the pride? Or is there any other deliverance from pride except the spirit? Pride springs from supposed success in the high aim: with attainment itself comes humility. But here there is no room for ambition. Ambition is the desire to be above one's neighbor; and here there is no possibility of comparison with one's neighbor: no one knows what the white stone contains except the man who receives it. Here is room for endless aspiration towards the unseen ideal; none for ambition. Ambition would only be higher than others; aspiration would be high. Relative worth is not only unknown—to the children of the kingdom it is unknowable. Each esteems the other better than himself.

"God has cared to make me for himself," says the victor with the white stone, " and has called me that which I like best; for my own name must be what I should have it, seeing it is myself. What matter whether I be called a grass of the field, or an eagle of the air? A stone to build into his temple, or a Boanerges to wield his thunder? I am his; his idea, his making; perfect in my kind, yea, perfect in his sight; full of him, revealing him, alone with him. Let him call me what he will. The name shall be precious as my life. I seek no more."

Neither will he thus be isolated from his fellows. For that we say of one, we say of all. It is as *one* that the man has claims among his fellows. Each will feel the sacredness and awe of his neighbor's dark and silent speech with his God. Each will behold in the other a marvel of revelation, a present son or daughter of the Most High, come forth from him to reveal him afresh. In God each will draw nigh to each.

"The New Name," *Unspoken Sermons: Series One*
Psalms 91:9-16

God's Words Cannot Be Numbered   January 15

> *But he answered, "It is written, 'One does not live by bread alone, but by every word that comes from the mouth of God.'"* Matt. 4:4.

The Bible is *a* word of God, the chief of his written words, because it tells us of The Word, the Christ; but everything God has done and given man to know is a word of his, a will of his; and inasmuch as it is a will of his, it is a necessity to man, without which he cannot live: the reception of it is man's life.

For inasmuch as God's utterances are a whole, every smallest is essential: he speaks no foolishness—there are with him no vain repetitions. But by *the word* of the God and not Maker only, who is God just because he *speaks* to men, I must understand, in the deepest sense, every revelation of Himself in the heart and consciousness of man, so that the man knows that God is there, nay, rather, that he is here.

Even Christ himself is not the Word of God in the deepest sense *to a man*, until the Spirit that is the meaning in the Word has come to him—until the speech is not a sound as of thunder, but the voice of words; for a word is more than an utterance—it is a sound to be understood. No word, I say, is fully a Word *of* God until it is a Word *to* the man, until the man therein recognizes God. This is that for which the word is spoken.

The words of God are as the sands and the stars—they cannot be numbered; but the end of all and each is this—to reveal God. Nor, moreover, can the man know that any one of them is the word of God, save as it comes thus to him, is a revelation of God in him. It is *to* him that it may be *in* him; but till it is *in* him he cannot *know* that it was *to* him. God must be God *in* man before man can know that he is God, or that he has received aright, and for that for which it was spoken, any one of his words.

"The Temptation in the Wilderness," *Unspoken Sermons, Series One*
Psalms 19:7-11

January 16 — The Nature of Faith

"And when the tempter came to him, he said, If you be the Son of God, command that these stones be made bread.."   Matt. 4:3

"If ye have faith and doubt not, if ye shall say unto this mountain, Be thou removed, and be thou cast into the sea, it shall be done." Good people, among them John Bunyan, have been tempted to tempt the Lord their God upon the strength of this saying, just as Satan sought to tempt our Lord on the strength of the passage he quoted from the Psalms. Happily for such, the assurance to which they would give the name of faith generally fails them in time.

Faith is that which, knowing the Lord's will, goes and does it; for, not knowing it, stands and waits, content in ignorance as in knowledge, because God wills; neither pressing into the hidden future, nor careless of the knowledge which opens the path of action. It is its noblest exercise to act with uncertainty of the result, when the duty itself is certain, or even when a course seems with strong probability to be duty. But to put God to the question in any other way than by saying, What wilt thou have me to do? Is an attempt to compel God to declare himself, or to hasten his work.

This probably was the sin of Judas. It is presumption of a kind similar to the making of a stone into bread. It is, as it were, either a forcing of God to act where he has created no need for action, or the making of a case wherein he shall seem to have forfeited his word if he does not act. The man is therein dissociating himself from God so far that, instead of acting by the divine will from within, he acts in God's face, as it were, to see what he will do. Man's first business is, "what does God want me to do?" not "What will God do if I do so and so?"

The faith that will remove mountains is that confidence in God which comes from seeking nothing but his will. A man who was thus faithful would die of hunger sooner than say to the stone, *Be bread*; would meet the scoffs of the unbelieving without reply and with apparent defeat, sooner than say to the mountain, *Be thou cast into the sea*, even if he knew that it would be torn from its foundations at the word, except he knew first that God would have it so.

"The Temptation in the Wilderness," *Unspoken Sermons, Series One*
Psalms 119:9-16

Nothing to Conceal — January 17

"My God, my God, why hast thou forsaken me?" Matt. 27:46

I do not know that I should dare to approach this, of all utterances into which human breath has ever been molded, most awful in import, did I not feel that, containing both germ and blossom of the final devotion, it contains therefore the deepest practical lesson the human heart has to learn. The Lord, the Revealer, hides nothing that can be revealed, and will not warn away the foot that treads in naked humility even upon the ground of that terrible conflict between him and Evil, when the smoke of the battle that was fought not only with garments rolled in blood but with burning and fuel of fire, rose up between him and his Father, and for the one terrible moment ere he broke the bonds of life, and walked weary and triumphant into his arms, hid God from the eyes of his Son.

He will give us even to meditate the one thought that slew him at last, when he could bear no more, and fled to the Father to know that he loved him, and was well-pleased with him. For Satan had come at length yet again, to urge him with his last temptation; to tell him that although he had done his part, God had forgotten his; that although he had lived by the word of his mouth, that mouth had no word more to speak to him; that although he had refused to tempt him, God had left him to be tempted more than he could bear; that although he had worshiped none other, for that worship God did not care.

The Lord hides not his sacred sufferings, for truth is light, and would be light in the minds of men. The Holy Child, the Son of the Father, has nothing to conceal, but the Godhead to reveal. Let us put off our shoes, and draw near, and bow the head, and kiss those feet that bear for ever the scars of our victory.

"The Eloi," *Unspoken Sermons: Series One*
Psalms 22:1-11

January 18 — God Was Never Nearer

"My God, my God, why hast thou forsaken me?" Matt. 27:46.

It is with the holiest fear that we should approach the terrible fact of the sufferings of our Lord. Let no one think that those were less because he was more. The more delicate the nature, the more alive to all that is lovely and true, lawful and right, the more does it feel the antagonism of pain, the inroad of death upon life; the more dreadful is that breach of the harmony of things whose sound is torture. He felt more than man could feel, because he had a larger feeling.

He was even therefore worn out sooner than another man would have been. These sufferings were awful indeed when they began to invade the region about the will; when the struggle to keep consciously trusting in God began to sink in darkness; when the Will of The Man put forth its last determined effort in that cry after the vanishing vision of the Father: *My God, my God, why hast thou forsaken me?*

Never had it been so with him before. Never before had he been unable to see God beside him. Yet never was God nearer him than now. For never was Jesus more divine. He could not see, could not feel him near; and yet it is "*My* God" that he cries.

"The Eloi," *Unspoken Sermons: Series One*
Isa. 53:1-6

This Is The Truth   JANUARY 19

"My God, my God, why hast thou forsaken me?" Matt. 27:46

It is easy in pain, so long as it does not pass certain undefinable bounds, to hope in God for deliverance, or pray for strength to endure. But what is to be done when all feeling is gone? When a man does not know whether he believes or not, whether he loves or not? When art, poetry, religion are nothing to him, so swallowed up is he in pain, or mental depression, or disappointment, or temptation, or he knows not what? It seems to him then that God does not care for him, and certainly he does not care for God.

If he is still humble, he thinks that he is so bad that God cannot care for him. And he then believes for the time that God loves us only because and when and while we love him; instead of believing that God loves us always because he is our God, and that we live only by his love. Or he does not believe in a God at all, which is better.

God does not, by the instant gift of his Spirit, make us always feel right, desire good, love purity, aspire after him and his will. Therefore either he will not, or he cannot. If he will not, it must be because it would not be well to do so. If he cannot, then he would not if he could; else a better condition than God's is conceivable to the mind of God—a condition in which he could save the creatures whom he has made, better than he can save them.

The truth is this: He wants to make us in his own image, *choosing* the good, *refusing* the evil. How should he effect this if he were *always* moving us from within, as he does at divine intervals, towards the beauty of holiness? God gives us room *to be*; does not oppress us with his will; "stands away from us," that we may act from ourselves, that we may exercise the pure will for good.

"The Eloi," *Unspoken Sermons: Series One*
Psalms 42:5-11

January 20 — His Own Best Making

My God, my God, why hast thou forsaken me?" Matt. 27:46

Do not imagine me to mean that we can do anything of ourselves without God. If we choose the right at last, it is all God's doing, and only the more his that it is ours, only in a far more marvelous way his than if he had kept us filled with all holy impulses precluding the need of choice. For up to this very point, for this very point, he has been educating us, leading us, pushing us, driving us, enticing us, that we may choose him and his will, and so be tenfold more his children, of his own best making. . . .

For God made our individuality as well as, and a greater marvel than, our dependence; make our *apartness* from himself, that freedom should bind us divinely dearer to himself, with a new and inscrutable marvel of love; for the Godhead is still at the root, is the making root of our individuality, and the freer the man, the stronger the bond that binds him to him who made his freedom. He made our wills, and is striving to make them free; for only in the perfection of our individuality and the freedom of our wills can we be altogether his children. This is full of mystery, but can we not see enough in it to make us very glad and very peaceful?

> "The Eloi," *Unspoken Sermons: Series One.*
> Heb. 12:1-3

On this day in 1856: Greville, George and Louisa's first son is born.

BEING MADE PERFECT IN ONE   JANUARY 21

"My God, my God, why hast thou forsaken me?" Matt. 27:46

See, then, what lies within our reach every time that we are thus lapped in the folds of night. The highest condition of the human will is in sight, is attainable. I say not the highest condition of the Human Being; that surely lies in the Beatific Vision, in the sight of God. But the highest condition of the Human Will – as distinct, not as separated from God – is when, not seeing God, not seeming to itself to grasp him at all, it yet holds him fast. It cannot continue in this condition, for, not finding, not seeing God, the man would die; but the will thus asserting itself, the man has passed from death into life, and the vision is nigh at hand.

Then first, thus free, in thus asserting its freedom, is the individual will one with the Will of God; the child is finally restored to the father; the childhood and the fatherhood meet in one; the brotherhood of the race arises from the dust; and the prayer of our Lord is answered, "I in them and thou in me, that they may be made perfect in one."

Let us then arise in God-born strength every time that we feel the darkness closing, or become aware that it has closed around us, and say, "I am of the Light and not of the Darkness."

Then, if ever the time should come, as perhaps it must come to each of us, when all consciousness of well-being shall have vanished, when . . . man nor woman shall delight us more, nay, when God himself shall be but a name, and Jesus an old story, then, even then, when Death . . . is griping at our hearts. . . then we shall be able to cry out with our Lord, "My God, my God, why hast thou forsaken me?" Nor shall we die then, I think, without being able to take up his last words as well, and say, *"Father, into thy hands I commend my spirit."*

"The Eloi," *Unspoken Sermons: Series One*
Phil. 3:12-16

January 22 — Obedience Perfected

"Father, into thy hands I commend my spirit." Luke 23:46

Will the Lord ever tell us why he cried so? Was it the cry of relief at the touch of death? Was it the cry of victory? Was it the cry of gladness that he had endured to the end? Or did the Father look out upon him in answer to his *My God*, and the blessedness of it make him cry aloud because he could not smile? Was such his condition now that the greatest gladness of the universe could express itself only in a loud cry? Or was it but the last wrench of pain ere the final repose began?

It may have been all in one. But never surely in all books, in all words of thinking men, can there be so much expressed as lay unarticulated in that cry of the Son of God. Now had he made his Father Lord no longer in the might of making and loving alone, but Lord of right of devotion and deed of love. Now should inward sonship and the spirit of glad sacrifice be born in the hearts of men; for the divine obedience was perfected by suffering.

He had been among his brethren what he would have his brethren be. He had done for them what he would have them do for God and for each other. God was henceforth inside and beneath them, as well as around and above them, suffering with them and for them, giving them all he had, his very life-being, his essence of existence, what best he loved, what best he was. He had been among them, their God-brother. And the mighty story ends with a cry.

"The Hands of the Father," *Unspoken Sermons: Series One*
Isa. 55:1-7

How To Worship God January 23

"Father, into thy hands I commend my spirit." Luke 23:46

Every highest human act is just a giving back to God of that which he first gave to us. "Thou God hast given me: here again is thy gift. I send my spirit home."

Every act of worship is a holding up to God of what God has made us. "Here, Lord, look what I have got": feel with me in what thou hast made me, in this thy own bounty, my being. I am thy child, and know not how to thank thee save by uplifting the heave-offering of the overflowing of thy life, and calling aloud, 'It is thine: it is mine. I am thine, and therefore I am mine.'" The vast operations of the spiritual as of the physical world, are simply a turning again to the source.

The last act of our Lord, in thus commending his spirit at the close of his life, was only a summing up of what he had been doing all his life. He had been offering this sacrifice, the sacrifice of himself, all the years, and in thus sacrificing he had lived the divine life. Every morning when he went out ere it was day, every evening when he lingered on the night-lapt mountain after his friends were gone, he was offering himself to his Father in the communion of loving words, of high thoughts, of speechless feelings; and, between, he turned to do the same thing in deed, namely, in loving word, in helping thought, in healing action towards his fellows; for the way to worship God while the daylight lasts is to work; the service of God, the only "divine service," is the helping of our fellows.

"The Hands of the Father," *Unspoken Sermons: Series One*
Rom. 12:1-2

*On this day in 1867: George MacKay,
George and Louisa's eleventh and last child, is born.*

January 24 — Into God's Hands

"Father, into thy hands I commend my spirit.   Luke 23:46

Am I going out into the business and turmoil of the day, where so may temptations may come to do less honorably, less faithfully, less kindly, less diligently than the Ideal Man would have me do? Father, into thy hands. Am I going to do a good deed? Then, of all times—Father, into thy hands; lest the enemy should have me now.

Am I going to do a hard duty, from which I would gladly be turned aside—to refuse a friend's request, to urge a neighbor's conscience—Father, into thy hands I commend my spirit. Am I in pain? Is illness coming upon me to shut out the glad visions of a healthy brain, and bring me such as are troubled and untrue?—Take my spirit, Lord, and see that it has no more to bear than it can bear.

Am I going to die? Thou knowest, if only from the cry of thy Son, how terrible that is; and if it comes not to me in so terrible a shape as that in which it came to him, think how poor to bear I am beside him. I do not know what the struggle means; for, of the thousands who pass through it every day, not one enlightens his neighbor left behind. I will question no more: Father, into thy hands I commend my spirit.

For it is thy business, not mine. Thou wilt know every shade of my suffering; thou wilt care for me with thy perfect fatherhood; for that makes my sonship, and enwraps and infolds it. As a child I could bear great pain when my father was leaning over me, or had his arm about me: how much nearer my soul cannot thy hands come!—yea, with a comfort, father of me, that I have never yet even imagined. . . . I care not for the pain, so long as my spirit is strong, and into thy hands I commend that spirit. If thy love, which is better than life, receive it, then surely thy tenderness will make it great.

"The Hands of the Father," *Unspoken Sermons: Series One*
Psalms 23

The One Father   January 25

"Father, into thy hands I commend my spirit. Luke 23:46

Every uplifting of the heart is a looking up to The Father. Graciousness and truth are around, above, beneath us, yea, *in* us. When we are least worthy, then, most tempted, hardest, unkindest, let us yet commend our spirits into his hands. Whither else dare we send them?

How the earthly father would love a child who would creep into his room with angry, troubled face, and sit down at his feet, saying when asked what he wanted: "I feel so naughty, papa, and I want to get good"! Would he say to his child: "How dare you! Go away, and be good, and then come to me?" And shall we dare to think God would send us away if we came thus, and would not be pleased that we came, even if we were angry as Jonah?

Would we not let all the tenderness of our nature flow forth upon such a child? And shall we dare to think that if we being evil know how to give good gifts to our children, God will not give us his own spirit when we come to ask him? Bread, at least, will be given, and not a stone; water, at least, will be sure, and not vinegar mingled with gall.

Nor is there anything we can ask for ourselves that we may not ask for another. We may commend any brother, any sister, to the common fatherhood. And there will be moments when, filled with that spirit which is the Lord, nothing will ease our hearts of their love but the commending of all men, all our brothers, all our sisters, to the one Father.

For he cannot be our father save as he is their father; and if we do not see him and feel him as their father, we cannot know him as ours. Never shall we know him aright until we rejoice and exult for our race that he is *the* Father.

"The Hands of the Father," *Unspoken Sermons: Series One*
Heb. 4:14-16

January 26 — Help Him Be Himself

"But I say to you, Love your enemies and pray for those who persecute you, so that you may be children of your Father in heaven." Matt. 5:44, 45

"There is the person. Can you deny that that person is unlovely? How then can you love him?" I answer, *that* person, with the evil thing cast out of him, will be yet more the *person*, for he will be his real self. The thing that now makes you dislike him is separable from him, is therefore not he, makes himself so much less himself, for it is working death in him. Now he is in danger of ceasing to be a person at all.

When he is clothed and in his right mind, he will be a person indeed. You *could* not then go on hating him. Begin to love him now, and help him into the loveliness which is his. Do not hate him although you can. The personality, I say, though clouded, besmeared, defiled with the wrong, lies deeper than the wrong, and indeed, so far as the wrong has reached it, is by the wrong injured, yea, so far, it may be, destroyed.

Am I not refusing to acknowledge the child of the kingdom within his bosom, so killing the child of the kingdom within my own? Let us claim for ourselves no more indulgence than we give to him. Such honesty will end in severity at home and clemency abroad. For we are accountable for the ill in ourselves, and have to kill it; for the good in our neighbor, and have to cherish it.

He only, in the name and power of God, can kill the bad in him; we can cherish the good in him by being good to it across all the evil fog that comes between our love and his good.

"Love Thine Enemy," *Unspoken Sermons; Series One*
Matt. 5:43-48

This day in 1873: George, Louisa, and Greville are guests at Mark Twain's home in Elmira, New York.

ALL LIVE UNTO HIM — JANUARY 27

*"Now he is God not of the dead, but of the living;
for to him all of them are alive."* Luke 20:38

What God-like relation can the ever-living, life-giving, changeless God hold to creatures [if they] . . . partake not of his life, who have death at the very core of their being, are not worth their Maker's keeping alive? To let his creatures die would be to change, to abjure his Godhood, to cease to be that which he had made himself. If they are not worth keeping alive, then his creating is a poor thing, and he is not so great, nor so divine as even the poor thoughts of those his dying creatures have been able to imagine him. But our Lord says, "All live unto him."

With Him death is not. Thy life sees our life, O Lord. All of whom *all* can be said, are present to thee. Thou thinkest about us, eternally more than we think about thee. The little life that burns within the body of this death, glows unquenchable in thy true-seeing eyes. If you didst forget us for a moment then indeed death would be. But unto thee we live.

The beloved pass from our sight, but they pass not from thine. This that we call death, is but a form in the eyes of men. It looks something final, an awful cessation, an utter change. It seems not probable that there is anything beyond. But if God could see us before we were, and make us after his ideal, that we shall have passed from the eyes of our friends can be no argument that he beholds us no longer. "All live unto Him."

He takes to himself the name of *Their God*. The Living One cannot name himself after the dead, when the very Godhead lies in the giving of life. Therefore they must be alive. If he speaks of them, remembers his own loving thoughts of them, would he not have kept them alive if he could; and if he could not, how could he create them? Can it be an easier thing to call into life than to keep alive?

"The God of the Living," *Unspoken Sermons: Series One.*
Luke 20:27–40

January 28 — With What Body Do They Come?

*"Now he is God not of the dead, but of the living;
for to him all of them are alive."* Matt. 20:38

"But if they live to God, they are aware of God. And if they are aware of God, they are conscious of their own being: Whence then the necessity of a resurrection?" For their relation to others of God's children in mutual revelation; and for fresh revelation of God to all. But let us inquire what is meant by the resurrection of the body. "With what body do they come?" A man's material body will be to his consciousness at death no more than the old garment he throws aside at night, intending to put on a new and a better one in the morning.

Let us first ask what is the use of this body of ours. It is the means of Revelation to us, the *camera* in which God's eternal shows are set forth. It is by the body that we come into contact with Nature, with our fellow-men, with all their revelations of God to us. It is through the body that we receive all the lessons of passion, of suffering, of love, of beauty, of science. It is through the body that we are both trained outwards from our selves, and driven inwards into our deepest selves to find God.

We cannot yet have learned all that we are meant to learn through the body. How much of the teaching even of this world can the most diligent and most favored man have exhausted before he is called to leave it! Is all that remains to be lost? Who that has loved this earth can but believe that the spiritual body of which St. Paul speaks will be a yet higher channel of such revelation?

We need not only a body to convey revelation to us, but a body to reveal us to others. The thoughts, feelings, imaginations which arise in us, must have their garments of revelation whereby shall be made manifest the unseen world within us to our brothers and sisters. Now, if this be one of the uses my body served on earth before, the new body must be like the old. Nay, it must be the same body, glorified as we are glorified, with all that was distinctive of each from his fellows more visible than before.

"The God of the Living," *Unspoken Sermons: Series One*
I Cor. 15:35-49

WHAT WILL IT BE?   JANUARY 29

*Now he is God not of the dead, but of the living;
for to him all of them are alive."* Matt. 20:38

Ah, my friends! What will resurrection or life be to me, how shall I continue to love God as I have learned to love him through you, if I find he cares so little for this human heart of mine, as to take from me the gracious visitings of your faces and forms? True, I might have a gaze at Jesus, now and then; but he would not be so good as I had thought him. And how should I see him if I could not see you?

No, our God is an unveiling, a revealing God. He will raise you from the dead, that I may behold you; that that which vanished from the earth may again stand forth, looking out of the same eyes of eternal love and truth, holding out the same mighty hand of brotherhood, the same delicate and gentle, yet strong hand of sisterhood, to me, this me that knew you and loved you in the days gone by.

And in the changes which, thank God, must take place when the mortal puts on immortality, shall we not feel that the nobler our friends are, the more they are themselves; that the more the idea of each is carried out in the perfection of beauty, the more like they are to what we thought them in our most exalted moods, to that which we saw in them in the rarest moments of profoundest communion, to that which we beheld through the veil of all their imperfections when we loved them the truest?

Lord, evermore give us the Resurrection, like thine own in the body of thy Transfiguration. Let us see and hear, and know, and be seen, and heard, and known, as thou seest, hearest, and knowest. Give us glorified bodies through which to reveal the glorified thoughts which shall then inhabit us, when not only shalt thou reveal God, but each of us shall reveal thee.

"The God of the Living," *Unspoken Sermons: Series One*
Dan. 12:1-4

January 30 — Here Is My Answer

This letter, penned from Bordighera on January 31, 1886,
is as precise a summary of MacDonald's attitudes as exists in his writings.

Dear W_____

When I had the pleasure of being your guest I entered with you into a conversation such as I am in general far from favorable to, believing it not at all conducive to profit. Had you been a stranger, I should have avoided or declined the argument. But in answer to your letter, I reply thus far, that your presentation of your opinions, which are the same as from childhood I was familiar with, I refuse entirely as the truth, holding them as the merest invention of the human intellect in the attempt to explain things which the spirit of the Son of Man alone can make any man to understand for his salvation.

If however any man ask me, as you do in your letter, to give in its stead the attempt of my intellect to explain the same things, I answer, far be it from me to do so! I am not going to replace in the same kind in dried and petrified form, what I see of the truth, favoring thus the idea that anything else whatever than a vital union with Christ, as of the members with the body, as of the branches of the vine, is of any avail to the well-being of a man. It is in no sense what we believe about Christ, or what way we would explain his work, that constitutes or can be the object of faith.

No belief in the atonement, for instance, whether that atonement be explained or understood right or wrong, no belief in what the theologians call the merits of Christ, is in the smallest degree or approximation what the Lord or his apostles meant by faith in him. It is to take him as our Lord and Master, obey his words, be prepared to die for him; it is to take on us the yoke his father laid on him and regard the will of God as the one thing worthy of a man's care and endeavor—as indeed our very life—that, and nothing less than that, is faith in the Son of God. (*Continued in next entry*)

The Beinecke Rare Book and Manuscript Library
Gal. 1:6-10

NOTHING BETWEEN   JANUARY 31

(continued from prior entry)

Then as to all things that are necessary for our growth in the Divine life, that is, for growing like to him in whose image we are made, he promises to teach us by his spirit everything. Nor even if a man could, which is impossible, know with his understanding the deepest mysteries, would these avail him the least, that would not constitute the knowledge of them after the true fashion: they must be spiritually discerned—in a way that no man can by any possibility teach his neighbor, but which only the Spirit of God can teach. I think and believe that the mischief done to the kingdom of Christ by teaching of what is called doctrine by theologians, and calling that teaching the Gospel, instead of presenting Christ as he presented himself, and took a whole life of labor to present himself, is enormous, and the cause of a huge part of the infidelity in the world. Let us follow the Lord, studying the mind of him, and not what the scribes and the elders teach about him.

If any man come to me with theological questions, if I find that they are troubling him, and keeping him from giving himself to God, I do my best to remove any such obstructions as are the result of man's handling of the eternal things: what I count false, I will not spare. But if the man come to me only for the sake of conference on the matter, I will hold none. Let him get what teaching he is capable of receiving from his knowledge of Christ, and the spirit given him. If he is satisfied with the theology he has learned, I should give myself no trouble to alter his opinion. I should do him no good either by success or failure in the attempt. I have other things altogether to do. I have to take up my cross and follow the master first, and then persuade him who will be persuaded to come with me. He is the atonement, and through him, through knowing him and being every day, every hour, every moment taught by him, I shall become pure in heart, and shall at length see God. No doctrine shall come between me and him. Nor will he come between anyone and God save to lead him home to the Father. The whole mischief has come of people setting themselves to understand rather than to do, to arrange God's business for him, and tell other people what the Father meant, instead of doing what the Father tells them, and then teaching others to do the same.

(Continued in next entry)

The Beinecke Rare Book and Manuscript Library
John 8:31-47

February 1 — No *Hortus Siccus*

(continued from prior entry)

If I am told that I am not definite—that something more definite is needed, I say your definiteness is one that God does not care about, for he has given no such system as you desire. But, I ask, is not the living man, the human God, after his 3 and 30 years on earth, poor and scanty as are the records of him, a definite enough object of faith for your turn? He is not, I grant you, for the kind of definiteness you would have, which is to reduce the infinite within the bounds of a legal document; but for life, for the joy of deliverance, for the glory of real creation, for the partakings of the divine nature, for the gaining of a faith that shall remove mountains, and for deliverance from all the crushing commonplaces of would-be teachers of religion, who present us with a God so poor and small that to believe in him is an insult to him who created the human heart—the story of the eternal Son of God, who knew and loved his father so that he delighted to die in the manifestation of him to his brothers and sisters, is enough, triumphantly enough. To have to believe in the God of the Calvinist would drive me to madness or atheism; to believe in the God of our Lord Jesus Christ, is to feel that, if such God there be, all is well, he may do with me as he please. I am blest.

Thus, or somehow thus, I would answer any man who pressed me to be more definite. Not that I could not give what seemed to me the best of reasons why the Lord should die, but if I set them out, it shall be in a vital fashion, and not in a *hortus siccus* [a dry garden] of heavenly flowers.

So far, my dear sir, I have answered, so far I have declined to answer your letter. I have other reasons also, the result of a long life's experience in these regions, for doing as I have done. But the day will come for saying anything. May we be of those who walking the streets of the New Jerusalem hold sweet counsel together without danger of being misunderstood.

> The Beinecke Rare Book and Manuscript Library
> *Gal. 3:1-9*

Nothing Else Will Do

February 2

Consisting of 366, 7 line stanzas, one for each day of the year,
A Book of Strife in the Form of the Diary of an Old Soul
*is an intimate revelation of MacDonald's mind. John Ruskin aptly
called it "one of the three great sacred poems of the nineteenth century."*

My Lord, I find that nothing else will do
But follow where thou goest, sit at thy feet,
And where I have thee not, still run to meet.
Roses are scentless, hopeless are the morns,
Rest is but weakness, laughter crackling thorns,
If thou, the Truth, do not make them the true.
Thou art my life, O Christ, and nothing else will do.

--

Thou art here—in heaven, I know, but not *from* here—
Although thy separate self do not appear;
If I could part the light from out the day,
There I should have thee! But thou art too near:
How find thee walking, when thou art the way?
O present Christ, make my eyes keen as stings,
To see thee at their heart, the glory even of things!

--

That thou art nowhere to be found, agree
Wise men, whose eyes are but for surfaces;
Men with eyes opened by the second birth,
To whom the seen, husk of the unseen is,
Descry thee soul of everything on earth.
Who know thy ends, thy means and motions see;
Eyes made for glory soon discover thee.

I Cor. 1:4 -9

FEBRUARY 3 — TEMPTATIONS ARE NECESSARY

This is a comment on Christ's first miracle, the turning of water into wine at the wedding feast at Cana, recorded in John: 2:1-11.

"Fill the jars with water." And they filled them up to the brim. "Now draw some out, and take it to the steward of the feast." So they took it. "You have kept the good wine until now." It is such a thing of course that, when our Lord gave them wine, it would be of the best, that it seems almost absurd to remark upon it. What the Father would make and will make, and that towards which He is ever working, is *the Best*; and when our Lord turns the water into wine it must be very good.

It is like His Father, too, not to withhold good wine because men abuse it. Enforced virtue is unworthy of the name. That men may rise above temptation, it is needful that they should have temptation. It is the will of Him who makes the grapes and the wine. Men will even call Jesus himself a wine-bibber. What matters it, so long as He works as the Father works, and lives as the Father wills.

I dare not here be misunderstood. God chooses that men should be tried, but let a man beware of tempting his neighbor. God knows how and how much, and where and when: man is his brother's keeper, and must keep him according to his knowledge. A man may work the will of God for others, and be condemned therein because he sought his own will and not God's. That our Lord gave this company wine, does not prove that He would have given any company wine. To some He refused even the bread they requested at His hands. Because He gave wine to the wedding-guests, shall man dig a pit at the corner of every street, that the poor may fall therein, spending their money for that which is not bread, and their labor for that which satisfies not? Let the poor man be tempted as God wills, for the end of God is victory; let not man tempt him, for his end is his neighbor's fall. Or at best he heeds not his neighbor's end for the sake of gain, and he shall receive according to his works.

"The Beginning of Miracles," *The Miracles of Our Lord*
II Pet. 1:3-9

It's In The Seeing — February 4

This is a comment on Christ's first miracle, the turning of water into wine at the wedding feast at Cana, recorded in John: 2:1-11.

To him who can thank God with free heart for his good wine, there is a glad significance in the fact that Our Lord's first miracle was this turning of water into wine. It is a true symbol of what He had done for the world in glorifying all things. With His divine alchemy He turns not only water into wine, but common things into radiant mysteries, yes, every meal into a Eucharist, and the jaws of the sepulcher into an outgoing gate. I do not mean that He makes any change in the things or ways of God, but a mighty change in the hearts and eyes of men, so that God's facts and God's meanings become their faiths and their hopes.

The destroying spirit, who works in the commonplace, is ever covering the deep and clouding the high. For those who listen to that spirit great things cannot be. Such are there, but they cannot see them, for in themselves they do not aspire. They believe, perhaps, in the truth and grace of their first child: when they have spoiled him, they laugh at the praises of childhood. From all that is thus low and wretched, incapable and fearful, He who made the water into wine delivers men. He reveals heaven around them, God in all things, truth in every instinct, and evil withering and hope springing even in the path of the destroyer.

That the wine should be His first miracle, and that the feeding of the multitudes should be the only other creative miracle, will also suggest many thoughts in connection with the symbol He has left us of His relation to His brethren. In the wine and the bread of the Eucharist, He reminds us how utterly He has given, is giving, Himself for the gladness and the strength of His Father's children. Yea more; for in that He is the radiation of the Father's glory, this bread and wine is the symbol of how utterly the Father gives Himself to His children, how earnestly He would have them partakers of His own being. If Jesus was the son of the Father, is it hard to believe that He should give men bread and wine?

"The Beginning of Miracles," *The Miracles of our Lord*
John 2:1-11

February 5 — The Power of Power

This is a comment on Christ's first miracle, the turning of water into wine at the wedding feast at Cana, recorded in John: 2:1-11.

It was not His power, however, but his glory, that Jesus showed forth in the miracle. His power could not be hidden, but it was a poor thing beside His glory. Yes, power in itself is a poor thing. If it could stand alone, which it cannot, it would be a horror. No amount of lonely power could create. It is the love that is at the root of power, the power of power, which alone can create. What then was this His glory? What was it that made Him glorious?

It was that, like His Father, He ministered to the wants of men. Had they not needed the wine, He would not have made it, even for the sake of whatever show of His power. The concurrence of man's need and His love made it possible for that glory to shine forth. It is for this glory most that we worship Him. But power is no object of adoration, and they who try to worship it are as slaves. Their worship is no real worship. Those who trembled at the thunder from the mountain went and worshiped a golden calf, but Moses went into the thick darkness to find his God.

How far the expectation of the mother Mary—that her son would, by majesty of might, appeal to the wedding guests, and arouse their enthusiasm for Himself—was from our Lord's thoughts may be well seen in the fact that the miracle was not beheld even by the ruler of the feast. So quietly was it done, so entirely without pre-intimation of His intent, so stolenly, as it were, in the two simple-ordered acts—the filling of the water-pots with water, and drawing of it out again—as to make it manifest that it was done for the ministration. He did not do it even for the show of His goodness, but *to be good*. This alone could show His Father's goodness. It was done because here was an opportunity in which all circumstances combined with the bodily presence of the powerful and the prayer of His mother, to render it fit that the love of His heart should go forth in giving His merry-making brothers and sisters more and better wine to drink.

"The Beginning of Miracles," *The Miracles of our Lord*
Phil. 4:10-20

God Keeps Quiet   February 6

This is a comment on Christ's first miracle, the turning of water into wine at the wedding feast at Cana, recorded in John: 2:1-11.

Here is another point in which this miracle of Jesus resembles the working of His Father. For God ministers to us so gently, with such a quiet, tender, loving absence of display, that men often drink of His wine, as these wedding guests drank, without knowing whence it comes —without thinking that the giver is beside them, yea, in their very hearts. For God will not compel the adoration of men: that would be but a pagan worship. He will rouse in men a sense of need, which shall grow at length into a longing; He will make them feel after Him, until by their search becoming able to hold Him, He may at length reveal to them the glory of their Father. He works silently—keeps quiet behind His works, as it were, that He may truly reveal Himself in the right time. With this intent also, when men find His wine good and yet do not rise and search for the giver, He will plague them with sore plagues, that the good wine of life may not be to them, and therefore to Him and the universe, an evil thing.

It would seem that the correlative of creation is search; that as God has *made* us, we must *find* Him. Thus our action must reflect His. Thus He glorifies us with a share in the end of all things, which is that the Father and His children may be one in thought, judgment, feeling, and intent, in a word, that they may mean the same thing. St. John says that Jesus thus "manifested His glory, and His disciples believed in Him." I doubt if any but His disciples knew of the miracle; or of those others who might see or hear of it. It is possible to see a miracle, and not believe in it; while many of those who saw a miracle of our Lord believed in the miracle, and yet did not believe in Him.

> "The Beginning of Miracles," *The Miracles of our Lord*
> I Kings 19:9-13

February 7 — There's Good Wine Yet To Come

This is a comment on Christ's first miracle, the turning of water into wine at the wedding feast at Cana, recorded in John: 2:1-11.

I wonder how many Christians there are who so thoroughly believe God made them that they can laugh in God's name; who understand that God invented laughter and gave it to His children. Such belief would add a keenness to the zest in their enjoyment, and slay that feeble laughter in which neither heart nor intellect has a share.

It would help them also to understand the depth of this miracle. The Lord of gladness delights in the laughter of a merry heart. These wedding guests could have done without wine, surely without more wine and better wine. But the Father looks with no esteem upon a bare existence, and is ever working, even by suffering, to render life more rich and plentiful. His gifts are to the overflowing of the cup; but when the cup would overflow, He deepens its hollow, and widens its brim. Our Lord is profuse like His Father, yea, will, at His own sternest cost, be lavish to His brethren. He will give them wine indeed.

But even they who know whence the good wine comes, and joyously thank the giver, shall one day cry out, like the praiseful ruler of the feast to him who gave it not, "You have kept the good wine until now!"

> "The Beginning of Miracles," *The Miracles of our Lord*
> Isa. 35:3- 10

On this day in 1864: Maurice, George and Louisa's fourth son, is born.

What We Need in Sorrow   February 8

MacDonald wrote many moving letters of condolence, of which this, written from Bordighera on February 8, 1890, to Adelaide Pym, is an example.

My dear Adelaide,

Let my heart come near to yours, and talk a little bit to it. If you are not able to listen, you can easily say to my messenger, "Wait till I can hear you."

We are all just children in our Father's nursery. Some of us are taken before others away from it, and we are left without our playmates. But we know the father has them, and though we must miss them constantly, we must remember that we shall be sent for by and by, and must by patient waiting be ready to go. You know all this as well as I do, but let us think it together.

What is all this life but a waiting? You who have suffered so much, must know that better than most! For myself, I have never been content with this world as a place to live in. I mean it has always, more and less, had the feel of a foreign land. The feeling has not been caused by much suffering, neither by any sense of outside failure. No doubt the world has been less satisfactory because of my own evil and great lack; but allowing for all that, there remains a something that indicates that it was never intended to be our home, and we were never intended to feel at home in it.

We must not then be unhappy when one of us goes to make the others happier who have gone before, and were waiting for them, and are now waiting for us to join them! The very notion of heaven is to have all we love with us, and God is just carrying out that notion for us, by gentle recurrent removals as we are ready to go. It seems so commonplace when said to a sore heart—a missing heart—but surely what you and anyone like you, and in such sorrow, needs is to "have your pure mind stirred up by way of remembrance."

But God has a marvelous bliss, and yet a very homely one, waiting for us. Be sure it will run in the old grooves, but the grooves will be of gold and gems, not of iron and clay.

(Continued in the next entry.)

The Beinecke Rare Book and Manuscript Library
Rev. 21:1-4

February 9 — More Lovely Still

Letter of condolence to Adelaide Pym continued

And then what a thing it will be to feel our bodies as free, as little held down and oppressed, as our better part! Of course the great joy of heaven will be the same as that of this world—to know God and to be what he is; but we shall know him so much better then, and know how foolish it was of us to be troubled about anything when HE was looking after everything! There will be no question whether life is worth living to those who know what life means.

Things are just as right as they could be, so far as God is concerned, for the making us capable of his own joy in life. The only thing amiss is that we put our hope in other things than God, and wish things that are not worth giving us, and which therefore he does not care to give us, and so we do not work along with him for what he wants us to be and thereby delay the success of his work with us. For there is nothing good but being one with him in every desire and hope and joy.

My heart says these things to your heart, dear Adelaide, because they are life to it—or rather He who makes them truth, and is the truth, is life to it. He is our elder brother, watching ever for our good. We know what it is to have brothers to love; what is it to have a brother to love perfectly because he is a perfect brother!

So you must love Beatrice more than ever, and more yet, and wait in strong expecting patience; she will be more lovely still by the time we see her again—though that cannot be very long. Day runs so swiftly after day, and our "salvation" is nearer than when we believed . . .

> The Beinecke Rare Book and Manuscript Library
> *Psalms 130:5-8*

From Whence The Power

February 10

This is a comment on Christ's miracle of restoring to a man his withered hand, recorded in Matt. 12:9-14; Mark 3:1-6; and Luke 6:6-11.

Here, plainly by the record, our Lord gave the man his share, not of mere acquiescence, but of active will, in the miracle. If man is the child of God, he must have a share in the works of the Father. Without such share in the work as faith gives, cure will be of little avail. "Stretch out your hand," said the Healer; and the man made the effort. The withered hand obeyed, and was no more withered. *In* the act came the cure, without which the act had been confined to the will, and had never taken form in the outstretching. It is the same in all spiritual redemption.

Think for a moment with what delight the man would employ his new hand. This right hand would henceforth be God's hand. But was not the other hand God's too?—God's as much as his? Had not the power of God been always present in that left hand, whose unwithered life had ministered to him all these years? Was it not the life of God that inspired his whole frame? By the loss and restoration in one part, he would understand possession in the whole.

But as the withered and restored limb to the man, so is the maimed and healed man to his brethren. In every man the power by which he does the commonest things is the power of God. The power is not *of* us. Our power does it; but we do not make the power. This, plain as it is, remains, however, the hardest lesson for a man to learn with conviction and thanksgiving. For God has, as it were, put us just so far away from Him that we can exercise the divine thing in us, our own will, in returning towards our source. Then we shall learn the fact that we are infinitely more great and blessed in being the outcome of a perfect self-constituting will, than we could be by the conversion of any imagined independence of origin into fact for us. This is a truth no man *can* understand, feel, or truly acknowledge, save in proportion as he has become one with his perfect origin, the will of God.

"Miracles of Healing Unsolicited" *The Miracles of our Lord*
Matt. 12:9-14

February 11   A Glimpse Of Absolute Glory

*This is a comment on Christ's miracle of healing the
man blind from birth, recorded in John 9:1-41*

In this miracle as in all the rest, Jesus did in little the great work of the Father; for how many more are they to whom God has given the marvel of vision than those blind whom the Lord enlightened! What a divine *invention*, what a mighty gift of God is this very common thing—these eyes to see with—that light which enlightens the world, this sight which is the result of both. What a believer the man born blind must have become! Nothing should be too grand and good for him to believe thereafter—not even the doctrine hardest to commonplace humanity, though the most natural and reasonable to those who have beheld it—that the God of the light is a faithful, loving, upright, honest, and self-denying being, utterly devoted to the uttermost good of those whom He has made.

Such is the Father of lights who enlightens the world and every man that comes into it. Every pulsation of light on every brain is from Him. Every feeling of law and order is from Him. Every hint of right, every desire after the true, whatever we call aspiration, all longing for the light, every perception that this is true, that that ought to be done, is from the Father of lights. His infinite and varied light gathered into one point—for how can we speak at all of these things if we do not speak in figures?—concentrated and embodied in Jesus, became *the* light of the world. For the light is no longer only diffused, but in Him man "beholds the light *and whence it flows.*

Not merely is our chamber enlightened, but we see the lamp. And so we turn again to God, the Father of lights, yea even the Light of the World. Hence forth we know that all the light wherever diffused has its center in God, as the light that enlightened the blind man flowed from its center in Jesus. In other words, we have a glimmering, faint, human perception of the absolute glory. We know what God is in recognizing Him as our God.

    "Miracles of Healing Unsolicited," *The Miracles of our Lord.*
    Psalms 36:5-10

Fit To Be Christ's Apostle   FEBRUARY 12

This is a comment on Christ's miracle of healing the Gadarene Demoniac, recorded in Matt. 8:28-34; Mark 5:1-20, and Luke 8:26-39. After he was healed, the demoniac begged Christ that he might go with him.

But who can imagine the delight of the man when that wild troop of maddening and defiling demons, which had possessed him with all uncleanness, vanished! Scarce had he time to know that he was naked, before the hands of loving human beings, in whom the good Spirit ruled, were taking off their own garments and putting them upon him. He was a man once more, and among men with human faces, human hearts, human ways. He was with his own, and that supreme form and face of the man who had set him free was binding them all into one holy family.

Now he could pray of himself the true prayer of a soul which knew what it wanted, and could say what it meant. He sat down like a child at the feet of the man who had cured him. When, yielding at once to the desire of those who would be rid of his presence, Jesus went down to the boat, he followed, praying that he might be with Him. What could he desire but to be near that power which had restored him his divine self, and the consciousness thereof—his own true existence, that of which God was thinking when He made him?

But he would be still nearer the Lord in doing His work than in following Him about. It is remarkable that while more than once our Lord charged the healed to be silent, He leaves this man as his apostle—his witness with those who had banished Him from their coasts. Something may be attributed to the different natures of the individuals; some in preaching Him would also preach themselves, and so hurt both. But this man was not of such. To be with the Lord was all his prayer. Therefore he was fit to be without Him, and to aid His work apart.

"The Casting Out of Devils," *The Miracles of our Lord*
Luke 8:26-39

February 13 — The Prayer For Us

> *This is a comment on Christ's miracle of healing the lunatic boy, recorded in Matt. 17:14-20, Mark 9:14-29, and Luke 9:37-43.*

The Lord will care for the father as much as for the child. He will help his growing faith.

"How long has he had this?"
"From childhood. And it has often cast him into the fire and into the water to destroy him; but if you can do anything, have pity on us and help us."
"*If you can?* All things are possible to him who believes."
"I believe; help my unbelief."

Whether the words of Jesus, "him who believes," meant Himself as believing in the Father, and therefore gifted with all power, or the man as believing in Him, and therefore capable of being the recipient of the effects of that power, I am not sure. I incline to the former. The result is the same, for the man resolves the question practically and personally. What was needful in him should be in him. "I believe; help my unbelief."

In the honesty of his heart, lest he should be saying more than was true—for how could he be certain that Jesus would cure his son? Or how could he measure and estimate his own faith?—he appeals to the Lord of Truth for all that he ought to be, and think, and believe. "Help my unbelief." It is the very triumph of faith. The unbelief itself cast like any other care upon Him who cares for us, is the highest exercise of belief. It is the greatest effort lying in the power of man.

No man can help doubt. The true man alone, that is, the faithful man, can appeal to the Truth to enable him to believe what is true, and refuse what is false. How this applies especially to our own time and the need for the living generations, is easy to see. Of all prayers it is the one for us.

"The Casting out of Devils," *The Miracles of our Lord*
Mark 9:14-29

Out Of Us Also — February 14

This is a comment on Christ's miracle of healing the lunatic boy, recorded in Matt. 17:14-20, Mark 9:14-29, and Luke 9:37-43.

The disciples, although they had already the power to cast out demons, could not cast this one out, and were surprised to find it so. There appears to me no absurdity, if we admit the demons at all, in admitting also that some had greater force than others, be it regarded as courage or obstinacy, or merely as grasp upon the captive mortal.

But we all need like healing. No man who does not yet love the truth with his whole being, who does not love God with all his heart and soul and strength and mind, and his neighbor as himself, is in his sound mind, or can act as a rational being, save more or less approximately. This is as true as it would be of us if possessed by other spirits than our own.

Every word of unkindness, God help us! Every unfair hard judgment, every trembling regard of the outward and fearless disregard of the inward life, is a siding with the spirit of evil against the spirit of good, with our lower and accidental selves against our higher and essential—our true selves. These the Spirit of God would set free from all possession but His own, for that is their original life. Out of us, too, the evil spirits can go by that prayer alone in which a man draws nigh to the Holy. Nor can we have any power over the evil spirit in others except in proportion as by such prayer we cast the evil spirit out of ourselves.

"The Casting out of Devils," *The Miracles of our Lord*
Eph. 4:29-32

February 15   Oneness With God Makes It A Necessity

It may seem strange that our Lord says so little about the life to come, as we call it—though in truth it is one life with the present, as the leaf and the blossom are one life. Even in argument with the Sadducees He supports His side upon words accepted by them, and upon the nature of God, but says nothing of the question from a human point of regard. He seems always to have taken it for granted, ever turning the minds of His scholars towards that which was deeper and lay at its root—the life itself—the oneness with God and His will, upon which the continuance of our conscious being follows of a necessity, and without which if the latter were possible, it would be for human beings an utter evil.

When He speaks of the world beyond, it is as *His Father's house*. He says there are many mansions there. He attempts in no way to explain. Man's own imagination enlightened of the spirit of truth, and working with his experience and affections, was a far safer guide than his intellect with the best schooling even our Lord could have given it. The memory of the poorest home of a fisherman on the shore of the Galilean lake, where He as a child had spent His years of divine carelessness in His father's house, would, at the words of our Lord *my Father's house*, convey to Peter or James or John more truth concerning the many mansions than a revelation to their intellect, had it been possible, as clear as the Apocalypse itself is obscure.

When He said, "I have overcome *the world*," He had overcome the cause of all doubt, the belief in the outside appearances and not in the living truth. He left it to His followers to say, from their own experience knowing the thing, not merely from the belief of His resurrection, "He has conquered death and the grave." "O death, where is thy victory? O death, where is thy sting?" It is the inward life of truth that conquers the outward death of appearances; and nothing else, no revelation from without, could conquer it.

"The Raising of the Dead," *The Miracles of our Lord*.
I Cor. 2:6-12

Though He Knew It Not

February 16

Robert Falconer as a child, living with his stern but loving Calvinist grandmother, first tries to pray:

But now began to appear in Robert the first signs of a practical outcome of such truth as his grandmother had taught him, operating upon the necessities of a simple and earnest nature. Reality, however lapt in vanity, or even in falsehood, cannot lose its power. It *is*—the other is not. She had taught him to look up—he would put it to the test. Not that he doubted it yet: he only doubted whether there was a hearing God. But was that not worse? It was, I think. For it is of far more consequence what kind of a God, than whether a God or no.

He had no comfort, and, without reasoning about it, he felt that life ought to have comfort----from which point he began to conclude that the only thing left was to try whether the God in whom his grandmother believed might not help him. If the God would but hear him, it was all he had yet learned to require of his Godhood. And that must ever be the first thing to require. More demands would come, and greater answers he would find. But now—if God would but hear him! If he spoke to him but one word, it would be the very soul of comfort; he could no more be lonely.

A fountain of glad imaginations gushed up in his heart at the thought. What if, from the cold winter of his life, he had but to open the door of his garret-room, and, kneeling by the bare bedstead, enter into the summer of God's presence! What if God spoke to him face to face! He had so spoken to Moses. He sought him from no fear of the future, but from present desolation; and if God came near to him, it would not be with storm and tempest, but with the voice of a friend. And surely, if there was a God at all, that is, not a power greater than man, but a power by whose power man was, he must hear the voice of the creature whom he had made, a voice that came crying out of the very need which he had created. Younger people than Robert are capable of such divine metaphysics.

Night after night he returned to the parlour cold to the very heart. God was not to be found, he said then. He said afterwards that even then 'God was with him though he know it not.'

Robert Falconer, Part II, Chapter 1
Matt. 7:7-12

February 17   But God Was With Him

Robert Falconer as a child, living with his stern but loving Calvinist grandmother, first tries to pray, but finds the stern doctrines of election and limited atonement an impassable barrier.
(There are strong echoes here of MacDonald's own struggles as a child.)

For the very first, night, the moment that he knelt and cried, "O Father in heaven, hear me, and let thy face shine upon me"—like a flash of burning fire the words shot from the door of his heart: "I dinna care for him to love me, gin he doesna love ilka [every] body"; and no more prayer went from the desolate boy that night, although he knelt an hour of agony in the freezing dark. Loyal to what he had been taught, he struggled hard to reduce his rebellious will to what he supposed to be the will of God. It was all in vain.

For a voice within him—surely the voice of that God who he thought was not hearing—told him that what he wanted was the love belonging to his human nature, his human needs—not the preference of a court-favorite. He had a dim consciousness that he would be a traitor to his race if he accepted a love, even from God, given him as an exception from his kind. But he did not care to have such a love. It was not what his heart yearned for. It was not *love*. He could not love such a love.

Robert had not the vaguest fancy that God was with him—the spirit of the Father groaning with the spirit of the boy in intercession that could not be uttered. If God had come to him then and comforted him with the assurance of individual favor—but the very supposition is a taking of his name in vain—had Robert found comfort in the fancied assurance that God was his friend in especial, that some private favor was granted to his prayers, that, indeed, would have been to be left to his own inventions, to bring forth not fruits meet for repentance, but fruits for which repentance alone is meet. But God *was* with him, and was indeed victorious in the boy when he rose from his knees, for the last time, as he thought, saying, "I cannot yield—I will pray no more" . . . .

                                   Robert Falconer, Part II, Chapter 1
                                   I John 2:1-2

Shall Life Itself Be Any Less?   February 18

*The young Robert Falconer is walking
amidst the beauties of a rural Scottish garden:*

He . . . went out into the garden, now in the height of its summer. Great cabbage roses hung heavy-headed splendour towards purple-black heartseases, and thin-filmed silvery pods of honesty; tall white lilies mingled with the blossoms of currant bushes, and at their feet the narcissi of old classic legend pressed their warm-hearted paleness into the plebeian thicket of the many-striped gardener's garters. It was a lovely type of a commonwealth indeed, of the garden and kingdom of God. His whole mind was flooded with a sense of sunny wealth. The farmer's neglected garden blossomed into higher glory in his soul. The bloom and the richness and the use were all there; but instead of each flower was a delicate ethereal sense or feeling about that flower. . . . Alas! He was no poet. . . he could see; he could not say.

Let him who doubts recall one of his own vain attempts to convey that which made the oddest of dreams entrancing in loveliness—to convey that aroma of thought, the conscious absence of which made him a fool in his own eyes when he spoke such silly words as alone presented themselves for the service. I can no more describe the emotion aroused in my mind by a gray cloud parting (sic) over a gray stone, by the smell of a sweet-pea, by the sight of one of those long upright pennons of striped grass with the homely name, than I can tell what the glory of God is who made these things. . . . Every dawn of such a feeling is a light-brushed bubble rendering visible for a moment the dark unknown sea of our being which lies beyond the lights of our consciousness, and is the stuff and region of our eternal growth.

And shall life itself be less beautiful than one of its days? Do not believe it, young brother. Men call the shadow, thrown upon the universe where their own dusky souls come between it and the eternal sun, life, and then mourn that it should be less bright than the hopes of their childhood. Keep thou thy soul translucent, that thou mayest never see its shadow; at least never abuse thyself with the philosophy which calls that shadow life. Or, rather would I say, become thou pure in heart, and thou shalt see God, whose vision alone is life.

Robert Falconer, Part II, Chapter 4.
Psalms 19:1-5

February 19 — Now First in Manhood

In an effort to come to terms with his grief at the death of close friends, Robert Falconer as a young man goes to the continent, and there has a deepening spiritual experience:

He soon recovered strength sufficiently to set out again upon his travels, great part of which he performed on foot. In this way he reached Avignon. Passing from one of its narrow streets into an open place in the midst, all at once he beheld, towering above him, on a height that overlooked the whole city and surrounding country, a great crucifix. The form of the Lord of Life still hung in the face of heaven and earth. He bowed his head involuntarily. No matter that when he drew nearer the power of it vanished. The memory of it remained with its first impression, and it had a share in what followed.

He made his way eastward towards the Alps. As he walked one day about noon over a desolate heath-covered height, reminding him not a little of the country of his childhood, the silence seized upon him. In the midst of the silence arose the crucifix, and once more the words which had often returned upon him sounded in the ears of the inner hearing, "My peace I give unto you." They were words he had known from the earliest memorial time. He had heard them in infancy, in childhood, in boyhood, in youth: now first in manhood it flashed upon him that the Lord did really mean that the peace of his soul should be the peace of their souls; that the peace wherewith his own soul was quiet, the peace at the very heart of the universe, was henceforth theirs—open to them, to all the world, to enter and be still. He fell upon his knees, bowed down in the birth of a great hope, held up his hands towards heaven, and cried, "Lord Christ, give me thy peace." He said no more, but rose, caught up his stick, and strode forward, thinking.

He had learned what the sentence meant; what that was of which it spoke he had not yet learned.

Robert Falconer, Part III, Chapter 1
John 14:25-27

Too Good To Last   February 20

In an effort to come to terms with his grief at the death of close friends,
Robert Falconer as a young man goes to the continent, and there has
a deepening spiritual experience from hearing in a dream
the words of Christ: "My peace I give unto you."

He had learned what the sentence meant; what that was of which it spoke he had not yet learned. The peace he had once sought, the peace that lay in the smiles and tenderness of a woman, had "overcome him like a summer cloud," and passed away. There was surely a deeper, a wider, a grander peace for him than that, if indeed it was the same peace wherewith the king of men regarded his approaching end, that he had left as a heritage to his brothers. Suddenly he was aware that the earth had begun to live again. The hum of insects arose from the heath around him; the odor of its flowers entered his dulled sense; the wind kissed him on the forehead; the sky domed up over his head; and the clouds veiled the distant mountain tops like the smoke of incense ascending from the altars of the worshiping earth. All Nature began to minister to one who had begun to lift his head from the baptism of fire. He had thought that Nature could never more be anything to him; and she was waiting on him like a mother. The next moment he was offended with himself for receiving ministrations the reaction of whose loveliness might no longer gather around the form of Mary St. John. Every wavelet of scent, every toss of a flower's head in the breeze, came with a sting in its pleasure—for there was no woman to whom they belonged. Yet he could not shut them out, for God and not woman is the heart of the universe.

I do not think this mood, wherein all forms of beauty sped to his soul as to their own needful center, could have lasted over many miles of his journey. But such delicate inward revelations are none the less precious that they are evanescent. Many feelings are simply to good to last—using the phrase not in the unbelieving sense in which it is generally used, expressing the conviction that God is a hard father, fond of disappointing his children, but to express the fact that intensity and endurance cannot yet coexist in the human economy. But the virtue of a mood depends by no means on its immediate presence. Like any other experience, it may be believed in, and, in the absence which leaves the mind free to contemplate it, work even more good than in its presence.

Robert Falconer, Part III, Chapter 1
Isa. 6:1-3

February 21   It Is After All, Simple

In an effort to come to terms with his grief at the death of close friends,
Robert Falconer as a young man goes to the continent,
and there has a deepening spiritual experience:

All this time he was in the wilderness as much as Moses at the back of Horeb, or St. Paul when he vanishes in Arabia: and he did nothing but read the four gospels and ponder over them. Therefore it is not surprising that he should have already become so familiar with the gospel story, that the moment these questions appeared, the following words should dart to the forefront of his consciousness to meet them: "If any man will do his will, he shall know of the doctrine, whether it be of God, or whether I speak of myself."

The next question naturally was: What is this will of God of which Jesus speaks? Here he found himself in difficulty. The theology of his grandmother rushed in upon him, threatening to overwhelm him with demands as to feeling and inward action from which his soul turned with sickness and fainting. That they were repulsive to him, that they appeared unreal, and contradictory to the nature around him, was not *proof* that they were not of God. But on the other hand, that they demanded what *seemed* to him unjust,—that these demands were founded on what *seemed* to him untruth attributed to God, on ways of thinking and feeling which are certainly degrading in a man,—these were reasons of the very highest nature for refusing to act upon them so long as, from whatever defects it might be in himself, they bore to him this aspect.

When at length he did see what the will of God was, he wondered, so simple did it appear, that he had failed to discover it at once. In trying to understand the words of Jesus by searching back, as it were, for such thoughts and feelings in him as would account for the words he spoke, the perception awoke that at least he could not have meant by the will of God any such theological utterances as those which troubled him. Next it grew plain that what he came to do, was just to lead his life. That he should do the work, such as recorded, and much besides, that the Father gave him to do—this was the will of God concerning him. With this perception arose the conviction that unto every man whom God had sent into the world, he had given a work to do in that world. He had to lead the life God meant him to lead.

Robert Falconer, Part III, Chapter 1
John 15:14-17

What Is Christ's Peace?   February 22

In an effort to come to terms with his grief at the death of close friends, Robert Falconer as a young man goes to the continent, and there has a deepening spiritual experience from hearing in a dream the words of Christ: "My peace I give unto you."

Walking up the edge of the valley, he came upon a little stream whose talk he had heard for some hundred yards . . . . and once more the words arose in his mind, "My peace I give unto you." Now he fell a-thinking what this peace could be. And it came into his mind as he thought, that Jesus had spoken in another place about giving rest to those that came to him, while here he spoke about *"my* peace." Could this *my* mean a certain *kind* of peace that the Lord himself possessed? Perhaps it was in virtue of that peace, whatever it was, that he was the Prince of Peace. Whatever peace he had must be the highest and best peace—therefore the one peace for a man to seek . . .

In the evening he returned to the brook, and fell to searching the story, seeking after the peace of Jesus. He found that the whole passage stood thus: "Peace I leave with you, my peace I give unto you: not as the world giveth give I unto you. Let not your heart be troubled, neither let it be afraid."

He did not leave the place for six weeks. Every day he went to the burn, as he called it, with his New Testament; every day tried yet again to make out something more of what the Savior meant. By the end of the month it had dawned upon him, he hardly knew how, that the peace of Jesus (although, of course, he could not know what it was like till he had it) must have been a peace that came from the doing of the will of his Father. From the account he gave of the discoveries he then made, I venture to represent them in the driest and most exact form that I can find they will admit of. . . . They were these: that Jesus taught—

First,—That a man's business is to do the will of God.

Second,—That God takes upon himself the care of the man.

Third,—Therefore, that a man must never be afraid of anything; and so,

Fourth,—be left free to love God with all his heart, and his neighbor as himself.

Robert Falconer, Part III, Chapter 1
Josh. 1:5-9

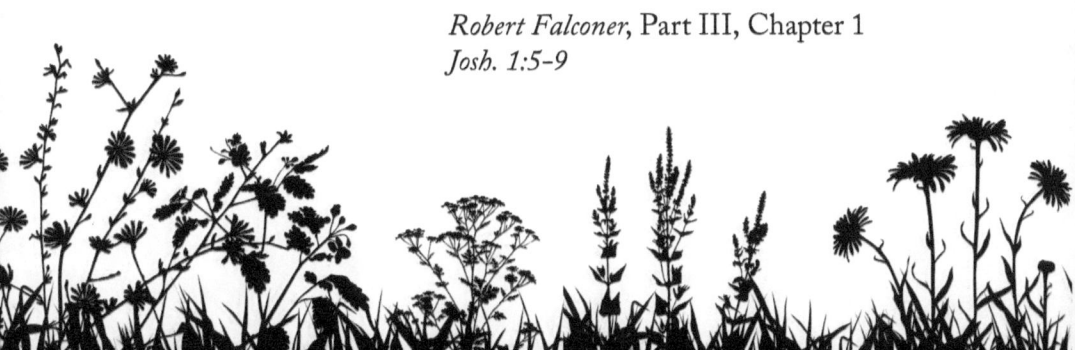

February 23 — Making Him Capable

Robert Falconer as a young man goes to the continent and, after having there a deepening spiritual experience, comes to the following conclusion:

Robert had not settled at any of the universities, but had moved from one to the other as he saw fit, report guiding him to the men who spoke with authority. The time of doubt and anxious questioning was far from over, but the time was long gone by—if in his case it had ever been—when he could be like a wave of the sea, driven of the wind and tossed. He had ever one anchor of the soul, and he found that it held—the faith of Jesus (I say the faith of Jesus, not his own faith in Jesus), the truth of Jesus, the life of Jesus.

However his intellect might be tossed on the waves of speculation and criticism, he found that the word the Lord had spoken remained steadfast; for in doing righteously, in loving mercy, in walking humbly, the conviction increased that Jesus knew the very secret of human life. Now and then some great vision gleamed across his soul of the working of all things towards a far-off goal of simple obedience to a law of life, which God knew, and which his son had justified through sorrow and pain. Again and again the words of the Master gave him a peep into a region where all was explicable, where all that was crooked might be made straight, where every mountain of wrong might be made low, and every valley of suffering exalted. Ever and again some one of the dark perplexities of humanity began to glimmer with light in its inmost depth. Nor was he without those moments of communion when the creature is lifted into the secret place of the Creator.

Looking back to the time when it seemed that he cried and was not heard, he saw that God had been hearing, had been answering, all the time; had been making him capable of receiving the gift for which he prayed.

Robert Falconer, Part III, Chapter 2
Micah 6:8

On this day in 1887: An earthquake shakes Bordighera, damaging a part of Casa Coraggio, the MacDonald's home.

Toning Down His Great Voice — February 24

MacDonald is here musing on the nature of Christ's miracles:

If He came to reveal His Father in miniature, as it were (for in these unspeakable things we can but use figures, and the homeliest may be the holiest), to tone down His great voice, which, too loud for men to hear it aright, could but sound to them as an inarticulate thundering, into such a still small voice as might enter their human hearts in welcome human speech, then the works that His Father does so widely, so grandly that they transcend the vision of men, the Son must do briefly and sharply before their very eyes.

This, I think is the true nature of the miracles, an epitome of God's processes in nature beheld in immediate connection with their source—a source as yet lost to the eyes and too often to the hearts of men in the far-receding gradations of continuous law. That men might see the will of God at work, Jesus did the works of His Father thus.

Here I will suppose some honest, and therefore honorable, reader objecting: "But do you not thus place the miracles in dignity below the ordinary processes of nature?" I answer: The miracles are mightier far than any goings on of nature as beheld by common eyes, dissociating them from a living Will; but the miracles are surely less than those mighty goings on of nature with God beheld at their heart. In the name of Him who delighted to say "My Father is greater than I," I will say that His miracles in bread and in wine were far less grand and less beautiful than the works of the Father they represented, in making the corn to grow in the valleys, and the grapes to drink the sunlight of the hill-sides of the world, with all their infinitudes of tender gradation and delicate mystery of birth.

But the Son of the Father be praised, who, as it were, condensed these mysteries before us, and let us see the precious gifts coming at once from gracious hands—hands that love could kiss and nails could wound.

"Introduction," *The Miracles of our Lord*
Job 37:1-13

February 25 — The Suffering Is Necessary

> "*. . . and you shall call his name Jesus, for he will save his people from their sins.*" Matt. 1:21

I would help some to understand what Jesus came from the home of our Father to be to us and do for us. Everything in the world is more or less misunderstood at first: we have to learn what it is, and come at length to see that it must be so, that it could not be otherwise. Then we know it; and we never know a thing *really* until we know it thus.

I presume there is scarce a human being who, resolved to speak openly, would not confess to having something that plagued him, something from which he would gladly be free, something rendering it impossible for him at the moment to regard life an altogether good thing. Most men, I presume, imagine that, free of such things antagonistic, life would be an unmingled satisfaction, worthy of being prolonged indefinitely.

The cause of their discomfort are of all kinds, and the degrees of it reach from simple uneasiness to a misery such as makes annihilation the highest hope of the sufferer. Perhaps the greater part of the energy of this world's life goes forth in the endeavor to rid itself of discomfort.

However absurd the statement may appear to one who has not yet discovered the fact for himself, the cause of every man's discomfort is evil, moral evil—first of all, evil in himself, his own sin, his own wrongness, his own unrightness; and then, evil in those he loves: with this latter I have not now to deal; the only way to get rid of it is for the man to get rid of his own sin. No special sin may be recognizable as having caused this or that special physical discomfort—which may indeed have originated with some ancestor—but evil in ourselves is the cause of its continuance, the source of its necessity.

The evil is *essentially* unnecessary, and passes with the attainment of the object for which it is permitted—namely the development of pure will in many. The suffering also is essentially unnecessary, but while the evil lasts, the suffering, whether consequent or merely concomitant, is absolutely necessary.

"Salvation from Sin," *The Hope of the Gospel*
Isa. 59:1-2

A Miserable Fancy

February 26

*"... and you shall call his name Jesus,
for he will save his people from their sins."* Matt. 1:21

The Lord never came to deliver men from the consequences of their sins while yet those sins remained: that would be to cast out of the window the medicine of cure while yet the man lay sick; to go dead against the very laws of being. Yet men, loving their sins, and feeling nothing of their dread hatefulness, have, consistent with their low condition, constantly taken this word concerning the Lord to mean that He came to save them from the punishment of their sins. This idea—this miserable fancy, rather—has terribly corrupted the preaching of the gospel. The message of the good news has not been truly delivered.

The mission of Jesus was from the same source and with the same object as the punishment of our sins. He came to work along with our punishment, He came to side with it, and set us free from our sins. No man is safe from hell until he is free from his sins; free of them, hell itself would be endurable to him.

For hell is God's and not the devil's. Hell is on the side of God and man, to free the child of God from the corruption of death. Not one soul will ever be redeemed from hell but by being saved from his sins, from the evil in him. If hell be needful to save him, hell will blaze, and the worm will writhe and bite, until he takes refuge in the will of the Father.

"Salvation from hell" is salvation as conceived by such to whom hell and not evil is the terror. But if even for dread of hell a poor soul seek the Father, he will be heard of Him in his terror, and, taught of Him to seek the immeasurably greater gift, will in the greater receive the less.

"Salvation from Sin," *The Hope of the Gospel*
Heb. 12:4-12

February 27   A Very Important Misapprehension

*". . . and you shall call his name Jesus,
for he will save his people from their sins."* Matt. 1:21

An important misapprehension of the words of the messengers of good tidings is that they threaten us with punishment because of the sins we have committed; whereas, their message is of forgiveness, not of vengeance; of deliverance, not of evil to come. Not for anything he has committed do they threaten a man with the outer darkness. Not for any or all of his sins that are past shall a man be condemned; not for the worst of them needs he dread remaining unforgiven. The sin he dwells in, the sin he will not come out of, is the sole ruin of a man.

His present, his live sins—those pervading his thoughts and ruling his conduct; the sins he keeps doing, and will not give up; the sins he is called to abandon, and clings to; the same sins which are the cause of his misery, though he may not know it—these are they for which he is even now condemned. "This is the judgment, that the light has come into the world, and men loved darkness rather than light, because their deeds were evil."

It is the indwelling badness, ready to produce bad actions, that we need to be delivered from. Against this badness if a man will not strive, he is left to commit evil and reap the consequences. To be saved from these consequences would be no deliverance; it would be an immediate, ever deepening damnation. It is the evil in our being—no essential part of it, thank God—the miserable fact that the very child of God does not care for his Father and will not obey Him, causing us to desire wrongly, act wrongly, or, where we try not to act wrongly, yet making it impossible for us not to feel wrongly—this is what He came to deliver us from—not the things we have done, but the possibility of doing such things any more.

With the departure of this possibility, and with the hope of confession hereafter to those we have wronged, will depart also the power over us of the evil things we have done, and so we shall be saved from them also.

"Salvation from Sin," *The Hope of the Gospel*
John 5:14

THE HIGHEST MUST MEET THE HIGHEST   FEBRUARY 28

*". . . and you shall call his name Jesus,
for he will save his people from their sins."* Matt. 1:21

One master-sin is at the root of all the rest. It is the absence in the man of harmony with the Being whose thought is the man's existence, whose word is the man's power of thought. For the highest creation of God in man is his will, and until the highest in man meets the highest in God, their true relation is not yet a spiritual fact.

The relation exists, but while one of the parties neither knows, loves, nor acts upon it, the relation is, as it were, yet unborn. The highest in man is neither his intellect nor his imagination nor his reason; all are inferior to his will, and indeed, in a grand way, dependent upon it: his will must meet God's—a will *distinct* from God's, else were no *harmony* possible between them.

Not the less, therefore, but the more, is all God's. For God creates in the man the power to will His will. It may cost God a suffering man can never know, to bring the man to the point at which he will will His will; but when he is brought to that point, and declares the truth—that is, for the will of God—he becomes one with God, and the end of God in the man's creation, the end for which Jesus was born and died, is gained.

But I would not be supposed, from what I have said, to imagine the Lord without sympathy for the sorrows and pains which reveal what sin is, and by means of which he would make men sick of sin. With everything human He sympathizes. Evil is not human; it is the defect and opposite of the human; but the suffering that follows it is human, belonging of necessity to the human that has sinned. While it is by cause of sin, suffering is *for* the sinner, that he may be delivered from his sin.

"Salvation from Sin," *The Hope of the Gospel*
Luke 13:34

February 29   Let's Join The Lord's Side

*". . . and you shall call his name Jesus,
for he will save his people from their sins."* Matt. 1:21

The bad that lives in us, our evil judgments, our unjust desires, our hate and pride and envy and greed and self-satisfaction—these are the souls of our sins, our live sins, more terrible than the bodies of our sins, namely, the deeds we do, inasmuch as they not only produce these loathsome things, but make us loathsome as they.

Our wrong deeds are our dead works; our evil thoughts are our live sins. These, the essential opposites of faith and love, the sins that dwell and work in us, are the sins from which Jesus came to deliver us. When we turn against them and refuse to obey them, they rise in fierce insistence, but the same moment begin to die. We are then on the Lord's side, as He has always been on ours, and he begins to deliver us from them.

As the love of Him who is love transcends ours as the heavens are higher than the earth, so must He desire in His child infinitely more than the most jealous love of the best mother can desire in hers. He would have him rid of all discontent, all fear, all grudging, all bitterness in word or thought, all gauging and measuring of his own with a different rod from that he would apply to another's. He will have no curling of the lip; no indifference in him to the man whose service in any form he uses; no desire to excel another, no contentment at gaining by his loss. He will not have him receive the smallest service without gratitude; would not hear from him a tone to jar the heart of another, a word to make it ache, be the ache ever so transient. From such, as from all other sins, Jesus was born to deliver us; not, primarily, or by itself, from the punishment of any of them. When all are gone, the holy punishment will have departed also. He came to make us good, and therein blessed children.

"Salvation from Sin," *The Hope of the Gospel*
Matt. 15:16-20

The Only Possible Way   March 1

> *". . . and you shall call his name Jesus,*
> *for he will save his people from their sins."* Matt. 1:21

Jesus is in Himself aware of every human pain. He feels it also. In Him, too, it is pain. ` With the energy of tenderest love He wills his brothers and sisters free, that He may fill them to overflowing with that essential thing, joy. For that they were indeed created. But the moment they exist, truth becomes the first thing, not happiness; and He must make them true.

Were it possible, however, for pain to continue after evil was gone, He would never rest while one ache was yet in the world. Perfect in sympathy, He feels in Himself, I say, the tortured presence of every nerve that lacks its repose. The man may recognize the evil in him only as pain; he may know little and care nothing about his sins; yet is the Lord sorry for his pain. He cries aloud, "Come unto me, all ye that labor and are heavy laden, and I will give you rest."

He does not say, "Come unto me, all ye that feel the burden of your sins." He opens His arms to all weary enough to come to Him in the poorest hope of rest. Right gladly would He free them from their misery—but He knows only one way: He will teach them to be like Himself, meek and lowly, bearing with gladness the yoke of His Father's will. This is the one, the only right, the only possible way of freeing them from their sins, the cause of their unrest. With them the weariness comes first; with Him the sins: there is but one cure for both—the will of the Father.

The disobedient and selfish would fain in the hell of their hearts possess the liberty and gladness that belong to purity and love, but they cannot have them; they are weary and heavy-laden, both with what they are, and because of what they were made for but are not. The Lord knows what they need; they know only what they want. They want ease; he knows they need purity.

> "Salvation from Sin," *The Hope of the Gospel*
> Isa. 63:7-10

March 2 — Our Highest Privlege

"... and you shall call his name Jesus, for he will save his people from their sins." Matt. 1:21

It may be my reader will desire me to say *how* the Lord will deliver him from his sins. That is like the lawyer's "Who is my neighbor?" The spirit of such a mode of receiving the offer of the Lord's deliverance is the root of all the horrors of corrupt theology, so acceptable to those who love weak and beggarly hornbooks of religion. Such questions spring from the passion for the fruit of the tree of knowledge, not the fruit of the tree of life. Men would understand: they do not care to *obey*—understand where it is impossible they should understand save by obeying.

For the sake of knowing, they postpone that which alone can enable them to know. They will not accept, that is, act upon, their highest privilege, that of obeying the Son of God. It is on them that do His will that the day dawns; to them the day-star arises in their hearts. Obedience is the soul of knowledge. By obedience, I intend no kind of obedience to man or submission to authority claimed by man or community of men. I mean obedience to the will of the Father, however revealed in our conscience.

God forbid I should seem to despise understanding. The New Testament is full of urgings to understand. Our whole life, to be life at all, must be a growth in understanding. What I cry out upon is the misunderstanding that comes of man's endeavor to understand while not obeying. Upon obedience our energy must be spent; understanding will follow.

"Salvation from Sin," *The Hope of the Gospel*
John 6:66-68

The Sum Of The Matter   March 3

> *". . . and you shall call his name Jesus,*
> *for he will save his people from their sins."* Matt. 1:21

Not anxious to know our duty, or knowing it and not doing it, how shall we understand that which only a true heart and a clean soul can ever understand? The power in us that would understand were it free, lies in the bonds of imperfection and impurity, and is therefore incapable of judging the divine. It cannot see the truth. If it could see it, it would not know it, and would not have it. Until a man begins to obey, the light that is in him is darkness.

Any honest soul may understand this much, however—for it is a thing we may of ourselves judge to be right—that the Lord cannot save a man from his sins while he holds to his sins. It is but common sense that a man, longing to be freed from suffering, or made able to bear it, should betake himself to the Power by whom he is. Equally is it common sense that, if a man would be delivered from the evil in him, he must himself begin to cast it out, himself begin to disobey it, and work righteousness. It is also common sense that a man should look for and expect the help of his Father in the endeavor. Alone, he might labor to all eternity and not succeed. He who has not made himself cannot set himself right without Him who made him. But his Maker is in him, and is his strength.

He cannot make himself pure, but he can leave that which is impure; he cannot save himself, but he can let the Lord save him. The struggle of his weakness is as essential to the coming victory as the strength of Him who resisted unto death, striving against sin.

The sum of the whole matter is this: the Son has come from the Father to set the children free from their sins; the children must hear and obey Him, that He may send forth judgment unto victory.

"Salvation from Sin," *The Hope of the Gospel*
Col. 3:5-10

March 4   The Only Possible Preparation

*John the baptizer appeared in the wilderness,
preaching a baptism of repentance for the forgiveness of sins.* Mark 1:4

God and man must combine for salvation from sin, and the same word, here and elsewhere translated *remission* [i.e., in the KJV], seems to be employed in the New Testament for the share of both in the great deliverance. Both God and man send away sins, but in the one case God sends away the sins of the man, and in the other the man sends away his own sins. That the phrase here intends repentance unto the ceasing from sin, the giving up of what is wrong, I will try to show at least probable.

In the first place, the user of the phrase either defines the change of mind he means as one that has for its object the pardon of God, or as one that reaches to a new life: the latter seems to me the more natural interpretation by far. The kind and scope of the repentance or change, and not any end to be gained by it, appears intended. The change must be one of will and conduct—a radical change of life on the part of the man: he must repent—that is, change his mind—not to a different opinion, not even to a mere betterment of his conduct—not to anything less than a sending away of sins.

Next, in St. Matthew's gospel, the Baptist's buttressing argument, or imminent motive for the change he is pressing upon the people, is that the kingdom of heaven is at hand: "Because the King of heaven is coming, you must give up your sinning." The same argument for immediate action lies in his quotation from Isaiah: "Prepare ye the way of the Lord; make straight in the desert a highway for our God." The only true, the only possible preparation for the coming Lord, is to cease from doing evil, and begin to do well—to send away sin.

      "The Remission of Sins," *The Hope of the Gospel*
      Rom. 13:11-14

THE BAPTISM OF FIRE   MARCH 5

John the baptizer appeared in the wilderness, preaching a baptism of repentance for the forgiveness of sins. Mark 1:4

When the multitudes came to the prophet, and all—along with the classes most obnoxious to the rest, the publicans and the soldiers—asked what he would have them do, his instruction was throughout in the same direction: they must send away their sins, and each must begin with the fault that lay next to him. The kingdom of heaven was at hand; they must prepare the way of the Lord by beginning to do as must be done in His kingdom.

They could not rid themselves of their sins, but they could set about sending them away; they could quarrel with them, and proceed to turn them out of the house: the Lord was on His way to do His part in their final banishment. Those who had repented to the sending away of their sins, He would baptize with a holy power to send them away indeed. The operant will to get rid of them would be baptized with a fire that should burn them up.

I think, then, that the part of the repentant man, and not the part of God, in sending away of sins, is intended here. It is the man's one preparation for receiving the power to overcome them, the baptism of fire.

"The Remission of Sins," *The Hope of the Gospel*
Rev. 2:4-7

On this day in 1879: The MacDonald's fifteen-year-old son Maurice dies unexpectedly in Porto Fino after a short illness. Because of restrictions by the local parish, the family had to bury his body on a rocky promontory outside the walls of the church cemetery.

March 6   The Call To Real Existence

*John the baptizer appeared in the wilderness,
preaching a baptism of repentance for the forgiveness of sins.* Mark 1:4

Not seldom, what comes in the name of the gospel of Jesus Christ must seem, even to one not far from the kingdom of heaven, no good news at all. It does not draw him; it wakes in him not a single hope. He has no desire after what it offers him as redemption. The God it gives him news of is not one to whom he would draw nearer. But when such a man comes to see that the very God must be his life, the heart of his consciousness; when he perceives that, rousing himself to put from him what is evil, and do the duty that lies at his door, he may fearlessly claim the help of Him who "loved him into being," then his will immediately sides with his conscience; he begins to try to *be*; and—first thing toward being—to rid himself of what is antagonistic to all being, namely, *wrong*.

Multitudes will not even approach the appalling task, the labor and pain of *being*. God is doing His part, is undergoing the mighty toil of an age-long creation, endowing men with power to be; but few as yet are those who take up their part, who respond to the call of God, who will to be, who put forth a divine effort after real existence. To the many the spirit of the prophet cries, "Turn ye, and change your way! The kingdom of heaven is near you. Let your King possess his own. Let God throne Himself in you, that His liberty be your life, and you free men. That He may enter, clear the house for him. Send away the bad things out of it. Depart from evil, and do good. The duty that lieth at thy door, do it, be it great or small."

For indeed in this region there is no great or small. "Be content with your wages," said the Baptist to the soldiers. To many people now, the word would be, "Rule you temper"; or "Be courteous to all"; or, "Let each hold the other better than himself", or, "Be just to your neighbor that you may love him." We must bestir ourselves in the very spot on which we stand.

> "The Remission of Sins," *The Hope of the Gospel*
> I Thess. 4:3-8

WHY WAS CHRIST BAPTISED?

John the baptizer appeared in the wilderness, preaching a baptism of repentance for the forgiveness of sins. Mark 1:4

He came to John to be baptized; and most would say John's baptism was of repentance for the remission or pardon of sins. But the Lord could not be baptized for the remission of sins, for He had never done a selfish, an untrue, or an unfair thing. He needed no forgiveness; there was nothing to forgive. No more could He be baptized for repentance: in Him repentance would have been to turn to evil! Where, then, was the propriety of His coming to be baptized by John, and insisting on being by him baptized? It must lie elsewhere.

If we take the words of John to mean "the baptism of repentance unto the sending away of sins"; and if we bear in mind that in His case repentance could not be, inasmuch as what repentance is necessary to bring about in man was already existent in Jesus; then, altering the words to fit the case, and saying "the baptism of willed devotion to the sending away of sin," we shall see at once how the baptism of Jesus was a thing right and fit.

That He had no sin to repent of, was not because He was so constituted that He could not sin if He would; it was because, of His own will and judgment, He sent sin away from Him—sent it from Him with the full choice and energy of His nature. God knows good and evil, and, blessed be His name, chooses good. Never will his righteous anger make Him unfair to us, make Him forget that we are dust. Like Him, his Son also chose good, and in that choice resisted all temptation to help His fellows otherwise than as their and His father would.

> "The Remission of Sins," *The Hope of the Gospel*
> II Cor. 5:21

March 8   The Ways Of Help Essential

John the baptizer appeared in the wilderness, preaching a baptism of repentance for the forgiveness of sins. Mark 1:4

Instead of crushing the power of evil by divine force; instead of compelling justice and destroying the wicked; instead of making peace on the earth by the rule of a perfect prince; instead of gathering the children of Jerusalem under His wings whether they would or not, and saving them from the horrors that anguished His prophetic soul— He let evil work its will while it lived; He contented himself with the slow unencouraging ways of help essential; making men good; casting out, not merely controlling Satan; carrying to their perfect issue on earth the old primeval principles because of which the Father honored Him: "You love righteousness and hate wickedness. Therefore God, your God, has anointed you with the oil of gladness above your fellows."

To love righteousness is to make it grow, not to avenge it; and to win for righteousness the true victory, He, as well as His brethren, had to send away evil. Throughout His life on earth, He resisted every impulse to work more rapidly for a lower good—strong, perhaps, when He saw old age and innocence and righteousness trodden under foot.

What but this gives any worth of reality to the temptation in the wilderness, to the devil's departing from Him for a season, to his coming again to experience a like failure? Ever and ever, in the whole attitude of His being, in his heart always lifted up, in His unfailing readiness to pull with the Father's yoke, He was repelling, driving away sin—away from Himself, and, as Lord of men, and their savior, away from others also, bringing them to abjure it like Himself.

No man, least of all any lord of men, can be good without willing to be good, without setting himself against evil, without sending away sin. Other men have to send it away out of them; the Lord had to send it away from before Him, that it should not enter into Him. Therefore is the stand against sin common to the Captain of salvation and the soldiers under Him.

        "The Remission of Sins," *The Hope of the Gospel*
        Luke 4:1-13

On this day in 1851: George MacDonald marries Louisa Powell at The Old Gravel Pits, a quaint old meeting house in Hackney

All That The Children Want   March 9

John the baptizer appeared in the wilderness, preaching a baptism of repentance for the forgiveness of sins. Mark 1:4

What did Jesus come into the world to do? The will of God in saving His people from their sins—not from the punishment of their sins, that blessed aid to repentance, but from their sins themselves, the paltry as well as the heinous, the venial as well as the loathsome. His whole work was and is to send away sin—to banish it from the earth, yea, to cast it into the abyss of non-existence behind the back of God. He resisted unto blood; the soldiers that followed Him He taught and trained to resist also unto blood, striving against sin; so He became the Captain of their salvation, and they, freed themselves, fought and suffered for others.

Such, then, as were baptized by John, were initiated into the company of those whose work was to send sin out of the world, and first, by sending it out of themselves, by having done with it. Their earliest endeavor in this direction would, as I have said, open the door for that help to enter without which a man could never succeed in the divinely arduous task—could not, because the region in which the work has to be wrought lies in the very roots of his own being, where, knowing nothing of the secrets of his essential existence, he can immediately do nothing, where the Maker of him alone is potent, alone is consciously present.

The change that must pass in him more than equals a new creation, inasmuch as it is a higher creation. But its necessity is involved in a former creation; and thence we have a right to ask help of our Creator, for He requires of us what He has created us unable to effect without Him.

For the well-being and perfecting of his existence, the sole thing necessary is, that the man should know his Maker present in him. All that the children want is their Father.

> "The Remission of Sins," *The Hope of the Gospel*
> Psalms 32

March 10 — Must We Fail Still?

"'Child, why have you treated us like this? Look, your father and I have been searching for you in great anxiety.' He said to them, 'Why were you searching for me? Did you not know that I must be in my Father's house?'" Luke 2:48, 49

Was that His saying? Why did they not understand it? Do we understand it? What did His saying mean? The Greek is not absolutely clear. Whether the Syriac words He used were more precise, who in this world can tell? But had we heard His very words, we too, with His father and mother, would have failed to understand them. Must we fail still?

Let us see what lies in the Greek to guide us to the thought in the mind of the Lord when He thus reasoned with the apprehensions of His father and mother. The Greek, taken literally, says, "Did you not know that I must be in the _____ of my Father?" The authorized version supplies *business*; the revised, *house*. There is no noun in the Greek, and the article "the" is in the plural. To translate it as literally as it can be translated, making of it an English sentence, the saying stands, "Did you not know that I must be in the things of my Father?"

The plural article implies the English *things*; and the question is then, What *things* does He mean? The word might mean *affairs* or *business*; but why the plural article should be contracted to mean *house*, I do not know. In a great wide sense, no doubt, the word *house* might be used, as I am about to show, but surely not as meaning the temple.

He was arguing for confidence in God on the part of His parents, not for a knowledge of His whereabouts. The same thing that made them anxious concerning Him prevented them from understanding His words—lack, namely, of faith in the Father. This, the one thing He came into the world to teach men, those words were meant to teach His parents. They are spirit and life, involving the one principle by which men shall live. They hold the same core as His words to His disciples in the storm, "Where is your faith?"

"Jesus in the World," *The Hope of the Gospel*
Col. 3:15-17

Not At Home Yet — March 11

"'Child, why have you treated us like this? Look, your father and I have been searching for you in great anxiety.' He said to them, 'Why were you searching for me? Did you not know that I must be in my Father's house?'" Luke 2:48, 49

The Lord meant to remind them, or rather to make them feel, for they had not yet learned the fact, that He was never away from home, could not be lost, as they had thought Him; that He was in His Father's house all the time, where no hurt could come to Him. "The things" about Him were the furniture and utensils of His home; He knew them all and how to use them. "I must be among my Father's belongings." The world was his home because it was his Father's house. He was not a stranger who did not know His way about in it. He was no lost child, but with His Father all the time.

Here we find one main thing wherein the Lord differs from us: we are not at home in this great universe, our Father's house. We ought to be, and one day we shall be, but we are not yet. This reveals Jesus more than man, by revealing Him more man than we. We are not complete men, we are not anything near it, and are therefore out of harmony, more or less, with everything in the house of our birth and habitation. When we are true children, if not the world, then the universe will be our home, felt and known as such, the house we are satisfied with, and would not change.

Hence, until then, the hard struggle, the constant strife we hold with *Nature*,—as we call the things of our Father—a strife invaluable for our development, at the same time manifesting us not yet men enough to be lords of the house built for us to live in. We cannot govern or command it as did the Lord, because we are not at one with His Father, therefore neither in harmony with His things, nor rulers over them. Our best power in regard to them is but to find out wonderful facts concerning them and their relations, and turn these facts to our uses or systems of our own.

"Jesus in the World," *The Hope of the Gospel*
Heb. 13:12-4

March 12   His Father's Things

"'Child, why have you treated us like this? Look, your father and I have been searching for you in great anxiety.' He said to them, 'Why were you searching for me? Did you not know that I must be in my Father's house?'" Luke 2:48, 49

Think for a moment how Jesus was at home among the things of His Father. It seems to me, I repeat, a spiritless explanation of His words—that the temple was the place where naturally He was at home. Does He make the least lamentation over the temple? It is Jerusalem He weeps over—the men of Jerusalem, the killers, the stoners. What was His place of prayer? Not the temple, but the mountain-top.

Where does He find symbols whereby to speak of what goes on in the mind and before the face of His Father in heaven? Not in the temple; not in its rites; not on its altars; not in its holy of holies; He finds them in the world and its lovely-lowly facts; on the roadside, in the field, in the vineyard, in the garden, in the house; in the family, and the commonest of its affairs—the lighting of the lamp, the leavening of the meal, the neighbor's borrowing, the losing of the coin, the straying of the sheep. Even in the unlovely facts also of the world which he turns to holy use—such as the unjust judge, the false steward, the faithless laborers—He ignores the temple.

The world has for Him no chamber of terror. He walks to the door of the sepulcher, the sealed cellar of his Father's house, and calls forth its four-day's dead. He rebukes the mourners, He stays the funeral, and gives back the departed children to the parents' arms. The roughest of its servants do not make Him wince; none of them are so arrogant as to disobey His word; he falls asleep in the midst of the storm that threatens to swallow His boat. Hear how, on that same occasion, he rebukes his disciples! The children to tremble at a gust of wind in the house! God's little ones afraid of the storm! Hear Him tell the watery floor to be still .... All His life he was among His Father's things, either in heaven or in the world.

"Jesus in the World," *The Hope of the Gospel*
Matt. 13:1-9

Traveling To Such a Home

"'Child, why have you treated us like this? Look, your father and I have been searching for you in great anxiety.' He said to them, 'Why were you searching for me? Did you not know that I must be in my Father's house?'" Luke 2:48, 49

Did He ever say, "This is mine, not yours"? Did He not say, "All things are mine, therefore they are yours"? That the things were His Father's made them precious things to Him. Oh, for His liberty among the things of the Father! Only by knowing them the things of our Father can we escape enslaving ourselves to them.

Through the false, the infernal idea of *having*, of *possessing* them, we make them our tyrants, make the relation between them and us an evil thing. The world was a blessed place to Jesus, because everything in it was His Father's. What pain must it not have been to Him, to see His brothers so vilely misuse the Father's house by grasping, each for himself, at the family things! If the knowledge that a spot in the landscape retains in it some pollution suffices to disturb our pleasure in the whole, how must it not have been with Him, how must it not be with Him now, in regard to the disfigurements and defilements caused by the greed of men, by their haste to be rich, in His Father's lovely house!

Jesus, then, would have His parents understand that He was in His Father's world among His Father's things, where was nothing to hurt Him. He knew them all, was in the secret of them all, could use and order them as did His Father. To this same I think all we humans are destined to rise. Though so many of us now are ignorant what kind of home we need, what a home we are capable of having, we too shall inherit the earth with the Son eternal, doing with it as we would—willing with the will of the Father. To such a home as we now inhabit, only perfected, and perfectly behold, we are traveling—never to reach it save by the obedience that makes us the children, therefore the heirs, of God. And, thank God! There the Father does not die that the children may inherit; for, bliss of heaven! We inherit with the Father.

"Jesus in the World," *The Hope of the Gospel*
John 16:12-15

March 14 — They Wanted Vengeance

He unrolled the scroll and found the place were it was written: "The Spirit of the Lord is upon me, because he has anointed me to bring good news to the poor. He has sent me to proclaim release to the captives and recovery of sight to the blind, to let the oppressed go free, to proclaim the year of the Lord's favor." And he rolled up the scroll, gave it back to the attendant, and sat down. The eyes of all in the synagogue were fixed on him. Then he began to say to them, "Today this scripture has been fulfilled in your hearing." Luke 4:17-21

The point at which the Lord stops in His reading is suggestive: He closes the book, leaving the words "and the day of vengeance of our God," or, as the Septuagint, "the day of recompense," unread: God's vengeance is as holy a thing as His love, yea, is love, for God is love and God is not vengeance; but, apparently, the Lord would not give the word a place in his announcement of his mission: his hearers would not recognize it as a form of the Father's love, but as vengeance on their enemies, not vengeance on the selfishness of those who would not be their brother's keeper.

He had not begun with Nazareth, neither with Galilee. "A prophet has no honor in his own country," He said, and began to teach where it was more likely He would be heard. It is true that He wrought his first miracle in Cana, but that was at His mother's request, not of His own intent, and He did not begin His teaching there. He went first to Jerusalem, there cast out the buyers and sellers from the temple, and did other notable things alluded to by St. John; then went back to Galilee, where, having seen the things He did in Jerusalem, His former neighbors were now prepared to listen to Him.

Such was the fame of the new prophet, that even they were willing to hear in the synagogue what He had to say to them—thence to determine for themselves what claim He had to an honorable reception. But the eye of their judgment was not single, therefore was their body full of darkness. Should Nazareth indeed prove, to their self-glorifying satisfaction, the city of the great Prophet, they were more than ready to grasp at the renown of having produced Him; he was indeed the great Prophet, and within a few minutes they would have slain Him for the honor of Israel. In the ignoble even the love of their country partakes largely of the ignoble.

"Jesus and His Fellow Townsmen," *The Hope of the Gospel*
Isa. 61:1-3

The Real Source of Misery — March 15

When he came to Nazareth, where he had been brought up, he went to the synagogue on the Sabbath day, as was his custom. He stood up to read, and the scroll of the prophet Isaiah was given to him. He unrolled the scroll and found the place were it was written: "The Spirit of the Lord is upon me, because he has anointed me to bring good news to the poor. He has sent me to proclaim release to the captives and recovery of sight to the blind, to let the oppressed go free, to proclaim the year of the Lord's favor." And he rolled up the scroll, gave it back to the attendant, and sat down. The eyes of all in the synagogue were fixed on him. Then he began to say to them, "Today this scripture has been fulfilled in your hearing." Luke 4:16-21

There was a shadow of the hateless vengeance of God in the expulsion of the dishonest dealers from the temple with which the Lord initiated His mission: that was His first parable to Jerusalem; to Nazareth he comes with the sweetest words of the prophet of hope in His mouth—good tidings of great joy—of healing and sight and liberty; followed by the godlike announcement, that what the prophet had promised He was come to fulfil. His heart, His eyes, His lips, his hands—His whole body is full of gifts for men, and that day was the Scripture fulfilled in their ears.

The prophecy had gone before that he should save His people from their sins; He brings an announcement they will better understand: He is come, he says, to deliver men from sorrow and pain, ignorance and oppression, everything that makes life hard and unfriendly. What a gracious speech, what a daring pledge to a world whelmed in tyranny and wrong!

Every one will, I presume, confess to more or less misery. Its apparent source may be this or that; its real source is, to use a poor figure, a dislocation of the juncture between the created and the creating life. This primal evil is the parent of evils unnumbered, hence of miseries multitudinous, under the weight of which the arrogant man cries out against life, and goes on to misuse it, while the child looks around for help—and who shall help him but his Father! The Father is with him all the time, but it may be long ere the child knows himself in his arms. The gospel according to this or that expounder of it may repel him unspeakably; the gospel according to Jesus Christ attracts him supremely, and ever holds where it has drawn him.

"Jesus and His Fellow Townsmen," *The Hope of the Gospel*
Phil. 4:4-7

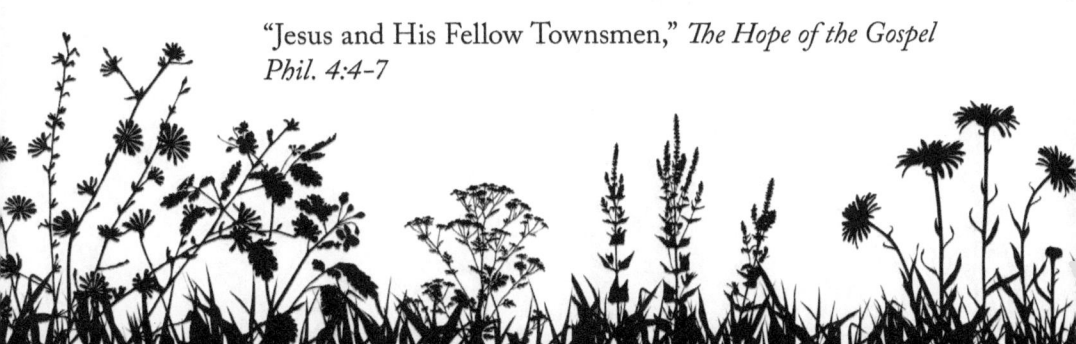

March 16   The False Gospel and the True

When he came to Nazareth, where he had been brought up, he went to the synagogue on the Sabbath day, as was his custom. He stood up to read, and the scroll of the prophet Isaiah was given to him. He unrolled the scroll and found the place were it was written: "The Spirit of the Lord is upon me, because he has anointed me to bring good news to the poor. He has sent me to proclaim release to the captives and recovery of sight to the blind, to let the oppressed go free, to proclaim the year of the Lord's favor." And he rolled up the scroll, gave it back to the attendant, and sat down. The eyes of all in the synagogue were fixed on him. Then he began to say to them, "Today this scripture has been fulfilled in your hearing." Luke 4:16-21

To the priest, the scribe, the elder. . . in refusing what they teach, [the true child of God] answers, "It is life or death to me. Your gospel I cannot take. To believe as you would have me believe would be to lose my God. Your God is not God to me. I do not desire Him. I would rather die the death than believe in such a God. In the name of the true God, I cast your gospel from me; it is not gospel, and to believe it would be to wrong Him in whom alone lies my hope.

"But to believe in such a man," he might go on to say, "with such a message as I read in the New Testament, is life from the dead. I have yielded myself, to live no more in the idea of self, but with the life of God. To Him I commit the creature He has made, that He may live in it, and work out its life—develop it according to the idea of it in His own creating mind. I fall in with His ways for me. I believe in Him. I trust Him. I try to obey Him. I look to be rendered capable of and receive a pure vision of His will, freedom from the prison-house of my limitation, from the bondage of a finite existence. For the finite that dwells in the infinite, and in which the infinite dwells, is finite no longer."

Those who are thus children indeed, are little Gods, the divine brood of the infinite Father. No mere promise of deliverance from the consequences of sin would be any gospel to me. Less than the liberty of a holy heart, less than the freedom of the Lord himself, will never satisfy one human soul. Father, set me free in the glory of thy will, so that I will only as thou willest. Thy will be at once thy perfection and mine. Thou alone art deliverance—absolute safety from every cause and kind of trouble that ever existed, anywhere now exists, or ever can exist in thy universe.

"Jesus and His Fellow Townsmen," *The Hope of the Gospel*
Heb. 10:19-23

Not For the Wise and Prudent   March 17

When he came to Nazareth, where he had been brought up, he went to the synagogue on the Sabbath day, as was his custom. He stood up to read, and the scroll of the prophet Isaiah was given to him. He unrolled the scroll and found the place were it was written: "The Spirit of the Lord is upon me, because he has anointed me to bring good news to the poor. He has sent me to proclaim release to the captives and recovery of sight to the blind, to let the oppressed go free, to proclaim the year of the Lord's favor." And he rolled up the scroll, gave it back to the attendant, and sat down. The eyes of all in the synagogue were fixed on him. Then he began to say to them, "Today this scripture has been fulfilled in your hearing." Luke 4:16-21

The people of the Lord's town, to whom He read, appropriating the gracious words of the prophet, were of the wise and prudent of their day. With one and the same breath they seem to cry, "These things are good, it is true, but they must come after our way. We must have the promise of our fathers fulfilled—that we shall rule the world, the chosen of God, the children of Abraham and Israel. We want to be a free people, manage our own affairs, live in plenty, and do as we please. Liberty alone can ever cure the woes of which you speak. We do not need to be better; we are well enough. Give us riches and honor, and keep us content with ourselves, that we may be satisfied with our own likeness, and thou shalt be the Messiah." Never, perhaps, would such be men's spoken words, but the prevailing condition of their minds might often well take form in such speech.

But the Lord knew what was in their hearts; He knew the false notion with which they were almost ready to declare for Him; He knew also the final proof to which they were in their wisdom and prudence about to subject Him. His mighty works were not meant for such as they—to convince them of what they were incapable of understanding or welcoming! Those who would not believe without signs and wonders could never believe worthily with any number of them, and none should be given them! His mighty works were to rouse the love and strengthen the faith of the meek and lowly in heart, of such as were ready to come to the light, and show that they were of the light.

"Jesus and His Fellow Townsmen," *The Hope of the Gospel*
I Cor. 1:20-25

1882: Caroline Grace (MacDonald) Jameson gives birth to MacDonald's grandchild, Octavia Grace. Caroline dies two months later.

March 18 — Why Indeed

When he came to Nazareth, where he had been brought up, he went to the synagogue on the Sabbath day, as was his custom. He stood up to read, and the scroll of the prophet Isaiah was given to him. He unrolled the scroll and found the place were it was written: "The Spirit of the Lord is upon me, because he has anointed me to bring good news to the poor. He has sent me to proclaim release to the captives and recovery of sight to the blind, to let the oppressed go free, to proclaim the year of the Lord's favor." And he rolled up the scroll, gave it back to the attendant, and sat down. The eyes of all in the synagogue were fixed on him. Then he began to say to them, "Today this scripture has been fulfilled in your hearing." Luke 4:16-21

Christ knew how poor the meaning the Nazarenes put on the word he had read; what low expectations they had of the Messiah when most they longed for His coming. They did not hear the prophet while he read the prophet! Salvation from their sins was not in their hearts, not in their imaginations, not at all in their thoughts. They had heard Him read His commission to heal the broken-hearted; they would rush to break hearts in His name. The Lord knew them and their vain expectations. He would have no such followers—no followers on false conceptions—no followers whom wonders would delight but nowise better! The Nazarenes were not yet of the sort that needed but one change to be His people. The Lord saw them on the point of challenging a display of His power, and anticipated the challenge with a refusal.

How could there be any miracle for such? They were well satisfied with themselves, and "Nothing almost sees miracles but misery." Need and the upward look, the mood ready to believe when and where it can, the embryonic faith, is dear to Him whose love would have us trust Him. Let any man seek Him—not in curious inquiry whether the story of Him may be true or cannot be true, but in humble readiness to accept Him altogether if only he can—and he shall find Him; we shall not fail of help to believe because we doubt. But if the questioner be such that the dispersion of his doubt would leave him in disobedience, the Power of truth has not care to effect his conviction. Why cast out a devil that the man may the better do the work of the devil?

"Jesus and His Fellow Townsmen," *The Hope of the Gospel*
I Cor 1:26-31

Only For The Meek And Lowley — March 19

When he came to Nazareth, where he had been brought up, he went to the synagogue on the Sabbath day, as was his custom. He stood up to read, and the scroll of the prophet Isaiah was given to him. He unrolled the scroll and found the place were it was written: "The Spirit of the Lord is upon me, because he has anointed me to bring good news to the poor. He has sent me to proclaim release to the captives and recovery of sight to the blind, to let the oppressed go free, to proclaim the year of the Lord's favor." And he rolled up the scroll, gave it back to the attendant, and sat down. The eyes of all in the synagogue were fixed on him. Then he began to say to them, "Today this scripture has been fulfilled in your hearing." Luke 4:16-21

The Lord could easily have satisfied the Nazarenes that He was the Messiah: they would but have hardened into the nucleus of an army for the subjugation of the world. To a warfare with their own sins, to the subjugation of their doing and desiring the will of the great Father, all the miracles in His power would never have persuaded them. A true convincement is not possible to hearts and minds like theirs. Not only is it impossible for a low man to believe a thousandth part of what a noble man can, but a low man cannot believe anything as a noble man believes it.

The men of Nazareth could have believed in Jesus as their savior from the Romans. As their savior from their sins they could not believe in Him, for they loved their sins. The King of heaven came to offer them a share in His kingdom; but they were not poor in spirit, and the kingdom of heaven was not for them. Gladly would they have inherited the earth; but they were not meek, and the earth was for the lowly children of the perfect Father.

"Jesus and His Fellow Townsmen," *The Hope of the Gospel*
Rom. 2:28-29

March 20 Strangers And Pilgrims

This excerpt is from a letter, headed Porto Fino, March 20, 1879, to their close friends and benefactors, the William Cowper-Temples, as they were searching for a place to settle in Italy. Their two children Mary and Maurice have both recently died.

... My wife says if we get this house we are looking after now she would like to put up in the hall "And they confessed that they were pilgrims and strangers on the earth." That is our mood, and may it last until we shall be no longer strangers or pilgrims but at home. ... Nothing comes to perfection—there is no time for anything but getting ready to go. But my faith and hope grow stronger. I seem very hard to teach. Imagination must be sent out of the throne of Faith, and taught to sit lowly on the footstool. A thousand things have to be set right. I have to be simply the child that tries to be good, and keeps close by his father. One day the door will open and we shall find ourselves at least started for home and the finding of our own. Meantime I must try to be better for the love of my children whom I cannot see, and that will bring me nearer to them.

Still I have the old story to tell you—more and more delight in my New Testament. I had no idea how inadequate was the English of the Epistles, nor how much I should learn from the Greek. Some day God will, I trust, reveal himself to me as he has never done yet, and I shall be as sure as St. Paul. I must try not to stand in the way of his redeeming will with me—for he is doing his best for me as for us all. Once I repeated to my lovely child—"Let patience have her perfect work that ye may be perfect and entire, wanting nothing"—and I delight to think that he asked for it again a minute after. Patient indeed he was—I think as quietly trusting as boy could be. May God make me a better father by the time I find him again, for my boy he must be to all eternity. ...

The Beinecke Rare Book and Manuscript Library
Jer. 15:16

Not As They Expected   March 21

> *Then he began to speak, and taught them, saying: "Blessed are the poor in spirit, for theirs is the kingdom of heaven. . . . Blessed are the meek, for they will inherit the earth."* Matt. 5:2, 3, 5

The words of the Lord are the seed sown by the sower. Into our hearts they must fall that they may grow. Meditation and prayer must water them, and obedience keep them in the sunlight. Thus will they bear fruit for the Lord's gathering.

Those of His disciples, that is, obedient hearers, who had any experience in trying to live, would, in part, at once understand them; but as they obeyed and pondered, the meaning of them would keep growing. This we see in the writings of the apostles. It will be so with us also, who need to understand everything He said neither more nor less than they to whom first He spoke; while our obligation to understand is far greater than theirs at the time, inasmuch as we have had nearly two thousand years' experience of the continued coming of the kingdom He then preached: it is not yet come; it has been all the time, and is now, drawing slowly nearer.

The sermon on the mount, as it is commonly called, seems the Lord's first free utterance, in the presence of any large assembly, of the good news of the kingdom. How different, at the first sound of it, must the good news have been from the news anxiously expected by those who waited for the Messiah! Even the Baptist in prison lay listening after something of quite another sort. The Lord had to send him a message, by eye-witnesses of His doings, to remind him that God's thoughts are not as our thoughts, or His ways as our ways—that the design of God is other and better than the expectation of men.

His summary of the gifts He was giving to men culminated with the preaching of the good news to the poor. If John had known these His doings before, he had not recognized them as belonging to the Lord's special mission: the Lord tells him it is not enough to have accepted Him as the Messiah; he must recognize His doings as the work He had come into the world to do, and as in their nature so divine as to be the very business of the Son of God in whom the Father was well pleased.

"The Heirs of Heaven and Earth," *The Hope of the Gospel*
Psalms 119:9-11

March 22   The Essential Spirit

Then he began to speak, and taught them, saying: "Blessed are the poor in spirit, for theirs is the kingdom of heaven. . . . Blessed are the meek, for they will inherit the earth." Matt. 5:2, 3, 5

All good news from heaven is of *truth*—essential truth, involving duty, and giving and promising help to the performance of it. There can be no good news for us men, except of uplifting love, and no one can be lifted up who will not rise. He will carry us in His arms till we are able to walk; He will carry us in His arms when we are weary with walking; He will not carry us if we will not walk.

The good news of Jesus was just the news of the thoughts and ways of the Father in the midst of His family. He told them that the way men thought for themselves and their children was not the way God thought for Himself and His children; that the kingdom of heaven was founded, and must at length show itself founded, on very different principles from those of the kingdoms and families of the world, meaning by the world that part of the Father's family which will not be ordered by Him, will not even try to obey Him.

The world's man, its great, its successful, its honorable man, is he who may have and do what he pleases. Whose strength lies in money and the praise of men. The greatest in the kingdom of heaven is the man who is humblest and serves his fellows the most. How many even of those who look for the world to come seek to the powers of this world for deliverance from its evils, as if God were the God of the world to come only! The oppressed of the Lord's time looked for a Messiah to set their nation free, and make it rich and strong; the oppressed of our time believe in money, knowledge, and the will of a people which needs but power to be in its turn the oppressor. The first words of the Lord on this occasion were: "Blessed are the poor in spirit, for theirs is the kingdom of heaven."

      "The Heirs of Heaven and Earth," *The Hope of the Gospel*
      Isa. 55:8-9

Those the Lord Calls Blessed   March 23

Then he began to speak, and taught them, saying: "Blessed are the poor in spirit, for theirs is the kingdom of heaven. . . . Blessed are the meek, for they will inherit the earth." Matt. 5:2, 3, 5

The Son of God will favor no smallest ambition, be it in the heart of him who leans on His bosom. The kingdom of God, the refuge of the oppressed, the golden age of the new world, the home of the children, will not open its gates to the most miserable who would rise above his equal in misery, who looks down on any one more miserable than himself. It is the home of perfect brotherhood.

The poor, the beggars in spirit, the humble men of heart, the unambitious, the unselfish; those who never despise men, and never seek their praises; the lowly, who see nothing to admire in themselves, therefore cannot seek to be admired of others; the men who give themselves away—these are the freemen of the kingdom, these are the citizens of the new Jerusalem.

The men who are aware of their own essential poverty; not the men who are poor in friends, poor in influence, poor in acquirements, poor in money, but those who are poor in spirit, who *feel themselves poor creatures*; who know nothing to be pleased with themselves for, and desire nothing to make them think well of themselves; who know that they need much to make their life worth living, to make their existence a good thing, to make them fit to live; these humble ones are the poor whom the Lord calls blessed.

> "The Heirs of Heaven and Earth," *The Hope of the Gospel*
> Isa 6:5

March 24   The Kingdom is Theirs

Then he began to speak, and taught them, saying: "Blessed are the poor in spirit, for theirs is the kingdom of heaven. . . . Blessed are the meek, for they will inherit the earth." Matt. 5:2, 3, 5

When a man says, I am low and worthless, then the gate of the kingdom begins to open to him, for there enter the true, and this man has begun to know the truth concerning himself. Whatever such a man has attained to, he straightway forgets; it is part of him and behind him. His business is with what he has not, with the things that lie above and before him.

The man who is proud of anything he thinks he has reached, has not reached it. He is but proud of himself, and imagining a cause for his pride. If he had reached, he would already have begun to forget. He who delights in contemplating whereto he has attained, is not merely sliding back; he is already in the dirt of self-satisfaction. The gate of the kingdom is closed, and he outside.

The man who does not house self has room to be his real self—God's eternal idea of him, He lives eternally; in virtue of the creative power present in him with momently unimpeded creation, he *is*. How should there be in him one thought of ruling or commanding or surpassing: he can imagine no bliss, no good in being greater than some one else.

He is unable to wish himself other then he is, except more what God made him for, which is indeed the highest willing of the will of God. His brother's well-being is essential to bliss. The thought of standing higher in the favor of God than his brother would make him miserable. He would lift every brother to the embrace of the Father. Blessed are the poor in spirit, for they are of the same spirit as God, and the kingdom of God is theirs.

    "The Heirs of Heaven and Earth," *The Hope of the Gospel*
    I Pet. 5:5-6

How to be Rich Indeed   March 25

Then he began to speak, and taught them, saying: "Blessed are the poor in spirit, for theirs is the kingdom of heaven. . . . Blessed are the meek, for they will inherit the earth." Matt. 5:2, 3, 5

"Blessed are the meek, for they shall inherit the earth" expresses the same principle as "Blessed are the poor"; the same law holds in the earth as in the kingdom of heaven. How should it be otherwise? Has the Creator of the ends of the earth ceased to rule it after His fashion, because His rebellious children have so long, to their own hurt, vainly endeavored to rule it after theirs? The kingdom of heaven belongs to the poor; the meek shall inherit the earth.

The earth as God sees it, as those to whom the kingdom of heaven belongs also see it, is good, all good, very good, fit for the meek to inherit; and one day they shall inherit it---not indeed as men of the world count inheritance, but as the Maker and Owner of the world has from the first counted it. So different are the two ways of inheriting, that one of the meek may be heartily enjoying his possession, while one of the proud is selfishly walling him out from the spot in it he loves best.

The meek are those that do not assert themselves, do not defend themselves, never dream of avenging themselves, or of returning aught but good for evil. They do not imagine it their business to take care of themselves. The meek man may indeed take much thought, but it will not be for himself. He never builds an exclusive wall, shuts any honest neighbor out. He will not always serve the wish, but always the good of his neighbor. His service must be true service. Because the man is meek, his eye is single; he sees things as God sees them, as He would have His child see them: to confront creation with pure eyes is to possess it.

"The Heirs of Heaven and Earth," *The Hope of the Gospel*
Eph. 4:1-2

March 26 — How To Make the Earth Ours

Then he began to speak, and taught them, saying: "Blessed are the poor in spirit, for theirs is the kingdom of heaven. . . . Blessed are the meek, for they will inherit the earth." Matt. 5:2, 3, 5

We cannot see the world as God means it, save in proportion as our souls are meek. In meekness only are we its inheritors. Meekness alone makes the spiritual retina pure to receive God's things as they are, mingling with them neither imperfection nor impurity of its own. A thing so beheld that it conveys to me the divine thought issuing in its form, is mine; by nothing but its mediation between God and my life can anything be mine.

The man so dull as to insist that a thing is his because he has bought it and paid for it, had better bethink himself that not all the combined forces of law, justice, and good-will can keep it his; while even death cannot take the world from the man who possesses it as alone the Maker of him and it cares that he should possess it. This man leaves it, but carries it with him; that man carries with him only its loss.

In the soul of the meek, the earth remains an endless possession—his because He who made it is his---his as nothing but his Maker could ever be the creature's. He has the earth by his divine relation to Him who sent it forth from Him as a tree sends out its leaves. To inherit the earth is to grow ever more alive to the presence, in it and in all its parts, of Him who is the life of men. How far one may advance in such inheritance while yet in the body will simply depend on the meekness he attains while yet in the body.

"The Heirs of Heaven and Earth," *The Hope of the Gospel*
Phil 2:1-5

You May Have It Now — March 27

Then he began to speak, and taught them, saying: "Blessed are the poor in spirit, for theirs is the kingdom of heaven. . . . Blessed are the meek, for they will inherit the earth." Matt. 5:2, 3, 5

It may be that the new heavens and the new earth are the same in which we now live, righteously inhabited by the meek, with their deeper-opened eyes. What if the meek of the dead be thus possessing it even now! But I do not care to speculate. It is enough that the man who refuses to assert himself, seeking no recognition by men, leaving the care of his life to the Father, and occupying himself with the will of the Father, shall find himself, by and by, at home in the Father's house, with all the Father's property his.

Which is more the possessor of the world—he who has a thousand houses, or he who, without one house to call his own, has ten in which his knock at the door would rouse instant jubilation? Which is the richer—the man who, his large money spent, would have no refuge; or he for whose necessity a hundred would sacrifice comfort? Which of the two possessed the earth—king Agrippa or tent-maker Paul?

The same spirit, then, is required for possessing the kingdom of heaven and for inheriting the earth. How should it not be so, when the one Power is the informing life of both? If we are the Lord's, we possess the kingdom of heaven, and so inherit the earth. How many who call themselves by his name would have it otherwise: they would possess the earth and inherit the kingdom! Such fill churches and chapels on Sundays. Anywhere suits for the worship of Mammon.

Yea verily, earth as well as heaven may be largely possessed even now.

"The Heirs of Heaven and Earth," *The Hope of the Gospel*
Luke 12:13-21

1868: MacDonald resigns his teaching post at King's College, London, in favor of making lecture tours.

March 28 — How To Change The Weather

Then he began to speak, and taught them, saying: "Blessed are the poor in spirit, for theirs is the kingdom of heaven. . . . Blessed are the meek, for they will inherit the earth." Matt. 5:2, 3, 5

Two men are walking abroad together. To the one, the world yields thought after thought of delight; he sees heaven and earth embrace one another; he feels an indescribable presence over and in them; his joy will afterwards, in the solitude of his chamber, break forth in song. To the other, oppressed with the thought of his poverty, or ruminating how to make much into more, the glory of the Lord is but a warm summer day; it enters in at no window of his soul; it offers him no gift; for, in the very temple of God, he looks for no God in it.

Nor must there needs be two men to think and feel differently. In what diverse fashion will any one subject to ever-changing mood see the same world of the same glad Creator! Alas for men, if it changed as we change, if it grew meaningless when we grow faithless! Thought for a morrow that may never come, dread of the dividing death which works for endless companionship, anger with one we love, will cloud the radiant morning, and make the day dark with the night.

At evening, having bethought ourselves, and returned to Him that feeds the ravens, and watches the dying sparrow, and says to His children, "Love one another," the sunset splendor is glad over us, the western sky is refulgent as the court of the Father when the glad news is spread abroad that a sinner has repented. We have mourned in the twilight of our little faith, but, having sent away our sin, the glory of God's heaven over His darkening earth has comforted us.

"The Heirs of Heaven and Earth," *The Hope of the Gospel*
Luke 12:27-34

Sorrow Is A Doorkeeper — March 29

"Blessed are those who mourn, for they will be comforted." Matt. 5:4

There is no evil in sorrow. True, it is not an essential good, a good in itself, like love; but it will mingle with any good thing, and is even so allied to good that it will open the door of the heart for any good. It is true also that joy is in its nature more divine than sorrow; for, although man must sorrow, and God share in his sorrow, yet in Himself God is not sorrowful, and the "glad Creator" never made man for sorrow: it is but a stormy strait through which he must pass to His ocean of peace.

Still, a man in sorrow is in general far nearer God than a man in joy. Gladness may make a man forget his thanksgiving; misery drives him to his prayers. For we *are* not yet, we are only *becoming*. The endless day will at length dawn whose every throbbing moment will heave our hearts God-ward; we shall scarce need to lift them up: now, there are two doorkeepers to the house of prayer, and Sorrow is more on the alert to open than her grandson Joy.

The promise to them that mourn is not *the kingdom of heaven,* but that their mourning shall be ended, that they shall be comforted. To mourn is not to fight with evil; it is only to miss that which is good. It is not an essential heavenly condition, like poorness of spirit or meekness. No man will carry his mourning with him into heaven—or if he does, it will speedily be turned into what will result in joy, namely, redemptive action.

The loss of the loved by death is the main cause of the mourning of the world. The Greek word here used to describe the blessed of the Lord generally means *those that mourn for the dead*. It is not in the New Testament employed exclusively in this sense, neither do I imagine it stands here for such only: there are griefs sorer far than death, and harder far to comfort—harder even for God Himself, with whom all things are possible; but it may give pleasure to know that the promise of comfort to those that mourn may specially apply to those that mourn because their loved have gone out of their sight, and beyond the reach of their cry.

"Sorrow the Pledge of Joy," *The Hope of the Gospel*
John 14:1-4

1890: Draft of first version of <u>Lilith</u> completed.

March 30   Bliss Divinely Purified

"Blessed are those who mourn, for they will be comforted." Matt. 5:4

"The Lord means of course," someone may say, "that the comfort of the mourners will be the restoration of that which they have lost. He means, 'Blessed are ye although ye mourn, for your sorrow will be turned into joy.'" But would restoration be comfort enough for the heart of Jesus to give? To call a man *blessed* in his sorrow because of something to be given him, surely implies a something better than what he had before!

True, the joy that is past may have been so great that the man might well feel blessed in the merest hope of its restoration; but would that be meaning enough for the word in the mouth of the Lord? That the interruption of his blessedness was but temporary would hardly be fit ground for calling the man *blessed* in the interruption. *Blessed* is a strong word, and in the mouth of Jesus means all it can mean. Can His saying here mean less than, "Blessed are they that mourn, for they shall be comforted with a bliss well worth all the pain of the medicinal sorrow"?

Besides, the benediction surely means that the man is blessed *because* of his condition of mourning, not in spite of it. His mourning is surely a part, at least, of the Lord's ground for congratulating him: is it not the present operative means whereby the consolation is growing possible? In a word, I do not think the Lord would be content to call a man blessed on the mere ground of his going to be restored a former bliss by no means perfect. I think He congratulated the mourners upon the grief they were enduring, because He saw the excellent glory of the comfort that was drawing nigh; because He knew the immeasurably greater joy to which the sorrow was at once clearing the way and conducting the mourner.

When I say *greater*, God forbid I should mean *other*! I mean the same bliss, divinely enlarged and divinely purified—passed again through the hands of the creative Perfection. God's comfort must ever be larger than man's grief.

      "Sorrow the Pledge of Joy," *The Hope of the Gospel*
      Heb 12:22-24

From Much Bad To All Good

March 31

"Blessed are those who mourn, for they will be comforted." Matt. 5:4

We shall all doubtless be changed, but in what direction?—to something less, or to something greater?—to something that is less we, which means degradation? To something that is not we, which means annihilation? Or to something that is more we, which means a further development of the original idea of us, the divine germ of us, holding in it all we ever were, all we can and must become?

Is it not of the very essence of the Christian hope, that we shall be changed from much bad to all good? If a wife so love that she would keep every opposition, every inconsistency in her husband's as yet but partially harmonious character, she does not love well enough for the kingdom of heaven. If its imperfections be essential to the individuality she loves, and to the repossession of her joy in it, she may be sure that, if he were restored to her as she would have him, she would soon come to love him less—perhaps to love him not at all; for no one who does not love perfection will ever keep constant in loving.

Fault is not lovable; it is only the good in which the alien fault dwells that causes it to seem capable of being loved. Neither is it any man's peculiarities that make him beloved; it is the essential humanity underlying those peculiarities. They may make him interesting, and, where not offensive, they may come to be loved for the sake of the man; but in themselves they are of smallest account. We must not, however, confound peculiarity with diversity. Diversity is in and from God; peculiarity in and from men. The real man is the divine idea of him.

"Sorrow the Pledge of Joy," *The Hope of the Gospel*
I John 3:1-3

April 1 — The Original God-Idea

"Blessed are those who mourn, for they will be comforted." Matt. 5:4

The real man is the man God had in view when He began to send him forth out of thought into thinking; the man He is now working to perfect by casting out what is not he, and developing what is he. But in God's real men, that is, His ideal men, the diversity is infinite; He does not repeat His creations; every one of His children differs from every other, and in every one the diversity is lovable. God gives in His children an analysis of himself, an analysis that will never be exhausted. It is the original God-idea of the individual man that will at length be given, without spot or blemish, into the arms of love.

Such, surely, is the heart of the comfort the Lord will give those whose love is now making them mourn; and their present blessedness must be the expectation of the time when the true lover shall find the restored the same as the lost----with precious differences: the things that were not like the true self, gone or going; the things that were loveliest, lovelier still; the restored not merely more than the lost, but more the person than he or she that was lost. For the things which made him or her what he or she was, the things that rendered lovable, the things essential to the person, will be more present, because more developed.

"Sorrow the Pledge of Joy," *The Hope of the Gospel*
II Cor. 3:18

Hope In God　　　　　　　　　　　　　　　April 2

Blessed are those who mourn, for they will be comforted." Matt. 5:4

There is one phase of our mourning for the dead which I must not leave unconsidered, seeing it is the pain within pain of all our mourning—the sorrow, namely with its keen recurrent pangs, because of things we have said or done, or omitted to say or do, while we companied with the departed. Would God be perfect if in His restitution of all things there were no opportunity for declaring our bitter grief and shame for the past? No room for making amends?

Whatever selfishness clouds the love that mourns the loss of love, that selfishness must be taken out of it—because of thy love's defect, thou must suffer that it may be supplied. God will not, like the unjust judge, avenge thee to escape the cry that troubles Him. No crying will make Him comfort thy selfishness. He will not render thee incapable of loving truly. He despises neither thy love, though mingled with selfishness, nor thy suffering that springs from both; He will disentangle thy selfishness from thy love, and cast it into the fire.

At the same time, when the desired moment comes, one look in the eyes may be enough, and we shall know one another even as God knows us. Like the purposed words of the prodigal in the parable, it may be that the words of our confession will hardly find place. Heart may so speak to heart as to forget there were such things. Mourner, hope in God, and comfort where thou canst, and the Lord of mourners will be able to comfort thee the sooner. It may be thy very severity with thyself has already moved the Lord to take thy part.

> "Sorrow the Pledge of Joy," *The Hope of the Gospel*
> Eph. 4:32

April 3 — Comfort For Every Grief

Blessed are those who mourn, for they will be comforted." Matt. 5:4

Begin to love as God loves, and your grief will assuage; but for comfort wait His time. What He will do for you, He only knows. It may be you will never know what He will do, but only what He has done: it was too good for you to know save by receiving it. The moment you are capable of it, yours it will be.

Whether or not the Lord was here thinking specially of the mourners for the dead, as I think He was, he surely does not limit the word of comfort to them, or wish us to believe less than that His Father has perfect comfort for every human grief. One thing is clear in regard to every trouble—that the natural way with it is straight to the Father's knee. The Father is father *for* his children, else why did He make Himself their father?

The Lord has come to wipe away our tears. He is doing it; he will have it done as soon as He can; and until He can, He would have them flow without bitterness; to which end He tells us it is a blessed thing to mourn, because of the comfort on its way. Accept his comfort now, and so prepare for the comfort at hand. He is getting you ready for it, but you must be a fellow-worker with Him, or He will never have done. He *must* have you pure in heart, eager after righteousness, a very child of His Father in heaven.

"Sorrow the Pledge of Joy," *The Hope of the Gospel*
II Cor. 1:3-4

On Seeing God   April 4

"Blessed are the pure in heart, for they will see God. Blessed are those who hunger and thirst for righteousness, for they will be filled. Blessed are the peacemakers, for they will be called children of God." Matt. 5:8, 6, 9

The cry of the deepest in man has always been to see God. It was the cry of Moses and the cry of Job, the cry of psalmist and of prophet; and to the cry there has ever been faintly heard a far approach of coming answer. In the fullness of time the Son appears with the proclamation that a certain class of men shall behold the Father: "Blessed are the pure in heart," He cries, "for they shall see God." He who saw God, who sees Him now, who always will see Him, says, "Be pure, and you also shall see Him."

To see God was the Lord's own, eternal, one happiness; therefore He knew that the essential bliss of the creature is to behold the face of the Creator. In that face lies the mystery of man's own nature, the history of a man's own being. He who can read no line of it can know neither himself nor his fellow; he only who knows God a little can at all understand man. The blessed in Dante's Paradise ever and always read each other's thoughts in God. Looking to Him, they find their neighbor.

All that the creature needs to see or know, all that the creature can see or know, is the face of Him from whom he came. Not seeing and knowing it, he will never be at rest; seeing and knowing it, his existence will yet indeed be a mystery to him and an awe, but no more a dismay.

"God's Family," *The Hope of the Gospel*
Psalms 63:1-3

April 5 — The End Of Our Creation

"Blessed are the pure in heart, for they will see God. Blessed are those who hunger and thirst for righteousness, for they will be filled. Blessed are the peacemakers, for they will be called children of God." Matt. 5:8, 6, 9

None but the pure in heart see God; only the growing-pure hope to see Him. Even those who saw the Lord, the express image of His person, did not see God. They only saw Jesus—and then but the outside Jesus, or a little more. They were not pure in heart; they saw Him and did not see Him. They saw Him with their eyes, but not with those eyes which alone can see God. Those were not born in them yet. Neither the eyes of the resurrection-body, nor the eyes of the unembodied spirits can see God; only the eyes of that eternal something that is of the very essence of God, the thought-eyes, the truth-eyes, the love-eyes, can see Him.

It is not because we are created and He uncreated, it is not because of any difference involved in that difference of all differences, that we cannot see Him. To see God is to stand on the highest point of created being. Not until we see God—no partial and passing embodiment of Him, but the abiding presence—do we stand upon our own mountain-top, the height of the existence God has given us, and up to which He is leading us. That there we should stand, is the end of our creation.

This truth is at the heart of everything, means all kinds of completions, may be uttered in many ways; but language will never compass it, for form will never contain it. Nor shall we ever see, that is, know, God perfectly. We shall indeed never absolutely know man or woman or child; but we may know God as we never can know human being—as we never can know ourselves. We not only may, but we must so know Him, and it can never be until we are pure in heart. Then shall we know Him with the infinitude of an ever-growing knowledge.

"God's Family," *The Hope of the Gospel*
Psalms 17:15

Dismiss The Care   April 6

This excerpt is from a letter written by MacDonald to Greville, his oldest son, from Bordighera, dated April 6, 1884:

My dearly Loved Son,

It puzzles me a little that you, to whom God has given more insight than many have into the necessities of the spiritual relations, should be so changeable and troubled by the appearances of things. "In quietness and confidence shall be your strength." "Wait on the Lord." You are so impatient! You will hardly give him time to do anything for you! As you are so easily troubled, as your faith in him seems so much in the abstract, and when it comes to the matter of next month or next year you are full of doubt—as if what the day was to bring forth must be evil and not good, notwithstanding that perfect goodness is at the head of your affairs—this being the case, I see why you should be troubled and tossed about as you are.

Do not be always speculating on your future and thinking what you shall do. You are not a bit nearer knowing for that; and it is a great waste of brain tissue, to say nothing of spiritual energy left dormant. . . . There is more action in dismissing a useless care than in a month's brooding over the possible or the probable. When the hour of decision arrives one moment's clear untroubled thought will do what weeks and weeks of brooding before hand will only make more uncertain and difficult . . . .

An Expression of Character: The Letters of George MacDonald,
Glen Edward Sadler, ed.
Isa. 27:14

April 7 — A Horror Of The Unfinished

Donal Grant, a young Scottish tutor and poet, is contemplating the ruins of an ancient fortress and recalling ancient wars:

Did not many an evil seem now as insurmountable as then? The world will change only as the heart of man changes. Growing intellect, growing civilization will heal man's wounds only to cause the deeper ill to break out afresh in new forms, nor can they satisfy one longing of the human soul. Its desires are deeper than that soul itself, whence it groans with the groanings that cannot be uttered.

As much in the times of civilization as in those of barbarity the soul needs an external presence to make its life a good to it. In the rougher times of violence men were less conscious of the need than in our own. Time itself, the starving, vacant, unlovely time, is to many the one dread foe they have to encounter. Others have the awful consciousness of a house empty and garnished in which neither Love nor Hope dwell, but doors and windows lie open to what evil things may enter. To others their very self, unrulable, insatiable, makes existence a hell.

For Godless man is a horror of the unfinished, a hopeless necessity for the unattainable, in which arise and revel monstrous dreams of truest woe. Money, ease, honor can help nothing: the most discontented are of those who have all that the truthless heart desires.

Donal Grant, Chapter 3
Jer. 10:23

An Essential In Its Time — April 8

Donal Grant, a young Scottish tutor and poet, having freshly arrived at a castle at which he has applied for a new position, is afforded a late lunch:

Their mid-day meal was long over, but Mistress Comin had kept and now cooked to perfection for him a piece of fish, and he dined to his entire content on what most English students would have regarded as very short commons indeed. Donal was in perfect health, thence able to make full use of whatever he ate, and so could do with less than many. He had not, indeed, learned to eat largely, or to find any enticement in variety. What was lacking to him of education by sickness, which in its time is an essential, had in part been made up for by what most men would call hardship, but he would have acknowledged only as the hardness which Paul says a good soldier of Jesus Christ must endure; with his cheerful and thorough response, he had not yet required more.

Suffering, more or less, awaits every youth. However he may count it the one thing to be avoided, he shall not succeed in avoiding it, neither are they to be counted specially fortunate who escape with the least share of it. If they would but await what will come, and accept the thing that is sent them, it would make men of them in half the time. There is more to be had out of the ordained oppositions in things than from the smoothest going of the world's wheels. Whatever makes the children feel that they are only out to nurse, and have here no abiding city, but a school of righteousness and truth and love, is a precious uplifting step to the only success.

Donal Grant, Chapter 4
I Pet. 5:10

April 9 — Simply The Way Home

Donal Grant, a young Scottish tutor and poet, having freshly acquired a new position at a castle, finds the handsome Lady Arctura, niece to the earl of the castle, enslaved to a false faith:

How was Lady Arctura to think aright without having had more than a glimmer of highest truths? How was she to please God, as she called it, who thought of him in a way repulsive to every loving soul? Is it any wonder that one in such a condition should neither enjoy nor recommend her religion? It would have been the worse for her if she had enjoyed it—the worse for others if she had recommended it. There was little of religion in her path but the difficulty of it, and that is hardly enough to make a religion.

Religion is simply the way home to the Father. The true way is difficult enough because of our unchildlikeness—uphill, steep, and difficult, but there is fresh life with every surmounted height, a purer air gained, more life for more climbing. But the path that is not the true one is not therefore an easy one. Uphill work is hard walking, but through a bog is worse. Those who seek God with their faces hardly turned towards him, who, instead of beholding the Father in the Son, take the stupidest opinions concerning him and his ways from men who, if they have themselves ever known him, have never taught him from their own knowledge of him, but from the dogmas of others, go wandering about in dark mountains, or through marshes, spending their strength in avoiding precipices and bog-holes, sighing and mourning over their sins instead of leaving them behind and fleeing to the Father, whom to know is eternal life. If they set themselves to find out what Christ thought and knew and meant, and to do it, they would soon forget their false teachers, and find a good riddance. But alas! They go on bowing before long-faced, big-worded authority, the more fatally when it is embodied in a good man who, himself a victim of faith in men, sees the Son of God only through the theories of others, and not with the clear sight of his own spiritual eyes.

Donal Grant, Chapter 6
Matt. 11:29

Nothing Too Good — April 10

Donal Grant, a young Scottish tutor and poet, is here strolling through the gardens of a castle..

Down a broad walk, on which his foot sank deep in velvety grass, he went wandering, and the loveliness of the dream did not fade. Hollyhocks, so gloriously impatient of development that their flowers could not wait to reach the top ere they burst into the flame of life, making splendid blots of color along their ascending stalks, received him like stately dames of enchantment, and enticed him, ever to see more and more of them, down the long walk between the two rows of them, deep red, and creamy white, primrose and yellow; and all the while below the present pleasure lay the dim assurance that they were leading him to some wonderful place, some nest of lovely dreams, if not more visions.

The walk itself led to a bower of roses—a bed surrounded with a trellis, on which they climbed, and made a huge bon-fire, incense altar, rather, of red and white flame. To Donal it seemed more glorious than his brain could receive. Herein seeing was hardly believing, but believing was more than seeing, and would ripen to a higher sight. Donal well understood that

though nothing can be too good to be true, there is nothing that is not too good to be grasped. Poor misbelieving birds of God, we hover about a whole wood of the trees of life, venturing here and there a peck, as if their fruit might be poison, and the design of our creation was our ruin: we shake our wise owl-feathered heads and declare they cannot be the trees of life, because that is too good to be true.

Ten times more consistent are they who deny there is a God at all than they who fancy they believe in a middling kind of a God, in whom they place indeed a fitting faith. Feelings such as these moving gently in his full heart, among flowers that came from the dark earth like the exhaled spirits of its hidden jewels which themselves could not reach the eye of the sun; over grass which fondled his feet like the lap of an old nurse, he walked slowly once round the bed of the roses, to return again towards the house.

Donal Grant, Chapter 11
Prov. 3:5-6

April 11 — Leaving Intellectual Idols

The handsome Lady Arctura, niece to the earl of the castle at which Donal Grant, a young Scottish tutor and poet, teaches, is slowly emerging from the throes of a false faith:

Lady Arctura's old troubles were gradually receding and fading into the limbo of vanities. Sometimes, however, and that in general when her health was worse, they would come in upon her like a flood—as if, after all, God was but the self-loving being the evil spirit of a false theology represented him—a being from whom no loving heart could but recoil with a holy instinct of dislike; and she of a nature so unregenerative that she could not receive the God in whom the priests and elders of her people believed.

Yet sometimes, even in the midst of a profoundest wretchedness from such a cause, a sudden flush from that nature which Jesus has told us to study. . . would break like gentlest strongest sunrise through the hellish fog, and she would feel a power upon her as from the heart of such a God as she would give her very self to believe in, and she would cast herself before him in speechless adoration—not of his greatness, for of that she felt little, but of his loving kindness, and the gentleness that was making her great. Then she would care only for God and his Christ, nothing for what men said about him, let them call themselves what they pleased, claim for themselves what they would: the Lord never meant his lambs to be under the tyranny of any, even his own Church! Then would God appear not only true, but real; and to the heart of the human she must cling, and there rest.

The corruption of all religion comes from leaving the human and God as the causing Humanity for something else imagined holier—which is indeed but a new idol, such as the heart of man that knows not the heart of the Father will forever be making. What but a human reality could the heart of man love! And what else was she offered in Jesus but the absolutely human! Of the mischievous fictions of theology the representation that Jesus has two natures is of the falsest.

Donal Grant, Chapter 36
II Sam. 22:31-36

A Man Within A Man — April 12

Donal Grant, a young Scottish tutor and poet, has strained relations with Lord Forgue, the son of the earl of the castle where he teaches, for reasons here described.

There was condescension in the politeness he showed Donal; and this, had there been nothing else, would have been enough to revolt Arctura, but the fact was that she felt him altogether, though she would not so have expressed herself perhaps, as a man of outsides—felt that in him you did not see the man he was, but the nearest approach he could make to the man he would be taken for. He was gracious, dignified, attentive, amusing, accurate, ready----everything but true; his outside everything but what it was meat for—a revelation of that which he was inside. Yet it was that too only that he did not mean it to be.

He was a man dressed in a man, and his dress was a revelation of much that he was, at the time he intended it to show much that he was not. For no man can help unveiling himself, however long he may escape detection. Neither is there anything covered that shall not be revealed. Things were meant to come out, and be read, and understood in the face of the universe. The soul of every man shall be as a book to be read of wise eyes—all its history, all its strife, all its victory, written in the pages thereof!—and oh, what a different book will it be thus read, from the biography that may have chanced to be written of it on the earth, where the very understanding of the man was chiefly a misunderstanding, where by some he was perhaps thought a god when on the very point of being eaten up of worms, or was by some taken for a fool when he was teaching the deepest wisdom. Each and all must one day be seen and known in the light.

Well for those who are humble enough and true enough not to shrink from the exposure of even their faults and sins—who hate them so much themselves that they would have them have no quarter.

Donal Grant, Chapter 36
Luke 12:1-3

April 13 — There Is No Escape

Letters from Hell, *a work written by an anonymous Danish author, was immediately popular in MacDonald's time and went through numerous editions. This is an excerpt from the Preface which MacDonald wrote for the English translation.*

I would not willingly be misunderstood: when I say the book is full of truth, I do not mean either truth of theory or truth in art, but something far deeper and higher—the realities of our relations to God and man and duty—all, in short, that belongs to the conscience. Prominent among these is the awful verity, that we make our fate in unmaking ourselves; that men, in defacing the image of God in themselves, construct for themselves a world of horror and dismay; that of *the outer darkness* our own deeds and character are the informing or inwardly creating cause; that if a man will not have God, he never can be rid of his weary and hateful self.

But there is one growing persuasion of the present age which I hope this book may somewhat serve to stem—not by any argument, but by such a healthy upstirring, . . . of the imagination and the conscience. In these days, when men are so gladly hearing afresh that "in Him is no darkness at all"; that God therefore could not have created any man if He knew that he must live in torture to all eternity; and that his hatred to evil cannot be expressed by injustice, itself the one essence of evil,—for certainly it would be nothing less than injustice to punish infinitely what was finitely committed, no sinner being capable of understanding the abstract enormity of what he does—in these days has arisen another falsehood—less, yet very perilous: thousands of half-thinkers imagine that, since it is declared with such authority that hell is not everlasting, there is then no hell at all. To such folly I for one have never given enticement or shelter. I see no hope for many, no way for the divine love to reach them, save through a very ghastly hell. Men have got to repent; there is no other escape for them, and no escape from that.

"Preface," *Letters from Hell*
Eze. 33:11

Ask Your Conscience   April 14

"Blessed are the pure in heart, for they will see God. Blessed are those who hunger and thirst for righteousness, for they will be filled. Blessed are the peacemakers, for they will be called children of God." Matt. 5:8, 6, 9

"What is it, then, to be pure in heart?"

I answer: It is not necessary to define this purity, or to have in the mind any clear form of it. For even to know perfectly (were that possible) what purity of heart is, would not be to be pure in heart.

"How then am I to try after it? Can I do so without knowing what it is?"

Though you do not know any definition of purity, you know enough to begin to be pure. You do not know what a man is, but you know how to make his acquaintance—perhaps even how to gain his friendship. Your brain does not know what purity is; you heart has some acquaintance with purity itself. Your brain is seeking to know what it is, may even obstruct your heart in bettering its friendship with it. To know what purity is, a man must already be pure; but he who can put the question already knows enough of purity, I repeat, to begin to become pure. If this moment you determine to start for purity, you conscience will at once tell you where to begin. If you reply, "My conscience says nothing definite," I answer, "You are but playing with your conscience. Determine, and it will speak.

If you care to see God, be pure. If you will not be pure, you will grow more and more impure; and instead of seeing God, will at length find yourself face to face with a vast inane—a vast inane, yet filled full of one inhabitant, that devouring monster, your own false self. If for this neither do you care, I tell you there is a Power that will not have it so; a Love that will make you care by the consequences of not caring.

"God's Family," *The Hope of the Gospel*
Phil. 4:8-9

April 15 — Love Is The Father

"Blessed are the pure in heart, for they will see God. Blessed are those who hunger and thirst for righteousness, for they will be filled. Blessed are the peacemakers, for they will be called children of God." Matt. 5:8, 6, 9

To hunger and thirst after anything implies a sore personal need, a strong desire, a passion for that thing. Those that hunger and thirst after righteousness seek with their whole nature the design of that nature. Nothing less will give them satisfaction; that alone will set them at ease. They long to be delivered from their sins, to send them away, to be clean and blessed by their absence—in a word, to become men, God's men; for sin gone, all the rest is good.

Righteousness itself, God's righteousness, rightness in their own being, in heart and brain and hands, is what they desire. Of such men as Nathanael, in whom was no guile; such perhaps, was Nicodemus too, although he did come to Jesus by night; such was Zacchaeus. The temple could do nothing to deliver them; but, by their very futility, its observances had done their work, developing the desires they could not meet, making the men hunger and thirst the more after genuine righteousness: the Lord must bring them this bread from heaven. With Him, the live, original rightness, in their hearts, they must speedily become righteous.

With that Love their friend, who is at once both the root and the flower of things, they would strive vigorously as well as hunger eagerly after righteousness. Love is the father of righteousness. It could not be, and could not be hungered after, but for love.

"God's Family," *The Hope of the Gospel*
Psalms 18:20-26

Our Primal Need — April 16

"Blessed are the pure in heart, for they will see God. Blessed are those who hunger and thirst for righteousness, for they will be filled. Blessed are the peacemakers, for they will be called children of God." Matt. 5:8, 6, 9

The Lord of Righteousness Himself could not live without Love, without the Father in Him. Every heart was created for, and can live no otherwise than in and upon love eternal. Perfect, pure, unchanging; and love necessitates righteousness.

In how many souls has not the very thought of a real God waked a longing to be different, to be pure, to be right! The fact that this feeling is possible, that a soul can become dissatisfied with itself, and desire a change in itself, reveals God as an essential part of its being; for in itself the soul is aware that it cannot be what it would, what it ought—that it cannot set itself right: a need has been generated in the soul for which the soul can generate no supply; a presence higher than itself must have caused that need; a power greater than itself must supply it, for the soul knows its very need, its very lack, is of something greater than itself.

But the primal need of the human soul is yet greater than this; the longing after righteousness is only one of the manifestations of it; the need is the man's need of God. A moral, that is, a human, spiritual being, must either be God, or one with God. This truth begins to reveal itself when the man begins to feel that he cannot cast out the thing he hates, cannot be the thing he loves. That he hates thus, that he loves thus, is because God is in him, but he finds he has not enough of God. His awakening strength manifests itself in his sense of weakness, for only strength can know itself weak. The negative cannot know itself at all. Weakness cannot know itself weak. It is a little strength that longs for more; it is infant righteousness that hungers after righteousness.

"God's Family," *The Hope of the Gospel*
Rom 8:37-39

April 17 — Forgetting Righteousness

"Blessed are the pure in heart, for they will see God. Blessed are those who hunger and thirst for righteousness, for they will be filled. Blessed are the peacemakers, for they will be called children of God." Matt. 5:8, 6, 9

To be filled with righteousness will be to forget even righteousness itself in the bliss of being righteous, that is, a child of God. The thought of righteousness will vanish in the fact of righteousness. When a creature is just what he is meant to be, what only he is fit to be; when, therefore, he is truly himself, he never thinks what he is. He *is* that thing; why think about it? It is no longer outside of him that he should contemplate or desire it.

God made man, and woke in him the hunger for righteousness; the Lord came to enlarge and rouse this hunger. The first and lasting effect of His words must be to make the hungering and thirsting long yet more. If their passion grow to a despairing sense of the unattainable, a hopelessness of ever gaining that without which life were worthless, let them remember that the Lord congratulates the hungry and the thirsty, so sure does He know them of being one day satisfied. Their hunger is a precious thing to have.

If your hunger seems long in being filled, it is well it should seem long. But what if your righteousness tarry because your hunger after it is not eager?

"God's Family," *The Hope of the Gospel*
Psalms 42:1-2

The Day Must Come

"Blessed are the pure in heart, for they will see God. Blessed are those who hunger and thirst for righteousness, for they will be filled. Blessed are the peacemakers, for they will be called children of God." Matt. 5:8, 6, 9

There are those who sit long at the table because their desire is slow; they eat as who would say, We need not food. In things spiritual, increasing desire is the sign that satisfaction is drawing nearer.

Hear another like word of the Lord. He assures us that the Father hears the cries of His elect—of those whom He seeks to worship Him because they worship in spirit and in truth. "Shall not God avenge His own elect," He says, "which cry day and night unto Him?" Now what can God's elect have to keep on crying for night and day, but righteousness? He allows that God seems to put off answering them, but assures us He will answer them speedily.

Even now He must be busy answering their prayers; increasing hunger is the best possible indication that He is doing so. For some divine reason it is well they should not yet know in themselves that He is answering their prayers; but the day must come when we shall be righteous even as He is righteous; when no word of His will miss being understood because of our lack of righteousness; when no unrighteousness shall hide from our eyes the face of the Father.

from "God's Family," *The Hope of the Gospel*
Luke 18:1-8

April 19   Helping Perfect The Father-Idea

"Blessed are the pure in heart, for they will see God. Blessed are those who hunger and thirst for righteousness, for they will be filled. Blessed are the peacemakers, for they will be called children of God." Matt. 5:8, 6, 9

These two promises, of seeing God and being filled with righteousness, have place between the individual man and his Father in heaven directly; the promise I now come to has place between a man and his God as the God of other men also, as the Father of the whole family in heaven and earth: "Blessed are the peacemakers, for they shall be called the children of God."

Those that are on their way to see God, those who are growing pure in heart through hunger and thirst after righteousness, are indeed the children of God; but specially the Lord calls those His children who, on their way home, are peacemakers in the traveling company; for, surely, those in any family are specially the children, who make peace with and among the rest.

The true idea of the universe is the whole family in heaven and earth. All the children in this part of it, the earth, at least, are not good children; but however far, therefore, the earth is from being a true portion of a real family, the life-germ at the root of the world—that by and for which it exists—is its relation to God the Father of men.

God, then, would make of the world a true, divine family. Now the primary necessity to the very existence of a family is peace. Many a human family is no family, and the world is no family yet, for the lack of peace. Wherever peace is growing, there, of course, is the live peace, counteracting disruption and disintegration, and helping the development of the true essential family. The peacemakers are the true children of that family, the allies and minsters of every clasping and consolidating force in it; fellow-workers they are with God in the creation of the family; they help Him to perfect His father-idea.

         from "God's Family," *The Hope of the Gospel*
         James 3:17-18

The One Haven

April 20

This letter was written in 1888 from Bordighera to the son of some friends, a sailor who came home seriously ill.

My dear Andy,

. . . . You have seen ever so much more of the outside world than I have, and when you are lying awake at night, or ill in the day, I suppose many scenes strange to me will come back to you with familiar looks, but there is another, the inside world, of thought and feeling and need and longing, into which, being so much older than you, I must have withdrawn more than you—like a snail to the inside of its shell; and I have learned to be sure that even if I had everything I could wish for in the outside world: if even I were strong enough to meet with delight the storms you know so well, and have battled with so often, there would be something wanting inside, in that other world, if I did not feel that the Power by which I am here, a glad human soul, was there present with one, and telling me he is my father, my friend, far too grand and good ever to forget the being he has called into life, and who cannot keep himself alive or do anything by his own power.

If I had made but a sparrow, I would be very careful over that sparrow; and the Lord who knows his father perfectly tells us that he cares for the sparrows he makes, and much more for us. You see what I am driving at, Andy: I want you to think over and again, for my sake, however often you think it for yourself, that God is just the one haven you have to make for in this storm. Say to him, My Father, I belong to thee, and I am ill, and I cannot help myself; be my Father and keep near me, and do what thou wilt with me, only take care of thy child, and let him know thou art taking care of him.

. . . . When I was child, and was hardly able to breathe for pain, I felt all right when my father came to me; and so now I am a man I feel of my higher father, the father of all fathers. . . .

The Beinecke Rare Book and Manuscript Library
James 4:10

April 21 — The Tragedy of Peace-Breakers

"Blessed are the pure in heart, for they will see God. Blessed are those who hunger and thirst for righteousness, for they will be filled. Blessed are the peacemakers, for they will be called children of God." Matt. 5:8, 6, 9

Ever radiating peace, the peacemakers welcome love, but do not seek it. They provoke no jealousy. They are the children of God, for, like Him, they would be one with His creatures.

His eldest Son, His very likeness, was the first of the family peacemakers. Preaching peace to them that were afar off and them that were nigh, He stood undefended in the turbulent crowd of His fellows, and it is only over His dead body that His brothers began to come together in the peace that will not be broken. He rose again from the dead; His peacemaking brothers, like Himself, are dying unto sin; and not yet have the evil children made their Father hate, or their Elder Brother flinch.

On the other hand, those whose influence is to divide and separate, causing the hearts of men to lean away from each other, make themselves the children of the evil one: born of God and not of the devil, they turn from God, and adopt the devil their father. They set their God-born life against God, against the whole creative, redemptive purpose of His unifying will, ever obstructing the one prayer of the First-born—that the children may be one with Him in the Father.

"God's Family," *The Hope of the Gospel*
Rom. 16:17-18

That Which Is Plain

April 22

"Blessed are the pure in heart, for they will see God. Blessed are those who hunger and thirst for righteousness, for they will be filled. Blessed are the peacemakers, for they will be called children of God." Matt. 5:8, 6, 9

Are we to treat persons known for liars and strife makers as the children of the devil or not? Are we to turn away from them, and refuse to acknowledge them, rousing an ignorant strife of tongues concerning our conduct? Are we guilty of connivance, when silent as to the ambush whence we know the wicked arrow privily shot? Are we to call the traitor to account? Or are we to give warning of any sort? I have no answer. Each must carry the question that perplexes to the Light of the World. To what purpose is the Spirit of God promised to them that ask it, if not to help them order their way aright?

One thing is plain—that we must love the strife-maker; another is nearly as plain—that, if we do not love him, we must leave him alone; for without love there can be no peacemaking, and words will but occasion more strife. To be kind neither hurts nor compromises. Kindness has many phases, and the fitting form of it may avoid offense, and must avoid untruth.

We must not fear what man can do to us, but commit our way to the Father of the Family. We must be nowise anxious to defend ourselves; and if not ourselves because God is our defense, then why our friends? Is He not their defense as much as ours?

Whatever our relation, then, with any peace-breaker, our mercy must ever be within call; and it may help us against an indignation too strong to be pure, to remember that when any man is reviled for righteousness' sake, then is he blessed.

"God's Family," *The Hope of the Gospel*
Luke 11:11-13

April 23 — Blessed Reward

"Blessed are the merciful, for they will receive mercy. Blessed are those who are persecuted for righteousness' sake, for theirs is the kingdom of heaven. Blessed are you when people revile you and persecute you and utter all kinds of evil against you falsely on my account. Rejoice and be glad, for your reward is great in heaven, for in the same way they persecuted the prophets who were before you." Matt. 5:7, 10-12

Mercy cannot get in where mercy goes not out. The outgoing makes way for the incoming. God takes the part of humanity against the man. The man must treat men as he would have God treat him. "If you forgive men their trespasses, your heavenly Father also will forgive you; but if you do not forgive men their trespasses, neither will your Father forgive your trespasses." And in the prophecy of the judgment of the Son of Man, He represents Himself as saying, "As you did it to one of the least of these my brethren, you did it to me."

But the demand for mercy is far from being for the sake only of the man who needs his neighbor's mercy; it is greatly more for the sake of the man who must show the mercy. It is a small thing to a man whether or not his neighbor be merciful to him; it is life or death to him whether or not he be merciful to his neighbor.

Unmerciful, we must be given up to the tormentors until we learn to be merciful. God is merciful; we must be merciful. There is no blessedness except in being such as God; it would be altogether unmerciful to leave us unmerciful. The reward of the merciful is, that by their mercy they are rendered capable of receiving the mercy of God—yea, God Himself, who is Mercy.

That men may be drawn to taste and see and understand, the Lord associates reward with righteousness. The Lord would have men love righteousness, but how are they to love it without being acquainted with it? How are they to go on loving it without a growing knowledge of it? To draw them toward it that they may begin to know it, and to encourage them when assailed by the disappointments that accompany endeavor, He tells them simply a truth concerning it—that in doing of it there is great reward.

"The Reward of Obedience," *The Hope of the Gospel*
Matt. 25:31-46

The Only Way To Learn — April 24

"Blessed are the merciful, for they will receive mercy. Blessed are those who are persecuted for righteousness' sake, for theirs is the kingdom of heaven. Blessed are you when people revile you and persecute you and utter all kinds of evil against you falsely on my account. Rejoice and be glad, for your reward is great in heaven, for in the same way they persecuted the prophets who were before you." Matt. 5:7, 10-12

The nature indeed of the Lord's promised rewards is hardly to be mistaken; yet the foolish remarks one sometimes hears make me wish to point out that neither is the Lord proclaiming an ethical system, nor does He make the blunder of representing as righteousness the doing of a good thing because of some advantage to be thereby gained. When He promises, He only states some fact that will encourage His disciples—that is, all who learn of Him—to meet the difficulties in the way of doing right and so learning righteousness, His object being to make men righteous, not to teach them philosophy.

It is the part of the enemy of righteousness to increase the difficulties in the way of becoming righteous, and to diminish those in the way of seeming righteous. Jesus desires no righteousness for the pride of being righteous, any more than for advantage to be gained by it; therefore, while requiring such purity as the man, beforehand, is unable to imagine, He gives him all the encouragement He can. He will not enhance his victory by difficulties—of them there are enough—but by completeness. He will not demand the loftiest motives in the yet far from loftiest soul: to those the soul must grow. He will hearten the child with promises, and fulfill them to the contentment of the man.

Men cannot be righteous without love; to love a righteous man is the best, the only way to learn righteousness: the Lord gives Himself to love, and promises His closest friendship to them that overcome.

"The Reward of Obedience," *The Hope of the Gospel*
Matt. 5:43-48

April 25 — Made Greater Than Oneself

"Blessed are the merciful, for they will receive mercy. Blessed are those who are persecuted for righteousness' sake, for theirs is the kingdom of heaven. Blessed are you when people revile you and persecute you and utter all kinds of evil against you falsely on my account. Rejoice and be glad, for your reward is great in heaven, for in the same way they persecuted the prophets who were before you." Matt. 5:7, 10-12

God's rewards are always in kind. "I am your Father; be my children, and I will be your Father." Every obedience is the opening of another door into the boundless universe of life. So long as the constitution of that universe remains, so long as the world continues to be made by God, righteousness can never fail of perfect reward. Before it could be otherwise, the government must have passed into other hands.

To be made greater than one's fellows is the offered reward of hell, and involves no greatness; to be made greater than one's self is the divine reward, and involves a real greatness. A man might be set above all his fellows, to be but so much less then he was before; a man cannot be raised a hair's-breadth above himself without raising nearer to God. The reward itself, then, is righteousness; and the man who was righteous for the sake of such reward, knowing what it was, would be righteous for the sake of righteousness—which yet, however, would not be perfection.

"The Reward of Obedience," *The Hope of the Gospel*
Matt. 20:25-28

THE HARDSHIPS OF THE WAY — APRIL 26

"Blessed are the merciful, for they will receive mercy. Blessed are those who are persecuted for righteousness' sake, for theirs is the kingdom of heaven. Blessed are you when people revile you and persecute you and utter all kinds of evil against you falsely on my account. Rejoice and be glad, for your reward is great in heaven, for in the same way they persecuted the prophets who were before you." Matt. 5:7, 10-12

The reward of mercy is not often of this world; the merciful do not often receive mercy in return from their fellows; perhaps they do not often receive much gratitude. None the less, being the children of their Father in heaven, will they go on to show mercy, even to their enemies. They must give like God, and like God be blessed in giving.

There is a mercy that lies in the endeavor to share with others the best things God has given: they who do so will be persecuted and reviled and slandered, as well as thanked and loved and befriended. The Lord not only promises the greatest possible reward; He tells His disciples the worst they have to expect. He not only shows them the fair countries to which they are bound; he tells them the truth of the rough weather and the hardships of the way. He will not have them choose in ignorance. At the same time He strengthens them to meet coming difficulty by instructing them in its real nature.

All this is part of His preparation of them for His work, for taking His yoke upon them, and becoming fellow-laborers with him in His Father's vineyard. They must not imagine, because they are the servants of His Father, that therefore they shall find their work easy; they shall only find the reward great.

"The Reward of Obedience," *The Hope of the Gospel*
Matt. 24:9-14

April 27   The Babes Must Not Yeild

At that time Jesus said, I thank you, Father, Lord of heaven and earth, because you have hidden these things from the wise and the intelligent and have revealed them to infants; yes, Father, for such was your gracious will.
Matt. 11:25-30 (cf. Matt. 18:10, 14; Luke 15:10)

The Lord makes no complaint against the wise and prudent [King James Version]; He but recognizes that they are not those to whom His Father reveals His best things, for which fact, and the reasons of it, He thanks or praises his Father. "I bless thy will: I see that thou art right: I am of one mind with thee": something of each of these phases of meaning seems to belong to the Greek word.

'But why not reveal true things first to the wise? Are they not the fittest to receive them?" Yes, if these things and their wisdom lie in the same region—not otherwise. No amount of knowledge or skill in physical science will make a man the fitter to argue a metaphysical question; and the wisdom of this world, meaning by the term, the philosophy of prudence, self-protection, precaution, specially unfits a man for receiving what the Father has to reveal: in proportion to our care about our own well-being is our incapability of understanding and welcoming the care of the Father. Their sagacity labors in earthly things, and so fills their minds with their own questions and conclusions that they cannot see the eternal foundations God has laid in man, or the consequent necessities of their own nature.

The babes must beware lest the wise and prudent come between them and the Father. They must yield no claim to authority over their belief, made by man or community, by church any more than by synagogue. That alone is for them to believe which the Lord reveals to their souls as true; that alone is it possible for them to believe with what He counts belief. The divine object for which teacher or church exists is the persuasion of the individual heart to come to Jesus, the Spirit, to be taught what He alone can teach.

         "The Yoke of Jesus," *The Hope of the Gospel*
         I Cor. 1:20-21

1878: Mary Josephine dies at the Palazzo Cattaneo, Nervi, Italy, after a long fight against tuberculosis.

It's Quite Other Than Just Intellectual — April 28

At that time Jesus said, I thank you, Father, Lord of heaven and earth, because you have hidden these things from the wise and the intelligent and have revealed them to infants; yes, Father, for such was your gracious will.
Matt. 11:25-30 (cf. Matt. 18:10, 14; Luke 15:10)

The wise and prudent, with all their energy of thought, could never see the things of the Father sufficiently to recognize them as true. They are proud of finding out things, but the things they find out are all less than themselves. Because, however they have discovered them, they imagine such things the goal of the human intellect.

They have not enthusiasm, and are shy of all forms of it—a clever, hard, thin people, who take *things* for the universe, and love of facts for love of truth. They know nothing deeper in man than mere surface mental facts and their relations. They do not perceive, or they turn away from any truth which the intellect cannot formulate. Zeal for God will never eat them up: why should it? He is not interesting to them: theology may be; to such men religion means theology.

How should the treasure of the Father be open to such? Even when they know their duty, they must take it to pieces, and consider the grounds of its claim before they will render it obedience. All those evil doctrines about God that work misery and madness have their origin in the brains of the wise and prudent, not in the hearts of the children.

These wise and prudent, careful to make the words of His messengers rime with their conclusions, interpret the great heart of God, not by their own hearts, but by their miserable intellects; and, postponing the obedience which alone can give power to the understanding, press upon men's minds their wretched interpretations of the will of the Father, instead of doing of that will upon their hearts. They call their philosophy the truth of God, and say men must hold it, or stand outside. They are the slaves of the letter in all its weakness and imperfection—and will be until the spirit of the Word, the spirit of obedience, shall set them free.

"The Yoke of Jesus," *The Hope of the Gospel*
Matt. 7:21-23

April 29 — How Would It Have Fared?

At that time Jesus said, I thank you, Father, Lord of heaven and earth, because you have hidden these things from the wise and the intelligent and have revealed them to infants; yes, Father, for such was your gracious will. All things have been handed over to me by my Father; and no one knows the Son except the Father, and no one knows the Father except the Son and anyone to whom the Son chooses to reveal him. Come to me, all you that are weary and are carrying heavy burdens, and I will give you rest. Take my yoke upon you, and learn from me; for I am gentle and humble in heart, and you will find rest for your souls. For my yoke is easy, and my burden is light." Matt. 11:25-30 (cf. Matt. 18:10, 14; Luke 15:10)

Terribly has His gospel suffered in the mouths of the wise and prudent: how would it be faring now, had its first messages been committed to persons of repute, instead of those simple fishermen? It would be nowhere, or, if anywhere, unrecognizable. From the first we should have had a system founded on a human interpretation of the divine gospel, instead of the gospel itself, which would have disappeared. As it is, we have had one dull, miserable human system after another usurping its place; but, thank God, the gospel remains!

Had the wise and prudent been the confidants of God, I repeat, the letter would at once have usurped the place of the spirit; the ministering slave would have been set over the household; a system of religion, with its rickety, malodorous plan of salvation, would not only have at once been put in the place of a living Christ, but would yet have held that place. The great Brother, the human God, the eternal Son, the living One, would have been as utterly hidden from the tearful eyes and aching hearts of the weary and heavy-laden as if He had never come from the deeps of love to call the children home out of the shadows of a self-haunted universe.

But the Father revealed the Father's things to His babes; the babes loved, and began to do them, therewith began to understand them, and went on growing in the knowledge of them and in the power of communicating them; while to the wise and prudent the deepest words of the most babe-like of them all, John Boanerges, even now appear but a finger-worn rosary of platitudes. The babe understands the wise and prudent, but is understood only by the babe.

"The Yoke of Jesus," *The Hope of the Gospel*
II Cor. 3:6

The One Eternal Relationship   April 30

At that time Jesus said, I thank you, Father, Lord of heaven and earth, because you have hidden these things from the wise and the intelligent and have revealed them to infants; yes, Father, for such was your gracious will. All things have been handed over to me by my Father; and no one knows the Son except the Father, and no one knows the Father except the Son and anyone to whom the Son chooses to reveal him. Come to me, all you that are weary and are carrying heavy burdens, and I will give you rest. Take my yoke upon you, and learn from me; for I am gentle and humble in heart, and you will find rest for your souls. For my yoke is easy, and my burden is light." Matt. 11:25-30 (cf. Matt. 18:10, 14; Luke 15:10)

The Father, then, revealed His things to babes because the babes were His own little ones, uncorrupted by the wisdom or the care of this world, and therefore able to receive them. The others, though His children, had not begun to be like Him, therefore could not receive them. The Father's things could not have got anyhow into their minds without leaving all their value, all their spirit, outside the unchildlike place.

The babes are near enough whence they come to understand a little how things go in the presence of their Father in heaven, and thereby to interpret the words of the Son. As God is the one only real Father, so is it only to God that any one can be a perfect child.

Having thanked His Father that he has done after his own "good and acceptable and perfect will," He turns to His disciples, and tells them that he knows the Father, being His Son, and that He only can reveal the Father to the rest of His children. It is almost as if His mention of the babes brought His thoughts back to Himself and His Father, between whom lay the secret of all life and all sending—yea, all loving. The relation of the Father and the Son contains the idea of the universe.

Jesus tells His disciples that His Father had no secrets from Him; that He knew the Father as the Father knew Him. The Son must know the Father; He only could know Him—and knowing, He could reveal Him; the Son could make the others, the imperfect children, know the Father, and so become such as He. All things were given unto Him by the Father, because He was the Son of the Father: for the same reason He could reveal the things of the Father to the child of the Father. The child-relation is the one eternal, ever-enduring, never-changing relation.

"The Yoke of Jesus," *The Hope of the Gospel*
Matt. 18:3-4

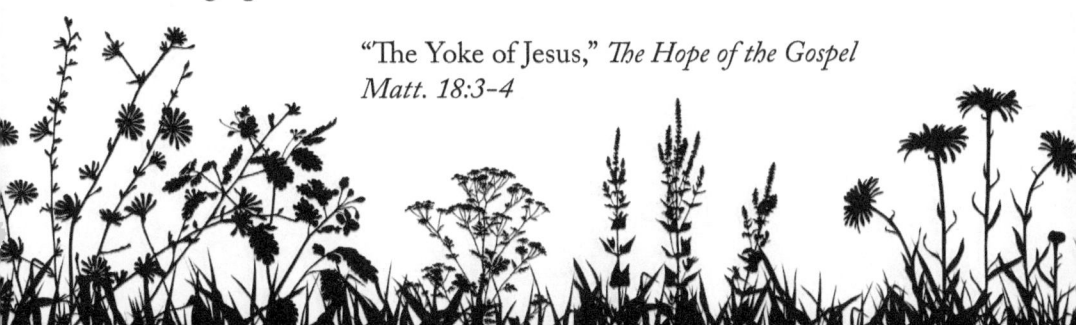

May 1 — Only To The Child

At that time Jesus said, I thank you, Father, Lord of heaven and earth, because you have hidden these things from the wise and the intelligent and have revealed them to infants; yes, Father, for such was your gracious will. All things have been handed over to me by my Father; and no one knows the Son except the Father, and no one knows the Father except the Son and anyone to whom the Son chooses to reveal him. Come to me, all you that are weary and are carrying heavy burdens, and I will give you rest. Take my yoke upon you, and learn from me; for I am gentle and humble in heart, and you will find rest for your souls. For my yoke is easy, and my burden is light." Matt. 11:25-30 (cf. Matt. 18:10, 14; Luke 15:10)

Note that, while the Lord here represents the knowledge His Father and He have each of the other as limited to themselves, the statement is one of fact only, not of design or intention: His presence in the world is for the removal of that limitation. The Father knows the Son, and sends Him to us that we may know Him; the Son knows the Father, and dies to reveal Him. The glory of God's mysteries is, that they are for His children to look into.

When the Lord took the little child in the presence of His disciples, and declared him His representative, He made him the representative of His Father also; but the eternal Child alone can reveal Him. To reveal is immeasurably more than to represent; it is to present to the eyes that know the true when they see it. Jesus represented God; the spirit of Jesus reveals God.

The represented God a man may refuse; many refused the Lord; the revealed God no one can refuse; to see God and to love Him are one. He can be revealed only to the child; perfectly, to the pure child only. All the discipline of the world is to make men children, that God may be revealed to them.

Drawn to Him, the children receive Him, and then He is able to reveal the Father to them. No wisdom of the wise can find out God; no words of the God-loving can reveal Him. The simplicity of the whole natural relation is too deep for the philosopher. The Son alone can reveal God; the child alone understand Him.

"The Yoke of Jesus," *The Hope of the Gospel*
Heb. 2:1-4

"Be As I Am" MAY 2

At that time Jesus said, I thank you, Father, Lord of heaven and earth, because you have hidden these things from the wise and the intelligent and have revealed them to infants; yes, Father, for such was your gracious will. All things have been handed over to me by my Father; and no one knows the Son except the Father, and no one knows the Father except the Son and anyone to whom the Son chooses to reveal him. Come to me, all you that are weary and are carrying heavy burdens, and I will give you rest. Take my yoke upon you, and learn from me; for I am gentle and humble in heart, and you will find rest for your souls. For my yoke is easy, and my burden is light." Matt. 11:25-30 (cf. Matt. 18:10, 14; Luke 15:10)

Having spoken to His Father first, and now to His disciples, the Lord turns to the whole world, and lets His heart overflow. St. Matthew alone has saved for us the eternal cry: "Come to me, all who labor and are heavy laden, and I will give you rest." He does not here call those who want to know the Father; His cry goes far beyond them; it reaches to the ends of the earth. He calls those who are weary; those who do not know that the ignorance of the Father is the cause of all their labor and the heaviness of their burden. "Come to me," He says, "and I will give you rest."

I will turn His argument a little: "I have rest because I know the Father. Be meek and lowly of heart toward Him as I am; let Him lay His yoke upon you as He lays it on me. I do His will, not my own. Take on you the yoke that I wear; be His child like me; become a babe to whom He can reveal His wonders. Then shall you too find rest to your souls; you shall have the same peace I have; you will be weary and heavy laden no more. I find my yoke easy, my burden light."

The best of the good wine remains; I have kept it to the last. A friend pointed out to me that the Master does not mean we must take on us a yoke like His; we must take on us the very yoke He is carrying. Dante, describing how, on the first terrace of Purgatory, he walked stooping, to be on a level with Oderisi, who went bowed to the ground by the ponderous burden of the pride he had cherished on earth, says, "I went walking with this heavy-laden soul, just as oxen walk in the yoke": this picture almost always comes to me with the words of the Lord, "Take my yoke upon you, and learn of me." Their intent is: Take the other end of my yoke, doing as I do, being as I am."

"The Yoke of Jesus," *The Hope of the Gospel*
Matt. 28:18-20

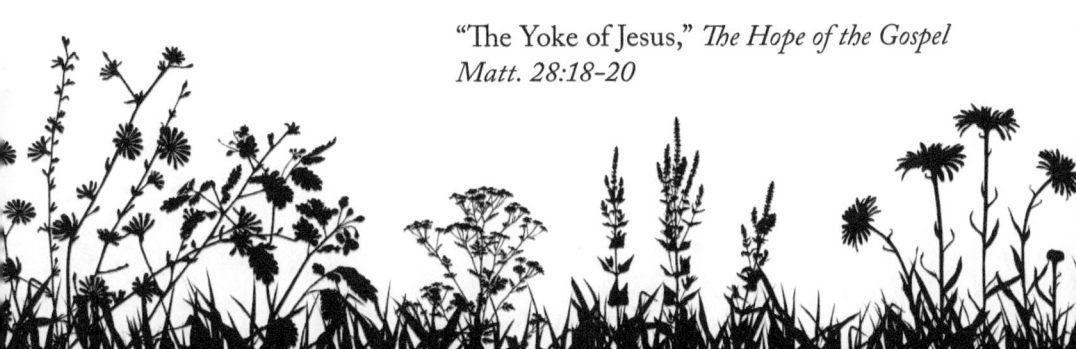

May 3 — What Is This Yoke?

At that time Jesus said, I thank you, Father, Lord of heaven and earth, because you have hidden these things from the wise and the intelligent and have revealed them to infants; yes, Father, for such was your gracious will. All things have been handed over to me by my Father; and no one knows the Son except the Father, and no one knows the Father except the Son and anyone to whom the Son chooses to reveal him. Come to me, all you that are weary and are carrying heavy burdens, and I will give you rest. Take my yoke upon you, and learn from me; for I am gentle and humble in heart, and you will find rest for your souls. For my yoke is easy, and my burden is light." Matt. 11:25-30 (cf. Matt. 18:10, 14; Luke 15:10)

Think of it a moment: to walk in the same yoke with the Son of Man, doing the same labor with Him, and having the same feeling common to Him and us! This, and nothing else, is offered the man who would have rest to his soul; is required of the man who would know the Father; is by the Lord pressed upon him to whom He would give the same peace which pervades and sustains His own eternal heart.

But a yoke is for drawing: what load is it the Lord is drawing? Wherewith is the cart laden which He would have us help Him draw? With what but the will of the eternal, the perfect Father? How should the Father honor the Son, but by giving Him His will to embody in deed? Specially in drawing this load must His yoke-fellow share. How to draw it, he must learn of Him who draws by his side.

Whoever, in the commonest duties that fall to him, does as the Father would have him do, bears his yoke along with Jesus. Bearing the same yoke with Jesus, the man learns to walk step for step with Him drawing---drawing the cart laden with the will of the Father of both, and rejoicing with the joy of Jesus.

"The Yoke of Jesus," *The Hope of the Gospel*
Col. 3:17

The One Thing Worth Living For   May 4

At that time Jesus said, I thank you, Father, Lord of heaven and earth, because you have hidden these things from the wise and the intelligent and have revealed them to infants; yes, Father, for such was your gracious will. All things have been handed over to me by my Father; and no one knows the Son except the Father, and no one knows the Father except the Son and anyone to whom the Son chooses to reveal him. Come to me, all you that are weary and are carrying heavy burdens, and I will give you rest. Take my yoke upon you, and learn from me; for I am gentle and humble in heart, and you will find rest for your souls. For my yoke is easy, and my burden is light." Matt. 11:25-30 (cf. Matt. 18:10, 14; Luke 15:10)

The glory of existence is to take up its burden, and exist for Existence eternal and supreme—for the Father who does His divine and perfect best to impart His glad life to us, making us sharers of that nature which is bliss, and that labor which is peace. He lives for us; we must live for Him. The little ones must take their full share in the great Father's work: His work is the business of the family.

He on whom lay the other half of the burden of God, the weight of His creation to redeem, says, "The yoke I bear is easy; the burden I draw is light"; and this He said, knowing the death he was to die. The yoke did not gall His neck, the burden did not overstrain His sinews, neither did the goal on Calvary fright Him from the straight way thither. He had the will of the Father to work out, and that will was His strength as well as His joy. He had the same will as His Father. To Him the one thing worth living for was the share the love of his Father gave Him in His work. He loved His Father even to the death of the cross, eternally beyond it.

        "The Yoke of Jesus," *The Hope of the Gospel*
        John 16:33

May 5   Knowing Only By Having

At that time Jesus said, I thank you, Father, Lord of heaven and earth, because you have hidden these things from the wise and the intelligent and have revealed them to infants; yes, Father, for such was your gracious will. All things have been handed over to me by my Father; and no one knows the Son except the Father, and no one knows the Father except the Son and anyone to whom the Son chooses to reveal him. Come to me, all you that are weary and are carrying heavy burdens, and I will give you rest. Take my yoke upon you, and learn from me; for I am gentle and humble in heart, and you will find rest for your souls. For my yoke is easy, and my burden is light." Matt. 11:25-30 (cf. Matt. 18:10, 14; Luke 15:10)

When we give ourselves up to the Father as the Son gave Himself, we shall not only find our yoke easy and our burden light, but that they communicate ease and lightness; not only will they not make us weary, but they will give us rest from all other weariness. Let us not waste a moment in asking how this can be; the only way to know that is to take the yoke on us. That rest is a secret for every heart to know, for never a tongue to tell. Only by having it can we know it.

If it seem impossible to take the yoke on us, let us attempt the impossible; let us lay hold of the yoke, and bow our heads, and try to get our necks under it. Giving our Father the opportunity, He will help and not fail us. He is helping us every moment, when least we think we need His help; when most we think we do, then may we most boldly, as most earnestly we must, cry for it.

What or how much His creatures can do or bear, God only understands; but when most it seems impossible to do or bear, we must be most confident that He will neither demand too much, nor fail with the vital creator-help. That help will be there when wanted----that is, the moment it can be help. To be able beforehand to imagine ourselves doing or bearing, we have neither claim nor need.

It is vain to think that any weariness, however caused, any burden, however slight, may be got rid of otherwise than by bowing the neck to the yoke of the Father's will. There can be no other rest for heart and soul that He has created. From every burden, from every anxiety, from all dread of shame or loss, even loss of love itself, that yoke will set us free.

"The Yoke of Jesus," The Hope of the Gospel
II Cor. 4:7-10

1884: Caroline Grace (MacDonald) Jameson dies in Bordighera

Where Would The World Be? May 6

You are the salt of the earth; but if salt has lost its taste, how can its saltiness be restored? It is no longer good for anything, but is thrown out and trampled under foot. You are the light of the world. A city built on a hill cannot be hid. No one after lighting a lamp puts it under the bushel basket, but on the lampstand, and it gives light to all in the house. In the same way, let your light shine before others, so that they may see your good works and give glory to your Father in heaven. Matt. 5:13-16

The Lord does not hesitate to call His few humble disciples the salt of the earth; and every century since has borne witness that such indeed they were—that He spoke of them but the simple fact. Where would the world be now but for their salt and their light!

The world that knows neither their salt nor their light may imagine itself now at least greatly retarded by the long-drawn survival of their influences; but such as have chosen aspiration and not ambition will cry, But for those men, whither should we at this moment be bound? Their Master set them to be salt against corruption, and light against darkness; and our souls answer and say, Lord, they have been the salt, they have been the light of the world.

No sooner had He used the symbol of the salt, than the Lord proceeds to supplement its incompleteness. They were salt which must remember that it is salt; which must live salt, and choose salt, and be salt. For the whole worth of salt lies in its being salt; and all the saltness of the moral salt lies in the will to be salt. To lose its saltness, then, is to cease to exist, save as a vile thing whose very being is unjustifiable. What is to be done with saltless salt? With such as would teach religion and know not God?

> "The Salt and Light of the World," *The Hope of the Gospel*
> Acts 4:13

May 7 — Make It So

You are the salt of the earth; but if salt has lost its taste, how can its saltiness be restored? It is no longer good for anything, but is thrown out and trampled under foot. You are the light of the world. A city built on a hill cannot be hid. No one after lighting a lamp puts it under the bushel basket, but on the lampstand, and it gives light to all in the house. In the same way, let your light shine before others, so that they may see your good works and give glory to your Father in heaven. Matt. 5:13-16

Salt only preserves from growing bad; it does not cause anything to grow better. His disciples are the salt of the world, but they are more. Therefore, having warned the human salt to look to itself that it be indeed salt, He proceeds: "You are the light of the world, a city, a candle," and so resumes His former path of persuasion and enforcement: "It is so; therefore make it so. You are the salt of the earth; therefore be salt. You are the light of the world; therefore shine. You are a city; be seen upon the hill. You are the Lord's candles; let no bushels cover you. Let your light shine. Every disciple of the Lord must be a preacher of righteousness.

Cities are the best lighted portions of the world; and perhaps the Lord meant, "You are a live city; therefore light up your city." Some connection of the city with light seems probably in His thought, seeing the allusion to the city on the hill comes in the midst of what He says about light in relation to His disciples as the light of the world. Anyhow the city is the best circle in which, and the best center from which, to diffuse moral light. A man brooding in the desert may find the very light of light, but he must go to the city to let it shine.

From the general idea of light, however associated with the city as visible to all the country around, the Lord turns at once, in this probably fragmentary representation of His words, to the homelier, the more individual and personally applicable figure of the lamp: "Nor do men light a lamp and put it under a bushel, but on a stand, and it gives light to all in the house."

Light unshared is darkness. To be light indeed, it must shine out. It is of the very essence of light, that it is for others. The thing is true of the spiritual as of the physical light—of the truth as of the type.

"The Salt and Light of the World," *The Hope of the Gospel*
II Tim. 2:15

The Danger Of The Self-Bushel   May 8

You are the salt of the earth; but if salt has lost its taste, how can its saltiness be restored? It is no longer good for anything, but is thrown out and trampled under foot. You are the light of the world. A city built on a hill cannot be hid. No one after lighting a lamp puts it under the bushel basket, but on the lampstand, and it gives light to all in the house. In the same way, let your light shine before others, so that they may see your good works and give glory to your Father in heaven. Matt. 5:13-16

The lamp that the Lord kindles is a lamp that can will to shine, a soul that must shine. Its true relation to the spirits around—to God and its fellows—is its light. Then only does it fully shine, when its love, which is its light, shows it to all the souls within its scope, and all those souls to each other, and so does its part to bring all together toward one. In the darkness each soul is alone; in the light the souls are a family. Take heed to your light that it be such, that it so shine, that in you men may see the Father—may see your works so good, so plainly His, that they recognize his presence in you, and thank Him for you.

There was the danger always of the shadow of the self-bushel clouding the lamp the Father had lighted; and the moment they ceased to show the Father, the light that was in them was darkness. God alone is the light, and our light is the shining of His will in our lives. If our light shine at all, it must be, it can be only in showing the Father; nothing is light that does not bear Him witness.

The man that sees the glory of God would turn sick at the thought of glorifying his own self, whose one only possible glory is to shine with the glory of God. When a man tries to shine from the self that is not one with God and filled with his light, he is but making ready for his own gathering contempt. The man who, like his Lord, seeks not his own, but the will of Him who sent him, he alone shines. He who would shine in the praises of men will, sooner or later, find himself but a Gideon's pitcher left broken on the field.

Let us bestir ourselves then, to keep this word of the Lord; and to this end inquire how we are to let our light shine.

"The Salt and Light of the World," *The Hope of the Gospel*
Gal. 2:20

May 9 — The Light Is From Him

You are the salt of the earth; but if salt has lost its taste, how can its saltiness be restored? It is no longer good for anything, but is thrown out and trampled under foot. You are the light of the world. A city built on a hill cannot be hid. No one after lighting a lamp puts it under the bushel basket, but on the lampstand, and it gives light to all in the house. In the same way, let your light shine before others, so that they may see your good works and give glory to your Father in heaven. Matt. 5:13-16

To the man who does not try to order his thought and feelings and judgments after the will of the Father, I have nothing to say; he can have no light to let shine. For to let our light shine is to see that in every, even the smallest thing, our lives and actions correspond to what we know of God; that, as the true children of our Father in heaven, we do everything as He would have us do it.

Need I say that to let our light shine is to be just, honorable, courteous, more careful over the claim of our neighbor than our own, as knowing ourselves in danger of overlooking it, and not bound to insist on every claim of our own? The man who takes no count of what is fair, friendly, pure, unselfish, lovely, gracious—where is his claim to Christianity? What saves his claim from being merest mockery?

The outshining of any human light must be obedience to truth recognized as such; our first show of light as the Lord's disciples must be in doing the things he tells us. Naturally thus we declare Him our Master, the ruler of our conduct, the enlightener of our souls; and while in the doing of His will a man is learning the loveliness of righteousness, he can hardly fail to let some light shine across the dust of his failures, the exhalations from his faults. Thus will His disciples shine as lights in the world, holding forth the Word of life.

To shine, we must keep in His light, sunning our souls in it by thinking of what He said and did, and would have us think and do. So shall we drink the light like some diamonds, keep it, and shine in the dark.

"The Salt and Light of the World," *The Hope of the Gospel*
John 15:5

Seeking His Will In The World   May 10

You are the salt of the earth; but if salt has lost its taste, how can its saltiness be restored? It is no longer good for anything, but is thrown out and trampled under foot. You are the light of the world. A city built on a hill cannot be hid. No one after lighting a lamp puts it under the bushel basket, but on the lampstand, and it gives light to all in the house. In the same way, let your light shine before others, so that they may see your good works and give glory to your Father in heaven. Matt. 5:13-16

Doing His will, men will see in us that we count the world His, hold that His will and not ours must be done in it. Our very faces will then shine with the hope of seeing Him, and being taken home where he is. Only let us remember that trying to look what we ought to be is the beginning of hypocrisy.

If we do indeed expect better things to come, we must let our hope appear. A Christian who looks gloomy at the mention of death, still more, one who talks of his friends as if he had lost them, turns the bushel of this little-faith over the lamp of the Lord's light. Death is but our visible horizon, and our look ought always to be focused beyond it. We should never talk as if death were the end of anything.

To let our light shine, we must take care that we have no respect for riches: if we have none, there is no fear of our showing any. To treat the poor man with less attention or cordiality than the rich is to show ourselves the servants of Mammon. In like manner we must lay no value on the praise of men, or in any way seek it. We must honor no man because of intellect, fame, or success. We must not shrink in fear of the judgment of men, from doing openly what we hold right; or at all acknowledge as a law-giver what calls itself Society, or harbor the least anxiety for its approval.

In business, the custom of the trade must be understood by both contracting parties, else it can have no place either as law or excuse, with the disciple of Jesus. The man to whom business is one thing and religion another is not a disciple. If he refuses to harmonize them by making his business religion, he has already chosen Mammon; if he thinks not to settle the question, it is settled. The most futile of all human endeavors is, to serve God and Mammon.

    "The Salt and Light of the World," *The Hope of the Gospel*
    James 2:1-4

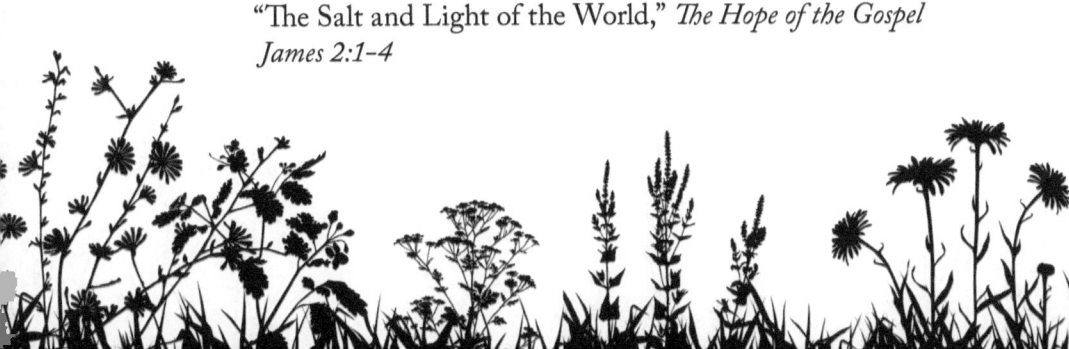

May 11 — It Is But Decent

"Beware of practicing your piety before others in order to be seen by them; for then you have no reward from your Father in heaven. But when you give alms, do not let your left hand know what your right hand is doing, so that your alms may be done in secret; and your Father who sees in secret will reward you." Matt. 6:, 3, 4

Let your light out freely, that men may see it, but not that men may see you. If I do anything in order that I may be seen as the doer, that I may be praised of men, that I may gain repute of others; be the thing itself ever so good, I may look to men for my reward, for there is none for me with the Father.

The injunction, however, is not to hide what you do from others, but to hide it from yourself.. The Master would have you not plume yourself upon it, not cherish the thought that you have done it, or confer with yourself in satisfaction over it. You must not count it to your praise. A man must not desire to be satisfied with himself. His right hand must not seek the praise of his left hand. His doing must not invite his after-thinking. The right hand must let the thing done go, as a thing done with.

When we have done all, we are unprofitable servants. Our very best is but decent. What more could it be? Why then think of it as anything more? What things could we or any one do, worthy of being brooded over as possessions? Good to do, they were; bad to pride ourselves upon, they are. Why should a man meditate with satisfaction on having denied himself some selfish indulgence, any more than on having washed his hands.

Even if our supposed merit were of the positive order, and we did every duty perfectly, the moment we began to pride ourselves upon the fact we should drop into a hell of worthlessness. What are we for but to do our duty? We must do it, and think nothing of ourselves for that, neither care what men think of us for anything. With the praise or blame of men we have nought to do.

"The Right Hand and the Left," *The Hope of the Gospel*
Luke 17:7-10

What Is The Reward?   May 12

"Beware of practicing your piety before others in order to be seen by them; for then you have no reward from your Father in heaven. But when you give alms, do not let your left hand know what your right hand is doing, so that your alms may be done in secret; and your Father who sees in secret will reward you." Matt. 6:, 3, 4

But there are some who, if the notion of reward is not naturally a trouble to them, yet have come to feel it such, because of the words of certain objectors who think to take a higher stand than the Christian, saying the idea of reward for doing right is a low, an unworthy idea.

What kind of a father were the man who, because there could be no merit or desert in doing well, would not give his child a smile or a pleased word when he saw him trying his best? Would not such acknowledgment from the father be the natural correlate of the child's behavior? And what would the father's smile be but the perfect reward of the child? Suppose the father to love the child so that he wants to give him everything, but dares not until his character is developed: must he not be glad, and show his gladness, at every shade of a progress that will at length set him free to throne his son over all that he has?

If you say, "No one ought to do right for the sake of reward," I go further and say, "No man *can* do right for the sake of reward. A man may do a thing indifferent, he may do a thing wrong, for the sake of reward, but a thing in itself right, done for reward, would, in the very doing, cease to be right." At the same time, if a man does right, he cannot escape being rewarded for it; and to refuse the reward would be to refuse life, and foil the creative love.

"The Right Hand and the Left," *The Hope of the Gospel*
Matt. 10:40-42

May 13 — What Other Reward Is Possible?

"Beware of practicing your piety before others in order to be seen by them; for then you have no reward from your Father in heaven. But when you give alms, do not let your left hand know what your right hand is doing, so that your alms may be done in secret; and your Father who sees in secret will reward you." Matt. 6:, 3, 4

The whole question is of the kind of reward expected. What first reward for doing well may I look for? To grow purer in heart, and stronger in the hope of at length seeing God. If a man be not after this fashion rewarded, he must perish. As to happiness or any lower rewards that naturally follow the first—is God to destroy the law of the universe, the divine sequence of cause and effect in order to say: "You must do well, but you shall gain no good by it; you must lead a dull, joyless existence to all eternity, that lack of delight may show you pure?" Could Love create with such end in view? A righteousness that created misery in order to uphold itself would be a righteousness that was unrighteous.

God will die for righteousness, but never create for a joyless righteousness. To call into being the necessarily and hopelessly incomplete would be to wrong creation in its very essence. To create for the knowledge of Himself, and then not give Himself, would be injustice even to cruelty; and if God give Himself, what other reward—there can be no *further*—is not included, seeing He is Life and all her children—the All in all?

To object to Christianity as selfish is utter foolishness; Christianity alone gives any hope of deliverance from selfishness. Is it selfish to desire love? Is it selfish to hope for purity and the sight of God? What better can we do for our neighbor than to become altogether righteous toward him? Will he not be the nearer sharing in the exceeding great reward of a return to the divine idea?

"The Right Hand and the Left," *The Hope of the Gospel*
Phil. 1:9-11

Thinkable Only By Men — May 14

"Beware of practicing your piety before others in order to be seen by them; for then you have no reward from your Father in heaven. But when you give alms, do not let your left hand know what your right hand is doing, so that your alms may be done in secret; and your Father who sees in secret will reward you." Matt. 6:, 3, 4

It seems to me that the only merit that could live before God is the merit of Jesus—who of Himself, at once, unimplored, laid Himself aside, and turned to the Father, refusing His life save in the Father. Like God, of Himself He chose righteousness, and so merited to sit on the throne of God. In the same spirit He gave himself afterward to His Father's children, and merited the power to transfuse the life-redeeming energy of His spirit into theirs: made perfect, He became the author of eternal salvation unto all them that obey Him. But it is a word of little daring, that Jesus had no thought of merit in what He did—that He saw only what He had to be, what He must do.

I suspect the notion of merit belongs to a low development, and the higher a man rises, the less will he find it worth a thought. Perhaps we shall come to see that it owes what being it has to man, that it is a thing thinkable only by men. I suspect it is not a thought of the eternal mind, and has in itself no existence, being to God merely a thing thought by man:

> For merit lives from man to man,
> And not from man, O Lord, to thee.

The man, then, who does right, and seeks no praise from men, while he merits nothing, shall be rewarded by his Father, and his reward will be right precious to him.

"The Right Hand and the Left," *The Hope of the Gospel*
Heb. 12:1-3

May 15 — The Sole Escape

"Beware of practicing your piety before others in order to be seen by them; for then you have no reward from your Father in heaven. But when you give alms, do not let your left hand know what your right hand is doing, so that your alms may be done in secret; and your Father who sees in secret will reward you." Matt. 6:, 3, 4

We must let our light shine, make our faith, our hope, our love, manifest—that men may praise, not us for shining, but the Father for creating the light. No man with faith, hope, love, alive in his soul, could make the divine possessions a show to gain for himself the admiration of men: not the less must they appear in our words, in our looks, in our carriage—above all, in honorable, unselfish, hospitable, helpful deeds.

Our light must shine in cheerfulness, in joy, yea, where a man has the gift, in merriment; in freedom from care save for one another, in interest in the things of others, in fearlessness and tenderness; in courtesy and graciousness. In our anger and indignation, specially, must our light shine. But we must give no quarter to the most shadowy thought of how this or that will look. From the faintest thought of the praise of men, we must turn away.

No man can be the disciple of Christ and desire fame. To desire fame is ignoble; it is a beggarly greed. In the noble mind, it is the more of an infirmity. There is not aspiration in it—nothing but ambition. It is simply selfishness that would be proud if it could. Fame is the applause of the many, and the judgment of the many is foolish; therefore the greater the fame, the more is the foolishness that swells it, and the worse is the foolishness that longs after it.

Aspiration is the sole escape from ambition. He who aspires—that is, does his endeavor to rise above himself—neither lusts to be higher than his neighbor, nor seeks to mount in his opinion. What light there is in him shines the more that he does nothing to be seen of men. He stands in the mist between the gulf and the glory, and looks upward. He loves not his own soul, but longs to be clean.

"The Right Hand and the Left," *The Hope of the Gospel*
Phil 3:12-15

WHAT IS PAUL SAYING — MAY 16

For the creation waits with eager longing for the revealing of the children of God. Rom. 8:19

Let us try, through these words, to get at the idea in St. Paul's mind for which they stand, and have so long stood. The words mean something which Paul believes vitally associated with the life and death of his Master.

First then, what does Paul, the slave of Christ, intend by "the creature" or "the creation"? If he means the visible world, he did not surely, and without saying so, mean to exclude the noblest part of it—the sentient! If he did, it is doubly strange that he should immediately attribute not merely sense, but conscious sense, to that part, the insentient, namely, which remained. If you say he does so but by a figure of speech, I answer that a figure that meant less than it said—and how much less would not this?---would be one altogether unworthy of the Lord's messenger.

Take another part of the same utterance: "We know that the whole creation has been groaning in travail together until now"; is it now manifest that to interpret such words as referring to the mere imperfections of the insentient material world would be to make of the phrase a worthless hyperbole? I am inclined to believe the apostle regarded the whole visible creation as, in far differing degrees of consciousness, a live outcome from the heart of the living one, who is all and in all: such view, at the same time, I do not care to insist upon; I only care to argue that the word *creature* or *creation* must include everything in creation that has sentient life.

My point is simply this: that in the term *creation* Paul comprises all creatures capable of suffering; the condition of which the sentient, therefore superior portion, gives him occasion to speak of the whole creation as suffering in the process of its divine evolution or development, groaning and travailing as in the pangs of giving birth to a better self, a nobler world.

> "The Hope of the Universe," *The Hope of the Gospel*
> James 4:7-10

May 17 — A Creative Demon?

For the creation waits with eager longing for the revealing of the children of God. Rom. 8:19

It is not necessary to the idea that the creation should know what it is groaning after, or wherein the higher condition constituting its deliverance must consist. The human race groans for deliverance: how much does the race know that its redemption lies in becoming one with the Father, and partaking of His glory? Here and there one of the race knows it—which is indeed a pledge for the race—but the race cannot be said to know its own lack, or to have even a far-off notion of what alone can stay its groaning.

In like manner the whole creation is groaning after an unforeseen yet essential birth—groans with the necessity of being freed from a state that is but a transitional and not a true one, from a condition that nowise answers to the intent in which existence began. In both the lower creation and the higher, this same groaning of the fettered idea after a freer life seems the first enforced decree of a holy fate, and itself the first movement of the hampered thing toward the liberty of another birth.

To believe that God made many of the lower creatures merely for prey, or to be the slaves of a slave, and writhe under the tyrannies of a cruel master who will not serve his own master; that He created and is creating an endless succession of them to reap little or no good of life but its cessation—a doctrine held by some, and practically accepted by multitudes—is to believe in a God who, as far as one portion at least of His creation is concerned, is a demon.

But a creative demon is an absurdity; and were such a creator possible, he would not be God, but must one day be found and destroyed by the real God.

> "The Hope of the Universe," *The Hope of the Gospel*
> Isa. 11:6-9

Are They Not Worth It?   May 18

For the creation waits with eager longing for the revealing of the children of God. Rom. 8:19

Miserable suffering abounds among [many animals], and, even supposing God did not foresee how creation would turn out for them, the thing lies at his door. He has besides made them so far dumb that they cannot move the hearts of the oppressors into whose hands He has given them, telling how hard they find the world, how sore their life in it. The apostle takes up their case, and give us material for an answer to such as blame God for their sad condition.

What many men call their beliefs are but the prejudices they happen to have picked up. But there are not a few who would be indignant at having their belief in God questioned, who yet seem greatly to fear imagining Him better than he is. "You see the plain facts of the case," they say, "There is no questioning them. What can be done for the poor things—except, indeed, you take the absurd notion into your head, that they too have a life beyond the grave?"

"Why should such a notion seem to you absurd?" I answer. The teachers of the nation have unwittingly, it seems to me through unbelief, wronged the animals deeply by their silence against the thoughtless popular presumption that they have no hereafter, thus leaving them deprived of a great advantage to their position among men. But I suppose they too have taken it for granted that the Preserver of man and beast never had a thought of keeping one beast alive beyond a certain time; in which case heartless men might well argue He did not care how they wronged them, for He meant them no redress.

Their immortality is no new faith with me, but as old as my childhood. "Do you believe in immortality for yourself?" I would ask any reader who is not in sympathy with my hope for the animals. If not, I have no argument with you. But if you do, why not believe in it for them? Are these not worth making immortal? How, then, were they worth calling out of the depth of no-being?

> "The Hope of the Universe," *The Hope of the Gospel*
> Eph. 3:20-21

May 19 — Not By A Little Only

For the creation waits with eager longing for the revealing of the children of God. Rom. 8:19

It is a greater deed, to make be that which was not, then to seal it with an infinite immortality: did God do that which was not worth doing? What He thought worth making, you think not worth continuing made? You would have Him go on forever creating new things with one hand, and annihilating those He had made with the other—for I presume you would not prefer the earth to be without animals. If it were harder for God to make the former go on living than to send forth new, then His creatures were no better than the toys which a child makes, and destroys as he makes them.

For what good, for what divine purpose is the Maker of the sparrow present at its death, if He does not care what becomes of it? What is He therefore, I repeat, if He have no care that it go well with His bird in its dying, that it be neither comfortless nor lost in the abyss? If His presence be no good to the sparrow, are you very sure what good it will be to you when your hour comes? Believe it is not by a little only that the heart of the universe is tenderer, more loving, more just and fair, then yours or mine.

If you did not believe you were yourself to outlive death, I could not blame you for thinking all was over with the sparrow; but to believe in immortality for yourself, and not care to believe in it for the sparrow, would be simply hard-hearted and selfish. If it would make you happy to think there was life beyond death for the sparrow as well as for yourself, I would gladly help you at least to hope that there may be.

I know of no reason why I should not look for the animals to rise again, in the same sense in which I hope myself to rise again—which is, to reappear, clothed with another and better form of life than before. If the Father will raise His children, why should he not also raise those whom He has taught His little ones to love?

"The Hope of the Universe," *The Hope of the Gospel*
Psalms 37:4

Why Indeed Not? May 20

For the creation waits with eager longing for the revealing of the children of God. Rom. 8:19

That there are difficulties in the way of believing [in the immortality of animals], I grant; that there are impossibilities, I deny. Perhaps the first difficulty that occurs is, the many forms of life which we cannot desire again to see. But while we would gladly keep the perfected forms of the higher animals, we may hope that those of any other kinds are as transitory as their bodies, belonging but to a stage of development. All animal forms tend to higher: why should not the individual, as well as the race, pass through stages of ascent?

The suggestion may appear very ridiculous, and no doubt lends itself to humorous comment; but what if it should be true? What I care to press is the question—if we believe in the progress of creation as hitherto manifested, also in the marvelous changes of form that take place in every individual of certain classes, why should there be any difficulty in hoping that old lives may appear in new forms? The typal soul reappears in higher formal type; why may not also the individual soul reappear in higher form?

Multitudes evidently count it safest to hold by a dull scheme of things. Those that hope little cannot grow much. To them the very glory of God must be a small thing, for their hope of it is so small as not to be worth rejoicing in. That He is a faithful creator means nothing to them for far the larger portion of the creatures he has made. Truly their notion of faithfulness is poor enough; how then, can their faith be strong?

I say, then, I know no cause of reasonable difficulty in regard to the continued existence of the lower animals, except the present nature of some of them. But what Christian will dare to say that God does not care about them?—and He knows them as we cannot know them. Great are all his results; small are all his beginnings.

> "The Hope of the Universe," *The Hope of the Gospel*
> I John 3:2

May 21 — Waiting In Hope

For the creation waits with eager longing for the revealing of the children of God. Rom. 8:19

At the head of one of his poems, Henry Vaughan has his Latin translation of the verse: I do not know whether he found or made it, but it is closer to its true sense than ours: "For the things created, watching with head thrust out, await the revelation of the sons of God."

Why? Because God has subjected the creation to vanity [RSV: futility], in the hope that the creation itself shall be delivered from the bondage of corruption into the glorious liberty of the children of God. For this double deliverance—from corruption and the consequent subjection to vanity, the creation is eagerly watching.

The bondage of corruption God encounters and counteracts by subjection to vanity. Corruption is the breaking up of the essential idea; the falling away from the original indwelling thought. It is met by the suffering which itself causes. That suffering is for redemption, for deliverance. It is the life in the corrupting thing that makes the suffering possible; it is the live part, not the corrupted part, that suffers; it is the redeemable, not the doomed thing, that is subjected to vanity.

The race in which evil—that is, corruption—is at work, needs, as the one means of its rescue, subjection to vanity; it is the one hope against the supremacy of corruption; and the whole encircling, harboring, and helping creation must, for the sake of man, its head, and for its own further sake too, share in this subjection to vanity with its hope of deliverance.

"The Hope of the Universe," *The Hope of the Gospel*
Isa. 45:5-8

The Unpleasant Cure — May 22

For the creation waits with eager longing for the revealing of the children of God. Rom. 8:19

Corruption brings in vanity, causes empty aching gaps in vitality. This aching is what most people regard as evil: it is the unpleasant cure of evil. It takes all shapes of suffering—of the body, of the mind, of the heart, of the spirit. It is altogether beneficent; without this ever invading vanity, what hope would there be for the rich and powerful, accustomed to and set upon their own way? What hope for the self-indulgent, the conceited, the greedy, the miserly? The more things men seek, the more varied the things they imagine they need, the more are they subject to vanity—all the forms of which may be summed in the word *disappointment*.

He who would not house with disappointment must seek the incorruptible, the true. He must break the bondage of havings and shows; of rumors, and praises, and pretenses, and selfish pleasures. He must come out of the false into the real; out of the darkness into the light; out of the bondage of corruption into the glorious liberty of the children of God. To bring men to break with corruption, the gulf of the inane yawns before them. Aghast in soul, they cry, "Vanity of vanities! All is vanity!" and beyond the abyss begin to espy the eternal world of truth.

The creation then is to share in the deliverance and liberty and glory of the children of God. Deliverance from corruption, liberty from bondage, must include escape from the very home and goal of corruption, namely death—and that in all its kinds and degrees.

"The Hope of the Universe," *The Hope of the Gospel*
Col. 1:12-14

On this day in 1873: A group of American literati, led by William Cullen Bryant, give MacDonald a formal farewell dinner at New York Association Hall.

May 23 — St. Paul's Heaven

For the creation waits with eager longing for the revealing of the children of God. Rom. 8:19

If such then be the words of the apostle, does he, or does he not, I ask, hold the idea of the immortality of the animals? If you say all he means is, that the creatures alive at the coming of the Lord will be set free from the tyranny of corrupt man, I refer you to the poverty of such an interpretation: Is God a mocker, who will not be mocked? Is there a past to God with which He has done? Is Time too much for Him? Is He God enough to care for those that happen to live at one present time, but not God enough to care for those that happen to live at another present time?

The new heaven and the new earth will at least be a heaven and an earth! What would the newest earth be to the old children without its animals? Barer than the heavens emptied of the constellations that are called by their names. Then, if the earth must have its animals, why not the old ones, already dear? The sons of God are not a new race of sons of God, but the old race glorified—why a new race of animals, and not the old ones glorified?

What lovelier feature in the newness of the new earth, than the old animals glorified with us, in their home with us—our common home, the house of our Father—each kind an unfailing pleasure to the other. Ah, what horses? Ah, what dogs! Ah, what wild beasts, and what birds in the air! The whole redeemed creation goes to make up St. Paul's heaven. He had learned of Him who would leave no one out; who made the excuse for His murderers that they did not know what they were doing.

"The Hope of the Universe," *The Hope of the Gospel*
Hos. 2:18

Total Freedom   May 24

For the creation waits with eager longing for the revealing of the children of God. Rom. 8:19

But what is this liberty of the children of God, for which the whole creation is waiting? The children themselves are waiting for it: when they have it, then will their house and retinue, the creation, whose fate hangs on that of the children, share it with them: what is this liberty?

All liberty must of course consist in the realization of the ideal harmony between the creative will and the created life; in the correspondence of the creature's active being to the creator's idea, which is his substantial soul. In other words, the creature's liberty is what his obedience to the law of his existence, the will of his maker, effects for him.

The instant a soul moves counter to the will of its prime cause, the universe is its prison; it dashes against the walls of it, and the sweetest of its uplifting and sustaining forces at once become its manacles and fetters. But St. Paul is not at the moment thinking either of the metaphysical notion of liberty, or of its religious realization; he has in his thought the birth of the soul's consciousness of freedom.

"Not only the creation, but we ourselves, who have the first fruits of the Spirit, groan inwardly as we wait for the adoption as sons, the redemption of our bodies." We are not free, he implies, until our bodies are redeemed; then all the creation will be free with us.

> "The Hope of the Universe," *The Hope of the Gospel*
> Isa. 65:25

On this day in 1873: George, Louisa, and Greville leave America for England aboard the steamship Calabria.

May 25 — The Body Made a "House-Alive"

For the creation waits with eager longing for the revealing of the children of God. Rom. 8:19

The whole creation is waiting for the manifestation of the sons of God—that is, the redemption of their bodies, the idea of which extends to the whole material envelopment, with all the life that belongs to it. For this as for them, the bonds of corruption must fall away; it must enter into the same liberty with them, and be that for which it was created—a vital temple, perfected by the unbroken indwelling of its divinity.

The liberty here intended, it may be unnecessary to say, is not that essential liberty—freedom from sin—but the completing of the redemption of the spirit by the redemption of the body, the perfecting of the greater by its necessary complement of the less. Evil has been constantly at work, turning our house of the body into a prison; rendering it more opaque and heavy and insensible; casting about it bands and cerements, and filling it with aches and pains.

The freest soul, the purest of lovers, the man most incapable of anything mean, would not, for all his liberty, yet feel absolutely at large while chained to a dying body. The redemption of the body, therefore, the making of it for the man a genuine, perfected, responsive house-alive, is essential to the apostle's notion of a man's deliverance. The new man must have a new body with a new heaven and earth.

"The Hope of the Universe," *The Hope of the Gospel*
Isa. 65:17-23

1904: Daughter Irene marries Cecil Brewer.

For Our Sakes and Theirs   May 26

For the creation waits with eager longing for the revealing of the children of God. Rom. 8:19

    St. Paul never thinks of himself as released from body; he desires a perfect one, and of a nobler sort; he would inhabit a heaven-made house, and give up the earth-made one, suitable only to this lower stage of life, infected and unsafe from the first, and now much dilapidated in the service of the Master who could so easily give him a better.

    He wants a spiritual body—a body that will not thwart, but second, the needs and aspirations of the spirit. He had in his mind, I presume, such a body as the Lord died with, changed by the interpenetrating of the creative indwelling will, to a heavenly body, the body with which He rose. A body like the Lord's is, I imagine, necessary to bring us into true and perfect contact with the creation, of which there must be multitudinous phases whereof we cannot now be even aware.

    When the sons, then, are free, when their bodies are redeemed, they will lift up with them the lower creation into their liberty. St. Paul seems to believe that perfection in their kind awaits also the humbler inhabitants of our world, its advent to follow immediately on the manifestation of the sons of God: for our sakes and their own they have been made subject to vanity; for our sakes and their own they shall be restored and glorified, that is, raised higher with us.

> "The Hope of the Universe," *The Hope of the Gospel*
> I Cor. 15:42-49

May 27 — A Selfish Person Indeed

For the creation waits with eager longing for the revealing of the children of God. Rom. 8:19

The word *adoption* is used by St. Paul as meaning the same thing with the phrase, "the redemption of the body." In the beginning of the fourth chapter of his epistle to the Galatians, he makes perfectly clear what he intends by it. His unusual word means the father's recognition, when he comes of age, of the child's relation to him, by giving him his fitting place of dignity in the house; and here the deliverance of the body is the act of this recognition by the great Father, completing and crowning and declaring the freedom of the man, the perfecting of the last lingering remnant of his deliverance.

St. Paul's word, I repeat, has nothing to do with *adoption* [as we use the term commonly today]; it means the manifestation of the grown-up sons of God; the showing of those as sons, who have always been His children; the bringing of them out before the universe in such suitable attire and with such fit attendance, that to look at them is to see what they are, the sons of the house—such to whom their Elder Brother applied the words: "I said ye are gods."

If then the sons groan within themselves, looking to be lifted up, and the other inhabitants of the same world groan with them and cry, shall they not also be lifted up? Have they not also a faithful creator? He must be a selfish man indeed who does not desire that it should be so.

> "The Hope of the Universe," *The Hope of the Gospel*
> Gal. 4:1-7

It Dawned Upon Him

Thomas Wingfold, although a curate in the Church of England, is here shown preparing a sermon and in so doing becoming aware that he is far from being a follower of Christ.

"Ah! said the curate to himself, "if I had but seen him, would not I have minded him! Would not I have haunted his steps, with question upon question, until I got at the truth!"

Again the more definite thought vanished in the seething chaos of reverie. . . until suddenly rose from memory to consciousness and attention the words, "Why call ye me, Lord, Lord, and do not the things which I say?"

"Good God!" he exclaimed, "here am I bothering over him and questioning about this and that, as if I were testing his fitness for a post I had to offer him, and he all the time claiming my obedience! I cannot even, on the spur of the moment at least, tell one thing he wants me to do; and as to doing anything because he told me—not once did I ever! But then how am I to obey him until I am sure of his right to command? I just want to know whether I am to call him Lord or not. No, that won't do either, for he says, Why, even of yourselves judge ye not what is right? And do I not know—have I ever even doubted that what he said we ought to do, was the right thing to do? Yet here have I, all these years been calling myself a Christian, ministering, forsooth, in the temple of Christ, as if he were a heathen divinity, who cared for songs and prayers and sacrifices, and cannot honestly say I ever once in my life did a thing because he said so, although the record is full of his earnest, even pleading words! I have *not* been an honest man, and how should a dishonest man be judge over that man who said he was the Christ of God? Would it be any wonder if the things he uttered should be too high and noble to be by such a man recognized as truth?

With this, yet another saying dawned upon him: *If any man will do his will, he shall know of the doctrine, whether it be of God, or whether I speak of myself.* He went into his closet and shut the door: came out again, and went straight to visit a certain grievous old woman.

Thomas Wingfold, Curate, Chapter 36
Luke 6:46-49

May 29 — Hear Then His Words

Thomas Wingfold, a curate in the Church of England, is here speaking to his parishioners, honestly confessing he has not been a true follower of Christ.

"The church wherein you now listen, my hearers, the pulpit wherein I now speak, stand here from of old in the name of Christianity. What is Christianity? I know but one definition, the analysis of which, if the thing in question be a truth, must be the joyous labor of every devout heart to all eternity. For Christianity does not mean what you think or what I think concerning Christ, but what *is of* Christ. My Christianity, if ever I come to have any, will be what of Christ is in me; your Christianity now is what of Christ is in you.

Last Sunday I showed you our Lord's very words—that he, and no other, was his disciple who did what he told him—and said, therefore, that I dared not call myself a disciple. I say the same thing in saying now that I dare not call myself a Christian, lest I should offend him with my 'Lord, Lord!' Still it is, and I cannot now help it, in the name of Christianity that I here stand. I have—alas! with blameful and appalling thoughtlessness!—subscribed my name, as a believer, to the articles of the Church of England, with no better reason than that I was unaware of any dissent therefrom, and have been ordained one of her ministers. The relations into which this has brought me I do not feel justified in severing at once, lest I should therein seem to deny that which its own illumination may yet show me to be true, and I desire therefore a little respite and room for thought and resolve.

But meantime it remains my business, as an honest man in the employment of the church, to do my best towards the setting forth of the claims of him upon whom that church is founded, and in whose name she exists. As one standing on the outskirts of a listening Galilean crowd, a word comes now and then to my hungry ears and hungrier heart: I turn and tell it again to you—'Do I then obey this word? Have I ever, have I once, sought to obey it? Am I a Christian?' Hear then his words. For me, they fill my heart with doubt and dismay.

Thomas Wingfold, Curate, Chapter 36
John 14:6

Psyches Half-Awake

This excerpt is from a letter of condolence written from Great Tangley Manor near Guildford on May 30, 1875, to John Ruskin, whose close friend, Rose La Touche, had recently died.

I want just to speak a word in your ear. I do not know what it shall be. I only want you to know it is my voice. Do not turn your head to look at me, or stop what you are doing to think a moment about me. Go on.

But the Psyche is aloft, and her wings are broad and white, and the world of flowers is under her, and the sea of sunny air is around her, and the empty chrysalis—what of that?

Now we are all but Psyches half awake, who see the universe in great measure only by reflection from the dull coffin-lid over us. But I hope, I hope, I hope infinitely. And ever the longer I live and try to live, & think, & long to love perfectly, I see the scheme of things grow more orderly and more intelligible, and am more and more convinced that all is on the way to be well with a wellness to which there was no other road than just this whereon we are walking.

Let us call a word now and then through the darkness as we go. There is a great sunrise behind the hill. But that hill Death alone can carry us over. I look to God to satisfy us all. It cannot be but that he will satisfy you to your heart's content. You have fought a better fight, I think, than you yourself know, and his gentleness will make you great in the Kingdom of love. . .

An Expression of Character: The Letters of George MacDonald,
Glenn Edward Sadler, ed.
John 11:25

May 31 — Do You Really Believe?

Thomas Wingfold, a curate in the Church of England, is here speaking to his parishioners, sharing the reasons for his new-found conviction of the reality of Christ's ministry.

Recall the tenderness which he received those from whom the religious of his day turned aside—the repentant women who wept sore-hearted from very love, the publicans who knew they were despised because they were despicable. With him they sought and found shelter. He was their savior from the storm of human judgment and the biting frost of public opinion, even when that opinion and that judgment were re-echoed by the justice of their own hearts. He received them, and the life within them rose up, and the light shone—the conscious light of life—despite even of shame and self-reproach.

If God be for us who can be against us? In his name they rose from the hell of their own heart's condemnation, and went forth to do the truth in strength and hope. They heard and believed and obeyed his words. And of all words that ever were spoken, were ever words gentler, tenderer, humbler, lovelier—if true, or more arrogant man-degrading, God-defying—if false, than these concerning which, *as his*, I now desire to speak to you: '*Come unto me, all ye that labor and are heavy-laden, and I will give you rest. Take my yoke upon you and learn of me; for I am meek and lowly in heart; and ye shall find rest unto your souls. For my yoke is easy, and my burden is light.*'

Surely these words, could they but be heartily believed, are such as every human heart might gladly hear! What man is there who has not had, has not now, or will not have to class himself among the weary and heavy-laden? You who call yourselves Christians profess to believe such rest is to be had, yet how many of you go bowed to the very earth, and take no single step towards him who says *Come*, lift not an eye to see whether a face of mercy may not be looking down upon you! Is it that, after all, you do not believe there ever was such a man as they call Jesus?

Thomas Wingfold, Curate, Chapter 46
Isa. 42:1-4

TRUE DIVINE SERVICE JUNE 1

Polwarth, a congenital cripple who is their spiritual mentor, is speaking to the Rev. Thomas Wingfold and Mr. Drew, a local merchant:

"When my child would serve me, he spies out some need I have, springs from his seat at my knee, finds that which will meet my necessity, and is my eager happy servant, of consequence in his own eyes inasmuch as he has done something for his father. His seat by my knee is love, delight, well-being, peace—not service, however pleasing in my eyes.

"Talk not of public worship as divine service: it is a mockery. Search the prophets, and you will find the observances, fasts and sacrifices and solemn feasts of the temple, by them regarded with loathing and scorn just because by the people they were regarded as *divine service.*"

"But," said Mr. Drew, while Wingfold turned towards him with some anxiety lest he should break the mood of the little prophet, "I can't help thinking I have you; for how are poor creatures like us—weak, blundering creatures, sometimes most awkward when best intentioned—how are we to minister to a perfect God—perfect in wisdom, strength, and everything—of whom Paul says that he is not worshiped with men's hands as though he needed anything . . . ."

"Were there no such thing as Divine Service in the true sense of the word, then indeed it scarcely would be worth while to quarrel with its misapplication. But I assert that true and genuine service may be rendered to the living God; and for the development of the divine nature in man, it is necessary that he should do something for God. Nor is it hard to discover how; for God is in every creature that he has made, and in their needs he is needy, and in all their afflictions he is afflicted. Therefore Jesus says that what ever is done to one of his little ones is done to him. And if the soul of a man be the temple of the Spirit, then is the place of that man's labor—his shop, his counting-house, his laboratory—the temple of Jesus Christ, where the spirit of the man is incarnate in work. Mr. Drew, . . . your shop is the temple of your service. . .your counter is, or ought to be, his altar; and everything thereon laid, with intent of doing as well as you can for your neighbor, in the name of *the* man Christ Jesus, is a true sacrifice offered to him, a service done to the eternal creating Love of the universe."

Thomas Wingfold, Curate, Chapter 60
Isa. 1:11-13

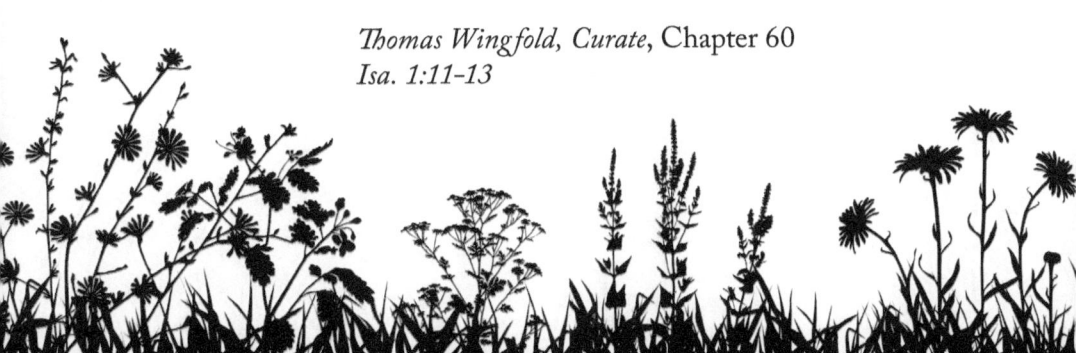

June 2 — No More Mathematics

Thomas Wingfold, a curate in the Church of England, is here contemplating the change within himself that his recent conversion has effected.

... whereas in former times the name Christ had been to him little more than a dull theological symbol, the thought of him and of his thoughts was now constantly with him; ever and anon some fresh light would break from the cloudy halo that enwrapped his grandeur; ever was he growing more the Son of Man to his loving heart, ever more the Son of God to his aspiring spirit. Testimony had merged almost in vision: he saw into, and partly understood, the perfection it presented: he looked upon the face of God and lived. Oftener and oftener, as the days passed, did it seem as if the man were by his side, and at times, in the stillness of the summer eve, when he walked alone, it seemed almost, as thoughts of revealing arose in his heart, that the Master himself was teaching him in spoken words.

What need now to rack his soul in following the dim-seen, ever-vanishing paths of metaphysics? He had but to obey the prophet of life, the man whose being and doing and teaching were blended in one three-fold harmony—or, rather were the three-fold analysis of one white essence—he had but to obey him, haunt his footsteps, and harken after the sound of his spirit, and all truth would in healthy process be unfolded in himself. What philosophy could carry him where Jesus would carry his obedient friends—into his own peace, namely, far above all fear and all hate, where his soul should breathe such a high atmosphere of strength at once and repose, that he should love even his enemies, and that with no such love as condescendingly overlooks, but with the real, hearty, and self-involved affection that would die to give them the true life! Alas! How far was he from such perfection now—from such a martyrdom, lovely as endless, in the consuming fire of God! And at the thought, he fell from the heights of his contemplation—but was caught in the thicket of prayer.

Thomas Wingfold, Curate, Chapter 66
Eph. 1:18-21

No Self-Satisfied Men   June 3

Thomas Wingfold, a curate in the Church of England, is here speaking to his parishioners on the text: "I came not to call the righteous, but sinners to repentance":

Was it then of the sinners first our Lord thought ere he came from the bosom of the Father? . . . If he were to come again visibly now, . . . certainly many a one would find the way to the feet of the Master from whom the respectable church-goer, the Pharisee of our time, and the priest who stands on his profession, would draw back in disgust. And doubtless it would be in the religious world that a man like Jesus, who, without a professional education, a craftsman by birth and early training, uttered scarce . . . a phrase endorsed by the religious cant of the day, but taught in simplest natural forms the eternal facts of faith and hope and love, would meet with the chief and perhaps the only *bitter* opponents of this doctrine and life.

But did our Lord not call the righteous? Did he not call honest men about him—James and John and Simon—sturdy fisher-folk, who faced the night and the storm, worked hard, fared roughly, lived honestly, and led good, cleanly lives with father and mother or with wife and children? I do not know that he said anything special to convince them that they were sinners before he called them. But it is to be remarked that one of the first effects of his company upon Simon Peter was that the fisherman grew ashamed of himself, and while ashamed was yet possessed with an impulse of openness and honesty no less than passionate. The pure man should not be deceived as to what sort of company he was in! "Depart from me, for I am a sinful man, O Lord!" I would I could clearly behold with my mind's eye what he than saw in Jesus that drew from him that cry!

He knew him for the Messiah: what was the working of the carpenter upon the fisher man that satisfied him of the fact? Would the miracle have done it but for the previous talk from the boat to the people? I think not. Anyhow St. Peter judged himself among the sinners, and we may be sure that if these fishers had been self-satisfied men, they would not have left all and gone after Him who called them.

Thomas Wingfold, Curate, Chapter 67
Luke 5:4-11

June 4 — First Came Sinners

Thomas Wingfold, a curate in the Church of England, is here speaking to his parishioners on the text: "I came not to call the righteous, but sinners to repentance":

Again, did not men such as the Lord himself regarded as righteous come to him—Nicodemus, Nathaniel, the young man who came running and kneeled to him, the scribe who was not far from the kingdom, the centurion, in whom he found more faith than in any Jew, he who had built a synagogue in Capernaum, and sculptured on its lintel the pot of manna? These came to him, and we know he was ready to receive them.

But he knew such would always come, drawn of the Father; they did not want much calling; they were not so much in his thought, therefore; he was not troubled about them; they were as the ninety-and-nine, the elder son at home, the money in the purse. Doubtless they had much to learn, were not yet in the kingdom, but they were crowding about its door. If I set it forth aright I know not, but thus it looks to me. And one thing I cannot forget—it meets me in the face—that some at least—who knows if not all—of the purest of men have counted themselves the greatest sinners!

Neither can I forget that other saying of our Lord, a stumbling-block to many—our Lord was not so careful as perhaps some would have had him, lest men should stumble at the truth—*the first shall be last and the last first.* While our Lord spoke the words, *The time cometh that whosoever killeth you will think that he doeth God service,* even then was Saul of Tarsus at the feet of Gamaliel, preparing to do God that service; but like one born out of due time, after all the rest he saw the Lord, and became the chief in labor and suffering. Thus the last became first. And I bethink me that the beloved disciple, he who leaned on the bosom of the Lord, who was bolder to ask him than any—with the boldness of love, he whom the meek and the lowly called a Son of thunder, was the last of all to rejoin the Master in the mansions of his Father. Last or first—if only we are with him! One thing is clear: that in the order of the Lord's business, first came sinners.

Thomas Wingfold, Curate, Chapter 67
Luke 5:27-32

No Such Distinction   June 5

Thomas Wingfold, a curate in the Church of England, is here speaking to his parishioners on the text: "I came not to call the righteous, but sinners to repentance":

"Nor must I fail to remind the man who has committed no grievous crime, that except he has repented of his evil self and abjured all wrong, he is not safe from any even the worst offence. There was a time when I could not understand that he who loved not his brother was a murderer: now I see it to be no figure of speech, but, in the realities of man's moral and spiritual nature, an absolute simple fact. The murderer and the unloving sit on the same bench before the judge of eternal truth.

The man who loves not his brother I do not say is at this moment capable of killing him, but if the natural working of his unlove be not checked, he will assuredly become capable of killing him. Until we love our brother—yes, until we love our enemy, who is yet our brother—we contain within ourselves the undeveloped germ of murder. And so with every sin in the tables or out of the tables. There is not one in this congregation who has a right to cast a look of reproach at the worst felon who ever sat in the prisoner's dock. I speak no hyperbole, but simple truth.

We are very ready to draw in our minds a distinction between respectable sins—human imperfections we call them, perhaps—and disreputable vices, such as theft and murder; but there is no such distinction in fact. Many a thief is a better man than many a clergyman, and miles nearer to the gate of the kingdom. The heavenly order goes upon other principles than ours, and there are first that shall be last, and last that shall be first. Only, at the root of all human bliss lies repentance.

Thomas Wingfold, Curate, Chapter 67
I John 3:14-15

June 6   The Perfecting Of Men

Rev. Thomas Wingfold is here conversing with Paul Faber, an agnostic physician:

"For my part," said the curate, "I think I *could* believe in a God who did but his imperfect best: in one all power, and not all goodness, I could not believe. But suppose that the design of God involved the perfecting of men as the *children of God*—'*I said ye are gods*' [Psa. 82:6] —that he would have them partakers of his own blessedness in kind—be as himself;—suppose his grand idea could not be contented with creatures perfect *only* by his gift, so far as that should reach, and having no willing casual share in the perfection—that is, partaking not at all of God's individuality and free-will and choice of good;—then suppose that suffering were the only way through which the individual soul could be set, in separate self-individuality, so far apart from God that it might *will*, and so become a partaker of his singleness and freedom; and suppose that this suffering must be and had been initiated by God's taking his share, and that the infinitely greater share; suppose, next, that God saw the germ of a pure affection, say in your friend and his wife, but saw also that it was a germ so imperfect and weak that it could not encounter the coming frosts and winds of the world without loss and decay, while, if they were parted now for a few years, it would grow and strengthen and expand to the certainty of an infinitely higher and deeper and keener love through the endless ages to follow—so that by suffering should come, in place of contented decline, abortion, and death, a troubled birth of joyous result in health and immortality;—suppose all this, and what then?"

Faber was silent a moment, and then answered, "Your theory has but one fault: it is too good to be true."

"My theory leaves plenty of difficulty, but has no such fault as that. . . . The only possibility of believing in a God seems to me to lie in finding an idea of a God large enough, grand enough, pure enough, lovely enough to be fit to believe in."

Thomas Wingfold, Curate, Chapter 73
I Peter 3:17-18

Nothing Less Than That

June 7

Thomas Wingfold, a curate in the Church of England, is here contemplating the discrepancy between the announced certainties of his sermon and the lingering uncertainties within him.

After preaching the sermon last recorded, there came a reaction of doubt and depression on the mind of the curate, greater than usual. Had he not gone farther than his right? Had he not implied more conviction than was his?

Words could not go beyond his satisfaction with what he found in the gospel, or his hopes for the range of his conscious life springing therefrom, but was he not now making people suppose him more certain of the *fact* of these things than he was? He was driven to console himself with the reflection that so long as he had had no such intention, even if he had been so carried away by the delight of his heart as to give such an impression, it mattered little: what was it to other people what he believed or how he believed? If he had not been untrue to himself, no harm would follow. Was a man never to talk from the highest in him to the forgetting of the lower? Was a man never to be carried beyond himself and the regions of his knowledge? If so, then farewell poetry and prophecy—yea, all grand discovery! For things must be foreseen ere they can be realised—apprehended ere they be comprehended.

This much he could say for himself, and no more: that he was ready to lay down his life for the mere *chance*, if he might so use the word, of these things being true; nor did he argue any devotion in that, seeing life without them would be to him a waste of unreality. He could bear witness to no facts, but to the truth, to the loveliness and harmony and righteousness and safety that he saw in the idea of the Son of Man—as he read it in the story.

At the same time he saw plain enough that even if he gave his body to be burned, it were no sufficing assurance of his Christianity: nothing could satisfy him of that less than the conscious presence of the perfect charity. Without that he was still outside the kingdom, wandering in a dream around its walls.

Thomas Wingfold, Curate, Chapter 74
II Cor. 4:7

June 8 — Lovely Because True

Thomas Wingfold, a curate in the Church of England, who formerly had felt that in honesty he should give up the curacy, is here asked if he is still thinking of doing so.

"I have almost forgotten I ever thought of such a thing. Whatever energies I may or may not have, I know one thing for certain: that I could not devote them to anything else I should think entirely worth doing. Indeed, nothing else seems interesting enough, nothing to repay the labor, but the telling of my fellow-men about the one man who is the truth, and to know whom is the life.

Even if there be no hereafter, I would live my time believing in a grand thing that ought to be true if it is not. No facts can take the place of truths; and if these be not truths, then is the loftiest part of our nature a waste. Let me hold by the better than the actual, and fall into nothingness off the same precipice with Jesus and John and Paul and a thousand more, who were lovely in their lives, and with their death make even the nothingness into which they have passed like the garden of the Lord. I go farther, and say I would rather die for evermore believing as Jesus believed, then live for evermore believing as those that deny him.

If there be no God, I feel assured that this existence is and could be but a chaos of contradictions whence can emerge nothing worthy to be called a truth, nothing worth living for. No, I will not give up my curacy. I will teach that which *is* good, even if there should be no God to make a fact of it, and I will spend my life on it in the growing hope, which *may* become assurance, that there is indeed a perfect God worthy of being the Father of Jesus Christ, and that it was *because* they are true that these things were lovely to me and to so many men and women, of whom some have died for them and some would be yet ready to die.

Thomas Wingfold, Curate, Chapter 75
Phil. 1:20-21

On this day in 1877: George MacDonald first plays the character Greatheart in the family public production in London of John Bunyan's <u>Pilgrim's Progress</u>, Part II.

On this day in 1901: MacDonald family gathers at their retirement home, St. George's Wood, near Haslemere, to celebrate George and Louisa's fiftieth wedding anniversary.

THE HIGHEST POSSIBLE CONDITION

Polwarth, a congenital dwarf, is speaking as spiritual mentor to Rev. Thomas Wingfold and Mr. Drew, a village merchant:

"Wherein consists the essential inherent worthiness of a life as life? The only perfect idea of life is—a unit, self-existent and creative. That is God, the only one."

"But to this idea, in its kind, must every life, to be complete as life, correspond; and the human correspondence to self-existence is that the man should round and complete himself by taking into himself his origin; by going back and in his own will adopting that origin, rooting therein afresh in the exercise of his own freedom and in all the energy of his own self-roused will; in other words, that the man say, 'I will be after the will of the creating *I*; that he see and say with his whole being that to will the will of God in himself and for himself and concerning himself is the highest possible condition of a man. Then has he completed his cycle by turning back upon his history, laying hold of his cause, and willing his own being in the will of the only I AM. This is the rounding, recreating, unifying of the man. This is religion; and all that gathers not with this, scatters abroad.'"

"And then," said Drew, with some eagerness, "lawfully comes the question, 'Shall I or shall I not live for ever?'"

"Pardon me; I think not," returned the little prophet. "I think rather we have done with it for ever. The man with life so in himself will not dream of asking whether he shall live. It is only in the twilight of a half-life, holding in it at once much wherefore it should desire its own continuance and much that renders it unworthy of continuance, that the doubtful desire of immortality can arise."

Thomas Wingfold, Curate, Chapter 75
Phil 3:7-9

Thomas Wingfold, a curate in the Church of England, is here contemplating one of the more enigmatic passages from the New Testament, the risen Christ's response to Mary in the garden:

"Why did he say, *Do not touch me?* It could not be that there was any defilement to one in the new body of the resurrection, from contact with one still in the old garments of humanity.

"One thing we can make sure of: it was nothing that should hurt her; for see what follows. But for that, when he said *Touch me not, for I am not yet ascended to my Father,* she might have thought—'Ah! Thou hast thy Father to go to and thou will leave us for him.' —*But* he went on, *go to my brethren and say unto them; I ascend unto my Father, AND YOUR FATHER; AND MY GOD AND YOUR GOD*. What more could she want? Think: the Father of Jesus, with whom, in all his knowledge and all his suffering, the grand heart was perfectly, exultingly satisfied, that Father he calls our Father too. He shares with his brethren—of his best, his deepest, his heartiest, most secret delight, and makes it their and his most open joy; he shares his eternal Father with us, his perfect God with his brethren. And whatever his not having ascended to him may mean, we see, with marvel and joy, that what delayed him—even though, for some reason perfect in tenderness as in truth, he would not be touched—was love to Mary Magdalene and his mother and his brethren. He could not go to the Father without comforting them first. And certainly whatever she took the *Touch me not* to mean or point at, it was nothing that hurt her.—It just strikes me—is it possible he said it in order to turn the overwhelming passion of her joy, which after such a restoration would have clung more than ever to the visible presence, and would be ready to suffer the pains of death yet again when he parted from her—might it be to turn that torrent into the wider and ever widening channel of joy in his everlasting presence to the innermost being, his communion, heart to heart, with every child of his Father?

"In our poor weakness and narrowness and self-love, even of Jesus the bodily may block out the spiritual nearness, which, however in most moods we may be unable to realize the fact, is and remains a thing unutterably lovelier and better and dearer—enhancing tenfold what vision of a bodily presence may at some time be granted us.

Thomas Wingfold, Curate, Chapter 83
John 16:7

WHAT WAS WINGFOLD MISSING?   JUNE 11

Thomas Wingfold, a curate in the Church of England, is here contemplating the growth of his own knowledge as to what it means to be a devoted follower of Jesus Christ.

But the thing that did carry him through became plain enough to him afterwards: his faith in God was all the time growing—and that through what seemed at the time only a succession of interruptions. Nothing is so ruinous to progress in which effort is needful, as satisfaction with apparent achievement; that ever sounds a halt; but Wingfold's experience was that no sooner did he set his foot on the lowest hillock of self-congratulation, than some fresh difficulty came that threw him prostrate; and he rose again only in the strength of the necessity for deepening and broadening his foundations that he might build yet higher, trust yet farther: that was the only way not to lose everything.

He was gradually learning that his faith must be an absolute one, claiming from God everything the love a perfect Father could give, or the needs he had created in his child could desire; that he must not look to himself first for help, or imagine that the divine was only the supplement to the weakness and failure of the human; that the highest effort of the human was to lay hold of the divine. He learned that he could keep no simplest law in its loveliness until he was possessed of the same spirit whence that law sprung; that he could not even love Helen aright, simply, perfectly, unselfishly, except through the presence of the originating Love; that the one thing wherein he might imitate the free creative will of God was, to will the presence and power of that will which gave birth to his.

It was the vital growth of this faith even when he was too much troubled to recognise the fact that made him strong in the midst of weakness; when the son of man cried out, *Let this cup pass,* the son of God in him could yet cry, *Let thy will be done.*

Thomas Wingfold, Curate, Chapter 86
I Peter 1:5-8

June 12   One Good Reason

Polwarth, a congenital cripple who is spiritual mentor to Rev. Thomas Wingfold, is here conversing with him and Mr. Drew, a local merchant, on death.

"Can you then imagine any good reason," said Drew, "why we should be kept in such absolute ignorance of everything that befalls the parted spirit from the moment it quits its house with us?

"I think I know one," answered Polwarth. "I have sometimes fancied it might be because no true idea of their condition could possibly be grasped by those who remain in the tabernacle of the body; that to know their state it is necessary that we also should be clothed in our new bodies, which are to the old as a house to a tent. I doubt if we have any words in which the new facts could be imparted to our knowledge, the facts themselves being beyond the reach of any senses whereof we are not in actual possession. I expect to find my new body provided with new, I mean *other* senses beyond what I now possess: many more may be required to bring us into relation with all the facts in himself which God may have shadowed forth in properties, as we say, of what we call matter. The spaces all around us, even to those betwixt star and star, may be the home of the multitudes of the heavenly host, yet seemingly empty to all who have but our provision of senses.

"But I do not care to dwell upon that kind of speculation. It belongs to a lower region, upon which I grudge to expend interest while the far loftier one invites me, where if I gather not the special barley of which I am in search, I am sure to come upon the finest of wheat.—Well then, my reason: There are a thousand individual events in the course of every man's life, by which God takes a hold of him—a thousand breaches by which he would and does enter, little as the man may know; but there is one universal and unchanging grasp he keeps upon the race, yet not as the race, for the grasp is upon every solitary single individual that has a part in it: that grasp is—death in its mystery. To whom can the man who is about to die in absolute loneliness and go he cannot tell whither, flee for refuge from the doubts and fears that assail him, but to the Father of his being?"

Thomas Wingfold, Curate, Chapter 94
I Cor. 2:9

What Would Be Gained?   June 13

Polwarth, a congenital cripple who is spiritual mentor to Rev. Thomas Wingfold, is here conversing with him and Mr. Drew, a local merchant, on death.

"But," said Drew, "I cannot see what harm would come of letting us know a little—as much at least as might serve to assure us that there was more of *something* on the other side."

"Just this," returned Polwarth, "that, their fears allayed, their hopes encouraged from any lower quarter, men would as usual, turn away from the fountain to the cistern of life, from the ever fresh original creative Love to that drawn off and shut in. That there are thousands who would forget God if they could but be assured of such a tolerable state of things beyond the grave as even this wherein we now live, is plainly to be anticipated from the fact that the doubts of so many in respect of religion concentrate themselves now-a-days upon the question whether there is any life beyond the grave; a question which, although no doubt nearly associated with religion,—as what question worth asking is not?—does not immediately belong to religion at all. Satisfy such people, if you can, that they shall live, and what have they gained? A little comfort perhaps—but a comfort not from the highest source, and possibly gained too soon for their well-being. Does it bring them any nearer to God than they were before? Is he filling one cranny more of their hearts in consequence? Their assurance of immortality has not come from a knowledge of him, and without him it is worse than worthless. Little indeed has been gained, and that with the loss of much. The word applies here which our Lord in His parable puts in the mouth of Abraham: *"If they hear not Moses and the prophets, neither will they be persuaded though one rose from the dead.* He does not say they would not believe in a future state though one rose from the dead—although most likely they would soon persuade themselves that the apparition after all was only an illusion—but that they would not be persuaded to repent, though one rose from the dead; and without that, what great matter whether they believed in a future state or not? It would only be the worse for them if they did.

"No, Mr. Drew! I repeat, it is not a belief in humanity, but faith in the God of life, the Father of lights, the God of all consolation and comfort. Believing in him, a man can leave his friends, and their and his own immortality, with everything else—even his and their love and perfection, with utter confidence in his hands.

Thomas Wingfold, Curate, Chapter 94
Heb. 12:22-24

June 14 — Under Holy Orders

At the conclusion of the novel, the Rev. Thomas Wingfold states to his parishioners what he has learned:

"All I now say is, that in the story of Jesus I have beheld such grandeur—to me apparently altogether beyond the reach of human invention, such a radiation of divine loveliness and truth, such hope for man, soaring miles above every possible pitfall of Fate; and have at the same time, from the endeavor to obey the word recorded as his, experienced such a conscious enlargement of mental faculty, such a deepening of moral strength, such an enhancement of ideal, such an increase of faith, hope, and charity towards all men, that I now declare with the consent of my whole man—I cast in my lot with the servants of the Crucified; I am content even to share their delusion, if delusion it be, for it is the truth of the God of men to me; I will stand or fall with the story of my Lord; I will take my chance—I speak not in irreverence but in honesty—my chance of failure or success in regard to whatever may follow in this life or the life to come, if there be a life to come—on the words and will of the Lord Jesus Christ, whom if, impressed as I am with the truth of his nature, the absolute devotion of his life, and the essential might of his being, I yet obey not, I shall not only deserve to perish but in that very refusal draw ruin upon my head.

Before God I say it—I would rather be crucified with that man, so it might be as a disciple and not as a thief that creeps, intrudes or climbs into the fold, than I would reign with him over such a kingdom of grandeur as would have satisfied the imagination and love-ambition of his mother. On such grounds as these I hope I am justified in declaring myself a disciple of the Son of Man, and in devoting my life and the renewed energy and enlarged, yea infinite hope which he has given me, to his brothers and sisters of my race, that if possible I may gain some to be partakers of the blessedness of my hope. Henceforth I am not *in holy orders*, I reject the phrase in all its professional vulgarity, but *under* holy orders, even the orders of Christ Jesus, which is the law of liberty, the law whose obedience alone can set a man free from in-burrowing slavery.

Thomas Wingfold, Curate, Chapter 96
Matt. 23:9-12

Who Is To Blame? — June 15

At the conclusion of the novel, the Rev. Thomas Wingfold leaves these concluding thoughts with his parishioners:

"The waves of infidelity are coming in with a strong wind and a flowing tide. Who is to blame? God it cannot be, and for unbelievers, they are as they were. It is the Christians who are to blame. I do not mean those who are called Christians, but those who call and count themselves Christians. I tell you, and I speak to each one of whom it is true, that you hold and present such a withered, starved, miserable, death's-head idea of Christianity; that you are yourself such poverty-stricken believers, if believers you are at all; that the notion you present to the world as your ideal, is so common-place, so false to the grand, gracious, might-hearted Jesus—that *you* are the cause why the truth hangs its head in patience, and rides not forth on the white horse, conquering and to conquer.

"Until you repent and believe afresh, believe in a nobler Christ, namely the Christ revealed by himself, and not the muffled form of something vaguely human and certainly not divine, which the false interpretations of men have substituted for him, you will be as, I repeat you are, the main reason why faith is so scanty in the earth, and the enemy comes in like a flood. . . . While you are not of those Christians who obey the word of the master, *doing* the things he says to them, you are of those Christians, if you *will* be called by the name, to whom he will say, *I never knew you: go forth into the outer darkness.*

But oh what unspeakable bliss of heart and soul and mind and sense remains for him who like St. Paul is crucified with Christ, who lives no more from his own self, but is inspired and informed and possessed with the same faith towards the Father in which Jesus lived and wrought the will of the Father! If the words attributed to Jesus are indeed the words of him whom Jesus declared himself, then truly is the fate of mankind a glorious one,—and that, first and last, because men have a God supremely grand, all-perfect in God-head; for that is, and that alone can be, the absolute bliss of the created."

Thomas Wingfold, Curate, Chapter 96
Luke 12:47-48

June 16   How Many Helps

Consisting of 366, 7 line stanzas, one for each day of the year, **A Book of Strife in the form of the diary of an old soul** *is an intimate revelation of MacDonald's mind. John Ruskin aptly called it "one of the three great sacred poems of the nineteenth century."*

Who sets himself not sternly to be good
Is but a fool, who judgment of true things
Has none, however oft the claim renewed.
And he who thinks, in his great plentitude,
To right himself, and set his spirit free,
Without the might of higher communings,
Is foolish also—save he willed himself to be.

How many helps thou giv'st to those would learn!
To some sore pain, to others a sinking heart;
To some a weariness worse than any smart;
To some a haunting, fearing, blind concern,
Madness to some; to some a shaking dart
Of hideous death still following as they turn;
To some a hunger that will not depart.

Me thou hast given an infinite unrest,
A hunger—not at first after known good,
But something vague I knew not, and yet would—
The veiled Isis, thy will not understood;
A conscience tossing ever in my breast;
And something deeper, that will not be expressed,
Save as the Spirit thinking in the Spirit's brood.

Lam. 3:25-33

GIVING SUFFERING ITS RIGHTFUL NAME   JUNE 17

In these excerpts from MacDonald's crowning fantasy, **Lilith***, the protagonist, Vane, traveling through the nether world, visits the house of Mara. Symbolizing suffering and bitterness, she here converses with him as he makes his acquaintance with her.*

"I saw you," she answered, still with her back to me, "in the light of the moon, just as she went down. I see badly in the day, but at night perfectly . . . . People are frightened if I come on them suddenly. They call me the Cat-woman. It is not my name."

"You shall not hear it from me," I answered. "Please tell me what I *may* call you."

"When you know me, call me by the name that seems to you to fit me," she replied. "That will tell me what sort you are. People do not often give me the right one. It is well when they do."

*   *   *

"The time will come when you must house with me many days and many nights," she murmured sadly through her muffling.

"Willingly," I replied.

"Nay, not willingly!" she answered.

I said to myself that she was right—I would not willingly be her guest a second time! But immediately my heart rebuked me, and I had scarce crossed the threshold when I turned again.

She stood in the middle of the room, her white garments lay like foamy waves at her feet, and among them the swathings of her face: it was lovely as a night of stars. Her great gray eyes looked up to the heaven, tears were flowing down her pale cheeks. She reminded me not a little of the sexton's wife [the redeemed Eve], although the one looked as if she had not wept for thousands of years, and the other as if she wept constantly behind the wrappings of her beautiful head. Yet something in the very eyes that wept seemed to say, "Weeping may endure for a night, but joy cometh in the morning."

"A Strange Hostess," *Lilith*, Chapter 15
Heb. 12:11

June 18   Why Should The Rich Fare Differently?

"How hard it will be for those who have wealth to enter the kingdom of God!"
Mark 10:23

He [the rich man] is apt to ask, "why should it be difficult for a rich man to enter into the kingdom of heaven?" He is ready to look upon the natural fact as an arbitrary decree, arising, shall I say? from some prejudice in the divine mind, or at least from some objection to the joys of well-being, as regarded from the creatures' side. Why should the rich fare differently from other people in respect to the world to come?

They do not perceive that the law is they *shall* fare like other people, whereas they want to fare as rich people. A condition of things in which it would be easy for a rich man to enter into the kingdom of heaven is to me inconceivable. There is no kingdom of this world into which a rich man may not easily enter—in which, if he be but rich enough, he may not be the first: a kingdom into which it would be easy for a rich man to enter could be no kingdom of heaven.

To the man born to riches they seem not merely a natural, but an essential condition of well-being; and the man who has *made* his money, feels it his by the labor of his soul, the travail of the day, the care of the night. Each feels a right to have and to hold the things he possesses; and if there is a necessity for his entering into the kingdom of heaven, it is hard indeed that right and necessity should confront each other, and constitute all by a bare impossibility! Why should he not "make the best of both worlds"?

He would compromise, if he might; he would serve Mammon a little, and God much. He would not have such a "best of both worlds" as comes of putting the lower in utter subservience of the higher—of casting away the treasure of this world and taking the treasure of heaven instead.

"The Hardness of the Way," *Unspoken Sermons: Second Series*
Acts 10:34-35

The Use Of Things

JUNE 19

"Children, how hard it is to enter the kingdom of God." Mark 10:24

Possessions are *Things*, and *Things* in general . . . are very ready to prove inimical to the better life. The man who for consciousness of well-being depends upon anything but life, the life essential, is a slave; he hangs on what is less than himself.

Things are given us, this body first of things, that through them we may be trained both to independence and true possession of them. We must possess them; they must not possess us. Their use is to mediate—as shapes and manifestations in lower kind of the things that are unseen, that is, in themselves unseeable, the things that belong, not to the world of speech, but the world of silence, not to the world of showing, but the world of being, the world that cannot be shaken, and must remain.

These things unseen take form in the things of time and space—not that they may exist, for they exist in and from eternal Godhead, but that their being may be known to those in training for the eternal; these things unseen the sons and daughters of God must possess. But instead of reaching out after them, they grasp at their forms, regard the things seen as the things possessed, fall in love with the bodies instead of the souls of them

Things can never be really possessed by the man who cannot do without them—who would not be absolutely divinely content in the consciousness that the cause of his being is within it—and *with him*. He who has God, has all things, after the fashion in which he who made them has them.

"The Hardness of the Way," *Unspoken Sermons: Second Series*
Matt. 6:24

June 20 — The Reason For Miracles

"And he said to them, "Do you not yet understand?" Mark 8:21

The lesson he would have had them learn from the miracle [the feeding of the four thousand], the natural lesson, the only lesson worthy of the miracle, was, that God cared for his children, and could, did, and would provide for their necessities. This lesson they had not learned.

No doubt the power of the miracle was some proof of his mission, but the love of it proved it better, for it made it worth proving: it was a throb of the Father's heart. The ground of the Master's upbraiding is not that they did not trust God; that, after all they had seen, they yet troubled themselves about bread. Because we easily imagine ourselves in want, we imagine God ready to forsake us.

The miracles of Jesus were the ordinary works of his Father, wrought small and swift that we might take them in. The lesson of them was that help is always within God's reach when his children want it—their design, to show what God is—not that Jesus was God, but that his Father was God—that is, was what he was, for no other kind of God could be, or be worth believing in; no other notion of God be worth having. The mission undertaken by the Son, was not to show himself as having all power in heaven and earth, but to reveal his Father, to show him to men such as he is, that men may know him, and knowing, trust him.

It were a small boon indeed that God should forgive men, and not give himself. It would be but to give them back themselves; and less than God just as he is will not comfort men for the essential sorrow of their existence. Only God the gift can turn that sorrow into essential joy: Jesus came to give them God, who is eternal life.

"The Cause of Spiritual Stupidity," *Unspoken Sermons: Second Series*
Phil 4:19

1870: James Powell, Louisa's father, dies.

It Is Hard On God

JUNE 21

"And he said to them, "Do you not yet understand?" Mark 8:21

With the disciples as with the rich youth, it was *Things* that prevented the Lord from being understood. Because of possessions the young man had not a suspicion of the grandeur of the call with which Jesus honored him. The disciples were a little further on than he; they had left all and followed the Lord; but neither had they yet got rid of *Things*. The paltry solitariness of a loaf was enough to hide the Lord from them, to make them unable to understand him.

In the former case it was the possession of wealth, in the latter the not having more than a loaf, that rendered incapable of receiving the word of the Lord: the evil principle was precisely the same. If it be *Things* that slay you, what matter whether things you have, or things you have not? The youth, not trusting in God, the source of his riches, cannot brook the word of his Son, offering him better riches, more direct from the heart of the Father. The disciples, forgetting who is lord of the harvests of the earth, cannot understand his word, because filled with the fear of a day's hunger. He did not trust in God as having given; they did not trust in God as ready to give.

We are like them when, in *any* trouble, we do not trust him. It is hard on God, when his children will not let him give; when they carry themselves so that he must withhold his hand, lest he harm them. To take no care that they acknowledge whence their help comes, would be to leave them worshipers of idols, trusters in that which is not.

"The Cause of Spiritual Stupidity," *Unspoken Sermons: Second Series*
Matt. 16:8-11

June 22 — Affairs Of The Spirit

"And he said to them, "Do you not yet understand?" Mark 8:21

Everything is an affair of the spirit. If God has a way, then that is the only way. Every little thing in which you would have your own way, has a mission for your redemption; and he will treat you as a naughty child until you take your Father's way for yours.

There will be this difference, however, between the rich that loves his riches and the poor that hates his poverty—that, when they die, the heart of the one will be still crowded with things and their pleasures, while the heart of the other will be relieved of their lack; the one has had his good things, the other his evil things. But the rich man who held his *things* lightly, nor let them nestle in his heart; who was a channel and no cistern; who was ever and always forsaking his money—starts, in the new world, side by side with the man who accepted, not hated, his poverty. Each will say, "I am free!"

For the only air of the soul, in which it can breathe and live, is the present God and the spirits of the just: that is our heaven, our home, our all-right place. Cleansed of greed, jealousy, vanity, pride, possession, all the thousand forms of the evil self, we shall be God's children on the hills and in the fields of that heaven, not one desiring to be before another, any more than to cast that other out; for ambition and hatred will then be seen to be one and the same spirit. "What thou hast, I have; what thou desirest, I will; I give to myself ten times in giving once to thee. My want that thou mightst have, would be rich possession."

"The Cause of Spiritual Stupidity," *Unspoken Sermons: Second Series*
Psalms 16:1-2

Am I A Fool?   June 23

"And he said to them, "Do you not yet understand?" Mark 8:21

Am I not a fool whenever loss troubles me more than recovery would gladden? God would have me wise, and smile at the trifle. Is it not time I lost a few things when I care for them so unreasonably?

This losing of things is of the mercy of God; it comes to teach us to let them go. Or have I forgotten a thought that came to me, which seemed of the truth, and a revelation to my heart? I wanted to keep it, have it, to use it by and by, and it is gone! I keep trying and trying to call it back, feeling a poor man till that thought be recovered—to be far more lost, perhaps, in a note-book, into which I shall never look again to find it!

I forget that it is live things God cares about—live truths, not things set down in a book, or in a memory, or embalmed in the joy of knowledge, but things lifting up the heart, things active in an active will. True, my lost thought might have so worked; but had I faith in God, the maker of thought and memory, I should know that, if the thought was a truth, and so alone worth anything, it must come again; for it is in God—so, like the dead, not beyond my reach: kept for me, I shall have it again.

"These are foolish illustrations—not worth writing!"

If such things are not, then the mention of them is foolish. If they are, then he is foolish who would treat them as if they were not. I choose them for their smallness, and appeal especially to all who keep house concerning the size of trouble that suffices to hide the word and face of God.

"The Cause of Spiritual Stupidity," *Unspoken Sermons: Second Series*
Job 1:20-22

June 24   We Must Be Free

"And he said to them, "Do you not yet understand?" Mark 8:21

If you tell me that but for care, the needful work of the world would be ill done—"What work," I ask, "can that be, which will be better done by the greedy or anxious than by the free, fearless soul? Can care be a better inspirer of labor than the sending of God?

If the work is not his work, then, indeed, care may well help it, for its success is loss. But is he worthy the name of man who, for the fear of starvation, will do better work than for the joy that his labor is not in vain in the Lord? I know as well as you that you are not likely to get rich that way; but neither will you block up the gate of the kingdom of heaven against yourself.

Ambition in every shape has to do with *Things*, with outward advantages for the satisfaction of self-worship; it is that form of pride, foul shadow of Satan, which usurps the place of aspiration to rise above oneself; all other is of the devil. Yet is it nursed and cherished in many a soul that thinks itself devout, filling it with petty cares and disappointments, that swarm like bats in its air, and shut out the glory of God.

The love of the praise of men, the desire of fame, the pride that takes offence, the puffing-up of knowledge, these and every other form of Protean self-worship—we must get rid of them all. We must be free. The man whom another enslaves may be free as God; to him who is a slave in himself, God will not enter in; he will not sup with him, for he cannot be his friend.

Will not, did I say? *Cannot*, I say. Men full of things would not once partake with God, were he by them all the day. Nor will God force any door to enter.

"The Cause of Spiritual Stupidity," *Unspoken Sermons: Second Series*
Matt. 6:25-27

Why We Need To Pray

June 25

"...they ought always to pray and not lose heart." Luke 18:1

The impossibility of doing what we would as we would, drives us to look for help. But there is a reality of being in which all things are easy and plain—oneness, that is, with the Lord of Life; to pray for this is the first thing; and to the point of this prayer every difficulty hedges and directs us.

But if I try to set forth something of the reasonableness of all prayer, I beg my readers to remember that it is for the sake of action and not speculation; if prayer be anything at all, it is a thing to be done: what matter whether you agree with me or not, if you do not pray? I would not spend my labor for that; I desire to serve for help to pray, not to understand how a man might pray and yet be a reasonable soul.

If, seeing we live not by our own will, we live by another will, then is there reason, and then only can there be reason in prayer. To him who refuses that other will, I have nothing to say.

If I find my position, my consciousness, that of one from home, nay, that of one in some sort of prison; if I find that I can neither rule the world in which I live nor my own thoughts or desires; that I cannot quiet my passions, order my likings, determine my ends, will my growth, forget when I would, or recall what I forget; that I cannot love where I would, or hate where I would; that I am no king over myself; that I cannot supply my own needs, do not even always know which of my seeming needs are to be supplied, and which treated as impostors; if, in a word, my own being is every way too much for me; if I can neither understand it, be satisfied with it, nor better it—may it not well give me pause—the pause that ends in prayer?

"The Word of Jesus on Prayer," *Unspoken Sermons; Second Series*
Phil. 4:6-7

June 26 — The Reality Behind the Look

"And the Lord said, 'Hear what the unrighteous judge says. And will not God vindicate his elect, who cry to him day and night? . . . I tell you, he will vindicate them speedily." Luke 18:7, 8

Here then is a word of the Lord about prayer; it is a comfort that he recognizes difficulty in the matter—sees that we need encouragement to go on praying, that it looks as if we were not heard, that it is no wonder we should be ready to faint and leave off. He tells a parable to which the suppliant has to go often and often to the man who can help her, gaining her end only at the long last.

Actual delay on the part of God, we know from what follows, he does not allow; the more plain is it that he recognizes how the things must look to those whom he would have go on praying. Here as elsewhere he teaches us that we must not go by the look of things, but by the reality behind the look.

A truth, a necessity to God's own willed nature, is enough to set up against a whole army of appearances. It looks as if he did not hear you; never mind; he does; it must be that he does; go on as the woman did; you too will be heard. She is heard at last, and in virtue of her much going; God hears at once, and will avenge speedily.

The unrighteous judge cared nothing for the woman; those who cry to God are his own chosen—plain in the fact that they cry to him. He has made and appointed them to cry: they do cry: will he not hear them? They exist that they may pray; he has chosen them that they may choose him; he has called them that they may call him—that there may be such communion, such interchange as belongs to their being and the being of their Father.

"A Word of Jesus on Prayer," *Unspoken Sermons: Second Series*
II Cor. 4:17-18

Try It

"I tell you, he will vindicate them speedily." Luke 18:8

Shall I not tell him my troubles—how he, even he, has troubled me by making me?—how unfit I am to be that which I am?—that my being is not to me a good thing yet?—that I need a law that shall account to me for it in righteousness—reveal to me how I am to make it a good—how I am to *be* a good, and not an evil? Shall I not tell him that I need him to comfort me? His breath to move upon the face of the waters of the Chaos he has made? Shall I not cry to him to be in me rest and strength? To quiet this uneasy motion called life, and make me live indeed? To deliver me from my sins, and make me clean and glad? Such a cry is of the child to the Father: if there be a Father, verily he will hear, *and let the child know that he hears!*

The sole assurance worth a man's having even if the most incontestable evidence were open to him from a thousand other quarters, is that to be gained only from personal experience-—that assurance is himself which he can least readily receive from another, and which is least capable of being transmuted into evidence for another. The evidence of Jesus Christ could not take the place of that.

A truth is of enormous import in relation to the life—that is the heart, and conscience, and will; it is of little consequence merely as a fact having relation to the understanding. God may hear all prayers that ever were offered to him, and a man may believe that he does, nor be one whit the better for it, so long as God has no prayers of his to hear, he no answers to receive from God. Nothing in this quarter will ever be gained by investigation.

Reader, if you are in any trouble, try whether God will not help you; if you are in no need, why should you ask questions about prayer? True, he knows little of himself who does not know that he is wretched, and miserable, and poor, and blind, and naked; but until he begins at least to suspect a need, how can he pray?

"The Word of Jesus on Prayer," *Unspoken Sermons: Second Series*
James 4:1-3

June 28 — Our Endless Need

Three times I besought the Lord about this, that it should leave me; but he said to me, "My grace is sufficient for you, for my power is made perfect in weakness." II Cor. 12:8,9

That God should as a loving father listen, hear, consider, and deal with the request after the perfect tenderness of his heart, is to me enough; it is little that I should go without what I pray for. If it be granted that any answer which did not come of love, and was not for the final satisfaction of him who prayed, would be unworthy of God; that it is the part of love and knowledge to watch over the wayward, ignorant child; than the trouble of seemingly unanswered prayers begins to abate, and a lovely hope and comfort takes its place in the child-like soul.

To hear is not necessarily to grant—God forbid! but to hear is necessarily to attend to—sometimes as necessarily to refuse. God had a better thing for Paul than granting his prayer and removing his complaint: he would make him strong; the power of Christ should descend and remain upon him; he would make him stronger than his suffering, make him a sharer in the energy of God. Verily, if we have God, we can do without the answer to any prayer.

"But if God is so good as you represent him, and if he knows all that we need, and better far than we do ourselves, why should it be necessary to ask him for anything?"

I answer, What if he knows prayer to be the thing we need first and most? What if the main object in God's idea of prayer be the supplying of our great, our endless need—the need of himself? What if the good of all our smaller and lower needs lies in this, that they help to drive us to God? Hunger may drive the runaway child home, and he may or may not be fed at once, but he needs his mother more than his dinner.

"The Word of Jesus on Prayer," *Unspoken Sermons: Second Series*
Luke 11:13

Our One Need

June 29

". . .they ought always to pray and not lose heart." Luke 18:1

Communion with God is the one need of the soul beyond all other need; prayer is the beginning of that communion, and some need is the motive of that prayer. Our wants are for the sake of our coming into communion with God, our eternal need.

If gratitude and love immediately followed the supply of our needs, if God our Saviour was the one thought of our hearts, than it might be unnecessary that we should ask for anything we need. But seeing we take our supplies as a matter of course, feeling as if they came out of nothing, or from the earth, or our own thoughts, instead of out of a heart of love and a will which alone is force, it is needful that we should be made feel some at least of our wants, that we may seek him who alone supplies all of them, and find his every gift a window to his heart of truth.

So begins a communion, a talking with God, a coming-to-one with him, which is the sole end of prayer, yea, of existence itself in its infinite phases. We must ask that we may receive; but that we should receive what we ask in respect of our lower needs is not God's end in making us pray, for he could give us everything without that: to bring his child to his knee, God withholds that man may ask.

In regard, however, to the high necessities of our nature, it is in order that he may be able to give that God requires us to ask—requires by driving us to it—by shutting us up to prayer. For how can he give into the soul of a man what it needs, while that soul cannot receive it? The ripeness for receiving is the asking.

"The Word of Jesus on Prayer," *Unspoken Sermons: Second Series*
Psalms 27:7-11

JUNE 30 — PURIFYING THE PRAYER

". . .they ought always to pray and not lose heart." Luke 18:1

Every gift of God is but a harbinger of his greatest and only sufficing gift—that of himself. No gift unrecognized as coming from God is at its own best; therefore many things that God would gladly give us, things even that we need because we are, must wait until we ask for them, that we may know whence they come: when in all gifts we find him, then in him we shall find all things.

Sometimes to one praying will come the feeling rather than question: "Were it not better to abstain? If this thing be good, will he not give it me? Would he not be better pleased if I left it altogether to him?" It comes, I think, of a lack of faith and childlikeness—taking form, perhaps, in a fear lest, asking for what was not good, the prayer should be granted. Such a thought has no place with St. Paul; he says, "Casting all your care upon him, for he careth for you;" "In everything making your request known unto him." It may even come of ambition after spiritual distinction.

In every request, heart and soul and mind ought to supply the low accompaniment, "Thy will be done;" but the making of any request brings us near to him, into communion with our Life. Does it not also help us to think of him in all our affairs, and learn in everything to give thanks? Anything large enough for a wish to light upon, is large enough to hang a prayer upon: the thought of him to whom that prayer goes will purify and correct the desire.

"The Word of Jesus on Prayer," *Unspoken Sermons: Second Series*
Psalms 40: 7-8

True Son-Faith

July 1

"...they ought always to pray and not lose heart." Luke 18:1

To say, "Father, I should like this or that," would be enough at once, if the wish were bad, to make us know it and turn from it. Such prayer about things must of necessity help to bring the mind into true simple relation with him; to make us remember his will even when we do not see what that will is.

Was it not thus the Lord carried himself towards his Father when he said, "If it be possible, let this cup pass from me"? But there was something he cared for more than his own fears—his Father's will: "Nevertheless, not my will, but thine be done." The true son-faith is that which comes with boldness, fearless of the Father doing anything but what is right fatherly, patient, and full of loving-kindness.

There could be no riches but for need. God himself is made rich by man's necessity. By that he is rich to give; through that we are rich by receiving.

As to any notion of prevailing by entreaty over an unwilling God, that is heathenish, and belongs to such as think him a hard master, or one like the unjust judge. What so quenching to prayer as the notion of unwillingness in the ear that hears! And when prayer is dull, what makes it flow like the thought that God is waiting to give, wants to give us everything!

"Let us therefore come boldly to the throne of grace, that we may obtain mercy, and find grace to help in time of need." We shall be refused our prayer if that be better; but what is good our Father will give us with divine good will. The Lord spoke his parable "to the end that they ought always to pray, *and not to faint.*"

"The Word of Jesus on Prayer," *Unspoken Sermons: Second Series*
John 14:13-14

July 2 — No Room For Change?

"...they ought always to pray and not lose heart." Luke 18:1

"How should any design of the All-wise be altered in response to prayer of ours! How are we to believe such a thing?"

By reflecting that he is the All-wise, who sees before him, and will not block his path. Such objection springs from poorest idea of God in relation to us. It supposes him to have cares and plans and intentions concerning our part of creation, irrespective of us. What is the whole system of things for, but our education?

He lays no plans irrespective of his children; and his design being that they shall be free, active, live things, he sees that space be kept for them: they need room to struggle out of their chrysalis, to undergo the change that comes with the waking will, and to enter upon the divine sports and labors of children in the house and domain of their Father. Surely he may keep his plans in a measure unfixed, waiting the free desire of the individual soul! Is not the design of the first course of his children's education just to bring them to the point where they shall pray?

True, in many cases, the prayer, far more than the opportunity of answering it, is God's end; but how will the further end of the prayer be reached, which is oneness between the heart of the child and of the Father? How will the child go on to pray if he knows the Father cannot answer him? *Will not* may be for love, but how with a self-imposed *cannot?* How could he be Father, who creating, would not make provision, would not keep room for the babbled prayers of his children?

What stupidity of perfection would that be which left no margin about God's work, no room for change of plan upon change of fact—yea, even the mighty change that, behold now at length, his child is praying!

"Man's Difficulty Concerning Prayer," *Unspoken Sermons: Second Series*
Psalms 91:14-16

Room In His Plans

"...they ought always to pray and not lose heart." Luke 18:1

Poor, indeed, was the making of the wine in the earthen pots of stone, compared with its making in the lovely growth of the vine with its clusters of swelling grapes—the live roots gathering from the earth the water that had to be borne in pitchers and poured into the great vases; but it is precious as the interpreter of the same, even in its being the outcome of our Lord's sympathy with ordinary human rejoicing. There is however an element in its origin that makes it yet more precious to me—the regard of our Lord to a wish of his mother.

His mother had suggested to him that here was an opportunity for appearing in his own greatness, the potent purveyor of wine for the failing feast. It was not in his plan, as we gather from his words; for the Lord never pretended anything, whether to his enemy or his mother; he is The True.

He lets her know that he and she have different outlooks, different notions of his work: "What to me and thee, woman?" he said: "My hour is not yet come.' But there was that in his look and tone whence she knew that her desire, scarce half-fashioned into request, was granted. What am I thence to conclude, worthy of the Son of God, and the Son of Mary, but that, at the prayer of his mother, he made room in his plans for the thing she desired? It was not his wish then to work a miracle, but if his mother wished it, he would!

Not always did he do as his mother would have him; but this was a case in which he could do so, for it would interfere nowise with the will of his Father. Alas for the son who would not willingly for his mother do something which in itself he would rather not do! His yielding makes the story doubly precious to my heart. The Son then could change his intent, and spoil nothing: so, I say, can the Father; for the Son does nothing but what he sees the Father do.

"Man's Difficulty Concerning Prayer," *Unspoken Sermons: Second Series*
Isa. 55:8-9

1857: Poems by George MacDonald is published

July 4 — I Help And You Help

"...they ought always to pray and not lose heart." Luke 18:1

Finding it possible to understand that God may answer prayers to those who pray for themselves, what are we to think concerning prayer for others? What fitness can there be in praying for others? Will God give to another for our asking what he would not give without it?

If God has made us to love like himself, and like himself long to help, and if all our hope for ourselves lies in God—what is there for us, what can we think of, what do, but go to God? What but go to him with this our own difficulty and need? If I can be helped through my friend, I think God will take the thing up, and do what I cannot do—help me to help him.

God is ever seeking to lift us up into the sharing of his divine nature. See the grandeur of the creative love of the Holy! Nothing less will serve it than to have his children, through his and their suffering, share the throne of his glory! If his glory be in giving himself, and we must share therein, giving ourselves, why should we not begin here and now? If he would have his children fellow-workers with him; if he has desired and willed that not only by the help of his eternal Son, but by the help also of the children who through him have been born from above, other and still other children shall be brought to his knee, to the plenty of his house, why should he not have kept some margin of room wherein their prayers may work for those whom they have to help? I cannot tell how, but may not those prayers in some way increase God's opportunity for working his best and highest will?

If I love and cannot help, does not my heart move me to ask him to help who loves and can? How if he should answer, "Pray on, my child; I am hearing you; it goes through me in help to him. We are of one mind about it; I help and you help. I shall have you all safe home with me by and by! We must work and not lose heart. Go, and let your light so shine before men that they may see your good things, and glorify me!" What then? Oh that lovely picture by Michelangelo, with the young ones and the little ones come to help God to make Adam!

"Man's Difficulty Concerning Prayer," *Unspoken Sermons: Second Series*
James 4:16

The End Of All Prayer

July 5

"...they ought always to pray and not lose heart." Luke 18:1

There are moods of such satisfaction in God that a man may feel as if nothing were left to pray for, as if he had but to wait with patience for what the Lord would work; there are moods of such hungering desire, that petition is crushed into an inarticulate crying; and there is a communion with God that asks for nothing, yet asks for everything. This last is the very essence of prayer, though not petition.

It is possible for a man, not indeed to believe in God, but to believe that there is a God, and yet not desire to enter into communion with him; but he that prays and does not faint will come to recognize that to talk with God is more than to have all prayers granted—that it is the end of all prayer, granted or refused. And he who seeks the Father more than anything he can give, is likely to have what he asks, for he is not likely to ask amiss.

Even such as ask amiss may sometimes have their prayers answered. The Father will never give the child a stone that asks for bread; but I am not sure that he will never give the child a stone that asks for a stone. If the Father say, "My child, that is a stone; it is not bread;" and the child answer, "I am sure it is bread; I want it;" may it not be well he should try his bread?

Man's Difficulty Concerning Prayer," *Unspoken Sermons: Second Series*
Psalms 106:15

July 6   God Loses No Time

". . .they ought always to pray and not lose heart." Luke 18:1

But now for another point in the parable, where I think I can give some help—I mean the Lord's apparent recognition of delay in the answering of prayer: in the very structure of the parable he seems to take delay for granted, and says notwithstanding, "He will avenge them speedily."

The reconciling conclusion is, that God loses no time, though the answer may not be immediate.

He may delay because it would not be safe to give us at once what we ask: we are not ready for it. To give ere we could truly receive, would be to destroy the very heart and hope of prayer, to cease to be our Father. The delay itself may work to bring us nearer to our help, to increase the desire, perfect the prayer, and ripen the receptive condition.

God is limited by regard for our best; our best implies education; in this we must ourselves have a large share; this share, being human, involves time. And perhaps, indeed, the better the gift we pray for, the more time is necessary to its arrival. To give us the spiritual gift we desire, God may have to begin far back in our spirit, in regions unknown to us, and do much work that we can be aware of only in the results.

To avenge speedily must mean to make no delay beyond what is absolutely necessary, to begin the moment it is possible to begin. Because the Son of Man did not appear for thousands of years after men began to cry out for a Savior, shall we imagine he did not come the first moment it was well he should come? Can we doubt that to come a moment sooner would have been to delay, not to expedite, his kingdom? For anything that needs a process, to begin to act at once is to be speedy.

"Man's Difficulty Concerning Prayer," *Unspoken Sermons: Second Series*
Psalms 27:14

A Summons To Fight   July 7

". . . I tell you, he will avenge them speedily." Luke 18:8

The Lord uses words without anxiety as to the misuse of them by such as do not search after his will in them; and the word *avenge* may be simply retained from the parable without its special meaning therein; yet it suggests a remark or two.

Of course, no prayer for any revenge that would gratify the selfishness of our nature, a thing to be burned out of us by the fire of God, needs think to be heard. But perhaps the Lord was here thinking, not of persecution, or any form of human wrong, but of the troubles that most trouble his true disciple; and the suggestion is comforting to those whose foes are within them, for, if so, then he recognizes the evils of self, against which we fight, not as parts of ourselves, but as our foes, on which he will avenge the true self that is at strife with them.

And certainly no evil is, or ever could be, of the essential being and nature of the creature God made! The thing that is not good, however associated with our being, is against that being, not of it—is its enemy, on which we need to be avenged. When we fight, he will avenge. Till we fight, evil shall have dominion over us, a dominion to make us miserable; other than miserable can no one be, under the yoke of a nature contrary to his own.

But from what ever quarter come our troubles, whether from the world outside or the world inside, still let us pray. In his own right way, the only way that could satisfy us, for we are of his kind, will God answer our prayers with help. He will avenge us of our adversaries, and that speedily. -

"Man's Difficulty Concerning Prayer," *Unspoken Sermons: Second Series*
Psalms 18:16-19

On this day in 1858: John, George's brother, dies of tuberculosis.
On this day in 1888: Ronald was married to Louise Vivenda Blandy

July 8 — The Purpose Of The Parables

"Truly, I say to you, you will never get out till you have paid the last penny."
Matt. 5:26

There is a thing wonderful and admirable in the parables, not readily grasped, but specially indicated by the Lord himself—their unintelligibility to the mere intellect. They are addressed to the conscience and not to the intellect, to the will and not to the imagination.

They are strong and direct but not definite. They are not meant to explain anything, but to rouse a man to the feeling, "I am not what I ought to be, I do not the thing I ought to do!" Many maundering interpretations may be given by the wise, with plentiful loss of labor, which the child who uses them for the necessity of walking in the one path will constantly receive light from them. The greatest obscuration of the words of the Lord, as of all true teachers, comes from those who give themselves to interpret rather than do them. Theologians have done more to hide the gospel of Christ than any of its adversaries.

It was not for our understandings, but our will, that Christ came. He who does that which he sees, shall understand; he who is set upon understanding rather than doing, shall go on stumbling and mistaking and speaking foolishness. He has not that in him which can understand that kind. The gospel itself, and in it the parables of the Truth, are to be understood only by those who walk by what they find. It is he that runneth that shall read, and no other.

It is not intended by the speaker of the parables that any other should know intellectually what, known but intellectually, would be for his injury—what knowing intellectually he would imagine he had grasped, perhaps even appropriated. When the pilgrim of the truth comes on his journey to the region of the parable, he finds its interpretation. It is not a fruit or a jewel to be stored, but a well springing by the wayside.

"The Last Farthing," *Unspoken Sermons: Second Series*
John 7:17

Punishment In Love

"With them indeed is fulfilled the prophecy of Isaiah which says: 'You shall indeed hear but never understand, and you shall indeed see but never perceive. For this people's heart has grown dull, and their hearts are heavy of hearing, and their eyes they have closed, lest they should perceive with their eyes, and hear with their ears, and understand with their heart, and turn for me to heal them.'" Matt. 13:14, 15

Let us try to understand what the Lord himself said about his parables. It will be better to take the reading of St. Matthew xiii.14, 15, as it is plainer, and the quotation from Isaiah (6:9, 10) is given in full. . . in its light should be read the corresponding passages in the other Gospels: the purport is, that those who by insincerity and falsehood close their deeper eyes, shall not be capable of using in the matter the more superficial eyes of their understanding.

Whether this follows as a psychical or metaphysical necessity, or be regarded as a special punishment, it is equally the will of God, and comes from him who is the live Truth. They shall not see what is not for such as they. It is the punishment of the true Love, and is continually illustrated and fulfilled. If I know anything of the truth of God, then the objectors to Christianity, so far as I am acquainted with them, do not; their arguments, not in themselves false, have nothing to do with the matter; they see the thing they are talking against, but they do not see the thing they think they are talking against.

This will help to remove the difficulty that the parables are plainly for the teaching of the truth, and yet the Lord speaks of them as for the concealing of it. They are for the understanding of that man only who is practical—who does the thing he knows, who seeks to understand vitally.

Ignorance may be at once a punishment and a kindness: all punishment is kindness, and the best of which the man at the time is capable: "Because you will not do, you shall not see; but it would be worse for you if you did see, not being of the disposition to do." They are not fit to know more; more shall not be given them yet; it is their punishment that they are in the wrong, and shall keep in the wrong until they come out of it.

"The Last Farthing," *Unspoken Sermons: Second Series*
Matt. 6:22-23

July 10 — An Appeal To Common Sense

"Truly, I say to you, you will never get out till you have paid the last penny." Matt. 5:26

What special meaning may be read in the different parts of magistrate, judge, and officer. . . I do not know; but I think I do know what is meant by "agree on the way" and "the uttermost farthing" [penny]. The parable is an appeal to the common sense of those that hear it, in regard to every affair of righteousness. Arrange what claim lies against you; compulsion waits behind it.

Do at once what you must do one day. As there is no escape from payment, escape at least the prison that will enforce it. Do not drive Justice to extremities. Duty is imperative; it must be done. It is useless to think to escape the eternal law of things; yield of yourself, nor compel God to compel you.

To the honest man, to the man who would fain be honest, the word is of right gracious import. To the untrue, it is a terrible threat; to him who is of the truth, it is sweet as most loving promise. He who is of God's mind in things, rejoices to hear the word of the changeless Truth; the voice of the Right fills the heavens and the earth, and makes his soul glad; it is his salvation. If God were not inexorably just, there would be no stay for the soul of the feeblest lover of right: "Thou art true, O Lord: one day I also shall be true!"

"Thou shalt render the right, cost you what it may," is a dread sound in the ears of those whose life is a falsehood: what but the last farthing would those who love righteousness more than life pay? It is a joy profound as peace to know that God is determined upon such payment, is determined to have his children clean, clear, pure as very snow; is determined that not only shall they with his help make up for whatever wrong they have done, but at length be incapable, by eternal choice of good, under any temptation, of doing the thing that is not divine, the thing God would not do.

"The Last Farthing," *Unspoken Sermons: Second Series*
Matt. 18:15-17

No Escape

"Truly, I say to you, you will never get out till you have paid the last penny."
Matt. 5:26

There has been much cherishing of the evil fancy, often without its taking formal shape, that there is some way of getting out of the region of strict justice, some mode of managing to escape doing *all* that is required of us; but there is not such escape. A way to avoid any demand of righteousness would be an infinitely worse way than the road to the everlasting fire, for its end would be eternal death.

No, there is no escape. There is no heaven with a little hell in it—no plan to retain this or that of the devil in our hearts or our pockets. Out Satan must go, every hair and feather! Neither shalt thou think to be delivered from the necessity of *being* good by being made good. There is no clothing in a robe of imputed righteousness, that poorest of legal cobwebs spun by spiritual spiders. It is apparently an old 'doctrine;' for St. John seems to point at it where he says, "Little children, let no man lead you astray; he that doeth righteousness is righteous even as he is righteous."

Christ is our righteousness, not that we should escape punishment, still less escape being righteous, but as the live potent creator of righteousness in us, so that we, with our wills receiving his spirit, shall like him resist unto blood, striving against sin; shall know in ourselves, as he knows, what a lovely thing is righteousness, what a mean, ugly, unnatural thing is unrighteousness. He *is* our righteousness, and that righteousness is no fiction, no pretence, no imputation.

"The Last Farthing," *Unspoken Sermons: Second Series*
II Cor. 5:21

July 12 — You Must

"Truly, I say to you, you will never get out till you have paid the last penny."
Matt. 5:26

One thing that tends to keep men from seeing righteousness and unrighteousness as they are, is, that they have been told many things are righteous and unrighteous, which are neither the one nor the other. Righteousness is just fairness—from God to man, from man to God and to man; it is giving every one his due—his large mighty due. He is righteous, and no one else, who does this.

And any system which tends to persuade men that there is any salvation but that of becoming righteous even as Jesus is righteous; that a man can be made good, as a good dog is good, without his own willed share in the making; that a man is saved by having his sins hidden under a robe of imputed righteousness—that system, so far as this tendency, is of the devil and not of God.

Thank God, not even error shall injure the true of heart; it is not wickedness. They grow in the truth, and as love casts out fear, so truth casts out falsehood.

I read, then, in this parable, that a man had better make up his mind to be righteous, to be fair, to do what he can to pay what he owes, in any and all the relations of life—all the matters, in a word, wherein one man may demand of another, or complain that he has not received fair play. Arrange your matters with those who have anything against you, while you are yet together and things have not gone too far to be arranged; *you will have to do it,* and that under less easy circumstances than now. Putting off is of no use. You must. The thing has to be done; there are means of compelling you.

"The Last Farthing," *Unspoken Sermons: Second Series*
I Peter 1:13-16

No Escape

July 11

"Truly, I say to you, you will never get out till you have paid the last penny."
Matt. 5:26

There has been much cherishing of the evil fancy, often without its taking formal shape, that there is some way of getting out of the region of strict justice, some mode of managing to escape doing *all* that is required of us; but there is not such escape. A way to avoid any demand of righteousness would be an infinitely worse way than the road to the everlasting fire, for its end would be eternal death.

No, there is no escape. There is no heaven with a little hell in it—no plan to retain this or that of the devil in our hearts or our pockets. Out Satan must go, every hair and feather! Neither shalt thou think to be delivered from the necessity of *being* good by being made good. There is no clothing in a robe of imputed righteousness, that poorest of legal cobwebs spun by spiritual spiders. It is apparently an old 'doctrine;' for St. John seems to point at it where he says, "Little children, let no man lead you astray; he that doeth righteousness is righteous even as he is righteous."

Christ is our righteousness, not that we should escape punishment, still less escape being righteous, but as the live potent creator of righteousness in us, so that we, with our wills receiving his spirit, shall like him resist unto blood, striving against sin; shall know in ourselves, as he knows, what a lovely thing is righteousness, what a mean, ugly, unnatural thing is unrighteousness. He *is* our righteousness, and that righteousness is no fiction, no pretence, no imputation.

"The Last Farthing," *Unspoken Sermons: Second Series*
II Cor. 5:21

July 12   You Must

"Truly, I say to you, you will never get out till you have paid the last penny."
Matt. 5:26

One thing that tends to keep men from seeing righteousness and unrighteousness as they are, is, that they have been told many things are righteous and unrighteous, which are neither the one nor the other. Righteousness is just fairness—from God to man, from man to God and to man; it is giving every one his due—his large mighty due. He is righteous, and no one else, who does this.

And any system which tends to persuade men that there is any salvation but that of becoming righteous even as Jesus is righteous; that a man can be made good, as a good dog is good, without his own willed share in the making; that a man is saved by having his sins hidden under a robe of imputed righteousness—that system, so far as this tendency, is of the devil and not of God.

Thank God, not even error shall injure the true of heart; it is not wickedness. They grow in the truth, and as love casts out fear, so truth casts out falsehood.

I read, then, in this parable, that a man had better make up his mind to be righteous, to be fair, to do what he can to pay what he owes, in any and all the relations of life—all the matters, in a word, wherein one man may demand of another, or complain that he has not received fair play. Arrange your matters with those who have anything against you, while you are yet together and things have not gone too far to be arranged; *you will have to do it*, and that under less easy circumstances than now. Putting off is of no use. You must. The thing has to be done; there are means of compelling you.

        "The Last Farthing," *Unspoken Sermons: Second Series*
        I Peter 1:13-16

It's For Your Sake

JULY 13

"Truly, I say to you, you will never get out till you have paid the last penny." Matt. 5:26

It is a very small matter *to you* whether the man give you your rights or not; it is life or death to you whether or not you give him his. Whether he pay you what you count his debt or no, you will be compelled to pay him all you owe him.

If, owing you love, he gives you hate, you, owing him love, have yet to pay it. A love unpaid you, a justice undone you, a praise withheld from you, a judgment passed on you without judgment, will not absolve you of the debt of a love unpaid, a justice not done, a praise withheld, a false judgment passed: these uttermost farthings—not to speak of such debts as the world itself counts grievous wrongs—you must pay him, whether he pay you or not.

The same holds with every demand of God: by refusing to pay, the man makes an adversary who will compel him—and that for the man's own sake. If you or your life say, "I will not," then he will see to it. There is a prison, and the one thing we know about that prison is, that its doors do not open until entire satisfaction is rendered, the last farthing paid.

Whatever in us can be or make an adversary, whatever could prevent us from doing the will of God, or from agreeing with our fellow—all must be yielded. Our every relation, both to God and our fellow, must be acknowledged heartily, met as a reality. Smaller debts, if any debt can be small, follow as a matter of course.

If the man acknowledge, and would pay if he could but cannot, the universe will be taxed to help him rather than he should continue unable. If the man accepts the will of God, he is the child of the Father, the whole power and wealth of the Father is for him, and the uttermost farthing will easily be paid.

"The Last Farthing," *Unspoken Sermons: Second Series*
Rom. 13:8-10

July 14 — God Is Forever Good

"Truly, I say to you, you will never get out till you have paid the last penny."
Matt. 5:26

I think I have seen from afar something of the final prison of all, the innermost cell of the debtor of the universe.

It is the vast outside; the ghastly dark beyond the gates of the city of which God is the light—where the evil dogs go ranging, silent as the dark, for there is no sound any more than sight. The time of signs is over. The man wakes from the final struggle of death, in absolute loneliness —such a loneliness as in the most miserable moment of deserted childhood he never knew.

In the midst of the live world he cared for nothing but himself; now in the dead world he is in God's prison, his own separated self. But no liveliest human imagination could supply adequate representation of what it would be to be left without a shadow of the presence of God. For not he who cares least about God was in this world ever left as God could leave him. I believe the man would be glad to come in contact with the worst-loathed insect: it would be a shape of life, something beyond and besides his own huge, void, formless being!

Can there be any way out of the misery? Self-loathing, and that for no sin, from no repentance, from no vision of better, would begin and grow and grow; and to what it might not come to no soul can tell. Nay, there must be hope while there is existence; for where there is existence there must be God; and God is for ever good, nor can be other than good.

All his years in the world he received the endless gifts of sun and air, earth and sea and human face divine, as things that came to him because that was their way; now the poorest thinning of the darkness he would hail as men of old the glow of a descending angel; it would be as a messenger from God. Not that he would think of God! It takes long to think of God; but hope, not yet seeming hope, would begin to dawn in his bosom.

"The Last Farthing," *Unspoken Sermons: Second Series*
Matt. 25:29-30

THE WEARY WAY   JULY 15

"Truly, I say to you, you will never get out till you have paid the last penny."
Matt. 5:26

Only then, if a being be capable of self-disgust, is there not some room for hope—as much as a pinch of earth in the cleft of a rock might yield for the growth of a pine? A man may well imagine it impossible ever to think so unpleasantly of himself! But he has only to let things go, and he will make it the real, right, natural way to think of himself.

True, all I have been saying is imaginary; but our imagination is made to mirror truth; all the things that appear in it are more or less after the model of things that are; I suspect it is the region whence issues prophecy; and when we are true it will mirror nothing but truth. I deal here with the same light and darkness the Lord dealt with, the same St. Paul and St. John and St. Peter and St. Jude dealt with.

So might I imagine a thousand steps up from the darkness, each a little less dark, a little nearer the light—but, ah, the weary way! He cannot come out until he have paid the uttermost farthing! Repentance once begun, however, may grow more and more rapid! If God once get a willing hold, if with but one finger he touch the man's self, swift as possibility will he draw him from the darkness into the light.

For that which the forlorn, self-ruined wretch was made, was to be a child of God, a partaker of the divine nature, an heir of God and joint heir with Christ. Out of the abyss into which he cast himself, refusing to be the heir of God, he must rise and be raised. To the heart of God, the one and only goal of the human race—the refuge and home of all and each, he must set out and go, or the last glimmer of humanity will die from him.

"The Last Farthing," *Unspoken Sermons: Second Series*
Psalms 86:8-11

1862: Robert Falconer, George and Louisa's third son, is born.

July 16 — For This We Were Created

"—the spirit of adoption, whereby we cry, Abba, Father." Romans 8:15

The word [for adoption] used by St. Paul does not imply that God adopts children that are not his own, but rather that a second time he fathers his own; that a second time they are born—this time from above; that he will make himself tenfold, yea, infinitely their father: he will have them back into the very bosom whence they issued, issued that they might learn they could live nowhere else; he will have them one with himself. It was for the sake of this that, in his Son, he died for them.

From the passage [Gal. 4:1-7] it is plain as St. Paul could make it, that, by the word translated *adoption*, he means the raising of a father's own child from the condition of tutelage and subjection to others, a state which, he says, is not better than that of a slave, to the position and rights of a son. None but a child could become a son; the idea is—a spiritual coming of age; *only when the child is a man is he really and fully a son.*

The thing holds in the earthly relation. How many children of good parents—good children in the main too—never know those parents, never feel towards them as children might, until, grown up, they have left the house—until, perhaps they are parents themselves, or are parted from them by death! To be a child is not necessarily to be a son or daughter.

The childship is the lower condition of the upward process towards the sonship, the soil out of which the true sonship shall grow, the former without which the latter were impossible.

He dies to give them himself, thereby to raise his own to his heart; he gives them a birth from above; they are born again out of himself and into himself—for he is the one and the all.

His children are not his real, true sons and daughters until they think like him, feel with him, judge as he judges, are at home with him, and without fear before him because he and they mean the same thing, love the same things, seek the same ends. For this are we created; it is the one end of our being, and includes all other ends whatever.

"Abba, Father!" *Unspoken Sermons: Second Series*
Phil. 2:3-5

"—the spirit of adoption, whereby we cry, Abba, Father." Romans 8:15

In my own childhood and boyhood my father was the refuge from all the ills of life, even sharp pain itself. Therefore I say to son or daughter who has no pleasure in the name *Father*, "You must interpret the word by all that you have missed in life. All that human tenderness can give or desire in the nearness and readiness of love, all and infinitely more must be true of the perfect Father—of the maker of fatherhood, the Father of all the fathers of the earth, specially the Father of those who have specially shown a father-heart."

This Father would make to himself sons and daughters indeed—that is, such sons and daughters as shall be his sons and daughters not merely by having come from his heart, but by having returned thither—children such as choose to be what he is. He will have them share in his being and nature—strong wherein he cares for strength; tender and gracious as he is tender and gracious; angry where and as he is angry.

He has made us, but we have to be. All things were made *through* the Word, but that which was made *in* the Word was life, and that life is the light of men: they who live by this light, that is, live as Jesus lived—by obedience, namely, to the Father, have a share in their own making; the light becomes life in them; they are, in their lower way, alive with the life that was first born in Jesus, and through him has been born in them—by obedience they become one with the godhead.

"As many as received him, to them gave he power to become the sons of God." He does not *make* them the sons of God, but he gives them power to become the sons of God: in choosing and obeying the truth, man becomes the true son of the Father of lights.

"Abba, Father!" *Unspoken Sermons: Second Series*
Isa. 64:8

July 18 — Sons In Body Also

". . . and not only the creation, but we ourselves, who have the first fruits of the Spirit, groan inwardly as we wait for the adoption as sons, the redemption of our bodies." Rom. 8:23

Until our outward condition is that of sons royal, sons divine; so long as the garments of our souls, these mortal bodies, are mean, torn and dragged and stained; so long as we groan under sickness and weakness and weariness, old age, forgetfulness, and all heavy things; so long we have not yet received the sonship in full. We groan being burdened; we groan, waiting for the sonship—to wit, the redemption of the body—the uplifting of the body to be a fit house and revelation of the indwelling spirit—nay, like that of Christ, a fit temple and revelation of the deeper indwelling God.

For we shall always need bodies to manifest and reveal us to each other—bodies, then, that fit the soul with absolute truth of presentment and revelation. Hence the revealing of the sons of God, spoken of in the 19th verse, is the same thing as the redemption of the body; the body is redeemed when it is made fit for the sons of God; then it is a revelation of them. When we are the sons of God in heart and soul, then shall we be the sons of God in body too: "we shall be like him, for we shall see him as he is."

I care little to speculate on the kind of this body; two things only I will say, as needful to be believed, concerning it: first, that it will be a body to show the same self as before—but, second, a body to show the being truly—without the defects, that is, and imperfections of the former bodily revelation. Even through their corporeal presence shall we then know our own infinitely better, and find in them endlessly more delight, than before.

These things we must believe, or distrust the Father of our spirits. Till this redemption of the body arrives, the [adoption as sons] is not wrought out, is only upon the way. Nor can it come but by our working out the salvation he is working in us.

"Abba, Father," *Unspoken Sermons: Second Series*
Heb. 12:22-23

That They May Have Life

". . . and not only the creation, but we ourselves, who have the first fruits of the Spirit, groan inwardly as we wait for the adoption as sons, the redemption of our bodies." Rom. 8:23

It comes to this then, after the grand theory of the apostle: The world exists for our education; it is the nursery of God's children, served by troubled slaves, troubled because the children are themselves slaves—children, but not good children. Beyond its own will or knowledge, the whole creation works for the development of the children of God into the sons of God.

When at last the children have arisen and gone to their Father; when they are clothed in the best robes, with a ring on their hands and shoes on their feet, shining out at length in their natural, their predestined sonship; then shall the mountains and the hills break forth before them into singing, and all the trees of the field shall clap their hands. Then shall the wolf dwell with the lamb, and the leopard lie down with the kid and the calf, and the young lion and fatling together, and a little child shall lead them.

Then shall the fables of a golden age, which faith invented, and unbelief threw into the past, unfold their essential reality, and the tale of paradise prove itself a truth by becoming a fact. Then shall every ideal show itself a necessity, aspiration although satisfied put forth yet longer wings, and the hunger after righteousness know itself blessed. Then first shall we know what was in the Shepherd's mind when he said, *"I came that they may have life, and may have it abundantly."*

"Abba, Father," *Unspoken Sermons: Second Series*
Isa. 51:11

July 20 — Which Is The Greater Deception?

In Paul Faber MacDonald depicts and deals at length with an unbelieving and skeptical mentality.

Paul Faber was a man who had espoused the cause of science with all the energy of a suppressed poetic nature. He had such a horror of all kinds of intellectual deception or mistake, that he would rather run the risk of rejecting any number of truths than of accepting one error. In this spirit he had concluded that, as no immediate communication had ever reached his eye, or ear, or hand from any creator of men, he had no ground for believing in the existence of such a creator; while a thousand unfitnesses evident in the world, rendered the existence of one perfectly wise and good and powerful, absolutely impossible.

If one said to him that he believed thousands of things he had never himself known, he answered he did so upon testimony. If one rejoined that there too we have testimony, he replied it was not credible testimony, but founded on such experiences as he was justified in considering imaginary, seeing they were like none he had ever had himself. When he was asked whether, while he yet believed there was such a being as his mother told him of, he had ever set himself to act upon that belief, he asserted himself fortunate in the omission of what might have riveted on him the fetters of degrading faith. For years he had turned his face toward all speculation favoring the non-existence of a creating Will, his back toward all tending to show that such a one might be. Argument on the latter side he set down as born of prejudice, and appealing to weakness; on the other, as springing from courage, and appealing to honesty.

He had never put to himself which would be the worse deception—to believe there was a God when there was none; or to believe there was no God when there was one.

Paul Faber, Surgeon, Chapter 1.
I Cor. 2:14

Better To Be An Athiest

Paul Faber holds unbelieving and skeptical attitudes, but is in many ways more upright than many confessing Christians.

But such as Faber was, he was both loved and honored by all whom he had ever attended; and with his fine tastes, his genial nature, his quiet conscience, his good health, his enjoyment of life, his knowledge and love of his profession, his activity, his tender heart—especially to women and children, his keen intellect, and his devising though not embodying imagination, if any man could get on without a God, Faber was that man. He was now trying it, and as yet the trial had cost him no effort: he seemed to himself to be doing very well indeed.

And why should he not do as well as the thousands, who counting themselves religious people, get through the business of the hour, the day, the week, the year, without one reference in any thing they do or abstain from doing, to the will of God, or the words of Christ? If he was more helpful to his fellow than they, he fared better; for actions in themselves good, however imperfect the motives that give rise to them, react blissfully upon character and nature. It is better to be an atheist who does the will of God, than a so-called Christian who does not. The atheist will not be dismissed because he said *Lord, Lord,* and did not obey.

The thing that God loves is the only lovely thing, and he who does it, does well, and is upon the way to discover that he does it very badly. When he comes to do it as the will of the perfect Good, then is he on the road to do it perfectly—that is, from love of its own inherent self-constituted goodness, born in the heart of the Perfect. The doing of things from duty is but a stage on the road to the kingdom of truth and love. Not the less must the stage be journeyed; every path diverging from it is "the flowery way that leads to the broad gate and the great fire."

Paul Faber, Surgeon, Chapter 1.
Isa. 64:6

July 22 — God's Awful Mystery

Paul Faber, an unbelieving surgeon, has just attended an attractive but seriously ill young woman.

Was he in love with her? I do not know. I could tell, if I knew what being in love is. I think no two loves were ever the same since the creation of the world. I know that something had passed from her eyes to his—but what? He may have been in love with her already; but ere long my reader may be more sure than I that he was not. The Maker of men alone understands His awful mystery between the man and the woman. But without it, frightful indeed as are some of its results, assuredly the world He has made would burst its binding rings and fly asunder in shards, leaving His spirit nothing to enter, no time to work His lovely will.

It must be to any man a terrible thing to find himself in wild pain, with no God of whom to entreat that his soul may not faint within him; but to a man who can think as well as feel, it were a more terrible thing still, to find himself afloat on the tide of a lovely passion, with no God to whom to cry, accountable to Himself for that which He has made. Will any man who has ever cast more than a glance into the mysteries of his being, dare think himself sufficient to the ruling of his nature? And if he rule it not, what shall he be but the sport of the demons that will ride its tempests that will rouse and torment its ocean? What help then is there? What high-hearted man would consent to be possessed and sweetly ruled by the loveliest of angels? Truly it were but a daintier madness.

Come thou, holy Love, father of my spirit, nearer to the unknown deeper me than my consciousness is to its known self, possess me utterly, for thou art more me than I am myself. Rule thou. Then first I rule. Shadow me from the too radiant splendors of thy own creative thought. Folded in thy calm, I shall love, and not die. And ye, women, be the daughters of Him from whose heart came your mothers; be the saviors of men, and neither their torment nor their prey!

Paul Faber, Surgeon, Chapter 6.
Prov. 23:26

Science Cannot Do It   July 23

Dorothy Drake's faith is shaken by the momentary doubt of her minister father and the proclaimed atheism of Paul Faber:

Ready to trust, and incapable of arrogance, it was hard for her to imagine how a man like Mr. Faber, upright and kind and self-denying, could say such things if he did not *know* them true. The very word *science* appeared to carry an awful authority. She did not understand that it was only because science had never come closer to Him than the mere sight of the fringe of the outermost folds of the tabernacle of His presence, that her worshipers dared assert there was no God.

She did not perceive that nothing ever science could find, could possibly be the God of men; that science is only the human reflex of truth, and that truth itself can not be measured by what of it is reflected from the mirror of the understanding. She did not see that no incapacity of science to find God, even touched the matter of honest men's belief that He made His dwelling with the humble and contrite. Nothing she had learned from her father either provided her with reply, or gave hope of finding argument of discomfiture; nothing of all that went on at chapel or church seemed to have any thing to do with the questions that presented themselves.

Such a rough shaking of so-called faith, has been of endless service to many, chiefly by exposing the insecurity of all foundations of belief, save that which is discovered in digging with the spade of obedience. Well indeed is it for all honest souls to be thus shaken, who have been building upon doctrines concerning Christ, upon faith, upon experiences, upon any thing but Christ Himself, as revealed by Himself and His spirit to all who obey Him, and so revealing the Father—a doctrine just as foolish as the rest to men like Faber, but the power of God and the wisdom of God to such who know themselves lifted out of darkness and an ever-present sense of something wrong—if it be only into twilight and hope.

Paul Faber, Surgeon, Chapter 12.
Psalms 14:1

On this day in 1853: Mary Josephine, George and Louisa's second child, is born.

July 24   To The Uttermost Lash

In Paul Faber MacDonald depicts and deals at length with an unbelieving and skeptical mentality.

To Faber it seemed the true and therefore right thing, to deny the existence of any such being as men call God. I heartily admit that such denial may argue a nobler condition than that of the man who will reason for the existence of what he calls a Deity, but omits to order his way after what he professes to believe His will. At the same time, his conclusion that he was not bound to believe in any God, seemed to lift a certain weight off the heart of the doctor—the weight, namely, that gathers partly from the knowledge of having done wrong things, partly from the consciousness of not *being* altogether right.

It would be unfair, however, to leave the impression that this was the origin of all the relief the doctor derived from the conclusion. For thereby he got rid, in a great measure at least, of the notion—horrible in proportion to the degree in which it is actually present to the mind, although, I suspect, it is not, in a true sense credible to any mind—of a cruel, careless, unjust Being at the head of affairs. That such a notion should exist at all, is mainly the fault of the mass of so-called religious people, for they seem to believe in, and certainly proclaim such a God. In their excuse it may be urged they tell the tale as it was told to them; but the fault lies in this, that, with the gospel in their hands, they have yet lived in such disregard of its precepts, that they have never discovered their representation of the God of Truth to be such, that the more honest a man is, the less can he accept it.

That the honest man, however, should not thereupon set himself to see whether there might not be a true God notwithstanding, whether such a God was not conceivable consistently with things as they are, whether the believers had not distorted the revelation they professed to follow. . . must arise from a condition of being . . . for which the man, I cannot but think, will one day discover that he was to blame—for which a living God sees that he is to blame, makes all the excuse he can, and will give the needful punishment to the uttermost lash.

Paul Faber, Surgeon, Chapter 17.
Psalms 50:21

The Most Valueless Thing — July 25

Paul Faber, an unbelieving and skeptical doctor who nevertheless has dedicated his life to serving others, is here conversing with Juliet Meredith, a woman of questionable faith with whom he is in love.

"Do not think me incapable," he said one day, "of seeing much that is lovely and gracious in the orthodox fancies of religion. . . . For my part, I do not see why two friends should not consent to respect each other's opinions, letting the one do his best without a God to hinder him, and the other his best with his belief in one to aid him. Such a pair might be the most emulous of rivals in good works."

Juliet returned no satisfactory response to this tentative remark; but it was from no objection any longer in her mind to such a relation in the abstract. She had not yet at all consented with herself to abandon the faith of her father, but she did not see, and indeed it were hard for any one in her condition to see, why a man and a woman, the one denying after Faber's fashion, the other believing after hers, should not live together, and love and help each other. Of all valueless things, a merely speculative theology is one of the most valueless. To her, God had never been much more than a name—a name, it is true, that always occurred to her in any vivid moment of her life; but the Being whose was that name, was vague to her as a storm of sand—hardly so much her father as was the first forgotten ancestor of her line.

Under the growing fascination of the handsome, noble-minded doctor, she was fast losing what little shadow of faith she had possessed. The theology she had attempted to defend was so faulty, so unfair to God, that Faber's atheism had an advantage over it as easy as it was great. His unbelief was less selfish than Juliet's faith; consequently her faith sank, as her conscience rose meeting what was true in Faber's utterances. How could it be otherwise when she opposed lies uttered for the truth, to truths uttered for the lie? The truth itself she had never been true enough to look in the face. As her arguments, yea the very things she argued for, went down before him, her faith, which, to be faith, should have been in the living source of all true argument, found no object, was swept away like the uprooted weed it was, and whelmed in returning chaos.

Paul Faber, Surgeon, Chapter 17.
Gal. 1:6-9

July 26   Has He Not The Right?

Juliet Meredith is a woman with whom Paul Faber, an atheist, is in love.

She would have been at first highly offended, but the next moment a little pleased at being told that in reality she had never believed one whit more than Faber, that she was at present indeed incapable of believing. Probably she would have replied, "Then wherein am I to blame?" But although a woman who sits with her child in her arms in the midst of a burning house, half asleep, and half stifled and dazed with the fierce smoke, may not be to blame, certainly the moment she is able to excuse herself she is bound to make for the door.

So long as men do not feel that they are in a bad condition and in danger of worse, the message of deliverance will sound to them as a threat. Yea, the offer of absolute well-being upon the only possible conditions of the well-being itself, must, if heard at all, rouse in them a discomfort whose cause they attribute to the message, not to themselves; and immediately they will endeavor to justify themselves in disregarding it. There are those doing all they can to strengthen themselves in unbelief, who, if the Lord were to appear plainly before their eyes, would tell Him they could not help it, for he had not until then given them ground enough for faith, and when He left them, would go on just as before, except that they would speculate and pride themselves on the vision.

If men say, "We want no such deliverance," then the Maker of them must either destroy them as vile things for whose existence He is to Himself accountable, or compel them to change. If they say, "We choose to be destroyed," He, as their Maker, has a choice in the matter too. Is He not free to say, "You can not even slay yourselves, and I choose that you shall know the death of living without Me; you shall learn to choose to live indeed. I choose that you shall know what *I know* to be good?" And however much any individual consciousness may rebel, surely the individual consciousness which called that other into being, and is the Father of that being, fit to be such because of Himself He is such, has a right to object that by rebellion His creature should destroy the very power by which it rebels, and from a being capable of a divine freedom by partaking of the divine nature, should make of itself the merest slave incapable of will of any sort! Is it wrong to compel His creature to soar aloft into the ether of its origin, and find its deepest, its only true self? It is God's knowing choice of life against man's ignorant choice of death.

Paul Faber, Surgeon, Chapter 29.
I Tim. 2:4

Our Hope Is In Thee   July 27

The Rev. Thomas Wingfold here is praying for a needy retired curate in despair:

"God of justice, Thou knowest how hard it is for us, and Thou wilt be fair to us. We have seen no visions; we have never heard the voice of Thy Son, of whom those tales, so dear to us, have come down the ages; we have to fight on in much darkness of spirit and of mind, both from the ignorance we can not help, and from the fault we could have helped; we inherit blindness from the error of our fathers; and when fear, or dread of shame, or the pains of death, come upon us, we are ready to despair, and cry out that there is no God, or, if there be, He has forgotten His children.

"There are times when the darkness closes about us like a wall, and Thou appearest nowhere, either in our hearts, or in the outer universe; we can not tell whether the things we seemed to do in Thy name, were not mere hypocrisies, and our very life is but a gulf of darkness. We cry aloud, and our despair is as a fire in our bones to make us cry; but to all our crying and listening, there seems neither hearing nor answer in the boundless waste. Thou who knowest Thyself God, who knowest Thyself that for which we groan, Thou whom Jesus called Father, we appeal to Thee, not as we imagine Thee, but as Thou seest Thyself, as Jesus knows Thee, to Thy very self we cry—help us, O Cause of us! O Thou from whom alone we are this weakness, through whom alone we can become strength, help us—be our Father. We ask for nothing beyond what Thy Son has told us to ask. We beg for no signs or wonders but for Thy breath upon our souls, Thy spirit in our hearts.

We pray for no cloven tongues of fire—for no mighty rousing of brain or imagination; but we do, with all our power of prayer, pray for Thy spirit; we do not even pray to know that it is given to us; let us, if so it please Thee, remain in doubt of the gift for years to come—but lead us thereby. Knowing ourselves only as poor and feeble, aware only of ordinary and common movements of mind and soul, may we yet be possessed by the spirit of God, led by His will in ours. For all things in a man, even those that seem to him the commonest and least uplifted, are the creation of Thy heart, and by the lowly doors of our wavering judgment, dull imagination, lukewarm love, and palsied will, Thou canst enter and glorify all. Give us patience because our hope is in Thee, not in ourselves. Work Thy will in us, and our prayers are ended. Amen.

                         Paul Faber, Surgeon, Chapter 21.
                         Matt. 20:29-34

July 28 — The Heavier Obligation

Dorothy Drake, the midst of her own spiritual struggles, finds she cannot communicate with her clerical father:

She could say nothing to her father. She loved him—oh, how dearly! And trusted him, where she could trust him at all!—oh how perfectly! But she had no confidence in his understanding of herself. The main cause whence arose this insufficiency and her lack of trust was, that all his faith in God was as yet scarcely more independent of thought-forms, word-shapes, dogma and creed, than that of the Catholic or Calvinist.

How few are there whose faith is simple and mighty in the Father of Jesus Christ, waiting to believe all that He will reveal to them! How many of those who talk of faith as the one needful thing, will accept as sufficient to the razing of the walls of partition between you and them, your heartiest declaration that you believe *in Him* with the whole might of your nature, lay your soul bare to the revelation of His spirit, and stir up your will to obey Him?—And then comes *your* temptation—to exclude, namely, from your love and sympathy the weak and boisterous brethren who, after the fashion possible to them, believe in your Lord, because they exclude you, and put as little confidence in your truth as in your insight. If you do know more of Christ then they, upon you lies the heavier obligation to be true to them, as was St. Paul to the Judaizing Christians, whom these so much resemble, who were his chief hindrance in the work his Master had given him to do.

In Christ we must forget Paul and Apollos and Cephas, pope and bishop and pastor and presbyter, creed and interpretation and theory. Careless of their opinions, we must be careful of themselves—careful that we have salt in ourselves, and that the salt lose not its savor, that the old man, dead through Christ, shall not, vampire-like, creep from his grave and suck the blood of the saints, by whatever name they be called, or however little they may yet have entered into the freedom of the gospel that God is light, and in Him is no darkness at all.

Paul Faber, Surgeon, Chapter 31.
Rom. 9:1-2

A Better Knowing — July 29

Dorothy Drake, who has had difficulty communicating with her clerical father, here is finding the barrier between them beginning to give way:

"I suspect," returned the minister, "that I have been greatly astray. But after this, we will seek our Father together, in our Brother, Jesus Christ."

It was the initiation of a daily lesson together in the New Testament, which, while it drew their hearts closer to each other, drew them, with growing delight, nearer and nearer to the ideal of humanity, Jesus Christ, in whom shines the glory of its Father.

A man may look another in the face for a hundred years and not know him. Men *have* looked Jesus Christ in the face, and not known either Him or his Father. It was needful that He should appear, to begin the knowing of Him, but speedily was His visible presence taken away, that it might not become, as assuredly it would have become, a veil to hide from men the Father of their spirits. Do you long for the assurance of some sensible sign? Do you ask why no intellectual proof is to be had? I tell you that such would but delay, perhaps altogether impair for you, that better, that best, that only vision, into which at last your world must blossom—such a contact, namely, with the heart of God Himself, such a perception of His being, and His absolute oneness with you, the child of His thought, the individuality softly parted from his spirit, yet living still and only by His presence and love, as, by its own radiance, will sweep doubt away forever. Being then in the light and knowing it, the lack of intellectual proof concerning that which is too high for it, will trouble you no more than would your inability to silence a metaphysician who declared that you had no real existence.

It is for the sake of such vision as God would give that you are denied such vision as you would have. The Father of our spirits is not content that we should know Him as we know each other. There is a better, closer, nearer than any human way of knowing, and that He is guiding us across all the swamps of our unteachableness, the seas of our faithlessness, the desert of our ignorance.

Paul Faber, Surgeon, Chapter 32.
Heb. 11:6

July 30 — How To Help

Polwarth, a misshapen dwarf who is a spiritual mentor, is here presented as considering how best to help two people in severe estrangement each from the other.

In his inmost being he knew that the mission of man is to help his neighbors. But in as much as he was ready to help, he recoiled from meddling. To meddle is to destroy the holy chance. Meddlesomeness is the very opposite of helpfulness, for it consists in forcing your self into another self, instead of opening your self as a refuge to the others.

They are opposite extremes, and, like all extremes, touch. It is not correct that extremes meet; they lean back to back. To Polwarth, a human self was a shrine to be approached with reverence, even when he bore deliverance in his hand. Anywhere, everywhere, in the seventh heaven or the seventh hell, he could worship God with the outstretched arms of love, the bended knees of joyous adoration, but in helping his fellow, he not only worshiped but served God—ministered, that is, to the wants of God—doing it unto Him in the least of His. He knew that, as the Father unresting works for the weal of men, so every son, following the master-Son, must work also. Through weakness and suffering he had learned it. But he never doubted that his work as much as his bread would be given him, never rushed out wildly snatching at something to do for God, never helped a lazy man to break stones, never preached to foxes.

It was what the Father gave him to do that he cared to do, and that only. It was the man next him that he helped—the neighbor in need of the help he had. He did not trouble himself greatly about the happiness of men, but when the time and the opportunity arrived in which to aid struggling birth of the eternal bliss, the whole strength of his being responded to the call. And now, having felt a thread vibrate, like a sacred spider he sat in the center of his web of love, and waited and watched.

In proportion as the love is pure, and only in proportion to that, can such be a pure and real calling. The least speck of self will defile it—a little more may ruin its most hopeful effort.

Paul Faber, Surgeon, Chapter 39.
Matt. 25:40

It's A Simple Necessity

JULY 31

In the final chapter of Paul Faber, Surgeon, MacDonald directly addresses the reader:

Why should I pursue the story further? And if not here, where better should I stop? The true story has no end—no end. But endlessly dreary would the story be, were there no Life living by its own will, no perfect Will, one with an almighty heart, no Love in whom we live and move and have our being. Offer me an eternity in all things else after my own imagination, but without a perfect Father, and I say, no; let me die, even as the unbelieving would have it.

Not believing in the Father of Jesus, they are *right* in not desiring to live. Heartily do I justify them therein. For all this talk and disputation about immortality, wherein is regarded only the continuance of consciousness beyond what we call death, it is to me, with whatever splendor of intellectual coruscation it be accompanied, but little better than a foolish babble, the crackling of thorns under a pot. Apart from Himself, God forbid there would be any immortality. If it could be proved apart from Him, then apart from Him it could be, and would be, infinite damnation. It is an impossibility, and were but an unmitigated evil. And if it be impossible without Him, it can not be believed without Him: if it could be proved without Him, the belief so gained would be an evil. Only with the knowledge of the Father of Christ, did the endlessness of being become a doctrine of bliss to men. If he be the first life, the Author of his own, to speak after the language of men, and the origin and source of all other life, it can be only by knowing Him that we can know whether we shall live or die.

Nay, more, far more!—the knowledge of Him by such innermost contact as is possible only between creator and created, and possible only when the created has aspired to be one with the will of the creator, such knowledge and such alone is life to the created; it is the very life, that alone for the sake of which God created us. If we are one with God in heart, in righteousness, in desire, no death can touch us, for we are life, and the garment of immortality, the endless length of days which is but the mere shadow of the eternal, follows as a simple necessity.

Paul Faber, Surgeon, Chapter 54.
Psalms 40:1-3

August 1 — Not The God Of Your Fancy

Thus ends the novel that MacDonald thought his finest, Paul Faber, Surgeon.:

He is not the God of the dead, or of the dying, but of the essentially alive. Without this inmost knowledge of Him, this oneness with Him, we have no life in us, for *it is life*, and that for the sake of which all this outward show of things, and our troubled condition in the midst of them, exists. All that is mighty, grand, harmonious, therefore in its own nature true, is. If not, then dearly I thank the grim Death, that I shall die and not live. Thus undeceived, my only terror would be that the unbelievers might be but half right, and there might be a life, so-called, beyond the grave without a God.

My brother man, is the idea of a God too good or too foolish for thy belief? Or is it that thou art not great enough or humble enough to hold it? In either case, I will believe it for thee and for me. Only be not stiff-necked when the truth begins to draw thee: thou wilt find it hard if she has to go behind and drive thee—hard to kick against the divine goads, which, be thou ever so mulish, will be too much for thee at last. Yea, the time will come when thou wilt goad thyself toward the divine. But hear me this once more: the God, the Jesus in whom I believe, are not the God, the Jesus, in whom you fancy I believe: you know them not; your idea of them is not mine. If you knew them you would believe in them, for to know them is to believe in them.

Say not, "Let Him teach me, then," except you mean it in submissive desire; for He has been teaching you all this time: if you have been doing His teaching, you are on the way to learn more; if you hear and do not heed, where is the wonder that the things I tell you sound in your ears as the muttering of a dotard? They convey to you nothing, it may be: but that which makes of them words—words—words, lies in you, not in me. Yours is the killing power. They would bring you life, but the death in him that knoweth and doeth not is strong; in your air they drop and die, winged things no more.

Paul Faber, Surgeon, Chapter 54.
Psalms 32:8-9

The Grand Result — August 2

"I came that they may have life, and have it abundantly." John 10:10

All things are possible with God, but all things are not easy. It is easy for him *to be*, for there he has to do with his own perfect will: it is not easy for him to create—that is, after the grand fashion which alone will satisfy his glorious heart and will, the fashion in which he is now creating us.

In the very nature of being—that is, God—it must be hard—and divine history shows how hard—to create that which shall be not himself, yet like himself. The problem is, so far to separate from himself that which must yet on him be ever and always and utterly dependent, that it shall have the existence of an individual, and be able to turn and regard him—choose him, and say, "I will arise and go to my Father," and so develop in itself the highest *Divine* of which it is capable—to be the thing the maker thought of when he willed, ere he began to work its being.

I imagine the difficulty of doing this thing, of effecting this creation, this separation from himself such that will in the creature shall be possible—I imagine, I say, the difficulty of such creation so great, that for it God must begin inconceivably far back in the infinitesimal regions of beginnings—not to say before anything in the least resembling man, but eternal miles beyond the last farthest-pushed discovery in *protoplasm*—to set in motion that division from himself which in its grand result should be individuality, consciousness, choice, and conscious choice—choice at last pure, being the choice of the right, the true, the divinely harmonious. Hence the final end of the separation is not individuality; that is but a means to it; the final end is oneness—an impossibility without it.

For there can be no unity, no delight of love, no harmony, no good in being, where there is but one. Two at least are needed for oneness; and the greater the number of individuals, the greater, the lovelier, the richer, the diviner is the possible unity.

"Life," *Unspoken Sermons: Second Series*
Isa. 65:17-19

August 3 — An Eternal Labor

"I came that they may have life, and have it abundantly." John 10:10

God is life, and the will-source of life. In the outflowing of that life, I know him; and when I am told that he is love, I see that if he were not love he would not, could not create. I know nothing deeper in him than love, nor believe there is in him anything deeper than love—nay, that there can be anything deeper than love.

The being of God is love, therefore creation. I imagine that from all eternity he has been creating. As he saw it was not good for man to be alone, so has he never been alone himself; from all eternity the Father has had the Son, and the never-begun existence of that Son I imagine an easy outgoing of the Father's nature; while to make other beings—beings like us, I imagine the labor of a God, an eternal labor.

Speaking after our poor human fashions of thought—the only fashions possible to us—I imagine that God has never been contented to be alone even with the Son of his love, the prime and perfect idea of humanity, but that he has from the first willed and labored to give existence to other creatures who would be blessed with his blessedness—creatures whom he is now and always has been developing into likeness with that Son—a likeness for long to be distant and small, but a likeness to be for ever growing: perhaps never one of them yet, though unspeakably blessed, has had even an approximate idea of the blessedness in store for him.

He knew what it would cost—sore suffering such as we cannot imagine, and could only be God's in the bringing out, call it birth or development, of the God-life in the individual soul—a suffering still renewed, a labor thwarted ever by that soul itself, compelling him to take, still at the cost of suffering, the not absolutely best, only the best possible means left him by the resistance of his creature.

"Life," *Unspoken Sermons: Second Series*
Col. 3:9-11

An Infinite Embrace   August 4

"I came that they may have life, and have it abundantly." John 10:10

Man finds it hard to get what he wants, because he does not want the best; God finds it hard to give, because he would give the best, and man will not take it.

What Jesus did, was what the Father is always doing; the suffering he endured was that of the Father from the foundation of the world, reaching its climax in the person of his Son. God provides the sacrifice; the sacrifice is himself. He is always, and has ever been sacrificing himself to and for his creatures. It lies in the very essence of his creation of them.

The worst heresy, next to that of dividing religion and righteousness, is to divide the Father from the Son—in thought or feeling or action or intent; to represent the Son as doing that which the Father does not himself do. Jesus did nothing but what the Father did and does. If Jesus suffered for men, it was because his Father suffers for men; only he came close to men through his body and their senses, that he might bring their spirits close to his Father and their Father, so giving them life, and losing what could be lost of his own.

He is God our Savior: it is because God is our Savior that Jesus is our Savior. The unbeliever may easily imagine a better God than the common theology of the country offers him; but not the lovingest heart that ever beat can even reflect the length and breadth and depth and height of that love of God which shows itself in his Son—one, and of one mind, with himself.

The outcome of that agony, the victory of that creative and again creative energy, will be radiant life, whereof joy unspeakable is the flower. Every child will look in the eyes of the Father, and the eyes of the Father will receive the child with an infinite embrace.

        "Life," *Unspoken Sermons: Second Series*
        Rom. 3:23-26

1853: Charlotte Powell, Louisa's sister, marries John Godwin, principal of Highbury Seminary and George MacDonald's former mentor.

August 5 — The Only Reality

"I came that they may have life, and have it abundantly." John 10:10

The Father has given to the Son to have life in himself; that life is our light. We know life only as light; it is the life in us that makes us see. All the growth of the Christian is the more and more life he is receiving.

At first his religion may hardly be distinguishable from the mere prudent desire to save his soul; but at last he loses that very soul in the glory of love, and so saves it; self becomes but the cloud on which the white light of God divides into harmonies unspeakable.

"In the midst of life we are in death," said one; it is more true that in the midst of death we are in life. Life is the only reality; what men call death is but a shadow—a word for that which cannot be—a negation, owing the very idea of itself to that which it would deny. But for life there could be no death. If God were not, there would not even be nothing. Not even nothingness preceded life. Nothingness owes it very idea to existence.

"Life," *Unspoken Sermons: Second Series*
John 10:10

Live Indeed

August 6

"I came that they may have life, and have it abundantly." John 10:10

We who *are*, have nothing to do with death; our relations are alone with life. The thing that can mourn can mourn only from lack; it cannot mourn because of being, but because of not enough being. All the being must partake of essential being; life must be assisted, upheld, comforted, every part, with life. Life is the law, the food, the necessity of life. Life is everything.

Many doubtless mistake the joy of life for life itself; and, longing after the joy, languish with a thirst at once poor and inextinguishable; but even that thirst points to the one spring. These love self, not life, and self is but the shadow of life. When it is taken for life itself, and set as the man's center, it becomes a live death in the man, a devil he worships as his god; the worm of the death eternal he clasps to his bosom as his own joy!

The soul compact of harmonies has more life, a larger being, than the soul consumed of cares; the sage is a larger life than the clown; the poet is more alive than the man whose life flows out that money may come in; the man who loves his fellow is infinitely more alive than he whose endeavor is to exalt himself above him; the man who strives to be better, than he who longs for the praise of the many; but the man to whom God is all in all, who feels his life-roots hid with Christ in God, who knows himself the inheritor of all wealth and worlds and ages, yea, of power essential and in itself, that man has begun to be alive indeed.

"Life," *Unspoken Sermons: Second Series*
Prov. 4:18

August 7 — Our Real Need

"I came that they may have life, and have it abundantly." John 10:10

Let us in all the troubles of life remember—that our one lack is life—that what we need is more life—more of the life-making presence in us making us more, and more largely, alive.

When most oppressed, when most weary of life, as our unbelief would phrase it, let us bethink ourselves that it is in truth the inroad and presence of death we are weary of. When most inclined to sleep, let us rouse ourselves to live. Of all things let us avoid the false refuge of a weary collapse, a hopeless yielding to things as they are. It is life in us that is discontented; we need more of what is discontented, not more of the cause of its discontent.

Discontent, I repeat, is the life in us that has not enough of itself, is not enough to itself, so calls for more. He has the victory who, in the midst of pain and weakness, cries out, not for death, not for the repose of forgetfulness, but for strength to fight; for more power, more consciousness of being, more God in him; who when sorest wounded, says with Sir Andrew Barton in the old ballad:

> Fight on my men, says Sir Andrew Barton,
>   I am hurt, but I am not slain;
> I'll lay me down and bleed awhile,
>   And then I'll rise and fight again.

And that with no silly notion of playing the hero—what have creatures like us to do with heroism who are not yet barely honest!—but because so to fight is the true, and the only way.

"Life," *Unspoken Sermons: Second Series*
II Cor. 20:17

No Limit

August 8

"I came that they may have life, and have it abundantly." John 10:10

The true man trusts in a strength which is not his, and which he does not feel, does not even always desire; believes in a power that seems far from him, which is yet at the root of his fatigue itself and his need of rest—rest as far from death as is labor.

To trust in the strength of God in our weakness; to say, "I am weak: so let me be: God is strong;" to seek from him who is our life, as the natural, simple cure of all that is amiss us, power to do, and be, and live, even when we are weary—this is the victory that overcometh the world. To believe in God our strength in the face of all seeming denial, to believe in him out of the heart of weakness and unbelief, in spite of numbness and weariness and lethargy—these are the broken steps up to the high fields where repose is but a form of strength, strength but a form of joy, joy but a form of love.

"I am weak," says the true soul, "but not so weak that I would not be strong; not so sleepy that I would not see the sun rise; not so lame but that I would walk! Thanks be to him who perfects strength in weakness, and gives to his beloved while they sleep."

If we will but let our God and Father work his will with us, there can be no limit to his enlargement of our existence, to the flood of life with which he will overflow our consciousness.

"Life," *Unspoken Sermons: Second Series*
II Cor. 9:10

August 9 — What Must It Not Be?

"I came that they may have life, and have it abundantly." John 10:10

The ignorant soul understands by this life eternal only an endless elongation of consciousness; what God means by it is a being like his own, a being beyond the attack of decay or death, a being so essential that it has no relation whatever to nothingness; a something which is, and can never go to that which is not, for with that it never had to do, but came out of the heart of Life, the heart of God, the fountain of being; an existence partaking of the divine nature, and having nothing in common, any more than the Eternal himself, with what can pass or cease: God owes his being to no one, and his child has no lord but his Father.

This life, this eternal life, consists for man in absolute oneness with God and all divine modes of being, oneness with every phase of right and harmony. It consists in a love as deep as it is universal, as conscious as it is unspeakable; a love that can no more be reasoned about than life itself—a love whose presence is its all-sufficing proof and justification, whose absence is an annihilating defect: he who has it not cannot believe in it: how should death believe in life, though all the birds of God are singing jubilant over the empty tomb!

The delight of such a being, the splendor of a consciousness rushing from the wide open doors of the fountain of existence, the ecstasy of the spiritual sense into which the surge of life essential, immortal, flows in silent fulness from the heart of hearts—what may it, what must it not be, in the great day of God and the individual soul!

"Life," *Unspoken Sermons: Second Series*
Psalms 18:31-35

Two Wills In Harmony   August 10

"I came that they may have life, and have it abundantly." John 10:10

For the *will* is the deepest, the strongest, the divinest thing in man; so, I presume, is it in God, for such we find it in Jesus Christ. Here, and here only, in the relation of the two wills, God's and his own, can a man come into vital contact---in willed harmony of dual oneness—with the All-in-all.

When a man can and does entirely say, "not my will, but thine be done"—when he so wills the will of God as to do it, then is he one with God—one, as a true son with a true father. When a man wills that his being be conformed to the being of his origin, which is the life in his life, causing and bearing his life, therefore absolutely and only of its kind, one with it more and deeper than words or figures can say—to the life which is itself, only more of itself, causing itself—when the man thus accepts his causing life, *and sets himself to live the will of that causing life,* humbly eager after the privileges of his origin—thus receiving God, he becomes, in the act, a partaker of the divine nature, a true son of the living God, and an heir of all he possesses: by the obedience of a son, he receives into himself the very life of the Father.

Obedience is the joining of the links of the eternal round. Obedience is but the other side of the creative will. Will is God's will, obedience is man's will; the two make one. The Root-Life, knowing well the thousand troubles it would bring upon him, has created, and goes on creating other lives, that, though incapable of self-being, they may, by willed obedience, share in the bliss of his essential self-ordained being.

Our souls shall be vessels ever growing, and ever as they grow, filled with the more and more life proceeding from the Father and the Son, from God the ordaining, and God the obedient. What the delight of the being, what the abundance of the life he came that we might have, we can never know until we have it.

"Life," *Unspoken Sermons: Second Series*
John 17:20-21

On this day in 1853: MacDonald sees his brother John embark for Moscow, where he will be a tutor in a boy's school.

August 11 — Our Demon-Foe

"I came that they may have life, and have it abundantly." John 10:10

For we are made for love, not for self. Our neighbor is our refuge; *self* is our demon-foe. Every man is the image of God to every man, and in proportion as we love him, we shall know the sacred fact.

The precious thing to human soul is, and one day shall be known to be, every human soul. And if it be so between man and man, how will it not be betwixt the man and his maker, between the child and his eternal Father, between the created and the creating Life? Must not the glory of existence be endlessly redoubled in the infinite love of the creature—for all love is infinite—to the infinite God, the great one life, than whom is no other—only shadows, lovely shadows of him!

Reader to whom my words seem those of inflation and foolish excitement, it can be nothing to you to be told that I seem to myself to speak only the words of truth and soberness; but what if the cause why they seem other to your mind be—not merely that you are not whole, but that your being nowise thirsts after harmony, that you are not of the truth, that you have not yet begun to live?

Little can you, with your mind full of petty cares, or still more petty ambitions, understand the groanings and travailings of the creation. It may indeed by that you are honestly desirous of saving you own wretched soul, but as yet you can know but little of your need of him who is *the first and the last and the living one.*

"Life," *Unspoken Sermons: Second Series*
Matt. 13:22

Why They Fear Him   August 12

"And when I saw him, I fell at his feet as one dead. And he laid his right hand upon me, saying, Fear not; I am the first and the last and the Living one." Rev. 1:17, 18

It is not alone the first beginnings of religion that are full of fear. So long as love is imperfect, there is room for torment. That love only which fills the heart is able to cast out fear, leaving no room for its presence. What we find in the beginnings of religion, will hold in varying degree, until the religion, that is the love, be perfected.

According to the nature of the mind which occupies itself with the idea of the Supreme, whether regarded as maker or ruler, will be the kind and degree of the terror. To this terror need belong no exalted ideas of God; those fear him most who most imagine him like their own evil selves, only beyond them in power, easily able to work his arbitrary will with them. Power without love, dependence where is no righteousness, wake a worship without devotion, a loathsomeness of servile flattery.

Where it is possible that fear exist, it is well it should exist, cause continual uneasiness, and be cast out by nothing but love. Until love, which is the truth towards God, is able to cast out fear, it is well that fear should hold.

Verily, God must be terrible to those that are far from him; for they fear he will do, yea, he is doing with them what they do not, cannot desire, and can ill endure.   Such as many men are, such as all without God would become, they must prefer a devil, because of his supreme selfishness, to a God who will die for his creatures, and insists upon giving himself to them, insists upon their being unselfish and blessed like himself. That which is the power and worth of life they must be, or die; and the vague consciousness of this makes them afraid. They love their poor existence as it is; God loves it as it must be—and they fear him.

> "The Fear of God," *Unspoken Sermons: Second Series*
> I Thess. 3:12

August 13 — The Fire Of God

"And when I saw him, I fell at his feet as one dead. And he laid his right hand upon me, saying, Fear not; I am the first and the last and the Living one." Rev. 1:17, 18

The fire of God, which is his essential being, his love, his creative power, is a fire unlike its earthly symbol in this, that it is only at a distance it burns—that the farther from him, it burns the worse, and that when we turn and begin to approach him, the burning begins to change to comfort, which comfort will grow to such bliss that the heart at length cries out with a gladness no other gladness can reach, "Whom have I in heaven but thee? And there is none upon earth that I desire besides thee!"

The glory of being, the essence of life and its joy, shining upon the corrupt and deathly, must needs, like the sun, consume the dead, and send corruption down to the dust; that which it burns in the soul is not of the soul, yea, is at utter variance with it; yet so close to the soul is the foul fungous growth sprung from and subsisting upon it, that the burning of it is felt through every spiritual nerve: the evil parasites are consumed away, that is when the man yields his self and all that self's low world and returns to his lord and God, then that which, before, he was aware of only as burning, he will feel as love, comfort, strength—an eternal, ever-growing life in him.

For now he lives, and life cannot hurt life; it can only hurt death, which needs and ought to be destroyed. God is life essential, eternal, and death cannot live in his sight; for death is corruption, and has not existence in itself, living only in the decay of the things of life.

"The Fear of God," *Unspoken Sermons: Second Series*
Heb. 12:28-29

Oh, The Joy   August 14

"And when I saw him, I fell at his feet as one dead. And he laid his right hand upon me, saying, Fear not; I am the first and the last and the Living one." Rev. 1:17, 18

But the appearance of the Son of Man was not intended to breed terror in the son of man to whom he came. Why than was John afraid? Why did the servant of the Lord fall at his feet as one dead? Joy to us that he did, for the words that follow! They bear best sign of their source: however given to his ears, they must be from the heart of our great Brother, the one Man, Christ Jesus, divinely human!

It was still and only the imperfection of the disciple, unfinished in faith, so unfinished in everything a man needs, that was the cause of his terror. This is surely implied in the words the Lord said to him when he fell! The thing that made John afraid, he speaks of as the thing that ought to have taken from him all fear. For the glory that he saw, the head and hair pouring from it such a radiance of light that they were white as white wool—snow-white, as his garments on mount Hermon; in the mist of the radiance his eyes like a flame of fire, and his countenance as the son shines in his strength; the darker glow of the feet, yet as of fine brass burning in a furnace; the girdle under his breast, golden between the snow and the brass—what were they all but the effulgence of his glory who was himself the effulgence of the Father's? "He laid his right hand upon me, saying unto me, 'Fear not; I am the first and the last, and the living one.'"

Endless must be our terror, until we come heart to heart with the fire-core of the universe, the first and the last and the living one! But oh, the joy to be told, by Power himself, the first and the last, the living one—told what we can indeed then see *must* be true, the cure for trembling is the presence of Power; that fear cannot stand before Strength; that the visible God is the destruction of death; the one and only safety in the universe, is the perfect nearness of the Living One!

        "The Fear of God," *Unspoken Sermons: Second Series*
        II Cor. 4:6

August 15 — Punishment Or Favor?

"Oh that thou wouldest hide me in Sheol, that thou wouldest conceal me until thy wrath be past...." Job 14:13

The book of Job seems to me the most daring of poems: from a position of the most vantageless realism, it assaults that very citadel of the ideal! Its hero is a man seated among the ashes, covered with loathsome boils from head to foot, scraping himself with a potsherd. Sore in body, sore in mind, sore in heart, sore in spirit, he is the instance-type of humanity in the depths of its misery—all the waves and billows of a world of adverse circumstances rolling free over its head.

Job, I say, is *the human being*—a center to the sickening assaults of pain, the ghastly invasions of fear. These, one time or another, I presume, threaten to overwhelm every man, reveal him to himself as enslaved to the external, and stir him up to find some way out into the infinite, where alone he can rejoice in the liberty that belongs to his nature. Seated in the heart of a leaden despair, Job cries aloud to the Might unseen, scarce known, which yet he regards as the God of his life.

He cannot, will not believe *him* a tyrant; but, while he pleads against his dealing with himself, he loves him, and looks to him as the source of life, the power and gladness of being. He dares not think God unjust, but not therefore can he allow that he has done anything to merit the treatment he is receiving at his hands. Hence is he of necessity in profoundest perplexity, for how can the two things be reconciled?

The thought has not yet come to him that that which it would be unfair to lay upon him as punishment, may yet be laid upon him as favor—by a love supreme which would give him blessing beyond all possible prayer—blessing for which, once known and understood, he would be willing to endure yet again all that he had undergone.

"The Voice of Job," *Unspoken Sermons: Second Series*
I Peter 1:6-7

PHARISAIC FRIENDS   AUGUST 16

"Oh that thou wouldest hide me in Sheol, that thou wouldest conceal me until thy wrath be past...." Job 14:13

Job refused the explanation of his friends because he knew it false; to have accepted such as would by many in the present day be given him, would have been to be devoured at once of the monster. He simply holds on to the skirt of God's garment—besieges his door—keeps putting his question again and again, ever haunting the one source of true answer and reconciliation. No answer will do for him but the answer that God only can give; for who but God can justify God's ways to his creature?

His friends, good men, religious men, but of the pharisaic type—that is, men who would pay their court to God, instead of coming into his presence as children; men with traditional theories which have served their poor turn, satisfied their feeble intellectual demands, they think others therefore must accept or perish; men anxious to appease God rather than trust in him; men who would rather receive salvation from God, than God their salvation—these his friends would persuade Job to the confession that he was a hypocrite, insisting that such things could not have come upon him but because of wickedness, and as they knew of none open, it must be for some secret vileness. They grow angry with him when he refuses to be persuaded against his knowledge of himself. They insist on his hypocrisy, he on his righteousness.

The poem prepares us for the right understanding of the man by telling us in the prologue, that God said thus to the accuser of men: "Hast thou considered my servant Job, that there is none like him in the earth, a perfect and an upright man, one that feareth God, and escheweth evil?" God gives Job into Satan's hand with confidence in the result; and at the end of the trial approves of what Job has said concerning himself.

> "The Voice of Job," *Unspoken Sermons: Second Series*
> Psalms 4:1-3

August 17 — Not To Be Found?

"Oh that thou wouldest hide me in Sheol, that thou wouldest conceal me until thy wrath be past. . . ." Job 14:13

But let us look a little closer at Job's way of thinking and speaking about God, and his manner of addressing him—so different from the pharisaic in all ages, in none more than our own.

He uses language which, used by any living man, would horrify the religious of the present day, in proportion to the lack of truth in them, just as it horrified his three friends, the honest pharisees of the time, whose religion was "doctrine" and rebuke. God speaks not a word of rebuke to Job for the freedom of his speech: he has always been seeking such as Job to worship him.

It is those who know only and respect the outsides of religion, such as never speak or think of God but as *the Almighty* or *Providence*, who will say of the man who would go close up to God, and speak to him out of the deepest in the nature he has made, "he is irreverent." They pay court to God, not love him; they treat him as one far away, not as the one whose bosom is the only home.

In the desolation of this man, the truth of God seems to him, yet more plainly than hitherto, the one thing that holds together the world which by the word of his mouth came first into being. He would cast his load at the feet of his maker! God is the God of comfort, known of man as the refuge, the life-giver, or not known at all. But alas—he cannot come to him! Nowhere can he see his face! He has hid himself from him!

He cannot find him! Yet is he in his presence all the time, and his words enter into the ear of God his Savior.

"The Voice of Job," *Unspoken Sermons: Second Series*
Psalms 145:17-19

His Most Divine Gift — August 18

"Oh, that thou wouldest appoint me a set time, and remember me!" Job 14:13

The grandeur of the poem is that Job pleads his cause with God against all the remonstrance of religious authority, recognizing no one but God, and justified therein. And the grandest of all is this, that he implies, if he does not actually say, that God *owes* something to his creature.

This is the beginning of the great discovery of all—that God owes *himself* to the creature he has made in his image, for so he has made him incapable of living without him. This, his creatures' highest claim upon him, is his divinest gift to them. For the fulfilling of this their claim he his sent his son, that he may himself, the father of him and of us, follow into our hearts. Perhaps the worst thing in a theology constructed out of man's dull *possible,* and not out of the being and deeds and words of Jesus Christ, is the impression it conveys throughout that God acknowledges no such obligation.

Are not we the clay, and he the potter? How can the clay claim from the potter? We are the clay, it is true, but *his* clay, but spiritual clay, live clay, with needs and desires—and *rights*; we are clay, but clay worth the Son of God's dying for, that it might learn to consent to be shaped unto honor. We can have no merits—a *merit* is a thing impossible; but God has given us rights. Out of him we have nothing; but, created by him, come forth from him, we have even rights towards him—ah, never, never *against* him! His whole desire and labor is to make us capable of claiming, and induce us to claim of him the things whose rights he bestowed in creating us.

No claim had we to be created: that involves an absurdity; but, being made, we have claims on him who made us: our needs are our claims. A man who will not provide for the hunger of his child, is condemned by the whole world.

"The Voice of Job," *Unspoken Sermons: Second Series*
Isa. 45:18-22

August 19   Claiming Our Claims

"Oh, that thou wouldest appoint me a set time, and remember me!" Job 14:13

"Ah, but," says the partisan of God, "the Almighty stands in a relation very different from that of an earthly father: there is no parallel." I grant it: there is no parallel. The man did not create the child, he only yielded to an impulse created in himself: God is infinitely more bound to provide for *his* child than any man is to provide for his.

The relation is infinitely, divinely closer. It is God to whom every hunger, every aspiration, every desire, every longing of our nature is to be referred; he made all our needs—made us the creatures of a thousand necessities—and have we no claim on him? Nay, we have claims innumerable, infinite; and his one great claim on us is that we should claim our claims of him.

It is terrible to represent God as unrelated to us in the way of appeal to his righteousness. How should he be righteous without owing us anything? How would there be any right for the judge of all the earth to do if he owed nothing? Verily he owes us nothing that he does not pay like a God; but it is of the devil to imagine imperfection and disgrace in obligation. So far is God from thinking so that in every act of his being he lays himself under obligation to his creatures.

Oh, the grandeur of his goodness, and righteousness, and fearless unselfishness! When doubt and dread invade, and the voice of love in the soul is dumb, what can please the father of men better than to hear his child cry to him from whom he came, "Here I am, O God! Thou hast made me: give me that which thou hast made me needing." The child's necessity, his weakness, his helplessness, are the strongest of all his claims.

I am a child; this beyond all other claims, I claim: that, if any of my needs are denied me, it shall be by the love of a father, who will let me see his face, and allow me to plead my cause before him. And this must be just what God desires. What would he have, but that his children should claim their father?

        "The Voice of Job," *Unspoken Sermons: Second Series*
        Isa. 45:23-25

Will He Not Be Pleased?   August 20

"Oh, that thou wouldest appoint me a set time, and remember me!" Job 14:13

Our Lord teaches us that the truth, known by obedience to him, will make us free: our freedom lies in living the truth of our relations to God and man. For a man to be alone in the universe would be to be a slave to unspeakable longings and loneliness.

And again to speak after the manner of men: God could not be satisfied with himself without doing all that a God and Father could do for the creatures he had made—that is, without doing just what he has done, what he is doing, what he will do, to deliver his sons and daughters, and bring them home with rejoicing.

To answer the cry of the human heart, "Would that I could see him! Would that I might come before him, and look upon him face to face!" he sent his son, the express image of his person. That we might know him he came; that we might go to him he went.

If we dare, like Job, to plead with him in any of the heart-eating troubles that arise from the impossibility of loving such misrepresentations of him as are held out to us to love by our would-be teachers; if we think and speak out before him that which seems to us to be right, will he not be heartily pleased with his children's love of righteousness—with the truth that will not part him and his righteousness?

Verily, he will not plead against us with his great power, but will put strength in us, and where we are wrong will instruct us. For the heart that wants to do and think aright, the heart that seeks to worship him as no tyrant, but as the perfectly, absolutely righteous God, is the delight of the Father.

        The Voice of Job," *Unspoken Sermons: Second Series*
        John 14:9-10

August 21 — The Rights He Has Given

"Thou wouldst call, and I would answer thee; thou wouldest long for the work of thy hands." Job 14:15

But be it well understood that when I say *rights,* I do not mean *merits*—of any sort. We can deserve from him nothing at all, in the sense of any right proceeding from ourselves.

All our rights are such as the bounty of love inconceivable has glorified our being with—bestowed for the one only purpose of giving the satisfaction, the fulfilment of the same—rights so deep, so high, so delicate, that their satisfaction cannot be given until we desire it—yea long for it with our deepest desire. The giver of them came to men, lived with men, and died by the hands of men, that they might possess these rights abundantly: more not God could do to fulfil his part—save indeed what he is doing still every hour, every moment, for every individual.

Our rights are rights with God himself at the heart of them. He could recall them if he pleased, but only by recalling us, by making us cease. While we exist, by the being that is ours, they are ours. If he could not fulfil our rights to us—because we would not have them, that is—if he could not make us such as to care for these rights which he has given us out of the very depth of his creative being, I think he would have to uncreate us.

But as to deserving, that is absurd: he had to die in the endeavor to make us listen and receive. "When ye shall have done all the things that are commanded you, say, We are unprofitable servants; we have done that which was our duty to do." Duty is a thing prepaid: it can never have desert. There is no claim on God that springs from us: all is from him.

"The Voice of Job," *Unspoken Sermons: Series Two*
Psalms 8:3-5

The Rights of The Unchildlike — August 22

"Thou wouldst call, and I would answer thee; thou wouldest long for the work of thy hands." Job 14:15

But, lest it should be possible that any unchildlike soul might, in arrogance and ignorance, think to stand upon his rights *against* God, and demand of him this or that after the will of the flesh, I will lay before such a possible one some of the things to which he has right, yea, perhaps has first of all a right to, from the God of his life, because of the beginning he has given him—because of the divine germ that is in him.

He has a claim on God, then, a divine claim, for any pain, want, disappointment, or misery, that would help to show him to himself as the fool he is; he has a claim to be punished to the last scorpion of the whip, to be spared not one pang that may urge him towards repentance; yea, he has a claim to be sent out into the outer darkness, whether what we call hell, or something speechlessly worse, if nothing less will do. He has a claim to be compelled to repent; to be hedged in on every side; to have one after another of the strong, sharp-toothed sheep-dogs of the great shepherd sent after him, to thwart him in any desire, foil him in any plan, frustrate him of any hope, until he come to see at length that nothing will ease his pain, nothing make life a thing worth having, but the presence of the living God within him.

Nothing is good but the will of God; nothing noble enough for the desire of the heart of man but oneness with the eternal. For this God must make him yield his very being, that He may enter in and dwell with him.

"The Voice of Job," *Unspoken Sermons: Series Two*
Rom. 11:32

August 23 — Bound By His Will

"Thou wouldst call, and I would answer thee; thou wouldest long for the work of thy hands." Job 14:15

That the man would enforce none of these claims, is nothing; for it is not a man who owes them to him, but the eternal God, who by his own will of right towards the creature he has made, is bound to discharge them.

God has to answer to himself for his idea; he has to do with the need of the nature he made, not with the self-born choice of the self-ruined man. His candle yet burns dim in the man's soul; that candle must shine as the sun. For what is the all-pervading dissatisfaction of his wretched being but an unrecognized hunger after the righteousness of his father. The soul God made is thus hungering, though the selfish usurping self, which is its consciousness, is hungering only after low and selfish things, every trying, but in vain, to fill its mean, narrow content, with husks too poor for its poverty-stricken desires.

For even that most degraded chamber of the soul which is the temple of the deified Self, cannot be filled with less than God; even the usurping Self must be miserable until it cease to look at itself in the mirror of Satan, and open the door of its innermost closet to the God who means to dwell there, and make peace.

He that has looked on the face of God in Jesus Christ, whose heart overflows, if ever so little, with answering love, sees God standing with full hands to give the abundance for which he created his children, and those children hanging back, refusing to take, doubting the God-heart which knows itself absolute in truth and love.

"The Voice of Job," *Unspoken Sermons: Series Two*
Psalms 22:26-31

THE PUZZLING ANSWER   AUGUST 24

"Thou wouldst call, and I would answer thee; thou wouldest long for the work of thy hands." Job 14:15

It is not at first easy to see wherein God gives Job any answer; I cannot find that he offers him the least explanation of why he has so afflicted him. He justifies him in his words; he says Job has spoken what is right concerning him, and his friends have not; and he calls up before him, one after another, the works of his hands.

The argument implied, not expressed, seems to be this—that Job, seeing God so far before him in power, and his works so far beyond his understanding that they filled him with wonder and admiration—that Job, beholding these things, ought to have reasoned that he who could work so grandly beyond his understanding, must certainly use wisdom in things that touched him nearer, though they came no nearer his understanding.

If Job could not search his understanding in these things, why should he conclude his own case wrapt in the gloom of injustice? Did he understand his own being, history, and destiny? Should not God's ways in these also be beyond his understanding? Might he not trust him to do him justice? The maker of Job was so much greater than Job, that his ways with him might well be beyond his comprehension! God's thoughts were higher than his thoughts, as the heavens were higher than the earth.

The true child, the righteous man, will trust absolutely, against all appearances, the God who has created in him the love of righteousness. God does not, I say, tell Job why he had afflicted him: he rouses his child-heart to trust. How much more than Job are we bound, who know him in his Son as Love, to trust God in all the troubling questions that force themselves upon us concerning the motions and results of things.

"The Voice of Job," *Unspoken Sermons: Series Two*
Psalms 33:20-22.

1858: George MacDonald, Sr., dies of a heart attack.

August 25 — Nature's Meanings

"Thou wouldst call, and I would answer thee; thou wouldest long for the work of thy hands." Job 14:15

The appearances of nature are the truths of nature. Nature exists primarily for her face, her look, her appeals to the heart and the imagination, her simple service to human need, and not for the secrets to be discovered in her and turned to man's further use. What in the name of God is our knowledge of the elements of the atmosphere to our knowledge of the elements of Nature?

What are its oxygen, its hydrogen, its nitrogen, its carbonic acid, its ozone, and all the possible rest, to the blowing of the wind on our faces? What is the analysis of water to the babble of a running stream? What is any knowledge of things to the heart, beside its child-play with the Eternal! And by an infinite decomposition we should know nothing more of what a thing really is, for, the moment we decompose it, it ceases to be, and all its meaning is vanished.

Think for a moment what would be our idea of greatness, of God, of infinitude, of aspiration, if, instead of a blue, far withdrawn, light-spangled firmament, we were born and reared under a flat white ceiling!

I would not be supposed to depreciate the labors of science, but I say its discoveries are unspeakably less precious than the merest gifts of Nature, those which, from morning to night, we take unthinking from her hands. One day, I trust, we shall be able to enter into their secrets from within them—by natural contact between our heart and theirs. When we are one with God we may well understand in an hour things that no man of science, prosecuting his investigations from the surface with all the aids that keenest human intellect can supply, would read in the longest lifetime.

"The Voice of Job," *Unspoken Sermons: Series Two*
Isa. 40:26-28

THOSE INEVITABLE DOUBTS

"If a man die, shall he live again? All the days of my service I would wait, till my release should come." Job 14:14

In the confusion of Job's thoughts—that God was just, yet *punishing* a righteous man as if he were wicked—while he was not yet able to generate, or to receive the thought, that approving love itself might be inflicting the torture—that such suffering as his was granted only to a righteous man, that he might be made perfect—I can well imagine that at times, as the one moment he doubted God's righteousness, and the next cried aloud, "Though he slay me, yet will I trust in him" there must in the chaos have mingled some element of doubt as to the existence of God.

To deny the existence of God may, paradoxical as the statement will at first seem to some, involve less unbelief than the smallest yielding to doubt of his goodness. I say *yielding*; for a man may be haunted with doubts, and only grow thereby in faith. Doubts are the messengers of the Living One to rouse the honest. They are the first knock at our door of things that are not yet, but have to be, understood; and theirs in general is the inhospitable reception of angels that do not come in their own likeness. Doubt must precede every deeper assurance; for uncertainties are what we first see when we look into a region hitherto unknown, unexplored, unannexed. In all Job's begging and longing to see God, then, may well be supposed to mingle the mighty desire to be assured of God's being.

To acknowledge is not to be sure of God. One great point in the poem is—that when Job hears the voice of God, though it utters no word of explanation, it is enough to him to hear it: he knows that God is, and that he hears the cry of his creature. That he is there, knowing all about him, and what had befallen him, is enough; he needs no more to reconcile seeming contradictions, and the worst ills of outer life become endurable.

"The Voice of Job," *Unspoken Sermons: Series Two*
Psalms 18:30-32

August 27 — The Greatest Injustice

"If a man die, shall he live again? All the days of my service I would wait, till my release should come." Job 14:14

God settled everything for Job when, by answering him out of the whirlwind, he showed him that he had not forsaken him. It is true that nothing but a far closer divine presence can ever make life a thing fit for a son of man—and that for the simplest of all reasons, that he is made in the image of God, and it is for him absolutely imperative that he should have in him the reality of which his being is the image: while he has it not in him, his being, his conscious self, is but a mask, a spiritual emptiness; but for the present, Job, yielding to God, was calmed and satisfied.

Perhaps he came at length to see that, if anything God could do to him would trouble him so as to make him doubt God—if he knew him so imperfectly who could do nothing ill, then it was time that he should be so troubled, that the imperfection of his knowledge of God and his lack of faith in him should be revealed to him—that an earthquake of his being should disclose its hollowness, and at the same time bring to the surface the gold of God that was in him.

To know that our faith is weak is the first step towards its strengthening; to be capable of distrusting is death; to know that we are, and cry out, is to begin to live—to begin to be made such that we cannot distrust—such that God may do anything with us and we shall never doubt him. Until doubt is impossible, we are lacking in the true, the childlike knowledge of God; for either God is such that one *may* distrust him, or he is such that to distrust him is the greatest injustice of which a man can be guilty.

If then we are able to distrust him, either we know God imperfect, or we do not know him. Perhaps Job learned something like this; anyhow, the result of what he had had to endure was a greater nearness to God.

"The Voice of Job," *Unspoken Sermons: Series Two*
Job. 13:15

On Self-Contempt — August 28

"Behold, I am vile; what shall I answer thee? Job 40:4 (KJV)

Seeing God, Job forgets all he wanted to say, all he thought he should say if he could but see him. The close of the poem is grandly abrupt. Job had his desire: he saw the face of God—and abhorred himself in dust an ashes.

He sought justification; he found self-abhorrence. Was this punishment? The farthest from it possible. It was the best thing—to begin with—that the face of God could do for him. Blessedest gift is self-contempt, when the giver of it is the visible glory of the Living One. For there to see is to partake; to be able to behold that glory is to live; to turn from and against self is to begin to be pure of heart.

Job was in the right when he said that he did not deserve to be in such wise punished for his sins: neither did he deserve to see the face of God, yet had he that crown of all gifts given him—and it was to see himself vile, and abhor himself. By very means of the sufferings against which he had cried out, the living one came near to him, and he was silent. Oh the divine generosity that will grant us to be abashed and self-condemned before the Holy!

Verily we must be of his kind, else no show of him could make us feel small and ugly and unclean! Oh the love of the Father, that he should give us to compare ourselves with him, and be buried in humility and shame. To be rebuked before him is to be his. Good man as Job was, he had never yet been right near to God; now God has come near to him, has become very real to him; he knows now in very deed that God is he with whom he has to do. He had laid all these troubles upon him that He might through them draw nigh to him, and enable him to know him.

"The Voice of Job," *Unspoken Sermons: Series Two*
Lam. 3:25-33

August 29 — Nearer Than Any Wrong

"Behold, I am vile; what shall I answer thee?" Job 40:4 (KJV)

Two things are clearly contained in, and manifest from, this poem: that not every man deserves for his sins to be punished everlastingly from the presence of the Lord; and that the best of men, when he sees the face of God, will know himself vile. Any man may, like Job, plead his cause with God—though possibly it may not be to like justification: he gives us liberty to speak, and will hear with absolute fairness.

But, blessed be God, the one result for all who so draw nigh to him will be—to see him plainly, surely right, the perfect Savior, the profoundest refuge even from the wrongs of their own being, yea, nearer to them always than any wrong they could commit; so seeing him, they will abhor themselves, and rejoice in him. And, as the poem indicates, when we turn from ourselves to him, becoming true, that is, being to God and to ourselves what we are, he will turn again our captivity; they that have sown in tears shall reap in joy; they shall doubtless come again with rejoicing, bring their sheaves with them.

For the prosperity that follows upon Job's submission, is the embodiment of a great truth. Although a man must do right if it send him to hades, yea, even were it to send him for ever to hell itself, yet, while the Lord lives, we need not fear: *all* good things must grow out of and hang upon the one central good, the one law of life—the Will, the One Good.

To submit absolutely to him is the only reason: circumstance as well as all being must then bud and blossom as the rose. And it will! What matter whether in this world or the next, if one day I know my life as a perfect bliss, having neither limitation nor hindrance nor pain nor sorrow more than it can dominate in peace and perfect assurance?

> "The Voice of Job," *Unspoken Sermons: Series Two*
> Psalms 16:11

WE MUST   AUGUST 30

"'My servant Job shall pray for you, and I will accept his prayer not to deal with you according to your folly; for you have not spoken of me what is right, as my servant Job has.'" Job 42:8

I care not whether the book of Job be a history or a poem. I think it is both—I do not care how much relatively of each. It was probably, in the childlike days of the world, a well-known story in the east, which some man, whom God had made wise to understand his will and his ways, took up, and told after the fashion of a poem. What its age may be, who can certainly tell! It must have been before Moses.

The poem is for many reasons difficult, and in the original to me inaccessible; but, through all the evident inadequacy of our translation, who can fail to hear two souls, that of the poet and that of Job, crying aloud with an agonized hope that, let the evil shows around them be what they may, truth and righteousness are yet the heart of things. The faith, even the hope of Job seems at times on the point of giving way; he struggles like a drowning man when the billow goes over him, but with the rising of his head his courage revives.

Friends, our cross may be heavy, and the *via dolorosa* rough; but we have claims on God, yea the right to cry to him for help. He has spent, and is spending himself to give us our birthright, which is righteousness. Though we shall not be condemned for our sins, we cannot be saved but by leaving them; though we shall not be condemned for the sins that are past, we shall be condemned if we love the darkness rather than the light, and refuse to come to him that we may have life.

God is offering us the one thing we cannot live without—his own self: we must make room for him; we must cleanse our hearts that he may come in; we must do as the Master tells us, who knew all about the Father and the way to him: *we must deny ourselves, and take up our cross daily, and follow him.*

The Voice of Job," *Unspoken Sermons: Series Two*
Psalms 19:9-11

August 31   The Highest Must Meet The Highest

". . . and you shall call his name Jesus, for he will save his people from their sins." Matt. 1:21

One master-sin is at the root of all the rest. It is the absence in the man of harmony with the Being whose thought is the man's existence, whose word is the man's power of thought. For the highest creation of God in man is his will, and until the highest in man meets the highest in God, their true relation is not yet a spiritual fact.

The relation exists, but while one of the parties neither knows, loves, nor acts upon it, the relation is, as it were, yet unborn. The highest in man is neither his intellect nor his imagination nor his reason; all are inferior to his will, and indeed, in a grand way, dependent upon it: his will must meet God's—a will *distinct* from God's, else were no *harmony* possible between them.

Not the less, therefore, but the more, is all God's. For God creates in the man the power to will His will. It may cost God a suffering man can never know, to bring the man to the point at which he will will His will; but when he is brought to that point, and declares the truth—that is, for the will of God—he becomes one with God, and the end of God in the man's creation, the end for which Jesus was born and died, is gained.

But I would not be supposed, from what I have said, to imagine the Lord without sympathy for the sorrows and pains which reveal what sin is, and by means of which he would make men sick of sin. With everything human He sympathizes. Evil is not human; it is the defect and opposite of the human; but the suffering that follows it is human, belonging of necessity to the human that has sinned. While it is by cause of sin, suffering is *for* the sinner, that he may be delivered from his sin.

                     "Salvation from Sin," *The Hope of the Gospel*
                     Heb. 4:14-16

On this day in 1857: Daughter Irene is born.

What We Need

September 1

These are excerpts from a letter to Mrs Russell Gurney, written from Porto Fino, Italy, and dated September 1, 1878. Her husband had died a few months earlier.

.... Sometimes the change that must come in me seems so immense, it is nothing less than a birth from above. But if there be One who could call us into thought, He is able for this too. We have but a poor glimmering notion of what life means. If we were *one with* the life eternal, the delight of mere consciousness of being would, I think, be something unspeakable. The greatest bliss is just the one thing we cannot do without. As often as we get a little glimmer of truth, we are ready to feel as if now we could get on and be at peace a while; whereas it is every moment a breathing of God's breath, a walking with God, a thinking of God's thoughts, a consciousness of His presence as our deepest being: this is what we need, to live other than a broken, half-slavish life. ...

I think I can almost tell, that now in your loneliness, now that the noise of the surf of the tide of the world has receded, and will recede yet further from your dwelling, you will find more unexpected doors opening around you, and will learn more clearly than ever that you are all the time in the heart of the Father, where your beautiful husband is also. It cannot be very long. We will go on cheerfully. Our life might be a call to those beyond: "We are coming friends!" Christ be with us and teach us. I am generally, I think, perhaps always, sooner or later sent back to Him when I get into a hedge. That he knew God and was satisfied is a lovely comfort. If He lived really, all is well, and we will trust even when we cannot get things all right in our thoughts. To what a bliss we are called—to be the heirs of God! I shall one day live in the universe as God lives in it, with a pure, potent, perfect existence, at home with every form of life, because one with the Heart of all life.

You see I have been talking rather than writing to you. You will take what truth there is in it. .... I should get very sick of myself if I hadn't got God to refer the thing to ....

An Expression of Character: The Letters of George MacDonald,
Glenn Edward Sadler, ed.
Heb. 4:14-16

SEPTEMBER 2 — APPROACHING THAT HOLY ROOM

Rev. Harry Walton, as an elderly minister in the Church of England, muses on his past:

.... I find that, as I come nearer and nearer to the invisible world, all my brothers and sisters grow dearer and dearer to me; I feel towards them more and more as the children of my Father in heaven; and although some of them are good children and some naughty children, some very lovable and some hard to love, yet I never feel that they are below me, or unfit to listen to the story even of my love, if they only care to listen; and if they do not care, there is no harm done .... Even should they ... scoff at what seemed and seems to me the precious story, I have these defences: first, that it was not for them that I cast forth my precious pearls, for precious to me is the significance of every fact in my history—not that it is mine, for I have only been as clay in the hands of the potter, but that it is God's, who made my history as it seemed and was good to Him; and second, that even should they trample them under their feet, they cannot well get at me to rend me.

And more, the nearer I come to the region beyond, the more I feel that in that land a man needs not shrink from uttering his deepest thoughts, inasmuch as he that understands them will not therefore revile him.—"But you are not there yet. You are in the land in which the brother speaks evil of that which he understands not."—True, friend; too true. But I only do as Dr. Donne did in writing that poem in his sickness, when he thought he was near to the world of which we speak: I rehearse now, that I may find it easier then:

> Since I am coming to that holy room,
>   Where, with the choir of saints for evermore,
> I shall be made thy music, as I come,
>   I tune the instrument here at the door;
> And what I must do then, think here before.

Annals of a Quiet Neighbourhood, Chapter 33
Phil. 1:21-23

The World Defined

September 3

"And he said to all, 'If any man would come after me, let him deny himself and take up his cross daily and follow me. For whoever would save his life will lose it; and whoever loses his life for my sake, he will save it.'" Luke 9:23, 24

We must become as little children, and Christ must be born in us; we must learn of him, and the one lesson he has to give is himself: he does first all he wants us to do; he is first all he wants us to be. We must not merely do as he did; we must see things as he saw them, regard them as he regarded them; we must take the will of God as the very life of our being; we must neither try to get our own way, nor trouble ourselves as to what may be thought or said of us. The world must be to us as nothing.

I would not be misunderstood if I may avoid it: when I way *the world*, I do not mean the world God makes and means, yet less the human hearts that live therein; but the world man makes by choosing the perversion of his own nature—a world apart from and opposed to God's world. By *the world* I mean all ways of judging, regarding, and thinking, whether political, economical, ecclesiastical, social, or individual, which do not take God into account, do not set his will supreme, as the one only law of life; which do not care for the truth of things, but the customs of society, or the practice of the trade; which heed not what is right, but the usage of the time.

From everything that is against the teaching and thinking of Jesus, from the world in the heart of the best man in it, specially from the world in his own heart, the disciple must turn to follow him. The first thing in all progress is to leave something behind; to follow him is to leave one's self behind. "If any man would come after me, let him deny himself."

> "Self-Denial," *Unspoken Sermons: Series Two*
> *I John 2:15-17*

September 4   That The Self May Be Free

"And he said to all, 'If any man would come after me, let him deny himself and take up his cross daily and follow me. For whoever would save his life will lose it; and whoever loses his life for my sake, he will save it.'"   Luke 9:23, 24

Verily it is not to thwart or tease the poor self Jesus tells us. That was not the purpose for which God gave it to us! He tells us we must leave it altogether—yield it, deny it, refuse it, lose it: thus only shall we save it, thus only have a share in our own being.

The self is given to us that we may sacrifice it; it is ours that we like Christ may have somewhat to offer—not that we should torment it, but that we should deny it. It means this: we must refuse, abandon, deny self altogether as a ruling, or determining, or originating element in us. It is to be no longer the regent of our action. We are no more to think, "What should I like to do? But "What would the Living One have me do?" It is not selfish to take that which God has made us to desire; neither are we very good to yield it—we should only be very bad not to do so, when he would take it from us; but to yield it heartily, without a struggle or regret, is not merely to deny the Self a thing it would like, but to deny the Self itself, to refuse and abandon it.

The Self is God's making—only it must be the "slave of Christ," that the Son may make it also the free son of the same Father; it must receive all from him—not as from nowhere; as well as the deeper soul, it must follow him, not its own desires. The time will come when it shall be so possessed, so enlarged, so idealized, by the indwelling God, who is its deeper, its deepest self, that there will be no longer any enforced denial of it needful.

God's eternal denial of himself, revealed in him who for our sakes in the flesh took up his cross daily, will have been developed in the man; his eternal rejoicing will be in God—and in his fellows, before whom he will cast his glad self to be a carpet for their walk, a footstool for their rest, a stair for their climbing.

"Self-Denial," *Unspoken Sermons: Series Two*
Rom. 6:2-4

1890: Bernard marries Belinda Bird.

Taking His Yoke   September 5

"And he said to all, 'If any man would come after me, let him deny himself and take up his cross daily and follow me. For whoever would save his life will lose it; and whoever loses his life for my sake, he will save it.'"   Luke 9:23, 24

Christ is all for the Father; we must be all for the Father too, else are we not following him. To follow him is to be learning of him, to think his thoughts, to use his judgments, to see things as he saw them, to feel things as he felt them, to be hearted, souled, minded, as he was—that so also we may be of the same mind with his Father. This it is to deny self and go after him; nothing less, even if it be working miracles and casting out devils, is to be his disciple.

Busy from morning to night doing great things for him on any other road, we should but earn the reception, "I never knew you." When he says, "Take my yoke upon you," he does not mean a yoke which he would lay upon our shoulders; it is his own yoke he tells us to take, and to learn of him—it is the yoke he is himself carrying, the yoke his perfect Father had given him to carry. The will of the Father is the yoke he would have us take, and bear also with him. It is of this yoke that he says, *It is easy,* of this burden, *It is light.*

He is not saying, "The yoke I lay upon you is easy, the burden light"; what he says is " The yoke I carry is easy, the burden on my shoulders is light." With the garden of Gethsemane before him, with the hour and the power of darkness waiting for him, he declares his yoke easy, his burden light. There is no magnifying of himself. *He first* denies himself, and takes up his cross—then tells us to do the same. The Father magnifies the Son, not the Son himself; the Son magnifies the Father.

"Self-Denial," *Unspoken Sermons: Series Two*
Luke 10:38-42

September 6 — Increasing Joy

"And he said to all, 'If any man would come after me, let him deny himself and take up his cross daily and follow me. For whoever would save his life will lose it; and whoever loses his life for my sake, he will save it.'" Luke 9:23, 24

There is no joy belonging to human nature, as God made it, that shall not be enhanced a hundredfold to the man who gives up himself—though in so doing, he may seem to be yielding the very essence of life. To yield self is to give up grasping at things in their second causes, as men call them, but which are merely God's means, and to receive them direct from their source—to take them seeing whence they come, and not as if they came from nowhere, because no one appears presenting them.

The careless soul receives the Father's gifts as if it were a way things had of dropping into his hand. He thus grants himself a slave, dependent on chance and his own blundering endeavor—yet is he ever complaining, as if some one were accountable for the checks which meet him at every turn. For the good that comes to him, he gives no thanks—who is there to thank? At the disappointments that befall him he grumbles—there must be some one to blame! How could a God pour out his being to uphold the merest waste of such creatures? It is the children who shall inherit the earth; such as will not be children, cannot possess.

The hour is coming, when all that art, all that science, all that nature, all that animal nature---in ennobling subjugation to the higher even as man is subject to the Father—can afford, shall be the possession, to the endless delight, of the sons and daughters of God; to him to whom he is all in all, God is able to give these things; to another he cannot give them, for he is unable to receive them who is outside the truth of them. Assuredly we are not to love God for the sake of what he can give us; nay, it is impossible to love him save because he is our God, and altogether good and beautiful; but neither may we forget what the Lord does not forget, that, in the end, when the truth is victorious, God will answer his creature in the joy of his heart.

"Self-Denial," *Unspoken Sermons: Series Two*
Mark 10:29-31

1848: MacDonald is admitted to Highbury College, London, to study for the Congregational ministry

Made To Be Joyful

"And he said to all, 'If any man would come after me, let him deny himself and take up his cross daily and follow me. For whoever would save his life will lose it; and whoever loses his life for my sake, he will save it.'" Luke 9:23, 24

The good Father made his children to be joyful; only, ere they can enter into his joy, they must be like himself, ready to sacrifice joy to truth. No promise of such joy is an appeal to selfishness. Every reward held out by Christ is a pure thing; nor can it enter the soul save as a death to selfishness.

The heaven of Christ is a loving of all, a forgetting of self, a dwelling of each in all, and all in each.

Even in our nurseries, a joyful child is rarely selfish, generally righteous. It is not selfish to be joyful. What power could prevent him who sees the face of God from being joyful? That bliss is his which lies behind all other bliss, without which no other bliss could ripen or last. The one bliss of the universe is the presence of God—which is simply God being to the man, and felt by the man as being, that which in his own nature he is—the indwelling power of his life.

God must be to his creature what he is in himself, for it is by his essential being alone, that by which he *is*, that he can create. His presence is the unintermittent call and response of the creative to the created, of the father to the child. Where can be the selfishness in being so made happy? It may be deep selfishness to refuse to be happy. Is there selfishness in the Lord's seeing of the travail of his soul and being satisfied?

Selfishness consists in taking the bliss from another; to find one's bliss in the bliss of another is not selfishness. Joy is not selfishness; and the greater the joy thus reaped, the farther is that joy removed from selfishness.

"Self-Denial," *Unspoken Sermons: Series Two*
Rom. 12:11-13

SEPTEMBER 8 — THE ONE BLISS

"And he said to all, 'If any man would come after me, let him deny himself and take up his cross daily and follow me. For whoever would save his life will lose it; and whoever loses his life for my sake, he will save it.'" Luke 9:23, 24

The one bliss, next to the love of God, is the love of our neighbor. If any say, "You love because it makes you blessed," I deny it: "We are blessed," I say, "because we love." No one could attain to the bliss of loving his neighbor who was selfish and sought that bliss from love of himself.

Love is unselfishness. In the main we love because we cannot help it. There is no merit in it: how should there be in any love?—but neither is it selfish. There are many who confound righteousness with merit, and think there is nothing righteous where there is nothing meritorious. "If it makes you happy to love," they say, "where is your merit? It is only selfishness!" There is no merit, I reply, yet the love that is born in us is our salvation from selfishness. It is of the very essence of righteousness.

Because a thing is joyful, it does not follow that I do it for the joy of it; yet when the joy is in others, the joy is pure. That *certain* joys should be joys, is the very denial of selfishness. The man would be a demoniacally selfish man, whom love itself did not make joyful. It is selfish to enjoy in content beholding others lack; even in the highest spiritual bliss, to sit careless of others would be selfishness; but surely that bliss is right altogether of which a great part consists in labor that others may share it.

Such, I will not doubt—the labor to bring others in to share with us, will be a great part of our heavenly content and gladness. The making, the redeeming Father will find plenty of like work for his children to do.

"Self-Denial," *Unspoken Sermons: Series Two*
I Thess. 2:19-20

Beholding From Within — September 9

"And he said to all, 'If any man would come after me, let him deny himself and take up his cross daily and follow me. For whoever would save his life will lose it; and whoever loses his life for my sake, he will save it.'" Luke 9:23, 24

Dull are those, little at least can they have of Christian imagination, who think that where all are good, things must be dull. It is because there is so little good yet in them, that they know so little of the power or beauty of merest life divine. Let such make haste to be true. Interest will there be and variety enough, not without pain, in the ministration of help to those yet wearily toiling up the heights of truth—perhaps yet unwilling to part with their miserable self.

Some of the things a man may have to forsake in following Christ, he has not to forsake because what they are in themselves. Neither nature, art, science, nor fit society, is of those things a man will lose in forsaking himself: they are God's, and have no part in the world of evil, the false judgments, low wishes, and unrealities generally, that make up the conscious life of the self which has to be denied. But in forsaking himself to do what God requires of him—his true work in the world—a man may find he has to leave some of God's things—not to repudiate them, but for the time to forsake them, because they draw his mind from the absolute necessities of the true life in himself or in others.

He may have to deny himself in leaving them—not as bad things, but as things for which there is not room until those of paramount claim have been so heeded, that these will no longer impede but further them. Then he who knows God, will find that knowledge [will] open the door of his understanding to all things else. He will become able to behold them from within, instead of having to search wearily into them from without.

"Self-Denial," *Unspoken Sermons: Series Two*
Phil. 3:7-9

September 10 — Forsaking The False

"And he said to all, 'If any man would come after me, let him deny himself and take up his cross daily and follow me. For whoever would save his life will lose it; and whoever loses his life for my sake, he will save it.'" Luke 9:23, 24

There is another kind of forsaking that may fall to the lot of some, and which they may find very difficult: the forsaking of such notions of God and his Christ as they were taught in their youth—which they held, nor could help holding, at such time as they began to believe—of which they have begun to doubt the truth, but to cast which away seems like parting with every assurance of safety.

There are so-called doctrines long accepted of good people, which how any man can love God and hold, except indeed by fast closing of the spiritual eyes, I find it hard to understand. If a man care more for opinion than for life, it is not worth any other man's while to persuade him to renounce the opinions he happens to entertain; he would but put other opinions in the same place of honor—a place which can *belong* to no opinion whatever: it matters nothing what such a man may or may not believe, for he is not a true man. By holding with a school he supposes to be right, he but bolsters himself up with the worst of all unbelief—opinion calling itself faith—unbelief calling itself religion.

Good souls many will one day be horrified at the things they now believe of God. If they have not thought about them, but given themselves to obedience, they may not have done them much harm as yet; but they can make little progress in the knowledge of God, while, if but passively, holding evil things true of him. But there are those who find them a terrible obstruction, and yet imagine, or at least fear them true: such must take courage to forsake the false in *any* shape, to deny their old selves in the most seemingly sacred of prejudices, and follow Jesus, not as he is presented in the tradition of the elders, but as he is presented by himself, his apostles, and the spirit of truth.

But for him who is in earnest about the will of God, it is of endless consequence that he should think rightly about God. He will come to see that he must follow *no* doctrine, be it true as word of man could state it, but the living Truth, the Master himself.

"Self-Denial," *Unspoken Sermons: Series Two*
II Cor. 11:4-6

The One Terrible Heresy — September 11

"You did not so learn Christ!—assuming that you have heard about him and were taught in him, as the truth is in Jesus." Eph. 4:20

To the man who gives himself to the living Lord, every belief will necessarily come right; that Lord himself will see that his disciple believe aright concerning him. If a man cannot trust him for this, what claim can he make to faith in him?

It is because he has little or no faith, that he is left clinging to preposterous and dishonoring ideas, the traditions of men concerning his Father, and neither his teaching nor that of his apostles. The living Christ is to them but a shadow; the all but obliterated Christ of their theories no soul can thoroughly believe in: the disciple of such a Christ rests on his work, or his merits, or his atonement!

What I insist upon is, that a man's faith shall be in the living, loving, ruling, helping Christ, devoted to us as much as ever he was, and with all the powers of the Godhead for the salvation of his brethren. It is not faith that he did this, that his work wrought that. Do you ask, "What is faith in him?" I answer, The leaving of your way, your objects, your self, and the taking of his and him; the leaving of your trust in men, in money, in opinion, in character, in atonement itself, *and doing as he tells you.*. I can find no words strong enough to serve for the weight of this necessity—this obedience. It is the one terrible heresy of the church, that it has always been presenting something else than obedience as faith in Christ.

"The Truth in Jesus," *Unspoken Sermons: Series Two*
John 14:6-7

September 12 — Awake And Arise

"You did not so learn Christ!—assuming that you have heard about him and were taught in him, as the truth is in Jesus." Eph. 4:20

The reason that so many who believe *about* Christ rather than in him, get the comfort they do, is that, touching thus the mere hem of his garment, they cannot help believing a little in the live man inside the garment. It is not wonderful that such believers should so often be miserable: they lay themselves down to sleep with nothing but the skirt of his robe in their hand—a robe too, I say, that never was his, only by them supposed his—when they might sleep in peace with the living Lord in their hearts.

Instead of so knowing Christ that they have him in them saving them, they lie wasting themselves in soul-sickening self-examination as to whether they are believers, whether they are really trusting in the atonement, whether they are truly sorry for their sins—the way to madness of the brain and despair of the heart. Some even ponder the imponderable—whether they are of the elect, whether they have an interest in the blood shed for sin, whether theirs is a saving faith—when all the time the man who died for them is waiting to begin to save them from every evil—and first from this self which is consuming them with trouble about its salvation.

He will set them free, and take them home to the bosom of the Father—if only they will mind what he says to them—which is the beginning, middle, and end of faith. If, instead of searching into the mysteries of corruption in their own charnel-houses, they would but awake and arise from the dead, and come out into the light which Christ is waiting to give them, he would begin at once to fill them with the fulness of God.

The Truth in Jesus," *Unspoken Sermons: Series Two*
John 6:63

Do It

"You did not so learn Christ!—assuming that you have heard about him and were taught in him, as the truth is in Jesus." Eph. 4:20

"But I do not know how to awake and arise!"

I will tell you: Get up, and do something the master tells you; so make yourself his disciple at once. Instead of asking yourself whether you believe or not, ask yourself whether you have this day done one thing because he said, Do it, or once abstained because he said, Do not do it. It is simply absurd to say you believe, or even want to believe in him, if you do not anything he tells you.

If you can think of nothing he ever said as having had an atom of influence on your doing, or not doing, you have too good ground to consider yourself no disciple of his. Do not, I pray you, worse than waste your time in trying to convince yourself that you are his disciple notwithstanding—that for this reason or that you still have cause to think you believe in him. What though you should succeed in persuading yourself to absolute certainty that you are his disciple, if, after all, he say to you, "Why did you not do the things I told you? Depart from me: I do not know you!"

Instead of trying to persuade yourself, if the thing be true you can make it truer; if it be not true, you can begin at once to make it true, to *be* a disciple of the Living One—by obeying him in the first thing you can think of in which you are not obeying him. We must learn to obey him in everything, and so must begin somewhere: let it be at once, and in the very next thing that lies at the door of our conscience!

"The Truth in Jesus," *Unspoken Sermons: Series Two*
John 14:15

September 14 — He Meant What He Said

"You did not so learn Christ!—assuming that you have heard about him and were taught in him, as the truth is in Jesus." Eph. 4:20

There is but one plan of salvation, and that is to believe in the Lord Jesus Christ; that is, to take him for what he is—our master, and his words as if he meant them, which assuredly he did.

To do his words is to enter into vital relation with him, to obey him is the only way to be one with him. The relation between him and us is an absolute one; it can nohow begin to *live* but in obedience: it *is* obedience. There can be no truth, no reality, in any initiation of at-one-ment with him, that is not obedience. What! Have I the poorest notion of a God, and dare think of entering into relations with him, the very first of which is not that what he saith, I will do? The thing is absurd, and comes of the father of lies.

I know what he whispers to those to whom such teaching as this is distasteful: "It is the doctrine of works!" But one word of the Lord humbly heard and received will suffice to send all the demons of false theology into the abyss. He says the man that does not do the things he tells him, builds his house to fall in utter ruin. He instructs his messengers to go and baptize all nations, "teaching them to observe all things whatsoever I have commanded you."

Tell me it is faith he requires: do I not know it? and is not faith the highest act of which the human mind is capable? But faith in what? Faith in what he is, in what he says—a faith which can have no existence except in obedience—a faith which *is* obedience. To do what he wishes is to put forth faith in him.

"The Truth in Jesus," *Unspoken Sermons: Series Two*
Matt. 21:28-31

WHAT HAVE YOU DONE? SEPTEMBER 15

"You did not so learn Christ!—assuming that you have heard about him and were taught in him, as the truth is in Jesus." Eph. 4:20

You say you do not refuse to obey him? I care not whether you refuse or not, while you do not obey. Remember the parable: "I go, sir, and went not."

What have you done this day because it was the will of Christ? Have you dismissed, once dismissed, an anxious thought for the morrow? Have you ministered to any needy soul or body, and kept your right hand from knowing what your left hand did? Have you begun to leave all and follow him? Did you set yourself to judge righteous judgment? Are you being ware of covetousness? Have you forgiven your enemy? Are you seeking the kingdom of God and his righteousness before all things? Are you hungering and thirsting after righteousness? Have you given to some one that asked of you? Tell me something that you have done, are doing, or are trying to do because he told you.

If you do nothing that he says, it is no wonder that you cannot trust in him, and are therefore driven to seek refuge in the atonement, as if something he had done, and not he himself in his doing were the atonement.

That is not as you understand it? What does it matter how you understand, or what you understand, so long as you are not of one mind with the Truth, so long as you and God are not *at one*, do not atone together? How should you understand? Knowing that you do not heed his word, why should I heed your explanation of it? You do not his will, and so you cannot understand him; you do not know him, that is why you cannot trust in him.

It is the heart of the child that alone can understand the Father.

"The Truth in Jesus," *Unspoken Sermons: Series Two*
Matt. 21:28-31

September 16 — We May Be Sure

"You did not so learn Christ!—assuming that you have heard about him and were taught in him, as the truth is in Jesus." Eph. 4:20

We may be sure of this, that no man will be condemned for any sin that is past; that, if he be condemned, it will be because he would not come to the light when the light came to him; because he would not cease to do evil and learn to do well; because he hid his unbelief in the garment of a false faith, and would not obey; because he imputed to himself a righteousness that was not his; because he preferred imagining himself a worthy person, to confessing himself everywhere in the wrong and repenting.

We may be sure also of this, that, if a man becomes the disciple of Christ, he will not leave him in ignorance as to what he has to believe; he shall know the truth of everything it is needful for him to understand. If we do what he tells us, his light will go up in our hearts. Till then we could not understand even if he explained to us. If you cannot trust him to let you know what is right, but think you must hold this or that before you can come to him, then I justify your doubts in what you call your worst times, but which I suspect are your best times in which you come nearest to the truth—those, namely, in which you fear you have no faith.

So long as a man will not set himself to obey the word spoken, the word written, the word printed, the word read, of the Lord Christ, I would not take the trouble to convince him concerning the most obnoxious doctrines that they were false as hell. It is those who would fain believe, but who by such doctrines are hindered, whom I would help.

> "The Truth in Jesus," *Unspoken Sermons: Series Two*
> Luke 10:25-37

This day in 1854: Caroline Grace, George and Louisa's third child, is born.

The Whole Secret   September 17

"You did not so learn Christ!—assuming that you have heard about him and were taught in him, as the truth is in Jesus." Eph. 4:20

Disputation about things but hides the living Christ who alone can teach the truth, who is the truth, and the knowledge of whom is life. I write for the sake of those whom the false teaching that claims before all to be true has driven away from God—as well it might, for the God so taught is not a God worthy to be believed in.

He who believes in a God not altogether unselfish and good, a God who does not do all he can for his creatures, belongs to the same class; his is not the God who made the heaven and the earth and the sea and the fountains of water—not the God revealed in Christ. If a man see in God any darkness at all, and especially if he defend that darkness, attempting to justify it as one who respects the person of God, I cannot but think his blindness must have followed his mockery of *"Lord! Lord!"* Surely, if he had been strenuously obeying Jesus, he would ere now have received the truth that God is light, and in him is no darkness—a truth which is not acknowledged by calling the darkness attributed to him light, and the candle of the Lord in the soul of man darkness. It is one thing to believe that God can do nothing wrong, quite another to call whatever presumption may attribute to him right.

The whole secret of progress is the doing of the thing we know. There is no other way of progress in the spiritual life; no other way of progress in the understanding of that life: only as we do, can we know.

> "The Truth in Jesus," *Unspoken Sermons: Series Two*
> I Tim. 6:20-21

September 18 — How Can You?

"You did not so learn Christ!—assuming that you have heard about him and were taught in him, as the truth is in Jesus." Eph. 4:20

To let their light shine, not to force on them their interpretations of God's designs, is the duty of Christians towards their fellows. If you, who set yourselves to explain the theory of Christianity, had set yourselves instead to do the will of the Master, the one object for which the Gospel was preached to you, how different would now be the condition of that portion of the world with which you come in contact!

Had you given yourselves to the understanding of his word that you might do it, and not to the quarrying from it of material wherewith to buttress your systems, in many a heart by this time would the name of the Lord be loved where now it remains unknown. The word of life would then by you have been held out indeed. Men, undeterred by your explanations of Christianity---for you would not be forcing them of their acceptance---and attracted by your behavior, would be saying to each other, as Moses said to himself when he saw the bush that burned with fire and was not consumed, "I will now turn aside and see this great sight!" They would be drawing nigh to behold how these Christians loved one another, and how just and fair they were to every one that had to do with them! To note that their goods were the best, their prices most *reasonable,* their word most certain! That in their families was neither jealousy nor emulation! That mammon was not there worshiped! That in their homes selfishness was neither the hidden nor the openly ruling principle! That their children were as diligently taught to share, as some are to save, or to lay out only upon self! Their mothers more anxious lest a child should hoard than lest he should squander! That in no house of theirs was religion one thing, and the daily life another! That the ecclesiastic did not think first of his church, nor the peer of his privileges!

Refusing to obey him in your life, how can you trust him for your life?

"The Truth in Jesus," *Unspoken Sermons: Series Two*
II Tim. 2:15

1905: George MacDonald dies at his daughter Winifred's home in Ashtead, Surrey.

Presumptuous Doctrine?   September 19

"You did not so learn Christ!—assuming that you have heard about him and were taught in him, as the truth is in Jesus." Eph. 4:20

If any of you tell me my doctrine is presumptuous, that it is contrary to what is taught in the New Testament, and what the best of men have always believed, I will not therefore proceed to defend even my beliefs, the principles on which I try to live—how much less my opinions! I appeal to you instead, whether or not I have spoken the truth concerning our paramount obligation to do the word of Christ.

If you answer that I have not, I have nothing more to say; there is no other ground on which we can meet. But if you do not allow it *the* prime duty, then what I insist upon is, that you should do it, so and not otherwise recommending the knowledge of him. I do not attempt to change your opinions; if they are wrong, the obedience alone on which I insist can enable you to set them right; I only pray you to obey, and assert that thus only can you fit yourselves for understanding the mind of Christ.

I say none but he who does right can think right; you cannot *know* Christ to be right until you do as he does, as he tells you to do; neither can you set him forth, until you know him as he means himself to be known, that is, as he is. The true heart must see at once, that, however wrong I may or may not be in other things, at least I am right in this, that Jesus must be obeyed, and at once obeyed, in the things he did say: it will not long imagine to obey him in things he did not say.

      "The Truth in Jesus," *Unspoken Sermons: Series Two*
      Matt. 25:44-46

      This day in 1872: George, Louisa, and Greville set sail
      from Liverpool for their American lecture tour.

September 20 — Truth Will Grow

"You did not so learn Christ!—assuming that you have heard about him and were taught in him, as the truth is in Jesus." Eph. 4:20

The Lord did not die to provide a man with the wretched heaven he may invent for himself, or accept invented for him by others; he died to give him life, and bring him to the heaven of the Father's peace; the children must share in the essential bliss of the Father and the Son. This is and has been the Father's work from the beginning—to bring us into the home of his heart, where he shares the glories of life with the Living One, in whom was born life to light men back to the original life.

This is our destiny; and however a man may refuse, he will find it hard to fight with God—useless to kick against the goads of his love. For the Father is goading him, or will goad him, if needful, into life by unrest and trouble; hell-fire will have its turn if less will not do: can any need it more than such as will neither enter the kingdom of heaven themselves, nor suffer them to enter it that would? The old race of the Pharisees is by no means extinct; they were St. Paul's great trouble, and are yet to be found in every religious community under the sun.

The one only thing truly to reconcile all differences, is to walk in the light. So St. Paul teaches us in his epistle to the Philippians, the third chapter and the sixteenth verse. After setting forth the loftiest idea of human endeavor in declaring the summit of his own aspiration, he says—not, "this must be your endeavor also, or you cannot be saved"; but "If in anything ye be otherwise minded, God shall reveal even this unto you. Nevertheless whereto we have already attained, let us walk by the same." Observe what widest conceivable scope is given by the apostle to honest opinion, even in things of grandest import!—the one only essential point with him is, that whereto we have attained, what we have seen to be true, *we walk by that.* In such walking, and in such walking only, love will grow, truth will grow.

"The Truth in Jesus," *Unspoken Sermons: Series Two*
Phil. 3:16

Enjoying Their Leap-Frog

September 21

Rev. Harry Walton, an elderly parson in the Church of England, is ruminating on his past.

Ah! I should like to write for you, old men, old women, to help you to read the past, to help you to look for the future. Now is your salvation nearer than when you believed; for, however your souls may be at peace, however your quietness and confidence may give you strength, in the decay of your earthly tabernacle, in the shortening of its cords, in the weakening of its stakes, in the rents through which you see the stars, you have yet your share in the cry of the creation after sonship.

But the one thing I should keep saying to you, my companions in old age, would be "Friends, let us not grow old." Old age is but a mask; let us not call the mask the face. Is the acorn old, because its cup dries and drops it from its hold—because its skin has grown brown and cracks in the earth? Then only is a man growing old when he ceases to have sympathy with the young. That is a sign that his heart has begun to wither. And that is a dreadful kind of old age. The heart needs never be old. Indeed it should always be growing younger.

Some of us feel younger, do we not, than when we were nine or ten? It is not necessary to be able to play at leap-frog to enjoy the game. There are young creatures whose turn it is, and perhaps whose duty it would be, to play at leap-frog—if there was any necessity for putting the matter in that light; and for us, we have the privilege, or if we will not accept the privilege, then I say we have the duty, of enjoying their leap-frog.

The Seaboard Parish, Chapter 1
Heb. 12:1-3

September 22　　　　　　　　　　　　　　One Great Good

Rev. Harry Walton, now an elderly parson in the Church of England, is ruminating on his past.

For one of the great goods that come of having two parents, is that the one balances and rectifies the motions of the other. No one is good but God. No one holds the truth, or can hold it, in one and the same thought, but God.

Our human life is often, at best, but an oscillation between the extremes which together make the truth, and it is not a bad thing in a family, that the pendulums of father and mother should differ in movement so far, that when the one is at one extremity of the swing, the other should be at the other, so that they meet only in the middle; that the predominant tendency of the one should not be the predominant tendency of the other.

I was a very strict disciplinarian—too much so, perhaps, sometimes; Ethelwyn, on the other hand, was too much inclined, I thought, to excuse everything. I was law, she was grace. Yet she represented the higher; for in the ultimate triumph of grace, in the glad performance of the command from love of what is commanded, the law is fulfilled: the law is a schoolmaster to bring us to Christ.

I must say this for myself, however, that, although obedience was the one thing I enforced, believing it the one thing upon which all family economy primarily depends, yet my object always was to set my children free from my law as soon as possible; in a word, to help them to become, as soon as it might be, a law unto themselves. Then they would need no more of mine. Then I would go entirely over to the mother's higher side, and become to them, as much as in my lay, no longer law and truth, but grace and truth.

The Seaboard Parish, Chapter 2
Eph. 6:1-4

On Seeing The Unseen

Rev. Harry Walton, a parson in the Church of England, is speaking to his convalescing daughter.

As long as our Lord was with his disciples, they could not see him right: he was too near them. Too much light, too many words, too much revelation, blinds or stupifies.

The Lord had been with them long enough. They loved him dearly, and yet often forgot his words almost as soon as he said them. He could not get it into them, for instance, that he had not come to be a king. Whatever he said, they shaped it over again after their own fancy; and their minds were so full of their own worldly notions of grandeur and command, that they could not receive into their souls the gift of God present before their eyes. Therefore he was taken away, that his Spirit, which was more himself than his bodily presence, might come into them—that they might receive the gift of God into their innermost being.

After he had gone out of their sight, and they might look all around and down in the grave and up in the air, and not see him anywhere—when they thought they had lost him, he began to come to them again from the other side—from the inside. They found that the image of him which his presence with them had printed in light upon their souls, began to revive in the dark of his absence; and not that only, but that in looking at it without the overwhelming of his bodily presence, lines and forms and meanings began to dawn out of it which they had never seen before. And his words came back to them, no longer as they had received them, but as he meant them. The spirit of Christ filling their hearts and giving them new power, made them remember, by making them able to understand, all that he had said to them. So that after he had gone away, he was really nearer to them than he had been before.

The meaning of anything is more than its visible presence. There is a soul in everything, and that soul is the meaning of it. The soul of the world and all its beauty has come nearer, my dear, just because you are separated from it for a time.

The Seaboard Parish, Chapter 3
John 14:15-21

SEPTEMBER 24 — THE ONE GRAND THING

Rev. Harry Walton, a parson in the Church of England, is speaking:

Certainly I think Christ's trial on earth would not have been perfect had he known everything. He, too, had to live by faith in the father. And remember that for the Divine sonship on earth perfect knowledge was not necessary, only perfect confidence, absolute obedience, utter holiness.

There is a great tendency in our sinful natures to put knowledge and power on a level with goodness. It was one of the lessons of our Lord's life that they are not so; that the one grand thing in humanity is faith in God; that the highest in God is his truth, his goodness, his rightness. But if Jesus was a real man and no mere appearance of a man, is it any wonder that, with a heart full to the brim of the love of God, he should be for a moment surprised that his mother, whom he loved so dearly, the best human being he knew, should not have taken it as a matter of course that if he was not with her, he must be doing something his Father wanted him to do? For this is just what his answer means. To turn it into ordinary speech of our day, it is just this: "Why did you look for me! Didn't you know that I must of course be doing something my Father had given me to do?

Just think of the quiet sweetness of confidence in this. And think what a life his must have been up to that twelfth year of his, that such an expostulation with his mother was justified. It must have had reference to a good many things that had passed before then, which ought to have been sufficient to make Mary conclude that her missing boy must be about God's business somewhere. If her heart had been as full of God and God's business as his, she should not have been in the least uneasy about him.

And here is the lesson of his whole life: it was his Father's business. The boy's mind and hands were full of it. The man's mind and hands were full of it. And the risen conqueror was full of it still. For the Father's business is everything, and includes all work that is worth doing.

The Seaboard Parish, Chapter 7
I Cor. 8:1-3

What Was That Life?   September 25

"All things came into being through him, and without him not one thing came into being. What has come into being in him was life, and the life was the light of all people." John 1:3, 4

What was that life, the thing made *in* the Son—made by him inside himself, not outside him—made not *through* but *in* him—the life that was his own, as God's is his own?

It was, I answer, the act in him that corresponded in him, as the son, to the self-existence of his father. Now what is the deepest in God? His power? No, for power could not make him what we mean when we say *God*. In one word, God is Love.

Love is the deepest depth, the essence of his nature, at the root of all his being. Love is his right to create, and his power to create as well. The love that foresees creation is itself the power to create. Neither could he be righteous—that is, fair to his creatures—but that his love created them. His perfection is his love. All his divine rights rest upon his love.

What then is in Christ correspondent to the creative power of God? It must be something that comes also of love; and in the Son the love must be to the already existent. Because of that eternal love which has no beginning, the Father must have the Son. God could not love, could not be love, without making things to love: Jesus has God to love; the love of the Son is responsive to the love of the Father. The response to self-existent love is self-abnegating love. The refusal of himself is that in Jesus which corresponds to the creation of God. His love takes action, creates, in self-abjuration, in the death of self as motive; in the drowning of self in the life of God, where it lives only as love.

> "The Creation in Christ," *Unspoken Sermons: Series Three*
> John 17:24-26

On this day in 1877: Louisa, with Lily, Irene, and Ronald, leave for Italy with Mary, ill with tuberculosis.

September 26 — The Life Made In Him

"All things came into being through him, and without him not one thing came into being. What has come into being in him was life, and the life was the light of all people." John 1:3, 4

The life of Christ is this—negatively that he does nothing, cares for nothing for his own sake; positively, that he cares with his whole soul for the will, the pleasure of his father. Because his father is his father, therefore he will be his child. The truth in Jesus is his relation to his father; the righteousness of Jesus is his fulfilment of that relation.

Meeting this relation, loving his father with his whole being, he is not merely alive as born of God; but, giving himself with perfect will to God, choosing to die to himself and live to God, he therein creates in himself a new and higher life; and standing upon himself, has gained the power to awake life, the divine shadow of his own, in the hearts of us his brothers and sisters, who have come from the same birth-home as himself, namely, the heart of his God and our God, his father and our father, but who, without our elder brother to do it first, would never have chosen that self-abjuration which is life, never have become alive like him. To will, not from self, but with the Eternal, is to live.

This choice of his own being, in the full knowledge of what he did; this active willing to be the Son of the Father, perfect in obedience—is that in Jesus which responds and corresponds to the self-existence of God. When he died on the cross, he did that, in the torture of the body of his revelation, which he had done at home in glory and gladness. From the infinite beginning—from here I can speak only by contradictions—he completed and held fast the eternal circle of his existence in saying, "Thy will, not mine, be done!" This is the life that was made *in* Jesus: "That which was made in him was life."

"The Creation in Christ," *Unspoken Sermons: Series Three*
Heb. 12:2-3

We Must Choose

"All things came into being through him, and without him not one thing came into being. What has come into being in him was life, and the life was the light of all people." John 1:3, 4

Because we are come out of the divine nature, which chooses to be divine, we must *choose* to be divine, to be of God, to be one with God, loving and living as he loves and lives, and so be partakers of the divine nature, or we perish.

Man cannot originate this life; it must be shown him, and he must choose it. God is the father of Jesus and of us—of every possibility of our being; but while God is the father of his children, Jesus is the father of their sonship; for in him is made the life which is sonship to the Father—the recognition, namely, in fact and life, that the Father has his claim upon his sons and daughters. We are not and cannot become true sons without our will willing his will, our doing following his making. It was the will of Jesus to be the thing God willed and meant him, that made him the true son of God. He was not the son of God because he could not help it, but because he willed to be in himself the son that he was in the divine idea.

So with us: we must *be* the sons we are. We are not made to be what we cannot help being; sons and daughters are not after such fashion! We are sons and daughters in God's claim; we must be sons and daughters in our will. And we can be sons and daughters, saved into the original necessity and bliss of our being, only by choosing God for the father he is, and doing his will—yielding ourselves true sons to the absolute Father. Therein lies human bliss—only and essential. The working out of this our salvation must be pain, and the handing of it down to them that are below must ever be in pain; but the eternal form of the will of God in and for us, is intensity of bliss.

"The Creation in Christ," *Unspoken Sermons: Series Three*
Psalms 40:8

September 28 — God Goes On

MacDonald wrote many moving letters of condolence, of which this is an example. It is written to Eva Pym, and dated 28 September, 1889

My very dear Eva,

.... indeed I often put off writing to such as are in your sorrow, because I know that a time comes, worse than the first, and a word then is sometimes more of a help. I wish I could just flash into your minds all I think about these partings! Only perhaps you are thinking better things than I am thinking, and find the same impossibility of showing them.

I loved and love your father and look forward to having many talks with him yet. He is out of our sight, but God sees him alive—and many who love him also see him alive; and when our time comes to go—not like the demons out into the void, but home, home, home! we also shall see and love him more than ever. For God goes on to be good. He never changes, nor cares less, for his children one time than another.

We come into this world to learn to love, and have done with taking care of ourselves; and he whose one desire is to have his children love, cannot take them from each other after they have learned to love each other. The thing is not to be reasoned about, it does not need it.

Now for your outlook into the future, I send you a word I wrote since coming here:

> Go not forth to call thy sorrow
> From the dim fields of tomorrow;
> Let her roam there all unheeded;
> She will come when she is needed;
> But when she draws nigh the door,
> She will find God there before.

.... God be with you all, and then all is well. None of us will know, or I think will ever know, though we go on learning it forever, how perfectly glorious good and unselfish our Father in heaven is. We might let him have his way with us. ...

The Beinecke Rare Book and Manuscript Library
John 14:19

1865: Bernard Powell, George and Louisa's fifth son, is born.

Life Revealed In Light

"All things came into being through him, and without him not one thing came into being. What has come into being in him was life, and the life was the light of all people." John 1:3, 4

The life became light to men in the appearing of him in whom it came into being. The life became light that men might see it, and themselves live by choosing that life also, by choosing so to live, such to be.

The life is Christ. The light too is Christ, but only the body of Christ. The life is Christ himself. The light is what we *see* and shall see in him; the life is what we may *be* in him. The life is the unspeakable unknown; it must become light such as men can see before men can know it. Therefore the obedient human God appeared as the obedient divine man, doing the works of his father—the things, that is, which his father did—doing them humbly before unfriendly brethren.

The Son of the Father must take his own form in the substance of flesh, that he may be seen of men, and so become the light of men—not that men may have light, but that men may have life;—that, seeing what they could not originate, they may, through the life that is in them, begin to hunger after the life of which they are capable, and which is essential to their being;—that the life in them may long for him who is their life, and thirst for its own perfection.

That the child of God may become the son of God by beholding *the* Son, the life revealed in light; that the radiant heart of the Son of God may be the sunlight to his fellows; that the idea may be drawn out by the presence and drawing of the Ideal—that Ideal, the perfect Son of the Father, was sent to his brethren.

"The Creation in Christ," *Unspoken Sermons: Series Three*
I John 5:11-12

September 30   "Come Home With Me"

"All things came into being through him, and without him not one thing came into being. What has come into being in him was life, and the life was the light of all people." John 1:3, 4

Let us not forget that the devotion of the Son could never have been but for the devotion of the Father, who never seeks his own glory one atom more than does the Son; who is devoted to the Son, and to all his sons and daughters, with a devotion perfect and eternal, with fathomless unselfishness.

The whole being and doing of Jesus on earth is the same as his being and doing from all eternity, that whereby he is the blessed son-God of the father-God; it is the shining out of that life that men might see it. It is a being like God, a doing of the will of God, a working of the works of God, therefore an unveiling of the Father in the Son, that men may know him. It is the prayer of the Son to the rest of the sons to come back to the Father, to be reconciled to the Father, to behave to the Father as he does.

He seems to me to say: "I know your father, for he is my father; I know him because I have been with him from eternity. You do not know him; I have come to you to tell you that as I am, such is he; that he is just like me, only greater and better. He only is the true, original good; I am true because I seek nothing but his will. He only is all in all; I am not all in all, but he is my father, and I am the son in whom his heart of love is satisfied. Come home with me, and sit with me on the throne of my obedience. Together we will do his will, and be glad with him, for his will is the only good."

    "The Creation in Christ," *Unspoken Sermons: Series Three*
    I John 4:13-16

On this day in 1872: George, Louisa, and Greville arrive in Boston for their American lecture tour.

THE ONLY GOOD   OCTOBER 1

"All things came into being through him, and without him not one thing came into being. What has come into being in him was life, and the life was the light of all people." John 1:3, 4

The bond of the universe, the chain that holds it together, the one active unity, the harmony of things, the fact at the root of every vision, revealing that "love is the only good in the world," and selfishness the one thing hateful, in the city of the living God unutterable, is the devotion of the Son to the Father. It is the life of the universe.

It is not the fact that God created all things, that makes the universe a whole; but that he through whom he created them loves him perfectly, is eternally content in his father, is satisfied to be because his father is with him. It is not the fact that God is all in all, that unites the universe; it is the love of the Son to the Father. For of no onehood comes unity. There can be no oneness where there is only one. For the very beginnings of unity there must be two. Without Christ, therefore, there could be no universe. The reconciliation wrought by Jesus is not the primary source of unity, of safety to the world; that reconciliation was the necessary working out of the eternal antecedent fact, the fact making itself potent upon the rest of the family—that God and Christ are one, are father and son, the Father loving the Son as only the Father can love, the Son loving the Father as only the Son can love.

The prayer of the Lord for unity between men and the Father and himself, springs from the eternal need of love. The more I regard it, the more I am lost in the wonder and glory of the thing.

      "The Creation in Christ," *Unspoken Sermons: Series Three*
      John 17:23

        1877: MacDonald completes the manuscript of
        Paul Faber, Surgeon, the novel he thought his best.

October 2 — Our Only Necessity

"All things came into being through him, and without him not one thing came into being. What has come into being in him was life, and the life was the light of all people." John 1:3, 4

Light is not enough; light is for the sake of life. We too must have life in ourselves. We too must, like the Life himself, live. We can live in no way but that in which Jesus lived, in which life was made in him.

That way is, to give up our life. This is the one supreme action of life possible to us for the making of life in ourselves. Christ did it of himself, and so became light to us, that we might be able to do it in ourselves, after him, and through his originating act. We must do it ourselves, I say. The help that he has given and gives, the light and the spirit-working of the Lord, the spirit, in our hearts, is all in order that we may, as we must, do it ourselves. Till then we are not alive; life is not made in us.

The whole strife and labor and agony of the Son with every man, is to get him to die as he died. All preaching that aims not at this, is a building with wood and hay and stubble. If I say not with whole heart, "My father, do with me as thou wilt, only help me against myself and for thee;" if I cannot say, "I am thy child, the inheritor of thy spirit, thy being, a part of thyself, glorious in thee, but grown poor in me: let me be thine in any way, and my own or another's in no way but thine"—if we cannot, fully as this, give ourselves to the Father, then we have not yet laid hold upon that for which Christ has laid hold upon us.

The faith that a man may, nay, must put in God, reaches above earth and sky. The question is not at present, however, of moving mountains, a thing that will one day be simple to us, but of waking and rising from the dead *now*.

"The Creation in Christ," *Unspoken Sermons: Series Three*
II Cor. 5:14-15

Even In The Darkest Moments   October 3

> *"All things came into being through him, and without him not one thing came into being. What has come into being in him was life, and the life was the light of all people."*   John 1:3, 4

When a man truly and perfectly says with Jesus, and as Jesus said it, "Thy will be done," he closes the everlasting life-circle; the life of the Father and the Son flow through him; he is a part of the divine organism. Then is the prayer of the Lord in him fulfilled: "I in them and thou in me, that they may be perfect in one." The Christ in us, is the spirit of the perfect child toward the perfect father. The Christ in us is our own true nature made blossom in us by the Lord, whose life is the light of men that it may become the life of men; for our true nature is childhood to the Father.

Friends, those of you who know, or suspect, that these things are true, let us arise and live—arise even in the darkest moments of spiritual stupidity, when hope itself sees nothing to hope for. Let us not trouble ourselves about the cause of our earthliness, except we know it to be some unrighteousness in us, but go at once to the Life.

Thy will, O God, be done! Nought else is other than loss, than decay, than corruption. There is no life but that born of the life that the Word made in himself by doing thy will, which life is the light of men. Through that light is born the life of men—the same life in them that came first into being in Jesus. As he laid down his life, so must men lay down their lives, that as he liveth they may live also. That which was made in him was life, and the life is the light of men; and yet his own, to whom he was sent, *did not believe him.*

    "The Creation in Christ," *Unspoken Sermons: Series Three*
    Heb. 13:20-21

This day in 1850: Trinity Congregational Church, Arundel, Sussex, extends MacDonald a call to be their pastor.

October 4 — On Seeing God

"His voice you have never heard, his form you have never seen; and you do not have his word abiding in you, for you do not believe him whom he has sent. John 5: 37b, 38

If Jesus said these words, he meant more, not less, then lies on the surface. They were not intended to inform the Jews of a fact they would not have dreamed of denying. John himself says "No man has seen God at any time." Then he reproaches them that they had not seen God, when no man has seen God at any time, and Paul says no man can see him!

The word *see* is used in one sense in the one statement, and in another sense in the other. In the one it means *see with the eyes;* in the other, *with the soul.* The one statement is made of all men; the other is made to certain of the Jews of Jerusalem concerning themselves. It is true that no man has seen God, and true that some men ought to have seen him. No man has seen him with his bodily eyes; these Jews ought to have seen him with their spiritual eyes.

No man has ever seen God in any outward, visible, close-fitting form of his own: he is revealed in no shape save that of his son. But multitudes of men have with their mind's, or rather their heart's eye, seen more or less of God; and perhaps every man might have and ought to have seen something of him. We cannot follow God into his infinitesimal intensities of spiritual operation, any more than into the atomic life-potencies that lie deep beyond the eye of the microscope; God may be working in the heart of a savage, in a way that no wisdom of his wisest, humblest child can see, or imagine that it sees. Many who have never beheld the face of God, may yet have caught a glimpse of the hem of his garment; many who have never see his shape, may yet have seen the vastness of his shadow. The reproach in the words of the Lord is the reproach of men who ought to have had an experience they had not had.

"The Knowing of the Son," *Unspoken Sermons: Series Three*
Rom. 5:5

Who Would Know Him? October 5

"His voice you have never heard, his form you have never seen; and you do not have his word abiding in you, for you do not believe him whom he has sent. John 5: 37b, 38

If the Lord were to appear this day in England as once in Palestine, he would not come in the halo of the painters, or with that wintry shine of effeminate beauty, of sweet weakness, in which it is their helpless custom to represent him. Neither would he probably come as carpenter, or mason, or gardener. If he came in form altogether unlooked for, who would they be that recognized and received him?

Now, as then, it would of course be the childlike in heart, the truest, the least selfish. They would not be the highest in the estimation of any church, for the childlike are not yet the many. It might not even be those that knew most about the former visit of the Master, that had pondered every word of the Greek Testament. It would be no one with so little of the mind of Christ as to imagine him caring about stupid outside matters.

It would certainly, if any, be those who were likest the Master—those, namely, that did the will of their father and his father, that built their house on the rock by hearing and doing his sayings. But are there any enough like him to know him at once by the sound of his voice, by the look of his face? There are multitudes who would at once be taken by a false Christ fashioned after their fancy, and would at once reject the Lord as a poor impostor. One thing is certain: they who first recognized him would be those that most loved righteousness and hated iniquity.

"The Knowing of the Son," *Unspoken Sermons: Series Three*
Heb. 9:28

October 6 — Should The Lord Appear

"His voice you have never heard, his form you have never seen; and you do not have his word abiding in you, for you do not believe him whom he has sent. John 5: 37b, 38

I would not forget that there are many in whom foolish forms cover a live heart, warm toward everything human and divine; for the worst-fitting and ugliest robe may hide the loveliest form.

Every covering is not a clothing. The grass clothes the fields; the glory surpassing Solomon's clothes the grass; but the traditions of the worthiest elders will not clothe any soul—how much less the traditions of the unworthy! Its true clothing must grow out of the live soul itself. Some naked souls need but the sight of truth to rush to it, as Dante says, like a wild beast to his den; others, heavily clad in the garments the scribes have left behind them, and fearful of rending that which is fit only to be trodden underfoot, right cautiously approach the truth, go round and round it like a shy horse that fears a hidden enemy. But let each be true after the fashion possible to him, and he shall have the Master's praise.

If the Lord were to appear, the many who take the common presentation of thing or person for the thing or person, could never recognize the new vision as another form of the old: the Master has been so misrepresented by such as have claimed to present him, and especially in the one eternal fact of facts—the relation between him and his father—that it is impossible they should see any likeness. They are not true enough to desire that to be fact which would immediately demand the modeling of their lives upon a perfect idea, and the founding of their every hope upon the same.

For my part, I would believe in no God rather than in such a God as is generally offered for believing in.

"The Knowing of the Son," *Unspoken Sermons: Series Three*
Matt. 11:29

His Only Likeness

"And we all, with unveiled face, beholding the glory of the Lord, are being changed into his likeness from one degree of glory to another; for this comes from the Lord who is the Spirit." II Cor 3:18

What Paul cares about is plain enough to the true heart, however far from plain to the man whose desire to understand goes ahead of his obedience, who starts with the notion that Paul's design was to teach a system, to explain instead of help to see God, a God that can be revealed only to childlike insight, never to keenest intellect.

The energy of the apostle, like that of his master, went forth to rouse men to seek the kingdom of God over them, his righteousness in them; to dismiss the lust of possession and passing pleasure; to look upon the glory of the God and Father, and turn to him from all that he hates; to recognize the brotherhood of men, and the hideousness of what is unfair, unloving, and self-exalting. His design was not to teach any plan of salvation other than obedience to the Lord of Life.

He knew nothing of the so-called Christian systems that change the glory of the perfect God into the likeness of the low intellects and dull consciences of men—a worse corruption than the representing of him in human shape. What kind of soul is it that would not choose the Apollo of light to the notion of the dull, self-cherishing monarch, the law-dispensing magistrate, or the cruel martinet, accepted by the world in the church as the portrait of its God!

Jesus Christ is the *only* likeness of the living Father.

> "The Mirrors of the Lord," *Unspoken Sermons: Series Three*
> Matt. 16:24-25

October 8 — Willful Blindness

"And we all, with unveiled face, beholding the glory of the Lord, are being changed into his likeness from one degree of glory to another; for this comes from the Lord who is the Spirit." II Cor 3:18

Let us see what Paul teaches us in this passage about the life which is the light of men. It is his form of bringing to bear upon men the truth announced by John.

When Moses came out from speaking with God, his face was radiant; its shining was a wonder to the people, and a power upon them. But the radiance began at once to diminish and die away, as was natural, for it was not indigenous in Moses. Therefore Moses put a veil upon his face that they might not see it fade.

Paul says that the veil which obscured the face of Moses lies now upon the hearts of the Jews, so that they cannot understand him, but that when they turn to the Lord, go into the tabernacle with Moses, the veil shall be taken away, and they shall see God. Then will they understand that the glory is indeed faded upon the face of Moses, but by reason of the glory that excels, the glory of Jesus that overshines it.

Moses had put the veil for ever from his face, but they clutched it to their hearts, and it blinded them—admirable symbol of willful blindness. Paul says that the sight of the Lord will take that veil from their hearts. His light will burn it away. His presence gives liberty. Where he is, there is no more heaviness, no more bondage, no more wilderness or Mount Sinai. The Son makes free with sonship.

"The Mirrors of the Lord," *Unspoken Sermons: Series Three*
John 8:12

The Glory Itself — October 9

"And we all, with unveiled face, beholding the glory of the Lord, are being changed into his likeness from one degree of glory to another; for this comes from the Lord who is the Spirit." II Cor 3:18

We need no Moses, no earthly mediator, to come between us and the light, and bring out for us a little of the glory. We go into the presence of the Son revealing the Father—into the presence of the Light of men.

Our mediator is the Lord himself, the spirit of light, a mediator not sent by us to God to bring back his will, but come from God to bring us himself. We enter, like Moses, into the presence of the visible, radiant God—only how much more visible, more radiant! As Moses stood with uncovered face receiving the glory of God full upon it, so with open, with uncovered face, full in the light of the glory of God, in the place of his presence, stand we—you and I. It is no reflected light we see, but the glory of God shining *in*, shining out of, shining in and from the face of Christ, the glory of the Father, one with the Son. Israel saw but the fading reflection of the glory of God on the face of Moses; we see the glory itself in the face of Jesus.

Paul's idea is, that when we take into our understanding, our heart, our conscience, our being, the glory of God, namely Jesus Christ as he shows himself to our eyes, our hearts, our consciences, he works upon us, and will keep working, till we are changed to the very likeness we have thus mirrored in us; for with his likeness he comes himself, and dwells in us.

He will work until the same likeness is wrought out and perfected in us, the image, namely, of the humanity of God, in which image we were made at first, but which could never be developed in us except by the indwelling of the perfect likeness.

"The Mirrors of the Lord," *Unspoken Sermons: Series Three*
Phil 1:6

October 10 — His Door In

"And we all, with unveiled face, beholding the glory of the Lord, are being changed into his likeness from one degree of glory to another; for this comes from the Lord who is the Spirit." II Cor 3:18

The indwelling of Jesus in the soul of man, who shall declare! But let us note this, that the dwelling of Jesus in us is the power of the spirit of God upon us; for the Lord is the Spirit, and that Lord dwelling in us, we are changed even as from the Lord the Spirit.

When we think Christ, Christ comes; when we receive his image into our spiritual mirror, he enters with it. Our thought is not cut off from his. Our open receiving thought is his door to come in. When our hearts turn to him, that is opening the door to him, that is holding up our mirror to him; then he comes in, not by our thought only, not in our idea only, but he comes himself, and of his own will—comes in as we could not take him, but as he can come and we receive him—enabled to receive by his very coming the one welcome guest of the whole universe.

Thus the Lord, the spirit, becomes the soul of our souls, becomes spiritually what he always was creatively; and as our spirit informs, gives shape to our bodies, in like manner his soul informs, gives shape to our souls. It is that the deeper soul that willed and wills our souls, rises up, the infinite Life, into the Self we call *I* and *me*, but which lives immediately from him, and is his very own property and nature—unspeakably more his than ours.

This deeper creative soul makes the *I* and *me* more and more his, and himself more and more ours; until at length the glory of our existence flashes upon us, and we know ourselves alive with an infinite life, even the life of the Father.

"The Mirrors of the Lord," *Unspoken Sermons: Series Three*
Rom. 8:9-11

THEN INDEED

"And we all, with unveiled face, beholding the glory of the Lord, are being changed into his likeness from one degree of glory to another; for this comes from the Lord who is the Spirit." II Cor 3:18

Then indeed we *are*; then indeed we have life; the life of Jesus has, through light, become life in us; the glory of God in the face of Jesus, mirrored in our hearts, has made us alive; we are one with God for ever and ever.

What less than such a splendor of hope would be worthy the revelation of Jesus? Filled with the soul of their Father, men shall inherit the glory of their Father; filled with themselves, they cast him out, and rot. The company of the Lord, soul to soul, is that which saves with life, his life of God-devotion, the souls of his brethren. No other saving can save them. They must receive the Son, and through the Son the Father. What it cost the Son to get so near to us that we could say *Come in*, is the story of his life.

He stands at the door and knocks, and when we open to him he comes in, and dwells with us, and we are transformed to the same image of truth and purity and heavenly childhood. Where power dwells, there is not force; where the spirit-Lord is, there is liberty. The Lord Jesus, by free, potent communion with their inmost being, will change his obedient brethren till in every thought and impulse they are good like him, unselfish, neighborly, brotherly like him, loving the Father perfectly like him, ready to die for the truth like him, caring like him for nothing in the universe but the will of God, which is love, harmony, liberty, beauty, and joy.

"The Mirrors of the Lord," *Unspoken Sermons: Series Three*
I John 5:12

October 12 — So God Were There

"I am the truth." John 14:6

The highest truth to the intellect, the abstract truth, is the relation in which man stands to the source of his being—his will to the will whence it became a will, his love to the love that kindled his power to love, his intellect to the intellect that lighted his. If a man deal with these things only as things to be dealt with, as objects of thought, as ideas to be analyzed and arranged in their due order and right relation, he treats them as facts and not as truths, and is not better, probably much the worse, for his converse with them, for he knows in a measure, and is false to all that is most worthy of his faithfulness.

But when the soul, or what you please to call that which is the man himself and not his body, sooner or later becomes aware that he needs some one above him, whom to obey, in whom to rest, from whom to seek deliverance from what in himself is despicable, disappointing, unworthy even of his own interest; when he is aware of an opposition in him, which is not harmony; that, while he hates it, there is yet present with him, and seeming to be himself, what sometimes he calls *the old Adam*, sometimes *the flesh*, sometimes *his lower nature;* and sometimes recognizes as simply that part of his being where God is not; then indeed is the man in the region of truth, and beginning to come true in himself.

Nor will it be long ere he discover that there is no part in him with which he would be at strife, so God were there, so that it were true, what it ought to be—in right relation to the whole; for, by whatever name called, the old Adam, or antecedent horse, or dog, or tiger, it would then fulfil its part holily, intruding upon nothing, subject utterly to the rule of the higher, horse or dog or tiger, it would be a good horse, good dog, good tiger.

"The Truth," *Unspoken Sermons: Series Three*
Jer. 10:23

Not Merely *In* The Man

"I am the truth." John 14:6

When the man bows down before a power that can account for him, a power to whom he is no mystery as he is to himself; a power that knows whence he came and whither he is going; who knows why he loves this and hates that, why and where he began to go wrong; who can set him right, longs indeed to set him right, making of him a creature to look up to himself without shadow of doubt, anxiety or fear, confident as a child whom his father is leading by the hand, knowing that where he is wrong, the father is right and will set him right; when the man feels his whole being in the embrace of self-responsible paternity—then the man is bursting into his flower.

Then the truth of his being, the eternal fact at the root of his new name, his real nature, his idea—born in God at first, and responsive to the truth, the being of God, his origin—begins to show itself; then his nature is almost in harmony with itself. For, obeying the will that is the cause of his being, the cause of that which demands of itself to be true, and that will being righteousness and love and truth, he begins to stand on the apex of his being, to know himself divine. He begins to feel himself free.

The truth—not as known to his intellect, but as revealed in his own sense of being true, without which his nature is neither his own nor God's—trueness has made him free. Not any abstract truth, not all abstract truth, can make a man free; but the truth done, the truth loved, the truth lived by the man; the truth *of* and not merely *in* the man himself; the honesty that makes the man himself a child of the honest God.

"The Truth," *Unspoken Sermons: Series Three*
II Cor. 5:17

October 14   The Truth Of Everyman

"I am the truth." John 14:6

When a man is, with his whole nature, loving and willing the truth, he is than a live truth. But this he has not originated in himself. He has seen it and striven for it, but not originated it. The one originating, living, visible truth, embracing all truths in all relations, is Jesus Christ. He is true; he is the live Truth.

His truth, chosen and willed by him, the ripeness of his being, the flower of his sonship which is his nature, the crown of his own topmost perfect relation acknowledged and gloried in, is his absolute obedience to his father. The obedient Jesus is Jesus the Truth. He is true and the root of all truth and development of truth in men.

Their very being, however far from the true human, is the undeveloped Christ in them, and his likeness to Christ is the truth of a man, even as the perfect meaning of a flower is the truth of a flower. Every man, according to the divine idea of him, must come to the truth of that idea; and under every form of Christ is the Christ.

The truth of every man, I say, is the perfected Christ in him. The vital force of humanity working in him is Christ; he is his root—the generator and perfecter of his individuality.

> "The Truth," *Unspoken Sermons: Series Three*
> *John 15:5-6*

One With The Mighty Father — October 15

"I am the truth." John 14:6

He gives us the will wherewith to will, and the power to use it, and the help needed to supplement the power, whatever in any case the need may be; but we ourselves must will the truth, and for that the Lord is waiting, for the victory of God his father in the heart of his child. In this alone can he see the travail of his soul, in this alone be satisfied.

The work is his, but we must take our willing share. When the blossom breaks forth in us, the more it is ours the more it is his, for the highest creation of the Father, and that pre-eminently through the Son, is the being that can, like the Father and the Son, of his own self will what is right. The groaning and travailing, the blossom and the joy, are the Father's and the Son's and ours. The will, the power of willing, may be created, but the willing is begotten. Because God wills first, man wills also.

When my being is consciously and willedly in the hands of him who called it to live and think and suffer and be glad—given back to him by a perfect obedience—I thenceforward breathe the breath, share the life of God himself. Then I am free, in that I am true—which means one with the Father.

And freedom knows itself to be freedom. When a man is true, if he were in hell he could not be miserable. He is right with himself because right with him whence he came. To be right with God is to be right with the universe; one with the power, the love, the will of the mighty Father, the cherisher of joy, the lord of laughter, whose are all glories, all hopes, who loves everything, and hates nothing but selfishness, which he will not have in his kingdom.

"The Truth," *Unspoken Sermons: Series Three*
Deut. 30:6

October 16 — T̲r̲u̲e̲ T̲h̲o̲u̲g̲h̲ N̲o̲t̲ P̲e̲r̲f̲e̲c̲t̲

"... the truth shall make you free. ... every one who commits sin is a slave to sin. The slave does not continue in the house for ever; the son continues for ever. So if the Son makes you free, you will be free indeed" John 8:32; 34-36.

Those to whom God is not all in all, are slaves. They may not commit great sins; they may be trying to do right; but so long as they *serve* God, as they call it, from duty, and do not know him as their father, the joy of their being, they are slaves—good slaves, but slaves. If they did not try to do their duty, they would be bad slaves.

Where then are the sons? I know none, I answer, who are yet utterly and entirely sons or daughters. There may be such—God knows; I have not known them; or, knowing them, have not been myself such as to be able to recognize them. But I do know some who are enough sons and daughters to be at war with the slave in them, who are not content to be slaves to their father.

Nothing I have seen or known of sonship, comes near the glory of the thing; but there are thousands of sons and daughters, though their number be yet only a remnant, who are siding with the father of their spirits against themselves, against all that divides them from him from whom they have come, but out of whom they have never come, seeing that in him they live and move and have their being.

Such are not slaves; they are true though not perfect children; they are fighting along with God against the evil separation; they are breaking at the middle wall of partition. Only the rings of their fetters are left, and they are struggling to take them off. They are children—with more or less of the dying slave in them; they know it is there, and what it is, and hate the slavery in them, and try to slay it.

"Freedom," *Unspoken Sermons: Series Three*
Rev. 3:4-6

WHAT THEY DON'T GRUMBLE AT   OCTOBER 17

". . . the truth shall make you free. . . . every one who commits sin is a slave to sin. The slave does not continue in the house for ever; the son continues for ever. So if the Son makes you free, you will be free indeed"   John 8:32; 34-36.

The real slave is he who does not seek to be a child; who does not desire to end his slavery; who looks upon the claim of the child as presumption; who cleaves to the traditional authorized service of forms and ceremonies, and does not know the will of him who made the seven stars and Orion, much less cares to obey it; who never lifts up his heart to cry "Father, what would you have me to do?"

Such are continually betraying their slavery by their complaints. "Do we not well to be angry?" they cry with Jonah; and, truly, being slaves, I do not know how they are to help it. When they are sons and daughters, they will no longer complain of the hardships, and miseries, and troubles of life; no longer grumble at their aches and pains, at the pinching of their poverty, at the hunger that assails them; no longer be indignant at their rejection by what is called Society. Those who believe in their own perfect father, can ill blame him for anything they do not like. Ah, friend, it may be you and I are slaves, but there *are* such sons and daughters as I speak of.

The slaves of sin rarely grumble at that slavery; it is their slavery to God they grumble at; of that alone they complain—of the painful messengers he sends to deliver them from their slavery both to sin and to himself. They must be sons or slaves. They cannot rid themselves of their owner.

"Freedom," *Unspoken Sermons: Series Three*
Rom. 6:16-18

October 18 — What Does The *How* Mean?

". . . the truth shall make you free. . . . every one who commits sin is a slave to sin. The slave does not continue in the house for ever; the son continues for ever. So if the Son makes you free, you will be free indeed" John 8:32; 34-36.

But one who reads may call out, in the agony and thirst of a child waking from a dream of endless seeking and no finding: "I am bound like Lazarus in his grave-clothes! What am I to do?" Here is the answer, drawn from this parable of our Lord; for the saying is much like a parable, teaching more than it utters, appealing to the conscience and heart, not to the understanding:

"You are a slave; the slave has no hold on the house; only the sons and daughters have an abiding rest in the home of their father. God cannot have slaves about him always. You must give up your slavery, and be set free from it. That is what I am here for. If I make you free, you shall be free indeed; for I can make you free only by making you what you were meant to be, sons like myself. That is how the Son can work. But it is you who must become sons; you must will it, and I am here to help you."

It is as if he said, "Yourselves are your slavery. That is the darkness which you have loved rather than the light. You have given honor to yourselves, and not to the Father; you have sought honor from me, and not from the Father! Therefore, even in the house of your father, you have been but sojourning slaves. We in his family are all one; we have no party-spirit; we have no self-seeking; fall in with us, and you shall be free as we are free."

If then the poor starved child cry: "How, Lord?" the answer will depend on what he means by *how*. If he means, "What plan will you adopt? What is your scheme for cutting my bonds and setting me free?" the answer may be a deepening of the darkness. But if he means, "Lord, what would you have me to do?" the answer will not tarry.

"Freedom," *Unspoken Sermons: Series Three*
James 2:26

The Final Unity

". . . the truth shall make you free. . . . every one who commits sin is a slave to sin. The slave does not continue in the house for ever; the son continues for ever. So if the Son makes you free, you will be free indeed" John 8:32; 34-36.

Christ died to save us, not from suffering, but from ourselves; not from injustice, far less from justice, but from being unjust. He died that we might live—but live as he lives, by dying as he died who died to himself that he might live unto God. If we do not die to ourselves, we cannot live to God, and he that does not live to God, is dead.

"You shall know the truth," the Lord says, "and the truth shall make you free. I am the truth, and you shall be free as I am free. To be free, you must be sons like me. To be free you must *be* that which you have to be, that which you are created. To be free you must give the answer of sons to the Father who calls you. To be free you must fear nothing but evil, care for nothing but the will of the Father, hold to him in absolute confidence and infinite expectation. He alone is to be trusted."

He has shown us the Father not only by doing what the Father does, not only by loving his Father's children even as the Father loves them, but by his perfect satisfaction with him, his joy in him, his utter obedience to him. He has shown us the Father by the absolute devotion of a perfect son. He is the Son of God because the Father and he are one, have one thought, one mind, one heart. Upon this truth—I do not mean the dogma, but the truth itself of Jesus to his father—hangs the universe; and upon the recognition of this truth—that is, upon their becoming true—hangs the freedom of the children, the redemption of their whole world.

"I and the Father are one," is the center-truth of the universe; and the circumferenceing truth is, "that they also may be one in us."

"Freedom," *Unspoken Sermons: Series Three*
John 10:27-30

OCTOBER 20 — LESS TO BLAME

"Pilate said to him, 'So you are a king?' Jesus answered, 'You say that I am a king. For this I was born, and for this I have come into the world, to bear witness to the truth. Every one who is of the truth hears my voice.'" John 18:37

To understand his answer to Pilate, see wherein consists his kingship; what it is that makes him a king; what manifestation of his essential being gives him a claim to be king. The Lord's is a kingdom in which no man seeks to be above another; ambition is of the dirt of this world's kingdoms. He says, "I am a king, for I was born for the purpose, I came into the world with the object of bearing witness to the truth. Everyone that is of my kind, that is of the truth, hears my voice. He is a king like me, and makes one of my subjects."

Pilate thereupon—as would most Christians nowadays, instead of setting about being true—requests a definition of truth, a presentation to his intellect in set terms of what the word "truth" means; but instantly, whether confident of the uselessness of the inquiry, or intending to resume it when he has set the Lord at liberty, goes out to the people to tell them he finds no fault in him.

Whatever interpretation we put on his action here, he must be far less worthy of blame than those "Christians" who, instead of setting themselves to be pure "even as he is pure," to be their brother and sister's keeper, and to serve God by being honorable in shop and counting-house and labor-market, proceed to "serve" him, some by going to church, some by condemning the opinions of their neighbors, some by teaching others what they do not themselves heed.

Neither Pilate nor they ask the one true question, "How am I to be a true man?" The Lord is a king because his life, the life of his thoughts, of his imagination, of his will, of every smallest action, is true—true first to God in that he is altogether his, true to himself in that he forgets himself altogether, and true to his fellows in that he will endure anything they do to him. They will kill him, but it matters not: the truth is as he says!

"Kingship," *Unspoken Sermons: Series Three*
Rev. 3:15-18

The Principles of Hell — October 21

"Pilate said to him, 'So you are a king?' Jesus answered, 'You say that I am a king. For this I was born, and for this I have come into the world, to bear witness to the truth. Every one who is of the truth hears my voice.'" John 18:37

Jesus is a king because his business is to bear witness to the truth. What truth? All truth; all verity of relation throughout the universe—first of all, that his father is good, perfectly good; and that the crown and joy of life is to desire and do the will of the eternal source of will, and of all life.

He deals thus the death-blow to the power of hell. For the one principle of hell is—"I am my own. *I* am my own king and my own subject. *I* am the center from which go out my thoughts, *I* am the object and end of my thoughts; back upon *me* as the alpha and omega of life, my thoughts return. My own glory is, and ought to be, my chief care; my ambition, to gather the regards of men to the one center, myself. My pleasure is *my* pleasure. My kingdom is—as many as I can bring to acknowledge my greatness over them. My judgment is the faultless rule of things. My right is—what I desire. The more I am all in all to myself, the greater I am. The less I acknowledge debt or obligation to another; the more I close my eyes to the fact that I did not make myself; the more self-sufficing I feel or imagine myself; the greater I am. I will be free with the freedom that consists in doing whatever I am inclined to do, from whatever quarter may come the inclination. To do my own will so long as I feel anything to be my will, is to be free, is to live."

To all these principles of hell, or of this world—they are the same thing, and it matters nothing whether they are asserted or defended so long as they are acted upon—the Lord, the king, gives the direct lie.

"Kingship," *Unspoken Sermons: Series Three*
Gal. 2:20

October 22 — The Only Real King

"Pilate said to him, 'So you are a king?' Jesus answered, 'You say that I am a king. For this I was born, and for this I have come into the world, to bear witness to the truth. Every one who is of the truth hears my voice.'" John 18:37

The truth is *God*; the witness to the truth is Jesus. The kingdom of the truth is the hearts of men. The bliss of men is the true God. The thought of God is the truth of everything. All well-being lies in true relation to God.

The man who responds to this with his whole being, is of the truth. The man who knows these things, and but knows them; the man who sees them to be true, and does not order life and action, judgment and love by them, is of the worst of lying; with hand, and foot, and face he casts scorn upon that which his tongue confesses.

Little thought the sons of Zebedee and their ambitious mother what the earthly throne of Christ's glory was which they and she begged they might share. For the king crowned by his witnessing, witnessed then to the height of his uttermost argument, when he hung upon the cross—like a sin, as Paul in his boldness expresses it. When his witness is treated as a lie, then most he witnesses, for he gives it still. High and lifted up on the throne of his witness, on the cross of his torture, he holds to it: "I and the Father are one." Every mockery borne in witnessing, is a witnessing afresh. Infinitely more than had he sat on the throne of the whole earth, did Jesus witness to the truth when Pilate brought him out for the last time, and perhaps made him sit on the judgement-seat in his mockery of kingly garments and royal insignia, saying, "Behold your king!"

Just because of those robes and that crown, that scepter and that throne of ridicule, he was the only real king that ever sat on any throne.

"Kingship," *Unspoken Sermons: Series Three*
Psalms 2:6-8

We Are Bound — October 23

"Pilate said to him, 'So you are a king?' Jesus answered, 'You say that I am a king. For this I was born, and for this I have come into the world, to bear witness to the truth. Every one who is of the truth hears my voice.'" John 18:37

Is every Christian expected to bear witness? A man content to bear no witness to the truth is not in the kingdom of heaven. One who believes must bear witness. One who sees the truth, must live witnessing to it.

Is our life, then, a witnessing to the truth? Do we carry ourselves in bank, on farm, in house or shop, in study or chamber or workshop, as the Lord would, or as the Lord would not? Are we careful to be true? Do we endeavor to live to the height of our ideas? Or are we mean, self-serving, world-flattering, fawning slaves? When contempt is cast on the truth, do we smile? Wronged in our presence, do we make no sign that we hold by it? I do not say we are called upon to dispute, and defend with logic and argument, but we are called upon to show that we are on the other side.

But when I say *truth*, I do not mean *opinion*; to treat opinion as if that were truth, is grievously to wrong the truth. The soul that loves the truth and tries to be true, will know when to speak and when to be silent; but the true man will never look as if he did not care. We are not bound to say all we think, but we are bound not even to look what we do not think.

Kingship," *Unspoken Sermons: Series Three*
Matt. 5:13

October 24   He Alone

And steadfast love belongs to you, O Lord, for you repay to all according to their work. Psa. 62:12

The religious mind, however, educated upon the theories yet prevailing in the so-called religious world, must here recognize a departure from the presentation to which they have been accustomed; to make the psalm speak according to prevalent theoretic modes, the verse would have to be changed thus: "To thee, O Lord, belongs *justice*, for thou renderest to every man according to his work."

Suppose my watch has been taken from my pocket; I lay hold of the thief; he is dragged before the magistrate, proved guilty, and sentenced to a just imprisonment: must I walk home satisfied with the result? Have I had justice done me? The thief may have had justice done him—but where is my watch? That is gone, and I remain a man wronged. Who has done me the wrong? The thief. Who can set right the wrong? The thief, and only the thief; nobody but the man that did the wrong. God may be able to move the man to right the wrong, but God himself cannot right it without the man.

Suppose my watch found and restored, is the account settled between me and the thief? I may forgive him, but is the wrong removed? By no means. But suppose the thief to bethink himself, to repent. He has, we shall say, put it out of his power to return the watch, but he comes to me and says he is sorry he stole it, and begs me to accept for the present what little he is able to bring, as a beginning of atonement: how should I then regard the matter? Should I not feel that he had gone far to make atonement—done more to make up for the injury he had inflicted upon me, than the mere restoration of the watch, even by himself, could reach to?

Would it not indeed amount to a sufficing atonement as between man and man? I should still have a claim upon him for my watch, but should I not be apt to forget it? He who commits the offence can make up for it—and he alone.

        "Justice," *Unspoken Sermons: Series Three*
        Matt. 5:25-26

That Is Fair — October 25

And steadfast love belongs to you, O Lord, for you repay to all according to their work. Psa. 62:12

There is *no* opposition, *no* strife whatever, between mercy and justice. Those who say justice means the punishing of sin, and mercy the not punishing of sin, and attribute both to God, would make a schism in the very idea of God.

Human justice may be a poor distortion of justice, a mere shadow of it; but the justice of God must be perfect. We cannot frustrate it in its working; are we just to it in our idea of it? If you ask any ordinary Sunday congregation in England, what is meant by the justice of God, would not nineteen out of twenty answer, that it means his punishing of sin? In God shall we imagine a distinction of office and character? God is one; and the depth of foolishness is reached by that theology which talks of God as if he held different offices, and differed in each. It sets a contradiction in the very nature of God himself. It represents him, for instance, as having to do that as a magistrate which as a father he would not do! God is no magistrate; but, if he were, it would be a position to which his fatherhood alone gave him right; his rights as a father cover every right he can be analytically supposed to possess.

The justice of God is this, that—to use a boyish phrase, the best the language will now afford me because of misuse—he gives every man, woman, child, and beast, everything that has being, *fair play*; he renders to every man according to his work. And therein lies his perfect mercy; for nothing else could be merciful to the man, and nothing but mercy could be fair to him. God does nothing of which any just man, the thing set fairly and fully before him so that he understood, would not say, "that is fair."

"Justice," *Unspoken Sermons: Series Three*
II Cor. 5:10

October 26 — Not The Thing Required

And steadfast love belongs to you, O Lord, for you repay to all according to their work. Psa. 62:12

Punishment is *nowise* an *offset* to sin. If it were an offset to wrong, than God would be bound to punish for the sake of punishment; but he cannot be for he forgives. Then it is not for the sake of punishment, as a thing that in itself ought to be done, but for the sake of something else, as a means to an end, that God punishes. It is not directly for justice, else how could he show mercy, for that would involve injustice.

Primarily, God is not bound to *punish* sin; he is bound to *destroy* sin. If he were not the Maker, he might not be bound to destroy sin—I do not know; but seeing he has created creatures who have sinned, and therefore sin has, by the creating act of God, come into the world, God is, in his own righteousness, bound to destroy sin.

God does destroy sin; he is always destroying sin. In him I trust that he is destroying sin in me. He is always saving the sinner from his sins, and that is destroying sin. But vengeance on the sinner, the law of a tooth for a tooth, is not in the heart of God, neither in his hand. If the sinner and the sin in him, are the concrete object of the divine wrath, then indeed there can be no mercy. Then indeed there will be an end put to sin by the destruction of the sin and the sinner together. But thus would no atonement be wrought—nothing be done to make up for the wrong God has allowed to come into being by creating man. There must be an atonement, a making-up, a bringing together—an atonement which, I say, cannot be made except by the man who has sinned.

Punishment, I repeat, is not the thing required of God, but the absolute destruction of sin. What better is the world, what better is the sinner, what better is God, what better is the truth, that the sinner should suffer—continue suffering to all eternity?

"Justice," *Unspoken Sermons: Series Three*
Rev. 21:5

Wasted Cruelty   October 27

And steadfast love belongs to you, O Lord, for you repay to all according to their work. Psa. 62:12

The unjust word is an eternally evil thing; nothing but God in my heart can cleanse me from the evil that uttered it; but does it follow that I saw the evil of what I did so perfectly, that eternal punishment for it would be just? Sorrow and confession and self-abasing love will make up for the evil word; suffering will not.

For evil in the abstract, nothing can be done. It is eternally evil. But I may be saved from it by learning to loathe it, to hate it, to shrink from it with an eternal avoidance. The only vengeance worth having on sin is to make the sinner himself its executioner. Sin and suffering are not natural opposites; the opposite of evil is good, not suffering; the opposite of sin is not suffering, but righteousness. The path across the gulf that divides right from wrong is not the fire, but repentance.

Take any of those wicked people in Dante's hell, and ask wherein is justice served by their punishment. Mind, I am not saying it is not right to punish them; I am saying that justice is not, never can be, satisfied by suffering—nay, cannot have any satisfaction in or from suffering. Human resentment, human revenge, human hate may. Such justice as Dante's keeps wickedness alive in its most terrible forms.

The life of God goes forth to inform, or at least give a home to victorious evil. Is he not defeated every time that one of those lost souls defies him? All hell cannot make Vanni Fucci say "I was wrong." God is triumphantly defeated, I say, throughout the hell of his vengeance. Although against evil, it is but the vain and wasted cruelty of a tyrant.

"Justice," *Unspoken Sermons: Series Three*
Eze. 33:11-12

On this day in 1860: Ronald, George and Louisa's second son, is born.

October 28 — So Shall We Overcome

These portions are from a letter dated 28 October 1853 to "My dearest wife," during their transition away from the church at Arundel

.... How have you spent the day, dearest? It is a very good thing for us to be parted sometimes. It makes us think more, both more truly about each other, and less interruptedly about our God. He is the Truth, and all that we can see to be beautiful and true is in Him and we were taught by Him to see it. Perhaps it is a very bad want of faith in him to doubt whether he means what we see. But he knows too that it is impossible for us to be good all at once, and to be good at all without him. So we must seek him. We may however say to ourselves—one day these souls of ours will blossom into the full sunshine—when all that is desirable in the commonness of daily love, and all we long for of wonder and mystery and the look of Christmas time will be joined in one, and we shall walk as in a wondrous dream yet with more sense of reality than our most waking joy now gives us. . . .

A true Revival is springing up, and kept down I suppose in other quarters besides Arundel by those who cry most for it. But our great danger is of acting on feeling as a party. I wish to ignore and forget all opposition and be in a condition in which I can do my work for the Truth's sake, without any reference to others as opposing my teaching. We ought never to wish to overcome because *we* are the fighters. Never feel—there is *my* Truth—the hardest lesson to learn. Every higher stage of Truth brings with it its own Temptation like that in the Wilderness, and if one overcomes not in that, he overcomes not at all. The struggle may be hard. I would I could be sure of the struggle, and then I should of the victory. But Jesus overcame in the truest spiritual fight—So shall we overcome, too. Our God will surely help us to attain to that which he himself loves most. Oh dearest, whatever you may feel about our homeless condition at present, I hope it has helped to teach your husband some things. Pray for him that he may not forget them but that he may be all God's and then let God give him what he will. We may wait a little for a home here, for all the universe is ours and all time and the very thought of God himself.

I am your own
George MacDonald

The Beinecke Rare Book and Manuscript Library
Rev. 2:26-29

On this day in 1872: George, Louisa, and Greville are guests at the home of John Greenleaf Whittier in Massachusetts.

This Is The Reason

And steadfast love belongs to you, O Lord, for you repay to all according to their work. Psa. 62:12

If sin must be kept alive, then hell must be kept alive; but while I regard the smallest sin as infinitely loathsome, I do not believe that any being, never good enough to see the essential ugliness of sin, could sin so as to *deserve* such punishment.

I am not now, however, dealing with the question of the duration of punishment, but with the idea of punishment itself; and would only say in passing, that the notion that a creature born imperfect, nay, born with impulses to evil not of his own generating, and which he could not help having, a creature to whom the true face of God was never presented, and by whom it never could have been seen, should be thus condemned, is as loathsome a lie against God as could find place in heart too undeveloped to understand what justice is, and too low to look up into the face of Jesus. It never in truth found place in any heart, though in many a pettifogging brain. There is but one thing lower than deliberately to believe such a lie, and that is to worship the God of whom it is believed.

The one deepest, highest, truest, fittest, most wholesome suffering must be generated in the wicked by a vision, a true sight, more or less adequate, of the hideousness of their lives, of the horror of the wrongs they have done. Physical suffering may be a factor in rousing this mental pain; but "I would I have never been born!" must be the cry of Judas, not because of the hell-fire around him, but because he loathes the man that betrayed his friend, the world's friend.

Punishment is for the sake of amendment and atonement. God is bound by his love to punish sin in order to deliver his creation. Love is justice—is the fulfilling of the law, for God as well as for his children. This is the reason of punishment; this is why justice requires that the wicked shall not go unpunished—that they, through the eye-opening power of pain, may come to see and do justice, may be brought to desire and make all possible amends, and so become just.

"Justice," *Unspoken Sermons: Series Three*
Matt. 25:46

October 30 — Making Up For Wrong

And steadfast love belongs to you, O Lord, for you repay to all according to their work. Psa. 62:12

For Justice, that is God, is bound in himself to see justice done by his children—not in the mere outward act, but in their very being. He is bound in himself to make up for wrong done by his children, and he can do nothing to make up for wrong done but by bringing about the repentance of the wrong-doer.

When the man says, "I did wrong; I hate myself and my deed; I cannot endure to think that I did it!" Then, I say, is atonement begun. Without that, all that the Lord did would be lost. He would have made no atonement. Repentance, restitution, confession prayer for forgiveness, righteous dealing thereafter, is the sole possible, the only true make-up for sin. For nothing less than this did Christ die. When a man acknowledges the right he denied before; when he says to the wrong, "I abjure, I loathe you; I see now what you are; I could not see it before because I would not; God forgive me; make me clean, or let me die!" Then justice, that is God, has conquered—and not till then.

"What atonement is there?"

Every atonement that God cares for; and the work of Jesus Christ on earth was the creative atonement, because it works atonement in every heart. He brings and is bringing God and man, and man and man, into perfect unity: "I in them and thou in me, that they may be made perfect in one."

"That is dangerous doctrine!"

More dangerous than you think to many things—to every evil, to every lie, and among the rest to every false trust in what Christ did, instead of in Christ himself. Paul glories in the cross of Christ, but he does not trust in the cross: he trusts in the living Christ and his living father.

"Justice," *Unspoken Sermons: Series Three*
Acts 17:30-31

HE WILL SPARE NOTHING OCTOBER 31

And steadfast love belongs to you, O Lord, for you repay to all according to their work. Psa. 62:12

Justice requires that sin should be put an end to; and not that only, but that it should be atoned for; and where punishment can do anything to this end, where it can help the sinner to know what he has been guilty of, where it can soften his heart to see his pride and wrong and cruelty, justice requires that punishment shall not be spared.

And the more we believe in God, the surer we shall be that he will spare nothing that suffering can do to deliver his child from death. If suffering cannot serve this end, we need look for no more hell, but for the destruction of sin by the destruction of the sinner. That, however, would, it appears to me, be for God to suffer defeat, blameless indeed, but defeat.

If God be defeated, he must destroy—that is, he must withdraw life. How can he go on sending forth his life into irreclaimable souls, to keep sin alive in them throughout the ages of eternity? But then, I say, no atonement would be made for the wrongs they have done; God remains defeated, for he has created that which sinned, and which would not repent and make up for its sin. But those who believe that God will thus be defeated by many souls, must surely be of those who do not believe he cares enough to do his very best for them.

He *is* their Father; he had power to make them out of himself, separate from himself, and capable of being one with him: surely he will somehow save and keep them! Not the power of sin itself can close *all* the channels between creating and created.

"Justice," *Unspoken Sermons: Series Three*
Psalms 86:8-10

November 1   Not The Love We Want

And steadfast love belongs to you, O Lord, for you repay to all according to their work. Psa. 62:12

The notion of suffering as an offset for sin, the foolish idea that a man by suffering some may get out from under the hostile claim to which his wrong-doing has subjected him, comes first of all, I think, from the satisfaction we feel when wrong comes to grief.

Why do we feel this satisfaction? Because we hate wrong, but, not being righteous ourselves, more or less hate the wronger as well as his wrong, hence are not only righteously pleased to behold the law's disapproval proclaimed in his punishment, but unrighteously pleased with his suffering, because of the impact upon us of his wrong. In this way the inborn justice of our nature passes over to evil.

It is no pleasure to God, as it so often is to us, to see the wicked suffer. To regard any suffering with satisfaction, save it be sympathetically with its curative quality, comes of evil, is inhuman because undivine, is a thing God is incapable of. His nature is always to forgive, and just because he forgives, he punishes. Because God is so altogether alien to wrong, because it is to him a heart-pain and trouble that one of his little ones should do the evil thing, there is, I believe, no extreme of suffering to which, for the sake of destroying the evil thing in them, he would not subject them. A man might flatter, or bribe, or coax a tyrant; but there is no refuge from the love of God; the love will, for very love, insist upon the uttermost farthing.

"That is not the sort of love I care about!"

No; how should you? I well believe it! You cannot care for it until you begin to know it. But the eternal love will not be moved to yield you to the selfishness that is killing you. You may sneer at such love, but the Son of God who took the weight of that love, and bore it through the world, is content with it, and so is everyone who knows it.

        "Justice," *Unspoken Sermons: Series Three*
        Isa. 53:3-5

What Justice Demands

November 2

And steadfast love belongs to you, O Lord, for you repay to all according to their work. Psa. 62:12

The love of the Father is a radiant perfection. Love and not self-love is lord of the universe. Justice demands your punishment, because justice demands, and will have, the destruction of sin. Justice demands your punishment because it demands that your Father should do his best for you.

God, being the God of justice, that is of fair-play, and having made us what we are, apt to fall and capable of being raised again, is in himself bound to punish in order to deliver us—else is his relation to us poor beside that of an earthly father. A man's work is his character; and God in his mercy is not indifferent, but treats him according to his work.

The notion that the salvation of Jesus is a salvation from the consequences of our sins, is a false, mean, low notion. The salvation of Christ is salvation from the smallest tendency or leaning to sin. It is a deliverance into the pure air of God's ways of thinking and feeling. It is a salvation that makes the heart pure, with the will and choice of the heart to be pure. To such a heart, sin is disgusting. It sees a thing as it is—that is, as God sees it, for God sees everything as it is. The soul thus saved would rather sink into the flames of hell than steal into heaven and skulk there under the shadow of an imputed righteousness. No soul is saved that would not prefer hell to sin. Jesus did not die to save us from punishment; he was called Jesus because he should save his people from their sins.

"Justice," *Unspoken Sermons: Series Three*
Gal. 6:7-8

November 3 — Let Us Not Bury The Living

And steadfast love belongs to you, O Lord, for you repay to all according to their work. Psa. 62:12

A man who has not the mind of Christ—and no man has the mind of Christ except him who makes it his business to obey him—cannot have correct opinions concerning him; neither, if he could, would they be of any value to him: he would be nothing better, he would be the worse for having them.

Our business is not to think correctly, but to live truly; then first will there be a possibility of our thinking correctly. One chief cause of the amount of unbelief in the world is, that those who have seen something of the glory of Christ, set themselves to theorize concerning him rather than to obey him. In teaching men, they have not taught them Christ, but taught them about Christ. More eager after credible theory than after doing the truth, they have speculated in a condition of heart in which it was impossible they should understand; they have presumed to explain a Christ whom years and years of obedience could alone have made them able to comprehend.

Their teaching of him, therefore, has been repugnant to the common sense of many who had not half their privileges, but in whom, as in Nathanael, there was no guile. Such, naturally, press their theories, in general derived from them of old time, upon others, insisting on their thinking about Christ as they think, instead of urging them to go to Christ to be taught by him whatever he chooses to teach them. They do their unintentional worst to stop all growth, all life.

From such and their false teaching I would gladly help to deliver the true-hearted. Let the dead bury their dead, but I would do what I may to keep them from burying the living.

"Justice," *Unspoken Sermons: Series Three*
Phil. 2:5

WHAT I BELIEVE   NOVEMBER 4

And steadfast love belongs to you, O Lord, for you repay to all according to their work. Psa. 62:12

I will tell any man who cares to hear it what I believe. I believe in Jesus Christ, the eternal Son of God, my elder brother, my lord and master; I believe that he has a right to my absolute obedience whereinsoever I know or shall come to know his will; that to obey him is to ascend the pinnacle of my being; that not to obey him would be to deny him.

I believe that he died that I might die like him—die to any ruling power in me but the will of God—live ready to be nailed to the cross as he was, if God will it. I believe that he is my Savior from myself, and from all that has come of loving myself, from all that God does not love, and would not have me love—all that is not worth loving; that he died that the justice, the mercy of God, might have its way with me, making me just as God is just, merciful as he is merciful, perfect as my father in heaven is perfect. I believe and pray that he will give me what punishment I need to set me right, or keep me from going wrong. I believe that he died to deliver me from all meanness, all pretense, all falseness, all unfairness, all poverty of spirit, all cowardice, all fear, all anxiety, all forms of self-love, all trust or hope in possession; to make me merry as a child, the child of our father in heaven, loving nothing but what is lovely, desiring nothing I should be ashamed to let the universe of God see me desire.

I believe that God is just like Jesus, only greater yet, for Jesus said so. I believe that God is absolutely, grandly beautiful, even as the highest soul of man counts beauty, but infinitely beyond that soul's highest idea—with the beauty that creates beauty, not merely shows it, or itself exists beautiful. I believe that God has always done, is always doing his best for every man; that no man is miserable because God is forgetting him; that he is not a God to crouch before, but our father, to whom the child-heart cries exultant, "Do with me as thou wilt."

"Justice," *Unspoken Sermons: Series Three*
Psalms 119:46–48

November 5 — Such Is His Mercy

And steadfast love belongs to you, O Lord, for you repay to all according to their work. Psa. 62:12

I believe that there is nothing good for me or for any man but God, and more and more of God, and that alone through knowing Christ can we come nigh to him.

I believe that no man is ever condemned for any sin except one—that he will not leave his sins and come out of them, and be the child of him who is his father.

I believe that justice and mercy are simply one and the same thing; without justice to the full there can be no mercy, and without mercy to the full there can be no justice; that such is the mercy of God that he will hold his children in the consuming fire of his distance until they pay the uttermost farthing, until they drop the purse of selfishness with all the dross that is in it, and rush home to the Father and the Son, and the many brethren—rush inside the center of life-giving fire whose outer circles burn. I believe that no hell will be lacking which would help the just mercy of God to redeem his children.

I believe that to him who obeys, and thus opens the doors of his heart to receive the eternal gift, God gives the spirit of his son, the spirit of himself, to be in him, and lead him to the understanding of all truth; that the true disciple shall thus always know what he ought to do, though not necessarily what another ought to do, that the spirit of the Father and the Son enlightens by teaching righteousness. I believe that no teacher should strive to make me think as he thinks, but to lead them to the living Truth, to the Master himself, of whom alone they can learn anything, who will make them in themselves know what is true by the very seeing of it. I believe that the inspiration of the Almighty alone gives understanding. I believe that to be the disciple of Christ is the end of being; that to persuade men to be his disciples is the end of teaching.

"Justice," *Unspoken Sermons: Series Three*
Matt. 11:27

On this day in 1822: Louisa Powell born.

As God Means It

November 6

And steadfast love belongs to you, O Lord, for you repay to all according to their work. Psa. 62:12

I believe that Jesus Christ *is* our atonement; that through him we are reconciled to, made one with God. There is not one word in the New Testament about reconciling God to us; it is we that have to be reconciled to God.

Did not the Lord cast himself into the eternal gulf of evil yawning between the children and the Father? Did he not bring the Father to us, let us look on our eternal Sire in the face of his true son, that we might have that in our hearts which alone could make us love him—a true sight of him? Did he not insist on the one truth of the universe, the one saving truth, that God was just what he was? Did he not hold to that assertion to the last, in the face of contradiction and death? Did he not thus lay down his life persuading us to lay down ours at the feet of the Father? Has not his very life by which he died passed into those who received him, and re-created theirs, so that now they live with the life which alone is life? Did he not foil and slay evil by letting all the waves and billows of its horrid sea break upon him, go over him, and die without rebound—spend their rage, fall defeated, and cease? Verily, he made atonement!

We sacrifice to God!—it is God who has sacrificed his own son to us; there was no way else of getting the gift of himself into our hearts. Jesus sacrificed himself to his father and the children to bring them together—all the love on the side of the Father and the Son, all the selfishness on the side of the children. If the joy that alone makes life worth living, the joy that God is such as Christ, be a true thing in my heart, how can I but believe in the atonement of Jesus Christ? I believe it heartily, as God means it.

"Justice," *Unspoken Sermons: Series Three*
Heb. 9:26b-28

On this day in 1858: Winifred Louisa, George and Louisa's sixth child, is born.

November 7 — Making All Things Right

And steadfast love belongs to you, O Lord, for you repay to all according to their work. Psa. 62:12

Then again, as the power that brings about a making-up for any wrong done by man to man, I believe in the atonement. Who that believes in Jesus does not long to atone to his brother for the injury he has done him? What repentant child, feeling he has wronged his father, does not desire to make atonement?

Who is the mover, the causer, the persuader, the creator of the repentance, of the passion that restores fourfold?—Jesus, our propitiation, our atonement. He is the head and leader, the prince of the atonement. He could not do it without us, but he leads us up to the Father's knee: he makes us make atonement. Learning Christ, we are not only sorry for what we have done wrong, we not only turn from it and hate it, but we become able to serve both God and man with an infinitely high and true service, a soul-service. We are able to offer our whole being to God to whom by deepest right it belongs.

Have I injured anyone? With him to aid my justice, new risen with him from the dead, shall I not make good amends? Have I failed in love to my neighbor? Shall I not now love him with an infinitely better love than was possible to me before? That I will and can make atonement, thanks be to him who is my atonement, making me at one with God and my fellows! He is my life, my joy, my lord, my owner, the perfecter of my being by the perfection of his own. I dare not say with Paul that I am the slave of Christ; but my highest aspiration and desire is to be the slave of Christ.

"Justice," *Unspoken Sermons: Series Three*
I John 2:2

Go For It

Alister Macruadh entertains the dream of restoring his authority as chief of an ancient Scottish clan—for the noble purpose of serving his people well---in the modern period when clanship has long been disbanded.

The primary impulse became with Alister a large portion of his religion; he was the shepherd of the much ravaged and dwindled Macruadh-fold; it was his church, in which the love of the neighbor was intensified in the love of the relation and dependent. To aid and guard these his flock was Alister's divine service.

It was only towards the poor of a decayed clan he had opportunity of exercising the cherished relation; almost all who were not poor had emigrated before the lands were sold; and indeed it was only the poor who set sore by their unity with the old head. Not a few of the clan, removed elsewhere, would have smiled degenerate, and not without scorn in their amusement, at the idea of Alister's clinging to any supposed reality in the position he could claim. But in the hands of a man whom, from the top of their wealth, they regarded as but a poor farmer, they forgot all about it—along with a few other more important and older-world matters; for where Mammon gets in his foot, he will soon be lord of the house, and turn not merely Rank, his rival demon, out of doors, but God himself.

Alister indeed lived in a dream; he did not know how far the sea of hearts had ebbed, leaving him alone on the mount of his vision; but he dreamed a dream that was worth dreaming, comfort and help flowed from it to those about him, nor did his own soul fail to drink refreshment also. All dreams are not false; some dreams are truer than plainest facts. Fact at best is but a garment of truth, which has ten thousand changes of raiment woven in the same loom. Let the dreamer only do the truth of his dream. And one day he will realize all that was worth realizing in it—and a great deal more and better than it contained.

What's Mine's Mine, Chapter 5.
Exod. 33:12-13

NOVEMBER 9 — MY NEIGHBOR A REVOLUTION

Respect and graciousness from each to each is of the very essence of Christianity, independently of rank, or possession, or relation. A certain roughness and rudeness have usurped upon the intercourse of the century. It comes of the spread of imagined greatness; true greatness, unconscious of itself, cannot find expression other than gracious. In the presence of another, a man of true breeding is but faintly aware of his own self, and keenly aware of the other's self.

Before the human—that bush which, however trodden and peeled, yet burns with the divine presence—the man who thinks of the homage due to him, and not of the homage owing by him, is essentially rude. Mammon is slowly stifling and desiccating Rank; both are miserable deities, but the one is yet meaner than the other. Unrefined families with money are received with open arms and honors paid, in circles where a better breeding than theirs has hitherto prevailed: this, working along with the natural law of corruption where is no aspiration, has gradually caused the deterioration of which I speak.

Courtesy will never regain her former position, but she will be raised to a much higher; like Duty, she will be known as a daughter of the living God, "the first stocke father of gentilnes;" for in his neighbor every man will see a revelation of the Most High.

What's Mine's Mine, Chapter 8.
James 2:1-4

Human Chickens   November 10

Ian Macruadh, a young Scotchman with a probing Christian mind, is escorting home from a rural dance Mercy Palmer, a girl who is just barely awakening to divine realities

Ian had not proposed to Mercy that they should walk together; but when the issuing crowd began to break into twos and threes, they found themselves side by side. The company took its way along the ridge, and the road eastward. The night was clear, and like a great sapphire frosted with topazes—reminding Ian that, solid as is the world under our feet, it hangs in the will of God. Mercy and he walked for some time in silence. It was a sudden change from the low barn, the dull candles, and the excitement of the dance, to the awful space, the clear pure far-off lights, and the great stillness.

Both felt it, though differently. There was in both of them the quest after peace. It is not the banished demon only that wanders seeking rest, but souls upon souls, in ever growing numbers. The world and Hades swarm with them. They long after a repose that is not mere cessation of labor: there is a positive, an active rest. Mercy was only beginning to seek it, and that without knowing what it was she needed. Ian sought it in silence with God; she in creaking intercourse with her kind. Naturally ready to fall into gloom, but healthy enough to avoid it, she would rush at anything to do—not to keep herself from thinking, for she had hardly begun to think, but to escape that heavy sense of non-existence, that weary and restless want which is the only form life can take to the yet unliving, those who have not yet awaked and arisen from the dead.

She was a human chicken that had begun to be aware of herself, but had not yet attacked the shell that enclosed her: because it was transparent, and she could see life about her, she did not know that she was in a shell, or that, if she did not put forth the might of her own life, she was sealing herself up: a life in death, in her antenatal coffin. Many who think themselves free have never yet even seen the shell that imprisons them—know nothing of the liberty wherewith the Lord of our life would set them free. What they call the world is but their shell, which is all the time killing the infant Christ that houses with them!

What's Mine's Mine, Chapter 17
John 14:27

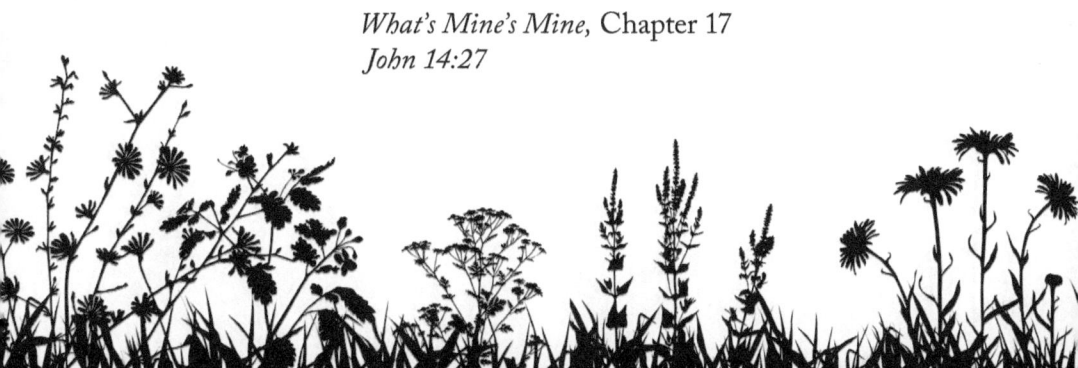

November 11 — The All-Sufficient Antidote

The following is an except from a letter written in 1894 to "My loved and honored old friend."

. . . The shadows of the evening that precedes a lovelier morning are drawing down around us both. But our God is in the shadows as in the shine, and all is and will be well; have we not seen his glory in the face of Jesus? And do we not know him a little? Have we not found the antidote to the theology of men in the Lord himself? I may almost say I believe in nothing but in Jesus Christ, and I know that when life was hardest for him, he was still thoroughly content with his father, whom he knew perfectly, and whom he has labored and is laboring to make known. We do know and we shall go on to know him. This life is a lovely school-time, but I never was content with it. I look for better—oh, so far better! I think we do not yet know the joy of mere existence. To exist is to be a child of God; and to know it, to feel it, is to rejoice evermore. May the loving father be near you and may you know it, and be perfectly at peace all the way into the home-country, and to the palace-home of the living one—the life of our life.

Next month I shall be 70, and I am humbler a good deal than when I was 20. To be rid of self is to have the heart bare to God and to the neighbor—to *have* all life ours, and possess all things. I see, in my mind's eye, the little children clambering up to sit on the throne with Jesus. My God, art thou not as good as we are capable of imagining thee? Shall we dream a better goodness than thou hast ever thought of? Be thyself, and all is well with us.

. . . It seems to me that the antidote to party-spirit is church history, and when the antidote itself has made you miserably ill, the cure is the gospel pure and simple—the story and words of Jesus. I care for no church but that of which every obedient disciple of the Lord, and no one else, is a member . . . .

The Beinecke Rare Book and Manuscript Library
Heb. 11:13-15

WHAT ELSE BUT LOOK ONWARD?   NOVEMBER 12

Ian Macruadh is here confiding to his brother Alister his hope for future life:

"Did he [Christ] say there would be no love there, Alister? Most people seem to fancy he did, for how else could they forget the dead as they do, and look so little for their resurrection? Few can be said really to believe in any hereafter worth believing in. How many go against the liking of the dead the moment they are gone—behave as if they were nowhere, and could never call them to account! Their plans do not recognize their existence; the life beyond is no factor in their life here. If God has given me a hope altogether beyond anything I could have generated for myself, beyond all the likelihoods and fulfilments around me, what can I do but give him room to verify it—what but look onward!

"Some people's bodies get so tired that they long for the rest of the grave; it is my soul that gets tired, and I know the grave can give that no rest; I look for the rest of more life, more strength, more love. But God is not shut up in heaven, neither is there one law of life there and another here; I desire more life here, and shall have it, for what is needful for this world is to be had in this world. In proportion as I become one with God, I shall have it. This world never did seem my home; I have never felt quite comfortable in it; I have yet to find, and shall find the perfect home I have not felt this world, even my mother's bosom to be. Nature herself is not lovely enough to satisfy me. Nor can it be that I am beside myself, seeing I care only for the will of God, not for my own. For what is madness but two or more wills in one body? Does the Bible itself not tell us that we are pilgrims and strangers in the world, that here we have no abiding city? It is but a place to which we come to be made ready for another.

"Yet I am sure those who regard it as their home are not half so well pleased with it as I. They are always grumbling at it. They complain that their plans are thwarted, and when they succeed they do not give them the satisfaction they expected. Yet they mock at him who says he seeks a better country!"

What's Mine's Mine, Chapter 22.
II Cor. 5:4-5

November 13   Selfishness Vaporizes Reality

Ian Macruadh has just rescued Christina Palmer from drowning:

How was it that, now first in danger, self came less to the front with her than usual? It was that now first she was face to face with reality. Until this moment her life had been an affair of unrealities. Her selfishness had thinned, as it were vaporized, every reality that approached her. Solidity is not enough to teach some natures reality; they must hurt themselves against the solid ere they realize its solidity.

It is when we are most aware of the *factitude* of things, that we are most aware of our need of God, and most able to trust him; when most aware of their presence, the soul finds it easiest to withdraw from them, and seek its safety with the maker of it and them. The recognition of inexorable reality in any shape, or kind, or way, tends to rouse the soul to the yet more real, to its relations with higher and deeper existence. It is not the hysterical alone for whom the great dash of cold water is good. All who dream life instead of living it, require some similar shock. Of the kind is every disappointment, every reverse, every tragedy of life. The true in even the lowest kind, is of the truth, and to be compelled to feel even that, is to be driven a trifle nearer to the truth of being, of creation, of God. Hence this sharp contact with Nature tended to make Christina less selfish; it made her forget herself, so far as to care for her helper as well as herself.

It must be remembered, however, that her selfishness was not the cultivated and ingrained selfishness of a long life, but that of an uneducated, that is undeveloped nature. Her being had not degenerated by sinning against light known as light; it had not been consciously enlightened at all; it had scarcely as yet begun to grow. It was not lying dead, only unawakened. I would not be understood to imply that she was nowise to blame—but that she was by no means so much to blame as one who has but suspected the presence of a truth, and from selfishness or self-admiration has turned from it. She was to blame wherever she had not done as her conscience feebly told her; and she had not made progress just because she had neglected the little things concerning which she had promptings. There are many who do not enter the kingdom of heaven just because they will not believe the tiny key that is handed them, fit to open its hospitable gate.

What's Mine's Mine, Chapter 22.
Eccl. 3:22a

A Common Human Mistake   November 14

Alister Macruadh has entertained the dream of restoring his authority as chief of an ancient Scottish clan—for the noble purpose of serving his people well---in the modern period when clanship has long been disbanded. He now discovers the bank has squandered the money he had hoped to use for this purpose.

We have to be delivered from the evils of which we are unaware as well as from those we hate; and the chief had to be set free from his unconscious worship of Mammon. He did not worship Mammon by yielding homage to riches; he did not make a man's money his pedestal; had he been himself a millionaire, he would not have connived at being therefore held in honor; but, ever consciously aware of the deteriorating condition of the country, and pitifully regarding the hundred and fifty souls who yet looked to him as their head, often turning it over in his mind how to shepherd them should things come to a crisis, his abiding, ever recurring comfort was the money from the last sale of the property, and now accumulating ever since, to be his in a very few years. He always thought, I say, first of this money and not first of God. He imagined it an exhaustible sum, a power with which for his clan he could work wonders. But he never thought of it otherwise than as belonging to the clan; never imagined the least liberty to use it save in the direct service of his people. And all the time, the very shadow of this money was disappearing from the face of the earth. It is the common human mistake to think of money as a power and not as a mere tool.

It had scarcely been deposited where the old laird judged it as safe as in the Bank of England, when schemes and speculations were entered into by the interested company which brought into jeopardy every thing it held, and things had been going from bad to worse ever since. Annihilation had long closed in upon the fund which the chief regarded as the sheet-anchor of his clan: he trusted in Mammon, and Mammon had played him a rogues' trick.

The most degrading wrong to ourselves, and the worst eventual wrong to others, is to trust in any thing or person but the living God: it was an evil thing from which the chief had sore need to be delivered. Even those who help us we must regard as the loving hands of the great heart of the universe, else we do God wrong, and will come to do them wrong also.

What's Mine's Mine, Chapter 32.
Psalms 33:16-22

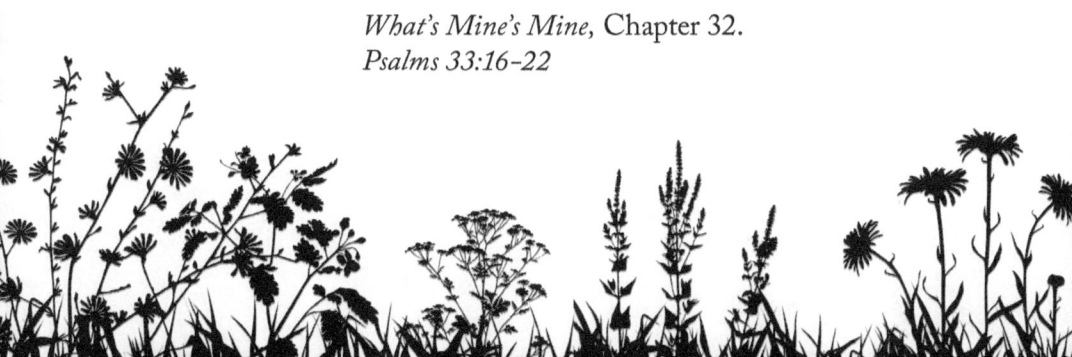

November 15   Righteous Are Worth Troubling

Ian Macruadh here perceives that his brother Alister, who in spite of his moral stature is deeply shaken by a recent loss of money, has been putting material things rather than God first in his life.

Ian, having himself learned the lesson that, so long as a man is dependent on anything earthly, he is not a free man, was very desirous to have his brother free also. Alister's love of the material world, of the soil of his ancestral acres, was, Ian plainly saw, not yet one with the meaning and will of God: he was not yet content that the home of his fathers should fare as the father of fathers pleased. He was therefore on the outlook for the right opportunity of having another talk with him on the subject.

That those who are trying to be good are more continuously troubled than the indifferent, has for ages been a puzzle. "I saw the wicked spreading like a green bay tree," says king David; and he was far from having fathomed the mystery when he got his mind at rest about it. Is it not simply that the righteous are worth troubling? That they are capable of receiving good from being troubled?

As a man advances, more and more is required of him. A wrong thing in the good man becomes more and more wrong as he draws nearer to freedom from it. His friends may say how seldom he offends; but every time he offends, he is the more to blame. Some are allowed to go on because it would be of no use to stop them yet; nothing would yet make them listen to wisdom. There must be many who, like Dives, need the bitter contrast between the good things of this life and the evil things of the next, to wake them up. In this life they are not only fools, and insist on being treated as fools, but would have God consent to treat them as if he too had no wisdom! The chief was one in whom was no guile, but he was far from perfect: any man is far from perfect whose sense of well-being could be altered by any change of circumstances. A man unable to do without this thing or that, is not yet in sight of his perfection, therefore not out of sight of suffering. They who do not know suffering, may well doubt if they have yet started on the way *to be*.

What's Mine's Mine, Chapter 32.
Phil. 4:12-13

True Possession

November 16

Alister Macruadh, having just been carefully told by his brother Ian that he has been putting material things rather than God first in his life, is here considering what his brother has said.

He did not know how much of the worldly mingled with the true was in him. He loved his people, and was unselfishly intent on helping them to the utmost; but [since] the thought that he was their chief was no small satisfaction and the relation between them was a grand one, self had there the more soil wherein to spread its creeping choke-grass roots.

In like manner, his love of nature nourished the parasite *possession*. He had but those bare hill-sides, and those few rich acres, yet when, from his eyry on the hill-top, he looked down among the valleys, his heart would murmur within him, "From my feet the brook flows gurgling to water my fields! The wild moors around me feed my sheep! Yon glen is full of my people!" Even with the pure smell of the earth, mingled the sense of its possession. When, stepping from his cave-house, he saw the sun rise on the outstretched grandeur of the mountain-world, and felt the earth a new creation as truly as when Adam first opened his eyes on its glory, his heart would give one little heave more at the thought that a portion of it was his own.

But all is man's only *because* it is God's. The true possession of anything is to see and feel in it what God made it for; and the uplifting of the soul by that knowledge, is the joy of true having. The Lord had no land of his own. He did not care to have it, any more than the twelve legions of angels he would not pray for: his pupils must not care for things he did not care for. He had no place to lay his head in—had not even a grave of his own. For want of a boat he had once to walk the rough Galilean sea. True, he might have gone with the rest, but he had to stop behind to pray: he could not do without that. Once he sent a fish to fetch him money, but only to pay a tax. He had even to borrow the few loaves and little fishes from a boy, to feed his five thousand with.

What's Mine's Mine, Chapter 32.
Luke 12:15

November 17   No Life But Love

As Mercy Palmer's love for Alister Macruadh dawns, so does her interest in spiritual things:

It was love, in part, that now awoke in Mercy a hunger and thirst after heavenly things. This is a direction of its power little heeded by its historians; its earthly side occupies almost all their care. Because lovers are not worthy of even its earthly aspect, it palls upon them, and they grow weary, not of love, but of their lack of it. The want of the heavenly in it has caused it to perish; it had no salt.

From those that have not is taken away that which they have. Love without religion is the plucked rose. Religion without love—there is no such thing. Religion is the bush that bears all the roses; for religion is the natural condition of man in relation to the eternal facts, that is the truths, of his own being. To live is to love; there is no life but love. What shape the love puts on, depends on the persons between whom is the relation. The poorest love with religion, is better, because truer, therefore more lasting, more genuine, more endowed with the possibility of persistence—that is, of infinite development, than the most passionate devotion between man and woman without it.

What's Mine's Mine, Chapter 35.
I Cor. 13:1-3

Living In Things Themselves   November 18

Alister Macruadh, in a period of uncertainty, is trying to surmise what the will of God is:

All the morning he was busy in the corn yard—with his hands in preparing new stances for ricks, with his heart in trying to content himself before hand with whatever fate the Lord might intend for him. As yet he was more of a Christian philosopher than a philosophical Christian. The thing most disappointing to him he would treat as the will of God for him, and try to make up his mind to it, persuading himself it was the right and best thing—as if he knew it the will of God.

He was thus working in the region of supposition, and not of revealed duty; in his own imagination, and not in the will of God. If this should not prove the will of God concerning him, then he was spending his strength for naught. There is something in the very presence and actuality of a thing to make one able to bear it; but a man may weaken himself for bearing what God intends him to bear, by trying to bear what God does not intend him to bear. The chief was forestalling the morrow like an unbeliever—not without some moral advantage, I dare say, but with spiritual loss.

We have no right to school ourselves to an imaginary duty. When we do not know, then what he lays upon us is *not to know*, and to be content not to know. The philosopher is he who lives in the thought of things, the Christian is he who lives in the things themselves. The philosopher occupies himself with God's decree, the Christian with God's will; the philosopher with what God may intend, the Christian with what God wants *him to do*.

What's Mine's Mine, Chapter 40.
Prov. 3:5-6

November 19 — A Painful Discovery

Alister Macruadh had long placed his faith in a legacy from his uncle, who in his lifetime had made it wrongfully, to help the poverty-stricken people of his Scottish clan. He here discovers that it has all been lost in bad investment:

Alister did not jump up and pace the room in the rage of disappointment; neither did he sit as one stunned and forlorn of sense. He felt some bitterness in the loss of the hope of making up to his people for his uncle's wrong; but it was clear that if God had cared for his having the money, he would have cared that he should have it. Here was an opportunity for absolute faith and contentment in the will that looks after all our affairs, the small as well as the great.

Those who think their affairs too insignificant for God's regard, will justify themselves in lying crushed under their seeming ruin. Either we live in the heart of an eternal thought, or we are the product and sport of that which is lower than we.

"It was evil money!" said the chief to himself' "it was the sale of a birthright for a mess of pottage! I would have turned it back into the right channel, the good of my people! But after all, what can money do? It was discontent with poverty that began the ruin of the highlands! If the heads of the people had but lived, pure, active, sober, unostentatious lives, content to be poor, poverty would never have overwhelmed them!"

Therewith it dawned upon Alister how, when he longed to help his people, his thoughts had always turned, not to God first; but to the money his uncle had left him. He had trust in a fancy; for trust in money that is, is less vain, and is farther from redress, than trust in money that is not. In God alone can trust repose. His heart had been so faithless that he did not know it was! He thought he loved God as the first and last, the beginning, middle, and end of all things, and he had been trusting, not in God, but in uncertain riches, that is in mammon! It was a painful and humiliating discovery.

What's Mine's Mine, Chapter 45.
Matt. 10:28-31

WE SHALL SEE LIGHT

This is the message we have heard from him and proclaim to you, that God is light and in him there is no darkness at all. And this is the judgment, that the light has come into the world, and people loved darkness rather than light because their deeds were evil. I John 1:5; John 3:19

    I love the light, and will not believe at the word of any man, or upon the conviction of any man, that that which seems to me darkness is in God. Where would the good news be if John said, "God is light, but you cannot see his light; you cannot tell, you have no notion, what light is; what God means by light, is not what you mean by light; what God calls light may be horrible darkness to you, for you are of another nature from him!" Where, I say, would be the good news of that?

    To say that what our deepest conscience calls darkness may be light to God, is blasphemy; to say light in God and light in man are differing kinds, is to speak against the spirit of light. God is light far beyond what we can see, but what we mean by light, God means by light; and what is light to God is light to us, or would be light to us if we saw it, and will be light to us when we do see it. God means us to be jubilant in the fact that he is light—that he is what his children, made in his image, mean when they say *light*; that what in him is dark to them, is dark by excellent glory, by too much cause of jubilation; that, however dark it may be to their eyes, it is light even as they mean it, light for their eyes and souls and hearts to take in the moment they are enough of eyes, enough of souls, enough of hearts, to receive it in its very being.

    Living Light, thou wilt not have me believe anything dark of thee! Thou wilt have me so sure of thee as to dare to say that is not of God which I see dark, see unlike the Master! If I am not honest enough, if the eye in me be not single enough to see thy light, thou wilt punish me, I thank thee, and purge my eyes from their darkness, that they may let the light in, and so I become an inheritor, with thy other children, of the light which is thy Godhead, and makes thy creatures need to worship thee. "In thy light we shall see light."

    "Light," *Unspoken Sermons: Series Three*
    Rev. 15:3-4

November 21 — God Our Savior

> *This is the message we have heard from him and proclaim to you, that God is light and in him there is no darkness at all. And this is the judgment, that the light has come into the world, and people loved darkness rather than light because their deeds were evil.* I John 1:5; John 3:19

All men will not, in our present imperfection, see the same light; but light is light not-withstanding, and what each does see, is his safety if he obeys it. In proportion as we have the image of Christ mirrored in us, we shall know what is and is not light. But never will anything prove to be light that is not of the same kind with that which we mean by light, with that in a thing which makes us call it light. The darkness yet left in us makes us sometimes doubt of a thing whether it be light or darkness; but when the eye is single, the whole body will be full of light.

To fear the light is to be untrue, or at least it comes of untruth. No being, for himself or for another, needs fear the light of God. Nothing can be in light inimical to our nature, which is of God, or to anything in us that is worthy. All fear of the light, all dread lest there should be something dangerous in it, comes of the darkness still in those of us who do not love the truth with all our hearts; it will vanish as we are more and more interpenetrated with the light. In a word, there is no way of thought or action which we count admirable in man, in which God is not altogether adorable. There is no loveliness, nothing that makes man dear to his brother man, that is not in God, only it is infinitely better in God.

He is God our savior. Jesus is our savior because God is our savior. He is the God of comfort and consolation. He will soothe and satisfy his children better than any mother her infant. The only thing we will not give them is—leave to stay in the dark.

"Light," *Unspoken Sermons: Series Three*
Psalms 36:9

A Handful Of Tares

November 22

This is the message we have heard from him and proclaim to you, that God is light and in him there is no darkness at all. And this is the judgment, that the light has come into the world, and people loved darkness rather than light because their deeds were evil. I John 1:5; John 3:19

Come to God, then, my brother, my sister, with all thy desires and instincts, all they lofty ideals, all thy longing for purity and unselfishness, all thy yearning to love and be true, all thy aspirations after self-forgetfulness and child-life in the breath of the Father; come to him with all thy weaknesses, all thy shames, all thy futilities; with all thy helplessness over thy own thoughts; with all thy failure, yea, with the sick sense of having missed the tide of true affairs; come to him with all thy doubts, fears, dishonesties, meannesses, paltrinesses, misjudgments, wearinesses, disappointments, and stalenesses: be sure he will take thee and all thy miserable brood.

For he is light, and in him is no darkness at all. If he were a king, a governor; if the name that described him were *the Almighty*, thou mightst well doubt whether there could be light enough in him for thee and thy darkness; but he is thy father, and more thy father than the word can mean in any lips but his who said, "my father and your father, my God and your God"; and such a father *is* light, an infinite, perfect light.

If anything seem to be in him that you cannot be content with, be sure that the ripening of thy love to thy fellows and to him, the source of thy being, will make thee at length know that anything else than just what he is would have been to thee an endless loss. Be not afraid to build upon the rock Christ, as if thy holy imagination might build too high and heavy for that rock, and it must give way and crumble beneath the weight of thy divine idea. Let no one persuade thee that there is in him a little darkness, because of something he has said which his creature interprets into darkness. The interpretation is the work of the enemy—a handful of tares of darkness sown in the light.

"Light," *Unspoken Sermons: Series Three*
Gen. 18:25

On this day in 1892: Lilia dies in her father's arms of tuberculosis.

November 23 — How Otherwise?

This is the message we have heard from him and proclaim to you, that God is light and in him there is no darkness at all. And this is the judgment, that the light has come into the world, and people loved darkness rather than light because their deeds were evil. I John 1:5; John 3:19

It may sound paradoxical, but no man is condemned for anything he has done; he is condemned for continuing to do wrong. He is condemned for not coming out of the darkness, for not coming to the light, the living God, who sent the light, his son, into the world to guide him home. Let us see what John says about the darkness.

For here also we have, I think, the word of the apostle himself: at the 13th verse he begins, I think to speak in his own person. In the 19th verse he says, "And this is the condemnation,"—not that men are sinners—not that they have done that which, even at the moment, they were ashamed of—not that they have committed murder, not that they have betrayed man or woman, not that they have ground the faces of the poor, making money by the groans of their fellows—not for any hideous thing are they condemned, but that they will not leave such doings behind, and do them no more: "This is the condemnation, that light is come into the world, and men" would not come out of the darkness to the light, but "loved darkness rather than light, because their deeds were evil."

Choosing evil, clinging to evil, loving the darkness because it suits with their deeds, therefore turning their backs on the in-breaking light, how can they but be condemned—if God be true, if he be light, and darkness be alien to him! What of honesty is in man, whatever of judgment is left in the world, must allow that their condemnation is in the very nature of things, that it must rest on them and abide.

"Light," *Unspoken Sermons: Series Three*
Deut. 32: 4

GOD GIVES TIME   NOVEMBER 24

This is the message we have heard from him and proclaim to you, that God is light and in him there is no darkness at all. And this is the judgment, that the light has come into the world, and people loved darkness rather than light because their deeds were evil. I John 1:5; John 3:19

It does not follow, because light has come into the world, that it has fallen upon this or that man. He has his portion of the light that lights every man, but the revelation of God in Christ may not yet have reached him. A man might see and pass the Lord in a crowd, nor be to blame like the Jews of Jerusalem for not knowing him.

A man like Nathanael might have started and stopped at the merest glimpse of him, but all growing men are not yet like him without guile. Everyone who has not yet come to the light is not necessarily keeping his face turned away from it. We dare not say that this or that man would not have come to the light had he seen it; we do not know that he will not come to the light the moment he does see it. God gives every man time.

There is a light that lightens sage and savage, but the glory of God in the face of Jesus may not have shined on this sage or that savage. The condemnation is of those who, having seen Jesus, refuse to come to him, or pretend to come to him but do not the things he says. They have all sorts of excuses at hand; but as soon as a man begins to make excuse, the time has come when he might be doing that from which he excuses himself. How many are there not who, believing there is something somewhere with the claim of light upon them, go on and on to get more out of the darkness! This consciousness, all neglected by them, gives broad ground to the expostulation of the Lord—"Ye will not come unto me that ye might have life."

> "Light," *Unspoken Sermons: Series Three*
> John 3:17-18

November 25 — That Cannot Be

This is the message we have heard from him and proclaim to you, that God is light and in him there is no darkness at all. And this is the judgment, that the light has come into the world, and people loved darkness rather than light because their deeds were evil. I John 1:5; John 3:19

"All manner of sin and blasphemy," the Lord said, "shall be forgiven unto men; but the blasphemy against the spirit shall not be forgiven." God speaks, as it were, in this manner:

"I forgive you everything. Not a word more shall be said about your sins—only come out of them; come out of the darkness of your exile; come into the light of your home, of your birthright, and do evil no more. Lie no more; cheat no more; oppress no more; slander no more; envy no more; be neither greedy nor vain; love your neighbor as I love you; be my good child; trust in your father. I am light; come to me, and you shall see things as I see them, and hate the evil thing. I will make you love the thing which now you call good and love not. I forgive all the past."

"I thank thee, Lord, for forgiving me, but I prefer staying in the darkness: forgive me that too."

"No; that cannot be. The one thing that cannot be forgiven is the sin of choosing to be evil, of refusing deliverance. It is impossible to forgive that sin. It would be to take part in it. To side with wrong against right, with murder against life, cannot be forgiven. The thing that is past I pass, but he who goes on doing the same, annihilates this my forgiveness, makes it of no effect. Let a man have committed any sin whatever, I forgive him; but to choose to go on sinning—how can I forgive that? It would be to nourish and cherish evil! It would be to let my creation go to ruin. Shall I keep you alive to do things hateful in the sight of all true men? If a man refuse to come out of his sin, he must suffer the vengeance of a love that would be no love if it left him there. Shall I allow my creature to be the thing my soul hates?"

"Light," *Unspoken Sermons: Series Three*
John 3:19-21

God Does All He Can   November 26

This is the message we have heard from him and proclaim to you, that God is light and in him there is no darkness at all. And this is the judgment, that the light has come into the world, and people loved darkness rather than light because their deeds were evil. I John 1:5; John 3:19

If we were punished for every fault, there would be no end, no respite; we should have no quiet wherein to repent; but God passes by all he can. He passes by and forgets a thousand sins, yea, tens of thousands, forgiving them all—only we must begin to be good, begin to do evil no more.

He who refuses must be punished and punished—punished through all the ages—punished until he gives way, yields, and comes to the light, that his deeds may be seen by himself to be what they are, and be by himself reproved, and the Father at last have his child again. For the man who in this world resists to the full, there may be, perhaps, a whole age or era in the history of the universe during which his sin shall not be forgiven; but *never* can it be forgiven until he repents. How can they who will not repent be forgiven, save in the sense that God does and will do all he can to make them repent? Who knows but such sin may need for its cure the continuous punishment of an aeon?

There are three conceivable kinds of punishment—first, that of mere retribution, which I take to be entirely and only human—therefore, indeed, more properly inhuman, for that which is not divine is not essential to humanity, and is of evil, and an intrusion upon the human; second, that which works repentance; and third, that which refines and purifies, working for holiness. But the punishment that falls on whom the Lord loves because they have repented, is a very different thing from the punishment that falls on those whom he loves indeed but cannot forgive because they hold fast by their sins.

       "Light," *Unspoken Sermons: Series Three*
       Rom. 8:1-2

November 27 — Ways Of Forgiveness

This is the message we have heard from him and proclaim to you, that God is light and in him there is no darkness at all. And this is the judgment, that the light has come into the world, and people loved darkness rather than light because their deeds were evil. I John 1:5; John 3:19

There are various ways in which the word *forgive* can be used. A man might say to his son—"My boy, I forgive you. You did not know what you were doing. I will say no more about it." Or he might say—"My boy, I forgive you; but I must punish you, for you have done the same thing several times, and I must make you remember." Or, again, he might say—"I am seriously angry with you. I cannot forgive you. I must punish you severely. The thing was too shameful! I cannot pass it by."

Or, once more, he might say—"Except you alter your ways entirely, I shall have nothing more to do with you. You need not come to me. I will not take the responsibility of anything you do. So far from answering for you, I shall feel bound in honesty to warn my friends not to put confidence in you. Never, never, till I see a greater difference in you than I dare hope to see in this world, will I forgive you. I can no more regard you as one of the family. I would die to save you, but I cannot forgive you. There is nothing in you now on which to rest forgiveness. To say, I forgive you, would be to say, Do anything you like; I do not care what you do."

So God may forgive and punish; and he may punish and not forgive, that he may rescue. To forgive the sin against the holy spirit would be to damn the universe to the pit of lies, to render it impossible for the man so forgiven ever to be saved. He cannot forgive the man who will not come to the light because his deeds are evil. Against that man his fatherly heart is moved with indignation.

"Light," *Unspoken Sermons: Series Three*
Matt. 12:31-32

Until Our Anger is Love   November 28

When Jesus saw her weeping, and the Jews who came with her also weeping, he was greatly disturbed in spirit and deeply moved. John 11:33

Let us know that the poverty of our idea of Jesus—how much more our disobedience to him!—thwarts his progress to victory, delays the coming of the kingdom of heaven. Many a man valiant for Christ, but not understanding him, and laying on himself and his fellows burdens against nature, has therein done will-worship and would-be service for which Christ will give him little thanks, which indeed may now be moving his holy anger.

Where we do that we ought not, and could have helped it, be moved to anger against us, O Christ! Do not treat us as if we were not worth being displeased with; let not our faults pass as if they were of no weight. Be angry with us, holy brother, wherein we are to blame; where we do not understand, have patience with us, and open our eyes, and give us strength to obey, until at length we are the children of the Father even as thou.

For though thou art lord and master and savior of them that are growing, thou art perfect lord only of the true and the safe and the free. Until we live in thy light and are divinely glad, we keep thee back from thy perfect lordship. Make us able to be angry and not sin; to be angry nor seek revenge the smallest; to be angry and full of forgiveness. We will not be content till our very anger is love.

"The Displeasure of Jesus," *Unspoken Sermons: Series Three*
Matt. 25:26-30

November 29   Why Was Jesus Angry?

After sternly warning him he sent him away at once, saying to him, "See that you say nothing to anyone, but go, show yourself to the priest.... But he went out and began to proclaim it freely, and to spread the word, so that Jesus could not longer go into a town openly, but stayed out in the country.... Mark 1:43-45

Literally, as, it seems to me, it reads, and ought to read, "And being 'angry' or 'displeased' or 'vexed, with him, he immediately dismissed him." [MacDonald justifies his translation in terms of his study of the Greek words of the text.] This adds something to the story, and raises the question, Why should Jesus have been angry?

Jesus had cured the leper—not with his word only, which would have been enough for the mere cure, but was not enough without the touch of his hand. The man, however, seems to have been unworthy of this delicacy of divine tenderness. The Lord, who could read his heart, saw that he made him no true response—that there was not awaked in him the faith he desired to rouse: he had not drawn the soul of the man to his. The leper was jubilant in the removal of his pain and isolating uncleanness, in his deliverance from suffering and scorn; he was probably elated with the pride of having had a miracle wrought for *him*. In a word, he was so full of himself that he did not think truly of his deliverer.

The Lord, I say, saw this, or something of this kind, and was not satisfied. He had wanted to give the man something so much better than a pure skin, and had only roused in him an unseemly delight in his own cleanness—*unseemly*, for it was such that he paid no heed to the Lord, but immediately disobeyed the positive command. The moral position the man took was that which displeased the Lord, made him angry. He saw in him positive and rampant self-will and disobedience, an impertinent assurance and self-satisfaction. Filled, not with pure delight at such deliverance; filled, not with gratitude, but gratification; filled with arrogance because of the favor shown to him by the great prophet, he left the presence of the healer to thwart his will, and, commanded to tell no man, began to blaze abroad the matter, insomuch that Jesus could no more openly enter into a city, but was without in desert places.

      "The Displeasure of Jesus," *Unspoken Sermons: Series Three*
      Heb. 10:36-39

He Knows What To Do — November 30

When Jesus saw her weeping, and the Jews who came with her also weeping, he was greatly disturbed in spirit and deeply moved. John 11:33

The Lord did not call the leprosy to return and seize again upon the man who disobeyed him [Mark 1:43-45]. He may have deserved it, but the Lord did not do it. He did not wrap the self-confident seeing men in the cloud of their old darkness because they wrapped themselves in the cloud of disobedience [Matt. 9:30-31]. He let them go.

Of course they failed of their well-being by it; for to say a man might disobey and be none the worse, would be to say that *no* may be *yes*, and light sometimes darkness; it would be to say that the will of God is not man's bliss. But the Lord did not directly punish them, any more than he does tens of thousands of wrongs in the world. Many wrongs punish themselves against the bosses of armed law; many wrong-doers cut themselves, like the priests of Baal, with the knives of their own injustice; and it is his will it should be so; but, whether he punish directly or indirectly, he is always working to deliver.

I think sometimes his anger is followed, yea, accompanied by an astounding gift, fresh from his heart of grace. He knows what to do, for he is love. He is love when he gives, and love when he withholds; love when he heals, and love when he slays. Lord, if thus thou look upon men in thine anger, what must a full gaze be from thine eyes of love!

"The Displeasure of Jesus," *Unspoken Sermons: Series Three*
Psalms 86:15

December 1 — He Expected More

When Jesus saw her weeping, and the Jews who came with her also weeping, he was greatly disturbed in spirit and deeply moved. John 11:33

Indignation—anger at the very tomb! In the presence of hearts torn by the loss of a brother four days dead, whom also he loved! Yes, verily, friends! Such indignation, such anger as, at such a time, in such a place, it was eternally right the heart of Jesus should be moved withal.

I can hardly doubt that he is in like manner moved by what he sees now at the death-beds and graves of not a few who are not his enemies, and yet in the presence of death seem no better than pagans. What have such gained by being the Christians they say they are? Weep freely, friends; but let your tears be those of expectant Christians, not hopeless pagans.

The Lord had all this time been trying to teach his friends about his father—what a blessed and perfect father he was, who had sent him that men might look on his very likeness, and know him greater than any likeness could show him; and all they had gained by it seemed not to amount to an atom of consolation when the touch of death came.

I do not mean that God would have even his closest presence make us forget or cease to desire that of our friend. God forbid! The love of God is the perfecting of every love. He is not the God of oblivion, but of eternal remembrance. His determination is that his sons and daughters shall love each other perfectly. He gave us to each other to belong to each other for ever. But is it nothing that he who is the life should be present, assuring the well-being of the life that has vanished, and the well-being of the love that misses it?

You may say they did not know Christ well enough yet. That is plain—but Christ had expected more of them, and was disappointed.

"The Displeasure of Jesus," *Unspoken Sermons, Series Three*
John 11:25

Lazarus's Sacrifice   December 2

When Jesus saw her weeping, and the Jews who came with her also weeping, he was greatly disturbed in spirit and deeply moved. John 11:33

How was he to comfort them? They would not be comforted! Was existence, the glorious out-gift of his father, to be the most terrible of miseries, because some must go home before others? It was all so sad!—and all because they would not know his father! Then came the reaction from his indignation, and the laboring heart of the Lord found relief in tears.

The Lord was standing, as it were, on the watershed of life. On one side of him lay what Martha and Mary called the world of life, on the other what he and his father and Lazarus called more abundant life. The Lord saw into both worlds—saw Martha and Mary on the one side weeping, on the other Lazarus waiting for them in peace. He would do his best for them—for the sisters—not for Lazarus! It was hard on Lazarus to be called back into the winding-sheet of the body, a sacrifice to their faithlessness, but it should be done! Lazarus should suffer for his sisters! Through him they should be compelled to believe in the Father, and so be delivered from bondage! Death should have no more dominion over them!

He was vexed with them, I have said, for not believing in God, his and their father; and at the same time was troubled with their trouble. The cloud of his loving anger and disappointed sympathy broke in tears; and the tears eased his heart of the weight of its divine grief. He turned, not to them, not to punish them for their unbelief, not even to chide them for their sorrow; he turned to his father to thank him.

"I thank thee, father, for hearing me; and I say it, not as if I had had any doubt of thy hearing me, but that the people may understand that I am not doing this thing of myself, but as thy messenger. It is thou, father, art going to do it; I am doing it as they right hand.—Lazarus, come forth." The thought of the Lord in uttering this prayer is not his own justification, but his father's reception by his children.

    "The Displeasure of Jesus," *Unspoken Sermons, Series Three*
    John 20:17b

December 3 — It Cannot Be

". . . that I may gain Christ and be found in him, not having a righteousness of my own that comes from the law, but one that comes through faith in Christ, the righteousness from God based on faith." Phil. 3:8, 9

What, then, is the righteousness which is of God by faith? It is God's righteousness wrought out in us, so that as he is righteous we too are righteous. It is to be so in love with what is fair and right as to make it impossible for a man to do anything that is less than absolutely righteous.

It is not the love of righteousness in the abstract that makes anyone righteous, but such a love of fair play toward everyone with whom we come into contact, that anything less than the fulfilling, with a clear joy, of our divine relation to him or her, is impossible. For the righteousness of God goes far beyond mere deeds and requires of us love and helping mercy as our highest obligation and justice to our fellow men—those of them too who have done nothing for us, those even who have done us wrong. Our relations with others, God first and then our neighbor in order and degree, must one day become, as in true nature they are, the gladness of our being; and nothing then will ever appear good for us, that is not in harmony with those blessed relations. Every thought will not merely be just, but will be just because it is something more, because it is live and true.

The light of our life, our sole, eternal, and infinite joy, is simply God—God—God—nothing but God, and all his creatures in him. He is all and in all, and the children of the kingdom know it. He includes all things; not to be true to anything he has made is to be untrue to him. God is truth, is life; to be in God is to know him and need no law. Existence will be eternal Godness. You would not like that way of it? There is, there can be, no other; but before you can judge of it, you must know at least a little of God as he is, not as you imagine. I say *as you imagine him*, because it cannot be that any creature should know him as he is and not desire him.

"Righteousness," *Unspoken Sermons: Series Three*
Eph. 2:10

Let Him Do It   December 4

". . . that I may gain Christ and be found in him, not having a righteousness of my own that comes from the law, but one that comes through faith in Christ, the righteousness from God based on faith." Phil. 3:8, 9

The wise and prudent interprets God by himself, and does not understand him; the child interprets God by himself, and does understand him. The wise and prudent must make a system and arrange things to his mind before he can say, *I believe.* The child sees, believes, obeys—and knows he must be perfect as his father in heaven is perfect.

If an angel, seeming to come from heaven, told him that God had let him off, that he did not require so much of him as that, but would be content with less; that he could not indeed allow him to be wicked, but would pass by a great deal, modifying his demands because it was so hard for him to be quite good, and he loved him so dearly, the child of God would at once recognize, woven with the angel's starry brilliancy, the flicker of the flames of hell, and would say to the shining one, "Get thee behind me, Satan."

"But how can God bring this about in me?"

Let him do it, and perhaps you will know. Help him to do it, or he cannot do it. He originates the possibility of your being his son, his daughter; he makes you able to will it, but you must will it. If he is not doing it in you—that is, if you have as yet prevented him from beginning, why should I tell you, even if I knew the process, how he would do what you will not let him do?

To teach your intellect what has to be learned by your whole being, what cannot be understood without the whole being, what it would do you no good to understand save you understood it in your whole being—if this be the province of any man, it is not mine.

"Righteousness," *Unspoken Sermons: Series Three*
Phil. 2:12-13

December 5 — God's Work

"... for nothing is covered up that will not be uncovered, and nothing secret that will not become known." Matt. 10:26; Luke 12:2

God is not a God that hides, but a God that reveals. His whole work in relation to the creatures he has made—and where else can lie his work?—is revelation—the giving them truth, the showing of himself to them, that they may know him, and come nearer and nearer to him, and so he have has children more and more of companions to him. That we are in the dark about anything is never because he hides it, but because we are not yet such that he is able to reveal that thing to us.

That God could not do the thing at once which he takes time to do, we may surely say without irreverence. His will cannot finally be thwarted; where it is thwarted for a time, the very thwarting subserves the working out of a higher part of his will. He gave man the power to thwart his will, that, by means of that same power, he might come at last to do his will in a higher kind and way than would otherwise have been possible to him. God sacrifices his will to man that man may become such as himself, and give all to the truth; he makes man able to do wrong, that he may choose and love righteousness.

In whatever mode the Lord may intend that it shall be wrought out, he gives us to understand, as an unalterable principle in the government of the universe, that all such things as the unrighteous desire to conceal, and such things as it is a pain to the righteous to have concealed, shall come out into the light.

"The Final Unmasking," *Unspoken Sermons; Series Three*
Psalms 145:18-19

Never Mind

". . . for nothing is covered up that will not be uncovered, and nothing secret that will not become known." Matt. 10:26; Luke 12:2

The Lord says also, "If they have called the master of the house Beelzebub, how much more shall they call them of his household! Fear them not therefore: for there is nothing covered, that shall not be revealed; and hid, that shall not be known." To a man who loves righteousness and his fellow men, it must always be painful to be misunderstood; and misunderstanding is specially inevitable where he acts upon principles beyond the recognition of those around him, who, being but half-hearted Christians, count themselves the lawgivers of righteousness, and charge him with the very things it is the aim of his life to destroy.

The Lord himself was accused of being a drunkard and a keeper of bad company—and perhaps would in the present day be so regarded by not a few calling themselves by his name, and teaching temperance and virtue. He lived upon a higher spiritual platform than they understand, acted from a height of the virtues they would inculcate, loftier than their eyes can scale. His Himalayas are not visible from their sand-heaps. The Lord bore with their evil tongues, and was neither dismayed nor troubled; but from this experience of his own, comforts those who, being his messengers, must fare as he.

While men count themselves Christians on any other ground than that they are slaves of Jesus Christ, the children of God, and free from themselves, so long will they use the servants of the Master despitefully. "Do not hesitate," says the Lord, "to speak the truth that is in you; never mind what they call you; proclaim from the housetop; fear nobody."

"The Final Unmasking," *Unspoken Sermons; Series Three*
Matt. 11:18-19

December 7 — The Truth Must Out

"... *for nothing is covered up that will not be uncovered, and nothing secret that will not become known.*" Matt. 10:26; Luke 12:2

If, in the endeavor to lead a truer life, a man merely lives otherwise than his neighbors, strange motives will be invented to account for it. To the honest soul it is a comfort to believe that the truth will one day be known, that it will cease to be supposed that he was and did as dull heads and hearts reported of him. Still more satisfactory will be the unveiling where a man is misunderstood by those who ought to know him better—who, not even understanding the point at issue, take it for granted he is about to do the wrong thing, while he is crying for courage to heed neither himself nor his friends, but only the Lord.

How many hear and accept the words, "Be not conformed to this world," without once perceiving that what they call Society and bow to as supreme, is the World and nothing else, or that those who mind what people think, and what people will say, are conformed to—that is, take the shape of—the world. The true man feels he has nothing to do with Society as judge or lawgiver; he is under the law of Jesus Christ, and it sets him free from the law of the World.

Let a man do right, nor trouble himself about worthless opinion; the less he heeds tongues, the less difficult will he find it to love men. Let him comfort himself with the thought that the truth must out. He will not have to pass through eternity with the brand of ignorant or malicious judgment upon him. He shall find his peers and be judged of them.

"The Final Unmasking," *Unspoken Sermons; Series Three*
Mark 13:13

The Bath Of Truth — December 8

". . . for nothing is covered up that will not be uncovered, and nothing secret that will not become known." Matt. 10:26; Luke 12:2

"Will all my weaknesses, all my evil habits, all my pettinesses, all the wrong thoughts which I cannot help—will all be set out before the universe?"

Yes, if they so prevail as to constitute your character—that is, if they are you. But if you have come out of the darkness, if you are fighting it, if you are honestly trying to walk in the light, you may hope in God your father that what he has cured, what he is curing, what he has forgiven, will be heard of no more, not now being a constituent part of you. Or if indeed some of your evil things must yet be seen, the truth of them will be seen—that they are things you are at strife with, not things you are cherishing and brooding over. God will be fair to you—so fair!—fair with the fairness of a father loving his own—who will have you clean, who will neither spare you any needful shame, nor leave you exposed to any that is not needful.

The thing we have risen above, is dead and forgotten, or if remembered, there is God to comfort us. "If any man sin, we have a comforter with the Father." We may trust God with our past as heartily as with our future. It will not hurt us so long as we do not try to hide things, so long as we are ready to bow our heads in hearty shame where it is fit we should be ashamed. For to be ashamed is a holy and blessed thing. Shame is a thing to shame only those who want to appear, not those who want to be. Shame is to shame those who want to pass their examination, not those who would get into the heart of things.

In the name of God let us henceforth have nothing to be ashamed of, and be ready to meet any shame on its way to meet us. For to be humbly ashamed is to be plunged in the cleansing bath of truth.

"The Final Unmasking," *Unspoken Sermons; Series Three*
Rom. 7:24-8:2

December 9 — The Only Victory

". . . for nothing is covered up that will not be uncovered, and nothing secret that will not become known." Matt. 10:26; Luke 12:2

Of all who will one day stand in dismay and sickness of heart, with the consciousness that their very existence is a shame, those will fare the worst who have been consciously false to their fellows; who pretending friendship, have used their neighbor to their own ends; and especially those who, pretending friendship, have divided their friends. To such Dante has given the lowest hell.

If there be one thing God hates, it must be treachery. Do not imagine Judas the only man of whom the Lord would say, "Better were it for that man if he had never been born!" Beyond all things pitiful is it that a man should carry about with him the consciousness of being such a person—should know himself and not another that false one! "O God," we think, "how terrible if it were I!" Just so terrible is it that it should be Judas! And have I not done things with the same germ in them, a germ which, brought to its evil perfection, would have shown itself the canker-worm, treachery? Except I love my neighbor as myself, I may one day betray him! Let us therefore be compassionate and humble, and hope for every man.

The good man, conscious of his own evil, and desiring no refuge but the purifying light, will chiefly rejoice that the exposure of evil makes for the victory of the truth, the kingdom of God and his Christ. He sees in the unmasking of the hypocrite, in the unveiling of the covered, in the exposure of the hidden, God's interference, for him and all the race, between them and the lie.

The only triumph the truth can ever have is its recognition by the heart of the liar.

"The Final Unmasking," *Unspoken Sermons; Series Three*
I John 4:7-8

NOT YET SOUNDED — DECEMBER 10

". . . for nothing is covered up that will not be uncovered, and nothing secret that will not become known." Matt. 10:26; Luke 12:2

There is no satisfaction of revenge possible to the injured. The severest punishment that can be inflicted upon the wrong-doer is simply to let him know what he is; for his nature is of God, and the deepest in him is the divine. Neither can any other punishment than the sinner's being made to see the enormity of his injury, give satisfaction to the injured. While the wrong-doer will admit no wrong, while he mocks at the idea of amends, or while, admitting the wrong, he rejoices in having done it, no suffering could satisfy revenge, far less justice. Both would continually know themselves foiled.

Therefore, while a satisfied justice is an unavoidable eternal event, a satisfied revenge is an eternal impossibility. For the moment that the sole adequate punishment, a vision of himself, begins to take true effect upon the sinner, that moment the sinner has begun to grow a righteous man, and the brother human whom he has offended has no choice, has nothing left him but to take the offender to his bosom—the more tenderly that his brother is a repentant brother, that he was dead and is alive again, that he was lost and is found.

Behold the meeting of the divine extremes—the extreme of punishment, the embrace of heaven! They run together; "the wheel is come full circle." For, I venture to think there can be no delight for created soul—short, that is, of being one with the Father—so deep as that of seeing the heaven of forgiveness open, and disclose the shining stair that leads to its own natural home, where the eternal Father has been all the time awaiting this return of his child.

We have not yet sounded the depths of forgiveness that are and will be required of such as would be his disciples.

"The Final Unmasking," *Unspoken Sermons; Series Three*
Job 42:5-6

1824: George MacDonald born in Huntly, Scotland

December 11 — The One Only Thing

Giving thanks to the Father, who has enabled you to share in the inheritance of the saints in the light." Col. 1:12

To have a share in any earthly inheritance, is to diminish the share of the other inheritors. In the inheritance of the saints, that which each has, goes to increase the possession of the rest. In this inheritance, then, a man may desire and endeavor to obtain his share without selfish prejudice to others; nay, to fail of our share in it, would be to deprive others of a portion of theirs. Let us look a little nearer, and see in what the inheritance of the saints consists.

It might perhaps be to commit some small logical violence on the terms of the passage to say that "the inheritance of the saints in light" *must* mean purely and only "the possession of light which is the inheritance of the saints." At the same time the phrase is literally "the inheritance of the saints *in the light;* and this perhaps makes it the more likely that, as I take it, Paul had in his mind the light as itself the inheritance of the saints—that he held the very substance of the inheritance to be the light. And if we remember that God is light; also that the highest prayer of the Lord for his friends was that they might be one in him and his father; and recall what the apostle said to the Ephesians, that "in him we live and move and have our being," we may be prepared to agree that, although he may not mean to include all possible phases of the inheritance of the saints in the one word *light*, as I think he does, yet the idea is perfectly consistent with his teaching.

For the one only thing to make existence a good, the one thing to make it worth having, is just that there should be no film of separation between our life and the life of which ours is an outcome; that we should not only *know* that God is our life, but be aware, in some grand consciousness beyond anything imagination can present to us, of the presence of the making God, in the very process of continuing us the live things he has made us.

"The Inheritance," *Unspoken Sermons: Series Three*
Psalms 37:4-6

The Faces of Some Flowers   December 12

Giving thanks to the Father, who has enabled you to share in the inheritance of the saints in the light." Col. 1:12

If you think of ten thousand things that are good and worth having, what is it that makes them good or worth having but the God in them? That the loveliness of the world has its origin in the making will of God, would not content me; I say, the very loveliness of it is the loveliness of God, for its loveliness is his own lovely thought, and must be a revelation of that which dwells and moves in himself. Nor is this all: my interest in its loveliness would vanish, I should feel that the soul was out of it, if you could persuade me that God had ceased to care for the daisy, and now cared for something else instead. The faces of some flowers lead me back to the heart of God; and, as his child, I hope I feel, in my lowly degree, what he felt when, brooding over them, he said, "They are good"; that is, "They are what I mean."

The thing I am reasoning toward is this: that, if everything were thus seen in its derivation from God, then the inheritance of the saints, whatever the form of their possession, would be seen to be light. All things are God's not as being in his power—that of course—but as coming from him. The darkness itself becomes light around him when we think that verily he hath created the darkness, for there could have been no darkness but for the light. Without God there would not even have been nothing; there would not have existed the idea of nothing, any more than any reality of nothing, but that he exists and called *something* into being.

Nothingness owes its very name and nature to the being and reality of God. There is not word to represent that which is not God, no word for the *where* without God in it; for it is not, could not be. So I think we may say that the inheritance of the saints is the share each has in the Light.

> The Inheritance," *Unspoken Sermons: Series Three*
> Psalm 19:1

December 13 — Each Revealing Him

Giving thanks to the Father, who has enabled you to share in the inheritance of the saints in the light." Col. 1:12

The true share, in the heavenly kingdom throughout, is not what you have to keep, but what you have to give away. The thing that is mine is the thing I have with the power to give it. The thing I have *no* power to give a share in, is nowise mine; the thing I cannot share with everyone, cannot be essentially my own. The cry of the thousand splendors which Dante, in the fifth canto of the "Paradiso," tells us he saw gliding toward them in the planet Mercury, was—

Lo, here comes one who will increase our loves!

All light is ours. God is all ours. Even that in God which we cannot understand is ours. If there were anything in God that was not ours, then God would not be one God. I do not say we must, or can ever know all in God; not throughout eternity shall we ever comprehend God, but he is our father, and must think of us with every part of him—so to speak in our poor speech; he must know us, and that in himself which we cannot know, with the same thought, for he is one. We and that which we do not or cannot know, come together in his thought. And this helps us to see how, claiming all things, we have yet shares. For the infinitude of God can only begin and only go on to be revealed, through his infinitely differing creatures—all capable of wondering at, admiring, and loving each other, and so bound all in one in him, each to the others revealing him.

For every human being is like a facet cut in the great diamond to which I may dare liken the father of him who likens his kingdom to a pearl. Every man, woman, child—for the incomplete also is his, and in its very incompleteness reveals him as a progressive worker in his creation—is a revealer of God. I have my message of my great Lord, you have yours.

"The Inheritance," *Unspoken Sermons: Series Three*
I John 4:12

Don't Kick That Dog — December 14

Giving thanks to the Father, who has enabled you to share in the inheritance of the saints in the light." Col. 1:12

Your dog, your horse tells you about him who cares for all his creatures. None of them came from his *hands*. Perhaps the precious things of the earth, the coal and the diamonds, the iron and clay and gold, may be said to have come from his hands; but the live things come from his heart—from near the same region whence ourselves we came. How much my horse may, in his own fashion—that is, God's equine way—know of him, I cannot tell, because he cannot tell. Also we do not know what the horses know, because they are horses, and we are at best, in relation to them, only horsemen.

The ways of God go down into microscopic depths, as well as up into telescopic heights—and with more marvel, for there lie the beginnings of life; the immensities of stars and worlds all exist for the sake of less things than they. So with mind; the ways of God go into the depths yet unrevealed to us; he knows his horses and dogs as we cannot know them, because we are not yet pure sons of God. When through our sonship, as Paul teaches, the redemption of these lower brothers and sisters shall have come, then we shall understand each other better.

But now the Lord of Life has to look on at the wilful torture of multitudes of his creatures. It must be that offences come, but woe unto that man by whom they come! The Lord may seem not to heed, but he sees and knows.

"The Inheritance," *Unspoken Sermons: Series Three*
Psalms 139:7-10

December 15   The Better Will Follow

Giving thanks to the Father, who has enabled you to share in the inheritance of the saints in the light." Col. 1:12

Little would any promise of heaven be to me if I might not hope to say, "I am sorry; forgive me; let what I did in anger or in coldness be nothing, in the name of God and Jesus!" Many such words will pass, many a self-humiliation have place.

The man or woman who is not ready to confess, who is not ready to pour out a heartful of regrets—can such a one be an inheritor of the light? It is the joy of a true heart of an heir of light, of a child of that God who loves an open soul—the joy of any man who hates the wrong the more because he has done it, to say, "I was wrong; I am sorry." Oh the sweet winds of repentance and reconciliation and atonement, that will blow from garden to garden of God, in the tender twilights of his kingdom! Whatever the place be like, one thing is certain, that there will be endless, infinite atonement, ever-growing love.

Certain too it is that whatever the divinely human heart desires, it shall not desire in vain. The light which is God, and which is our inheritance because we are the children of God, insures these things. For the heart which desires is made thus to desire. God is; let the heart be glad, and the heaven, and the heaven of heavens! Whatever a father can do to make his children blessed, that will God do for his children. Let us, then, live in continual expectation, looking for the good things that God will give to men, being their father and their everlasting savior.

If the things I have here come from him, and are so plainly but a beginning, shall I not take them as an earnest of the better to follow? How else can I regard them?

"The Inheritance," *Unspoken Sermons: Series Three*
Eph. 3:20

Not At Home Here December 16

Giving thanks to the Father, who has enabled you to share in the inheritance of the saints in the light." Col. 1:12

Never, in the midst of the good things of this lovely world, have I felt quite at home in it. Never has it shown me things lovely or grand enough to satisfy me. It is not all I should like for a place to live in. It may be that my unsatisfaction comes from not having eyes open enough, or keen enough, to see and understand what he has given; but it matters little whether the cause lie in the world or in myself, both being incomplete: God is, and all is well.

All that is needed to set the world right enough for me—and no empyrean heaven could be right for me without it—is, that I care for God as he cares for me; that my will and desires keep time and harmony with his music; that I have no thought that springs from myself apart from him; that my individuality have the freedom that belongs to it as born of his individuality, and be in no slavery to my body, or my ancestry, or my prejudices, or any impulse whatever from region unknown; that I be free by obedience to the law of my being, the live and live-making will by which life is life, and my life is myself.

What springs from myself and not from God, is evil; it is a perversion of something of God's. Whatever is not of faith is sin; it is a stream cut off—a stream that cuts itself off from its source, and thinks to run on without it. But light is my inheritance through him whose life is the light of men, to wake in them the life of their father in heaven. Loved be the Lord who in himself generated that life which is the light of men!

"The Inheritance," *Unspoken Sermons: Series Three*
Rom. 14:23b

December 17 — The Bliss Of Pure Being

Giving thanks to the Father, who has enabled you to share in the inheritance of the saints in the light." Col. 1:12

For my own part, I rejoice to think that there will be neither church nor chapel in the high countries; yea, that there will be nothing there called religion, and no law but the perfect law of liberty.

For how should there be law or religion where every throb of the heart says *God*? Where every song-throat is eager with thanksgiving! Where such a tumult of glad waters is for ever bursting from beneath the throne of God, the tears of the gladness of the universe! Religion? Where will be the room for it, when the essence of every thought must be God? Law? What room will there be for law, when everything upon which law could lay a *shalt not* will be too loathsome to think of? What room for honesty, where love fills full the law to overflowing—where a man would rather drop sheer into the abyss, than wrong his neighbor one hair's breath?

Heaven will be continuous touch with God. The very sense of being will in itself be bliss. For the sense of true life, there must be actual, conscious contact with the source of the life; therefore mere life—in itself, in its very essence good—good as the life of God which is our life—must be such bliss as, I think, will need the mitigation of the loftiest joys of communion with our blessed fellows; the mitigation of art in every shape, and of all combinations of arts; the mitigation of countless services to the incomplete, and hard toil for those who do not yet know their neighbor or their Father. The bliss of pure being will, I say, need these mitigations to render the intensity of it endurable by heart and brain.

"The Inheritance," *Unspoken Sermons: Series Three*
Isa. 65:17-19

The Kind Of Love Needed   December 18

Hester and her brother Cornelius are leaving a public meeting hall where they have heard a bumbling lecture on The Pilgrim's Progress given by a speaker apparently half-drunk.

When they came out and breathed again the blue, clean, rain-washed air instead of the musty smells of the hall, involuntarily Hester's eyes rose to the vault whose only keystone is the will of the Father, whose endless space alone is large enough to picture the heart of God: how was that old man to get up into the high regions and grow clean and wise? For all the look, he must belong there as well as she! And were there not thousands equally and more miserable in the world—people wrapped in no tenderness to whom none ministered, left if not driven—so it seemed at the moment to Hester—to fold themselves in their own selfishness? And was there nothing she, a favored one of the family, could do to help, to comfort, to lift up one such of her own flesh and blood?—to make this one or that feel there was a heart of love and refuge at the center of things?

Hestor had a large, though not hitherto entirely active, aspiration in her; and now, the moment she began to flutter her weak wings, she found the whole human family hanging upon her, and that she could not rise except in raising them along with her. For the necessities of our deepest nature are such as not to admit of a mere private individual satisfaction.

I well remember feeling as a child that I did not care for God to love me if he did not love everybody: the kind of love I needed was love essential to my nature—the love of me, a man, not of me a person—the love therefore that all men needed, the love that belonged to their nature as the children of the Father, a love he could not give me except he gave it to all men.

Weighed and Wanting, Chapter 3
Rom. 10:14-15

December 19 — Accompanying Christ

Hester Raymount, destined to become an admirable follower of Christ, is early in the novel shown to be seized with the sectarian spirit:

In religious politics, Hester was what is called a good churchwoman, which in truth means a good deal of a sectarian. She not merely recoiled from such as venerated the more primitive modes of church-government rather than those of later expediency and preferred far inferior extempore prayers to the best possible prayers in print, going therefore to some chapel instead of the church, but she looked down upon them as from a superior social standing—that is, with the judgment of this world, and not that of Christ the carpenter's son.

In short, she had a repugnance to the whole race of dissenters, and would not have soiled her dress with the dust of one of their school-rooms even. She regarded her own conscience as her Lord, but had not therefore any respect for that of another man where it differed from her in the direction of what she counted vulgarity. So she was scarcely in the kingdom of heaven yet, any more than thousands who regard themselves as choice Christians. I do not say these feelings were very active in her, for little occurred to call them out; but she did not love her dissenting neighbor and felt good and condescending when, brought into contact with one, she behaved kindly to him.

I will know that some of my readers will heartily approve of her in this very thing, and that not a few *good dissenters* on the other hand, who are equally and in precisely the same way sectarians, that is bad Christians, will scorn her for it; but for my part I would rather cut off my right hand than be so cased and stayed in a narrow garment of pride and satisfaction, condemned to keep company with myself instead of the Master as he goes everywhere—into the poorest companies of them that love each other, and so invite his presence.

Weighed and Wanting, Chapter 4
Rev. 3:15-17

Refinement Or Vulgarity?   December 20

Hester Raymount, destined to become an admirable follower of Christ, is early in the novel shown to be seized with the sectarian spirit:

The Lord of truth and beauty has died for us: shall we who, by haunting what we call his courts, have had our sense of beauty, our joy in grace tenfold exalted, gather around us, in the presence of those we count less refined than ourselves, skirts trimmed with the phylacteries of the world's law, turning up the Pharisaical nose, and forgetting both what painful facts self-criticism has revealed to ourselves, and the eyes upon us of the yet more delicate refinement and the yet gentle breeding of the high countries?

May these not see in us some malgrace which it needs the gentleness of Christ to get over and forget, some savagery of which we are not aware, some *gaucherie* that repels though it cannot estrange them? Casting from us our own faults first, let us cast from us and from him our neighbor's also. O gentle man, the common man is yet thy brother, and thy gentleness should make him great, infecting him with thy humility, not rousing in him the echo of a vile unheavenly scorn. Wilt thou, with thy lofty condescension, more intrinsically vulgar than even his ugly self-assertion, give him cause too good to hate thy refinement? It is not thy refinement makes thee despise him; it is thy own vulgarity.

That Hester had a tendency to high church had little or nothing to do with the matter. Such exclusiveness is simply a form of that pride, justify or explain it as you will, which found its fullest embodiment in the Jewish Pharisee—the evil thing that Christ came to burn up with his lovely fire, and which yet so many of us who call ourselves by his name keep hugging to our bosoms—I mean the pride that says, "I am better than thou." If these or those be in any true sense below us, it is of Satan to despise—of Christ to stoop and lay hold of and lift the sister soul up nearer to the heart of the divine tenderness.

Weighed and Wanting, Chapter 4
Phil. 2:3

December 21 — Which Is Uppermost?

The cry of the human heart in all ages and in every moment is "Where is God and how shall I find him"—No, friend, I will not accept your testimony to the contrary—not though you may be as well fitted as every one of eight hundred millions to come forward with it. You take it for granted that you know your own heart because you call it yours, but I say that your heart is a far deeper thing than you know or are capable of knowing. Its very nature is hid from you.

I use but a poor figure when I say that the roots of your heart go down beyond your knowledge—whole eternities beyond it—into the heart of God. If you have never yet made one discovery in your heart, your testimony concerning it is not worth a tuft of flue; and if you have made discoveries in it, does not the fact reveal that it is but little known to you, and that there must be discoveries innumerable yet to be made in it? To him who has been making discoveries in it for fifty years, the depths of his heart are yet a mystery—a mystery, however, peopled with loveliest hopes.

I repeat whether the man knows it or not, his heart in its depths is ever crying out for God. Where the man does not know it, it is because the unfaithful Self, a would-be monarch, has usurped the consciousness; the demon-man is uppermost, not the Christ-man; he is down in the crying heart, and the demon-man—that is the self that worships itself—is trampling on the heart and smothering it up in the rubbish of ambitions, lusts, and cares. If ever its cry reaches that Self, it calls it childish folly, and tramples the harder. It does not know that a child crying on God is mightier than a warrior dwelling in steel.

Weighed and Wanting, Chapter 5
Eccl. 3:11

The Only Way To Learn   December 22

Those who would do good to the poor must attempt it in the way in which best they could do good to people of their own standing. They must make their acquaintance first. They must know something of the kind of person they would help, to learn if help be possible from their hands. Only man can help man, money without man can do little or nothing, most likely less than nothing.

As our Lord redeemed the world by being a man, the true Son of the true Father, so the only way for a man to help men is to be a true man to this neighbor and that. But to seek acquaintance with design is a perilous thing, nor unlikely to result in disappointment, and the widening of the gulf both between the individuals, and the classes to which they belong. It seems to me that, in humble acceptance of common ways, we must follow the leading of providence, and make acquaintance in the so-called lower classes by the natural working of the social laws that bring men together. What is the divine intent in the many needs of humanity, and the consequent dependence of the rich on the poor, even greater than that of the poor on the rich, but to bring together, that in far-off ways at first they may be compelled to know each other? The man who treats his fellow as a mere mean for the supply of his wants, and not as a human being with whom he has to do, is an obstructing clot in the human circulation.

Does any one ask for rules of procedure? I answer, there are none to be had; such must be discovered by each for himself. The only way to learn the rules of any thing practical is to begin to do the thing.

Weighed and Wanting, Chapter 12
Luke 10:36-37

December 23 — Just Follow The Path

We have enough of knowledge in us—call it insight, call it instinct, call it inspiration, call it natural law, to begin anything required of us. The sole way to deal with the profoundest mystery that is yet not too profound to draw us, is to begin to do some duty revealed by the light from the golden fringe of its cloudy vast. If it reveal nothing to be done, there is nothing there for us. No man can turn his attention in the mere direction of a thing, without already knowing enough of that thing to carry him further in the knowledge of it by the performance of what it involves of natural action.

Let every simplest relation towards human being, if it be embodied but in the act of buying a reel of cotton or a knife, be recognized as a relation with, a meeting of that human soul. In its poor degree let its outcome be in truth and friendliness. Allow nature her course, and next time let the relation go farther. To follow such a path is the way to find both the persons to help and the real modes of helping them. In fact, to be true to a man in any way is to help him. He who goes out of common paths to look for opportunity, leaves his own door and misses that of his neighbor.

It is by following the path we are in that we shall first reach somewhere. He who does as I say will find his acquaintance widen and widen with growing rapidity; his heart will fill with the care of humanity, and his hands with its help. Such care will be death to one's own cares, such help balm to one's own wounds. In a word, he must cultivate, after a simple human manner, the acquaintance of his neighbors, who would be a neighbor where a neighbor may be wanted. So shall he fulfil the part left behind of the work of the Master, which He desires to finish through him.

Weighed and Wanting, Chapter 12
Col. 3:17

A Song Of The Child Jesus   December 24

MacDonald translated much German poetry into English, including many of Luther's hymns. The following is a sample.

A Song Of The Child Jesus, For Children at Christmas

From heaven on high I come to you,
I bring a story good and new:
Of goodly news so much I bring—
Of it I must both speak and sing.

To you a child is come this morn,
A child of holy maiden born;
A little babe so sweet and mild,
It is a joy to see the child.

'Tis Jesus Christ, our Lord and God,
He us will ease of all our load;
He will himself our Savior be,
And from all sinning set us free.

He brings the gladness which of yore
For you the Father had in store,
That you must in his heavenly house
Live now and evermore with us.

And this shall be the sign to you—
The crib, the swathing clothes so few.
Go find the infant just laid there,
Who all the world doth hold and bear.

Let all of us then gladsome be,
And with the shepherds go and see
What wondrous thing our God hath given,
Sent with his dear Son down from heaven. . .

"Luther the Singer," *Sunday Magazine*, Dec. 1, 1867
Gal. 4:4-5

December 25

That Holy Thing

That Holy Thing

They all were looking for a king
To slay their foes, and lift them high
   Thou cam'st a little baby thing
That made a woman cry.

   O son of man, to right my lot
Nought but thy presence can avail;
   Yet on the road thy wheels are not,
Nor on the sea thy sail!

   My fancied ways why shouldst thou heed?
Thou com'st down thine own secret stair;
   Com'st down to answer all my need,
Yea, every bygone prayer!

The Poetical Works of George MacDonald, vol.2, p 323
Phil. 4:19

HE SHINES IN SIDEWAYS — DECEMBER 26

Hester Raymount, in the process of learning how to become a true servant of Christ, is here pondering how to act Christianly with a doctor:

We are surrounded with things difficult to understand, and the way most people take is not to look at them lest they should find out they have to understand them. Hester suspected scepticism under the remarks of the doctor: most doctors, she believed, had more than a leaning in that direction. But she had herself begun to have a true notion of serving *man* at least; therefore she could not fail to finding out the word that belonged to the act: no one who does not serve him ever can find out what serving him means.

Some people are constantly rubbing their skylights, but if they do not keep their other windows clean also, there will not be much light in the house: God, like his body, the light, is all about us, and prefers to shine in upon us sideways: we could not endure the power of his vertical glory; no moral man can see God and live; and he who loveth not his brother whom he hath seen, shall not love his God whom he hath not seen. He will come to us in the morning through the eyes of a child, when we have been gazing all night at the stars in vain.

Weighed and Wanting, Chapter 13
I John 4:19-21

DECEMBER 27   LEARNING FROM OLD AGE

The first suspicion of the approach of old age and the beginning of that weakness whose end is sure, may well be a startling one. The man has begun to be a nobody in the world's race—is henceforth himself but the course of the race between age and death—a race in which the victor is known ere the start. Life with its self-discipline withdraws itself thenceforth more to the inside, and goes on with greater vigor. The man has now to trust and yield constantly.

He is coming to know the fact that he was never his own strength, had never the smallest power in himself at his strongest. But he is learning also that he is as safe as ever in the time when he gloried in his might—yea, as safe as then he imagined himself on his false foundation. He lays hold of the true strength, makes it his by laying hold of it. He trusts in the unchangeable thing at the root of all his strength, which gave it all the truth it had—a truth far deeper then he knew, a reality unfathomable, though not of the nature he had fancied. Strength has ever to be made perfect in weakness, and old age is one of the weaknesses in which it is perfected.

Weighed and Wanting, Chapter 22
Jer. 9:23-24

The Only Hope   December 28

Mrs. Raymount is here contemplating her son whom she has allowed to grow into a rather unloveable young man.

She was thinking of her boy, whom perhaps, in all the world, she was able to love heartily—there was so little in the personal being of the lad, that is, in the thing he was to himself, and was making of himself, to help anyone to love him! But in the absolute mere existence is reason for love, and upon that God does love—so love, that He will suffer and cause suffering for the development of that existence into a thing in its own full nature lovable, namely, an existence in its own will one with the perfect love whence it issued; and the mother's heart more than any other God has made is like Him in power of loving.

Alas that she is so seldom like Him in wisdom—so often thwarting the work of God, and rendering more severe His measures with her child by her attempts to shield him from His law, and save him from saving sorrow. How often from his very infancy—if she does not, like the very nurse she employs, actively teach him to be selfish—does she get between him and the right consequences of his conduct, as if with her one feeble loving hand, she would stay the fly-wheel of the holy universe. It is the law that the man who does evil shall suffer; it is the only hope for him, and a hope for the neighbor he wrongs.

Weighed and Wanting, Chapter 5
Gal. 6:7-10

December 29 — Individual Ardor Alone

The following instructions on serving effectively are given to Hester Raymount by a dedicated Christian layman, Mr. Christopher:

"Nothing worth calling good can or ever will be started full grown. The essential of any good is life, and the very body of created life, and essential to it, being its self operant, is growth. The larger start you make, the less room you leave for life to extend itself. . . . Small beginnings with slow growings have time to root themselves thoroughly. . . .God's beginnings are imperceptible, whether in the region of soul or of matter.

"Besides, I believe in no good done save in person—by personal operative presence of soul, body and spirit. God is the one only person, and it is our personality alone, so far as we have any, that can work with God's perfect personality. God can use us as tools, but to be a tool of, is not to be a fellow-worker with. How the devil would have laughed at the idea of a society for saving the world! But when he saw *one* take it in hand, one who was in no haste even to do that, one who would only do the will of God with all his heart and soul, and cared for nothing else, then indeed he might tremble for his kingdom! It is the individual Christians forming the church by their obedient individuality, that have done all the good done since men for the love of Christ began to gather together. It is individual ardor alone that can combine into larger flame.

"There is no true power but that which has individual roots. Neither custom nor habit nor law nor foundation is a root. The real roots are individual conscience that hates evil, individual faith that loves and obeys God, individual heart with its kiss of charity."

Weighed and Wanting, Chapter 48
James 1:4-5

It's Always Coming — December 30

This excerpt is from the final chapter of MacDonald's initial fantasy for adults, **Phantastes**, *published in 1858. Anodos, the protagonist, is speaking.*

"I will end my story with the relation of an incident which befell me a few days ago. I had been with my reapers, and, when they ceased their work at noon, I had lain down under the shadow of a great, ancient beech-tree, that stood on the edge of the field. As I lay, with my eyes closed, I began to listen to the sound of the leaves overhead. At first, they made sweet inarticulate music alone, but, by and by, the sound seemed to begin to take shape, and to be gradually molding itself into words, till, at last, I seemed able to distinguish these, half-dissolved in a little ocean of circumfluent tones: 'A great good is coming—is coming—is coming to thee, Anodos,' and so over and over again.

"I fancied that the sound reminded me of the voice of the ancient woman, in the cottage that was four-square. I opened my eyes, and, for a moment, almost believed that I saw her face, with its many wrinkles and its young eyes, looking at me from between two hoary branches of the beech overhead. But when I looked more keenly, I saw only twigs and leaves, and the infinite sky, in tiny spots, gazing through between. Yet I know that good is coming to me—that good is always coming, though few have at all times the simplicity and the courage to believe it. What we call evil, is the only and best shape, which, for the person and his condition at the time, could be assumed by the best good. . . ."

Phantastes, Chapter 25
Rom 8:28

December 31 — Believe In Nothing Else

This excerpt is taken from a letter to MacDonald's sister-in-law, written from Bordighera, dated "Last Sunday of 1884."

Yes, we are growing old; but the Ancient of Days cannot be old; and Jesus Christ is not old; his body must always be about thirty three, for it is embalmed with the light of life. He is child and man and one perfect friend. He is accountable for me, else I should not like to live. I look to the origin to make life worthy my having to all eternity. I can conceive by glimmers a vision of such worthiness, but such as I am I would rather be and cease altogether. He is my life and in the good to come I rejoice—in the hope of the glory of God. That the life in me should be of the same kind as that which makes God willing to live and be himself, can alone satisfy me—a life of absolute love and self-forgivefulness—from which at present [I] seem thousands of years away.

I believe in nothing but Jesus Christ, in whom are all the mysteries of reality. Less than the story of him could not satisfy me, though less might give me hope. But if he be such as that story says, then all is well. If God be indeed such a God as satisfies Jesus, then hail to the world with all its summers and snows, all its delights and its aching, all its jubilance and its old age! We shall come out of it the sons and daughters of life of God himself the only Father . . . .

An Expression of Character: The Letters of George MacDonald,
Glenn Edward Sadler, ed.
Psalms 73:23-26

TITLES OF DAILY READINGS BY MONTH

JANUARY

1. Becoming Ten Times a Man
2. The Offer is Ours
3. What a Scheme
4. Expecting Great Things
5. Turned Inside Out
6. Heed Those Inside Hands
7. Thousands More Could Not Speak Truth
8. Inexorable Love
9. The Outer Darkness
10. Our Childlike, Imperturbable God
11. Away with the Monstrosity!
12. What Seems vs. What Is
13. Our New Name
14. Ambition Vs. Aspiration
15. The Words of God Cannot Be Numbered
16. The Nature of Faith
17. Nothing to Conceal
18. God Was Never Nearer
19. This Is the Truth
20. His Own Best Making
21. Being Made Perfect in One
22. Obedience Perfected
23. How to Worship God
24. Into God's Hands
25. The One Father
26. Help Him Be Himself
27. All Live Unto Him
28. With What Body Do They Come?
29. What Will It Be?
30. Here's My Answer
31. Nothing Between

FEBRUARY

1. No *Hortus Siccus*
2. Nothing Else Will Do
3. Temptations Are Necessary
4. It's in the Seeing
5. The Power of Power
6. God Keeps Quiet
7. There's Good Wine Yet to Come
8. What We Need in Sorrow
9. More Lovely Still
10. From Whence the Power?
11. A Glimmering of Absolute Glory
12. Fit to Be Christ's Apostle
13. The Prayer for Us
14. Out of Us Also
15. Oneness with God Makes It A Necessity
16. Though He Knew It Not
17. But God *Was* With Him
18. Words of Spirit and Life
19. Now First in Manhood
20. Too Good to Last
21. It Is After All, Simple
22. What Is Christ's Peace?
23. Making Him Capable
24. Toning Down His Great Work
25. The Suffering Is Necessary
26. A Miserable Fancy
27. A Very Important Misapprehension
28. The Highest Must Meet the Highest
29. Let's Join the Lord's Side

MARCH

1. The Only Possible Way
2. Our Highest Privilege
3. The Sum of the Matter
4. The Only Possible Preparation
5. The Baptism of Fire
6. The Call to Real Existence
7. Why Was Christ Baptised?
8. The Ways of Help Essential
9. All That the Children Want
10. Must We Fail Still?
11. Not Yet at Home
12. His Father's Things
13. Traveling to Such a Home
14. The Wanted Vengeance
15. The Real Source of the Misery
16. The False Gospel and the True
17. Not for the Wise and Prudent
18. Why Indeed
19. Only for the Meek and Lowly
20. Strangers and Pilgrims
21. Not as They Expected
22. The Essential Spirit
23. Those the Lord Calls Blessed
24. The Kingdom Is Theirs
25. How to Be Rich Indeed
26. How to Make the Earth Ours
27. You May Have It Now
28. How To Change the Weather
29. Sorrow Is a Doorkeeper
30. Bliss Divinely Purified
31. From Much Bad to All Good

APRIL

1. The Original God-Idea
2. Hope in God
3. Comfort for Every Grief
4. On Seeing God
5. The End of Our Creation
6. Dismiss the Care
7. A Horror of the Unfinished
8. An Essential in Its Time
9. Simply the Way Home
10. Nothing too Good
11. Leaving Intellectual Idols
12. A Man within a Man
13. There is No Escape
14. Ask Your Conscience
15. Love Is the Father
16. Our Primal Need
17. Forgetting Righteousness
18. The Day Must Come
19. Helping Perfect the Father-Idea
20. The One Haven
21. The Tragedy of Peace-Breakers
22. The Which is Plain
23. Blessed Reward
24. The Only Way to Learn
25. Made Greater Than Oneself
26. The Hardships of the Way
27. The Babes Must Not Yield
28. It's Quite Other Than Just Intellectual
29. How Would It Have Fared?
30. The One Eternal Relationship

MAY

1. Only to the Child
2. "Be as I Am"
3. What Is the Yoke?
4. The One Thing Worth Living For
5. Knowing Only by Having
6. Where Wold the World Be?
7. Make It So
8. The Danger of the Self-Bushel
9. The Light Is from Him
10. Seeking His Will in the World
11. It Is But Decent
12. What is the Reward?
13. What Other Possible Reward?
14. Only People Think of It
15. The Sole Escape
16. What Is Paul Saying?
17. A Creative Demon?
18. Are They Not Worth It?
19. Not by a Little Only
20. Why Indeed Not?
21. Waiting in Hope
22. The Unpleasant Cure
23. St. Paul's Heaven
24. Total Freedom
25. The Body Made a House-Alive
26. For Our Sakes and Their's
27. A Selfish Person Indeed
28. It Dawned upon Him
29. Hear Then His Words
30. Psyches Half-Awake
31. Do Your Really Believe?

JUNE

1. True Divine Service
2. No More Metaphysics
3. No Self-Satisfied Men
4. Sinners Cane First
5. No Such Distinction
6. The Perfecting of Men
7. Nothing Less Than That
8. Lovely Because True
9. The Highest Possible Condition
10. Unutterably Lovelier
11. What Wingfold Was Learning
12. One Good Reason
13. What Would Be Gained?
14. Under Holy Orders
15. Who Is To Blame?
16. How Many Helps
17. Giving Suffering Its Rightful Name
18. Why Should the Rich Fare Differently?
19. The Use of Things
20. The Reason for the Miracles
21. It Is Hard on God
22. Affairs of the Spirit
23. Am I a Fool?
24. We Must Be Free
25. Why We Need to Pray
26. The Reality Behind the Look
27. Try It
28. Our Endless Need
29. Our Eternal Need
30. Purifying the Prayer

JULY

1. True Son-Faith
2. No Room for Change?
3. Room in His Plans
4. I Help and You Help
5. The End of All Prayer
6. God Loses No Time
7. A Summons to Fight
8. The Purpose of the Parables
9. Punishment in Love
10. An Appeal to Common Sense
11. No Escape.
12. You Must
13. It's for Your Sake
14. God Is Forever Good
15. The Weary Way
16. For This We Were Created
17. Power To Become
18. Sons in Body Also
19. That They May Have Life
20. Which is the Greater Deception?
21. Better to Be an Atheist
22. God's Awful Mystery
23. Science Cannot Do It
24. To the Uttermost Lash
25. The Most Valueless Thing
26. Has He Not the Right?
27. Our Hope Is in Thee
28. The Heavier Obligation
29. A Better Knowing
30. How To Help
31. It's a Simple Necessity

AUGUST

1. Not the God of Your Fancy
2. The Grand Result
3. An Eternal Labor
4. An Infinite Embrace
5. The Only Reality
6. Alive Indeed
7. Our Real Need
8. No Limit
9. What Must It Not Be?
10. Two Wills in Harmony
11. Our Demon-Foe
12. Why They Fear Him
13. The Fire of God
14. Oh, the Joy!
15. Punishment or Favor?
16. Pharisaic Friends
17. Not To Be Found?
18. His Most Divine Gift
19. Claiming our Claims
20. As False as Hell
21. Will He Not Be Pleased?
22. The Rights He Has Given
23. The Rights of the Childlike
24. Bound by His Will
25. The Puzzling Answer
26. Nature's Meanings
27. Those Inevitable Doubts
28. The Greatest Injustice
29. On Self-Contempt
30. Nearer Than Any Wrong
31. We Must

SEPTEMBER

1. What We Need
2. Approaching That Holy Room
3. The World Defined
4. That The Self May Be Free
5. Taking His Yoke
6. Increasing Joy
7. Made To Be Joyful
8. The One Bliss
9. Beholding from Within
10. Forsaking the False
11. The One Terrible Heresy
12. Awake and Arise
13. Do It
14. He Meant What He Said
15. What Have You Done?
16. We May Be Sure
17. The Whole Secret
18. How Can You?
19. Presumptuous Doctrine?
20. Truth Will Grow
21. Enjoying Their Leap-Frog
22. One Great Good
23. On Seeing the Unseen
24. The One Grand Thing
25. What Was That Life?
26. The Life Made in Him
27. We Must Choose
28. God Goes On
29. Life Revealed in Light
30. "Come Home with Me"

OCTOBER

1. The Only Good
2. Our One Necessity
3. Even in the Darkest Moments
4. On Seeing God
5. Who Would Know Him?
6. Should the Lord Appear
7. His Only Likeness
8. Wilful Blindness
9. The Glory Itself
10. His Door In
11. Then Indeed
12. So God Were There
13. Not Merely *in* the Man
14. The Truth of Every Man
15. One with the Mighty Father
16. True Though Not Perfect
17. What They Don't Grumble At
18. What Does the *How* Mean?
19. The Final Unity
20. Less To Blame
21. The Principles of Hell
22. The Only Real King
23. We Are Bound
24. He Alone
25. That Is Fair
26. Not the Thing Required
27. Wasted Cruelty
28. So Shall We Overcome
29. This Is the Reason
30. Making up for Wrong
31. He Will Spare Nothing

NOVEMBER

1. Not the Love We Want
2. What Justice Demands
3. Let Us Not Bury the Living
4. What I Believe
5. Such Is His Mercy
6. As God Means It
7. Making All Things Right
8. Go for It
9. My Neighbor a Revelation
10. Human Chickens
11. The All-Sufficient Antidote
12. What Else But Look Onward?
13. Selfishness Vaporizes Reality
14. A Common Human Mistake
15. Perhaps the Righteous Are Worth Troubling
16. True Possession
17. No Life but Love
18. Living in Things Themselves
19. A Painful Discovery
20. We Shall See Light
21. God Our Savior
22. A Handful of Tares
23. How Otherwise?
24. God Gives Time
25. That Cannot Be
26. God Does All He Can
27. Ways of Forgiveness
28. Until Our Anger Is Love
29. Why Jesus Was Angry
30. He Knows What To Do

DECEMBER

1. He Expected More
2. Lazarus's Sacrifice
3. It Cannot Be
4. Let Him Do It
5. God's Work
6. Never Mind
7. The Truth Must Out
8. The Bath of Truth
9. The Only Victory
10. Not Yet Sounded
11. The One Only Thing
12. The Faces of Some Flowers
13. Each Revealing Him
14. Don't Kick That Dog
15. The Bliss of Pure Being
16. The Better Will Follow
17. Not at Home Here
18. Accompanying Christ
19. The Kind of Love Needed
20. Refinement or Vulgarity?
21. Which Is Uppermost?
22. The Only Way To Learn
23. Just Follow the Path
24. A Song of the Child Jesus
25. That Holy Thing
26. He Shines in Sideways
27. Learning from Old Age
28. The Only Hope
29. Individual Ardor Alone
30. It's Always Coming
31. Believe in Nothing Else

ALPHABETICAL LIST OF SCRIPTURE PASSAGES

Colossians 1:12
    December 11, 12, 13, 14, 15, 16, 17

II Corinthians 3:18
    October 7, 8, 9, 10, 11

II Corinthians 12:8, 9:
    June 28

Eph. 4:20
    September 11, 12, 13, 14, 15, 16, 17, 18, 19, 20

Hebrews 12:29
    January 8, 9

Job 14:13-15
    August 15, 16, 17, 18, 19, 20, 21, 22, 23, 24, 25, 26, 27, 28

Job 40:4
    August 29, 30

Job 42:8
    August 31

John 1:3, 4
    September 25, 26, 27, 29, 30, October 1, 2, 3

John 2:1-11
    February 3, 4, 5, 6, 7

John 5:37b, 38
    October 4, 5, 6

John 8:32; 34-36
    October 16, 17, 18, 19

John 9:1-41
    February 11

John 10:10
    August 2, 3, 4, 5, 6, 7, 8, 9, 10, 11

John 11:33
    November 28, 29, 30, December 1, 2

John 14:6
    October 12, 13, 14, 15

John 14:27
    February 20, 22

John 18:37
    October 20, 21, 22, 23

I John 1:5
    November 20, 21, 22, 23, 24, 25, 26, 27

Luke 2:48, 49
    March 10, 11, 12, 13

Luke 4:16-21
    March 14, 15, 16, 17, 18, 19

Luke 6:6-11
    February 10

Luke 8:26-39
    February 12

Luke 9:23, 24
    September 3, 4, 5, 6, 7, 8, 9, 10

Luke 9:37-43
    February 13, 14

Luke 12:2
    December 5, 6, 7, 8, 9, 10

Luke 15:10
    April 27, 28, 29, 30, May 1, 2, 3, 4, 5

Luke 18:1
    June 25, 29, 30, July 1, 2, 3, 4, 5, 6, 7

Luke 18:7, 8
    June 26, 27

Luke 23:46
    January 22, 23, 24, 25

Mark 1:4
    March 4, 5, 6, 7, 8, 9, 10

Mark 3:1-6
    February 10

Mark 5:120
    February 12
Mark 8:21
    June 20, 21, 22, 23, 24
Mark 9:37
    January 10, 11
Mark 9:14-29
    February 13, 14
Mark 10:23
    June 18, 19

Matthew 1:21
    February 25, 26, 27, 28, 29,
    March 1, 2, 3
Matthew 5:2, 3, 5
    March 21, 22 23, 24, 25, 26, 27, 28
Matthew 5:4
    March 29, 30, 31,
    April 1, 2, 3
Matthew 5:7, 10-12
    April 23, 24, 25, 26
Matthew 5:8, 6, 9
    April 4, 5, 14, 15, 16, 17, 18, 19, 21, 22
Matthew 5:13-16
    May 6, 7, 8, 9, 10
Matthew 5:26
    July 8, 10, 11, 12, 13, 14, 15
Matthew 5:44, 45
    January 26
Matthew 6:3, 4
    May 11, 12, 13, 14, 15
Matthew 8:28-34
    February 12
Matthew 9:13
    May 3, 4, 5
Matthew 10:26
    December 5, 6, ,7, 8, 9, 10

Matthew 11:25-30
    April 27, 28, 29, 30,
    May 1, 2, 3, 4, 5
Matthew 12:9-14
    February 10
Matthew 13:14, 15
    July 9
Matthew 17:14-20
    February 13, 14
Matthew 18:10
    April 27, 28, 29, 30,
    May 1, 2, 3, 4, 5
Matthew 20:38
    January 27, 28, 29
Matthew 27:46
    January 17, 18, 19, 20, 21

Philippians 3:8, 9
    December 3, 4

Psalm 30:5
    June 17
Psalm 62:12
    October 24, 25, 26, 27, 29, 30, 31,
    November 1, 2, 3, 4, 5, 6, 7,

Revelation 1:17, 18
    August 12, 13, 14
Revelation 2:17
    January 13, 14, 15
Revelation 3:20
    January 2, 3

Romans 8:19
    May 16, 17, 18, 19, 20, 21, 22, 23, 24, 25, 26, 27
Romans 8:15
    July 16, 17, 18, 19

SUPPORTING SCRIPTURE PASSAGES BY MONTH

JANUARY

1: Matt. 11:25-30
2: Rev. 3:14-22
3. Psalms. 91:1-4
4. Isa. 35:10
5. Psalms 33:14-15
6. Eph 3:14-19
7. Psalms 18: 20-28
8. Heb. 12:18-29
9. Isa. 45:20 -25
10. Mark 9:33-37
11. Acts 17:22-28
12. Eph. 6:1-4
13. Rev. 2:12-17
14. Psalms 91:9-16
15 Psalms 19:7-11
16. Psalms 119:9-16
17. Psalms 22:1-11
18. Isa. 53:1-6
19. Psalms 42:5-11
20. Heb. 12:1-3
21. Phil. 3:12-16
22. Isa. 55:1-7
23. Rom 12:1-2
24. Psalms 23
25. Heb. 4:14-16
26. Matt. 5:43-48
27. Luke 20:27-40
28. I Cor. 15:35-49
29: Dan. 12:1-4
30. Gal. 1:6-10
31. John 8:31-47

FEBRUARY

1: Gal. 3:1-9
2: I Cor. 1:4-9
3: II Pet. 1:3-9
4. John 2:1-11
5. Phil 4:10-20
6. I Kings 19:9-13
7. Isa. 35:3-10
8. Rev. 21:1 -4
9. Psalms 130:5-8
10. Matt. 12:9-14
11. Psalms 36:5-10
12. Luke 8:26-39
13. Mark 9:14-29
14. Eph. 4: 29-32
15. I Cor. 2:6-12
16. Matt. 7:7-12
17. I John 2:1-2
18. Psalms 19:1-5
19. John 14:25-27
20. Isa. 6:1-3
21. John 15:14-17
22. Joshua 1:5-9
23. Micah 6:8
24. Job 37:1-13
25. Isa. 59:1-2
26. Heb. 12:4-12
27. John 5:14
28. Luke 13:34
29. Matt. 15:16-20

MARCH

1. Isa. 63:7-10
2. John 6:66-68
3. Col 3:5-10
4. Rom. 13:11-14
5. Rev. 2:4-7
6. I Thess. 4:3-8
7. II Cor. 5:21
8. Luke 4:1-13
9. Psalms 32
10. Col. 3:15-17
11. Heb. 13: 12-14
12. Matt. 13:1-9
13. John 16:12-15
14. Isa. 61:1-3
15. Phil. 4:4-7
16. Heb. 10:19-23
17. I Cor. 1:20-25
18. I Cor. 1: 26 -31
19. Rom. 2:28-29
20. Jer. 15:16
21. Psalms 119:9-11
22. Isa. 55:8-9
23. Isa. 6:5
24. I Pet. 5:5,6
25. Eph. 4:1-2
26. Phil. 2:1-5
27. Luke 12:13-21
28. Luke 12:27-34
29. John 14:1- 4
30. Heb. 12:22-24
31. I John 3:1-3

APRIL

1. II Cor. 3:18
2. Eph. 4:32
3. II Cor. 1:3-4
4. Psalms 63:1-3
5. Psalms 17:15
6. Isa. 27:14
7. Jer. 10:23
8. I Pet. 5:10
9. Matt. 11:29
10. Prov. 3:5-6
11. II Sam. 22:31 -36
12. Luke 12:1-3
13. Eze. 33:11
14. Phil. 4:8-9
15. Psalms 18:20-26
16. Rom. 8:37 -39
17. Psalms 42:1-2
18. Luke 18:1-8
19. James 3:17-18
20. James 4:10
21: Rom. 16:17-18
22. Luke 11:11-13
23. Matt. 25:31-46
24. Matt. 5:43-48
25. Matt. 20:25-28
26. Matt. 24:9-14
27. I Cor. 1:20-21
28. Matt. 7:21-23
29. II Cor. 3:6
30. Matt. 18:3-4

MAY

1. Heb. 2:1-4
2. Matt. 28:18-20
3. Col. 3:17
4. John 16:33
5. II Cor. 4:7-10
6. Acts. 4:13
7. II Tim. 2:15
8. Gal. 2:20
9. John 15:5
10. James 2:1-4
11. Luke 17:7-10
12. Matt. 10:40-42
13. Phil. 1:9-11
14. Heb. 12:1-3
15. Phil. 3:12-15
16. James 4:7-10
17. Isa. 11:6-9
18. Eph. 3:20-21
19. Psa. 37:4
20. I John 3:2
21: Isa. 45:5-8
22. Col. 1:12-14
23. Hos. 2:18
24. Isa. 65:25
25. Isa. 65:17-23
26. I Cor. 15:42-49
27. Gal. 4:1-7
28. Luke 6:46-49
29. John 14:6
30. John 11:25
31. Isa. 42:1-4

JUNE

1. Isa. 1:11-13
2. Eph. 1:18-21
3. Luke 5:4 -11
4. Luke 5:27-32
5. I John 3:14-15
6. I Peter 3:17-18
7. II Cor. 4:7
8. Phil. 1:20-21
9. Phil. 3:7-9
10. John 16:7
11. I Peter 1:5-8
12. I Cor. 2:9
13. Heb. 12:22-24
14. Matt. 23:9-12
15. Luke 12:47-48
16. Lam. 3:25-33
17. Heb. 12:11
18. Acts 10:34-35
19. Matt. 6:24
20. Phil. 4:19
21. Matt. 16:8-11
22. Psalms 16:1-2
23. Job. 1:20-22
24. Matt. 6:25 -27
25. Phil. 4:6-7
26. II Cor. 4:17-18
27. James 4:1-3
28. Luke 11:13
29. Psalms 27:7 -11
30. Psalms 40:7-8

JULY

1. John 14:13-14
2. Psalms 91:14-16
3. Isa. 55:8-9
4. James 4:16
5. Psalms 106:15
6. Psalms 27:14
7. Psalms 18:16-19
8. John 7:17
9. Matt. 6:22-23
10. Matt. 18:15-17
11. II Cor. 5:21
12. I Peter. 1:13-16
13. Rom. 13:8-10
14. Matt. 25:29-30
15. Psalms 86:8-11
16. Phil. 2:3-5
17. Isa. 64:8
18. Heb. 12:22-23
19. Isa. 51:11
20. I Cor. 2:14
21. Isa 64:6
22. Prov. 23:26
23. Psalms 14:1
24. Psalms 50:21
25. Gal. 1:6-9
26. I Tim. 2:4
27. Matt. 20:29-34
28. Rom. 9:1-2
29. Heb. 11:6
30. Matt. 25:40
31. Psalms 40:1-3

AUGUST

1. Psalms 32:8-9
2. Isa. 65:17-19
3. Col 3:9-11
4. Rom. 3:23-26
5. John 10:10
6. Prov. 4:18
7. II Cor. 20:17
8. II Cor. 9:10
9. Psalms 18:31-35
10. John 17:20-21
11. Matt. 13:22
12. I Thess. 3:12
13. Heb. 12:28-29
14. II Cor. 4:6
15. I Peter 1:6 -7
16. Psalms 4:1-3
17. Psalms 145:17-19
18. Isa. 45:18-22
19. Isa. 45:23-25
20. John 14:9-10
21. Psalms 8:3-5
22. Rom. 11:32
23. Psalms 22:26-31
24. Psalms 33:20-22
25. Isa. 40:26-28
26. Psalms 18:30-32
27. Job. 13:15
28. Lam. 3:25-33
29. Psalms 16:11
30. Psalms 19:9-11
31. Heb. 4:14-16

SEPTEMBER

1. Col 1:12-14
2. Phil 1:21-23
3. I John 2:15-17
4. Rom. 6:2-4
5. Luke 10:38-42
6. Mark 10:29-31
7. Rom. 12:11-13
8. I Thess. 2:19-20
9. Phil 3:7-9
10. II Cor. 11:4-6
11. John 14:6-7
12. John 6:63
13. John 14:15
14. Phil 2:12-13
15. Matt. 21:28-31
16. Luke 10:25-37
17. I Tim 6:20-21
18. II Tim. 2:15
19. Matt. 25:44-46
20. Phil. 3:16
21. Heb. 12:1-3
22. Eph. 6:1-4
23. John 14:15- 21
24. I Cor. 8:1-3
25. John 17:24-26
26. Heb. 12:2-3
27. Psalms 40:8
28. John 14:19
29. I John 5:11-12
30. I John 4:13-16

OCTOBER

1. John 17:23
2. II Cor. 5:14-15
3. Heb. 13:20, 21
4. Rom. 5:5
5. Heb. 9:28
6. Matt. 11:29
7. Matt. 16:24, 25
8. John 8:12
9. Phil. 1:6
10. Rom. 8:9-11
11. I John 5:12
12. Jer. 10:23
13. II Cor. 5:17
14. John 15:5, 6
15. Deut. 30:6
16. Rev. 3:4-6
17. Rom. 6:16-18
18. James 2:26
19. John 10:27-30
20. Rev. 3:15-18
21. Gal. 2:20
22. Psalms 2:6-8
23. Matt. 5:13
24. Matt. 5:25-26
25. II Cor. 5:10
26. Rev. 21:5
27. Eze. 33:11-12
28. Rev. 2:26-29
29. Matt. 25:46
30. Acts. 17:30-31
31. Psalms 86:8-10

NOVEMBER

1. Isa. 53:3-5
2. Gal. 6:7-8
3. Phil. 2:5
4. Psalms 119:46-48
5. Matt. 11:27
6. Heb. 9:26b-28
7. I John 2:2
8. Exod. 33:12-13
9. James. 2:1-4
10. John 14:27
11. Heb. 11:13-16
12. II Cor. 5:4-5
13. Eccl. 3:22a
14. Psalms 33:16-22
15. Phil. 4:12-13
16. Luke 12:15
17. I Cor. 13:1-3
18. Prov. 3:5-6
19. Matt. 10:29-31
20. Rev. 15:3-4
21. Psalms 36:9
22. Gen. 18:25
23. Deut. 32:4
24. John 3:17-18
25. John 3:19-21
26. Rom. 8:1-2
27. Matt. 12:31-32
28. Matt. 25:26-30
29. Heb. 10:36-39
30. Psalms 86:15

DECEMBER

1. John 11:25
2. John 20:17b
3. Eph. 2:10
4. Phil 2:12-13
5. Psalms 145:18-19
6. Matt. 11:18-19
7. Mark 13:13
8. Rom. 7:24-8:2
9. I Jn 4:7-8
10. Job. 42:5-6
11. Psalms 37:4 -6
12. Psalms 19:1
13. I Jn 4:12
14. Psalms 139:7-10
15. Eph. 3:20
16. Rom. 14:23b
17. Isa 65:17-19
18. Rom. 10:14-15
19. Rev. 3:15-17
20. Phil. 2:3
21. Eccl. 3:11
22. Luke 10:36-37
23. Col. 3:17
24. Gal. 4:4-5
25. Phil. 4:19
26. I John 4:19-21
27. Jer. 9:23 -24
28. Gal. 6:7-10
29. James 1:4-5
30. Rom. 8:28
31. Psalms 73:23-26

ABOUT THE EDITOR

Dr. Rolland Hein is a Professor Emeritus of English at Wheaton College, Wheaton, Illinois. He was a student at Wheaton College where he studied under Clyde Kilby, who was responsible for securing the papers of C. S. Lewis and other of the Inklings for the Marion E. Wade Center at Wheaton College. Dr. Hein is the author of several books, including *Growing with my Garden*; *Christian Mythmakers*; *The Harmony Within: The Spiritual Vision of Geroge MacDonald*; *George MacDonald: Christian Mythmaker*; and several editions of George MacDonald's works.

Readers are cordially invited to visit www.rollandhein.com for some additional material, including descriptions of his books and some summaries of lectures he has been giving at the Wade Center, a literary collection in Wheaton that houses the works and papers of George MacDonald, C. S. Lewis, Charles Williams, J. R. R. Tolkien, Dorothy Sayers, G. K. Chesterton, and Owen Barfield, as well as related artifacts. See http://www.wheaton.edu/wadecenter. He also maintains a blog, www.drhein.blogspot.com.

OTHER TITLES OF INTEREST

C. S. Lewis

C. S. Lewis: Views From Wake Forest - Essays on C. S. Lewis
Michael Travers, editor

Contains sixteen scholarly presentations from the international C. S. Lewis convention in Wake Forest, NC. Walter Hooper shares his important essay "Editing C. S. Lewis," a chronicle of publishing decisions after Lewis' death in 1963.

"Scholars from a variety of disciplines address a wide range of issues. The happy result is a fresh and expansive view of an author who well deserves this kind of thoughtful attention."
Diana Pavlac Glyer, author of *The Company They Keep*

The Hidden Story of Narnia:
A Book-By-Book Guide to Lewis' Spiritual Themes
Will Vaus

A book of insightful commentary equally suited for teens or adults – Will Vaus points out connections between the *Narnia* books and spiritual/biblical themes, as well as between ideas in the *Narnia* books and C. S. Lewis' other books. Learn what Lewis himself said about the overarching and unifying thematic structure of the Narnia books. That is what this book explores; what C. S. Lewis called "the hidden story" of Narnia. Each chapter includes questions for individual use or small group discussion.

Why I Believe in Narnia:
33 Reviews and Essays on the Life and Work of C. S. Lewis
James Como

Chapters range from reviews of critical books, documentaries and movies to evaluations of Lewis' books to biographical analysis.

"A valuable, wide-ranging collection of essays by one of the best informed and most acute commentators on Lewis' work and ideas."
Peter Schakel, author of *Imagination & the Arts in C. S. Lewis*

C. S. Lewis Goes to Heaven: A Reader's Guide to The Great Divorce
David G. Clark

This is the first book devoted solely to this often neglected book and the first to reveal several important secrets Lewis concealed within the story. Lewis felt his imaginary trip to Hell and Heaven was far better than his book *The Screwtape Letters*, which has become a classic. Clark is an ordained minister who has taught courses on Lewis for more than 30 years and is a New Testament and Greek scholar with a Doctor of Philosophy degree in Biblical Studies from the University of Notre Dame. Readers will discover the many literary and biblical influences Lewis utilized in writing his brilliant novel.

MORE INFORMATION AT WWW.WINGEDLIONPRESS.COM

C. S. Lewis & Philosophy as a Way of Life
Adam Barkman

C. S. Lewis is rarely thought of as a "philosopher" per se despite having both studied and taught philosophy for several years at Oxford. Lewis's long journey to Christianity was essentially philosophical – passing through seven different stages. This 624 page book is an invaluable reference for C. S. Lewis scholars and fans alike

C. S. Lewis: His Literary Achievement
Colin Manlove

"This is a positively brilliant book, written with splendor, elegance, profundity and evidencing an enormous amount of learning. This is probably not a book to give a first-time reader of Lewis. But for those who are more broadly read in the Lewis corpus this book is an absolute gold mine of information. The author gives us a magnificent overview of Lewis' many writings, tracing for us thoughts and ideas which recur throughout, and at the same time telling us how each book differs from the others. I think it is not extravagant to call C. S. Lewis: His Literary Achievement a tour de force."
    Robert Merchant, *St. Austin Review*, Book Review Editor

Mythopoeic Narnia:
Memory, Metaphor, and Metamorphoses in The Chronicles of Narnia
Salwa Khoddam

Dr. Khoddam, the founder of the C. S. Lewis and Inklings Society (2004), has been teaching university courses using Lewis' books for over 25 years. Her book offers a fresh approach to the Narnia books based on an inquiry into Lewis' readings and use of classical and Christian symbols. She explores the literary and intellectual contexts of these stories, the traditional myths and motifs, and places them in the company of the greatest Christian mythopoeic works of Western literature. In Lewis' imagination, memory and metaphor interact to advance his purpose – a Christian metamorphosis. *Mythopoeic Narnia* helps to open the door for readers into the magical world of the Western imagination.

Speaking of Jack: A C. S. Lewis Discussion Guide
Will Vaus

C. S. Lewis societies have been forming around the world since the first one started in New York City in 1969. Will Vaus has started and led three groups himself. *Speaking of Jack* is the result of Vaus' experience in leading those Lewis societies. Included here are introductions to most of Lewis' books as well as questions designed to stimulate discussion about Lewis' life and work. These materials have been "road-tested" with real groups made up of young and old, some very familiar with Lewis and some newcomers. *Speaking of Jack* may be used in an existing book discussion group, to start a C. S. Lewis society, or to guide your own exploration of Lewis' books.

George MacDonald

Diary of an Old Soul & The White Page Poems
George MacDonald and Betty Aberlin

The first edition of George MacDonald's book of daily poems included a blank page opposite each page of poems. Readers were invited to write their own reflections on the "white page." MacDonald wrote: "Let your white page be ground, my print be seed, growing to golden ears, that faith and hope may feed." Betty Aberlin responded to MacDonald's invitation with daily poems of her own.

"Betty Aberlin's close readings of George MacDonald's verses and her thoughtful responses to them speak clearly of her poetic gifts and spiritual intelligence."
    Luci Shaw, poet

George MacDonald: Literary Heritage and Heirs
Roderick McGillis, editor

This latest collection of 14 essays sets a new standard that will influence MacDonald studies for many more years. George MacDonald experts are increasingly evaluating his entire corpus within the nineteenth century context.

"This comprehensive collection represents the best of contemporary scholarship on George MacDonald."
    Rolland Hein, author of *George MacDonald: Victorian Mythmaker*

In the Near Loss of Everything: George MacDonald's Son in America
Dale Wayne Slusser

In the summer of 1887, George MacDonald's son Ronald, newly engaged to artist Louise Blandy, sailed from England to America to teach school. The next summer he returned to England to marry Louise and bring her back to America. On August 27, 1890, Louise died, leaving him with an infant daughter. Ronald once described losing a beloved spouse as "the near loss of everything". Dale Wayne Slusser unfolds this poignant story with unpublished letters and photos that give readers a glimpse into the close-knit MacDonald family.

A Novel Pulpit: Sermons From George MacDonald's Fiction
David L. Neuhouser

"In MacDonald's novels, the Christian teaching emerges out of the characters and story line, the narrator's comments, and inclusion of sermons given by the fictional preachers. The sermons in the novels are shorter than the ones in collections of MacDonald's sermons and so are perhaps more accessible for some. In any case, they are both stimulating and thought-provoking. This collection of sermons from ten novels serve to bring out the 'freshness and brilliance' of MacDonald's message."
    From the author's introduction

Behind the Back of the North Wind:
Critical Essays on George MacDonald's Classic Children's Book
John Pennington and Roderick McGillis, editors

The unique blend of fairy tale atmosphere and social realism in this novel laid the groundwork for modern fantasy literature. Sixteen essays by various authors are accompanied by an instructive introduction, extensive index, and beautiful illustrations.

Shadows and Chivalry:
C. S. Lewis and George MacDonald on Suffering, Evil, and Goodness
Jeff McInnis

Shadows and Chivalry studies the influence of George MacDonald, a nineteenth-century Scottish novelist and fantasy writer, upon one of the most influential writers of modern times, C.S. Lewis – the creator of Narnia, literary critic, and best-selling apologist. This study attempts to trace the overall affect of MacDonald's work on Lewis's thought and imagination. Without ever ceasing to be a story of one man's influence upon another, the study also serves as an exploration of each writer's thought on, and literary visions of, good and evil.

Christian Living

The Living Word of the Living God:
A Beginner's Guide to Reading and Understanding the Bible
Rev. Tom Furrer

This book is based on over 20 years experience of teaching the Bible to confirmation classes at Episcopal churches in Connecticut. Chapters from Genesis to Revelation.

Keys to Growth: Meditations on the Acts of the Apostles
Will Vaus

Every living things or person requires certain ingredients in order to grow, and if a thing or person is not growing, it is dying. *The Acts of the Apostles* is a book that is all about growth. Will Vaus has been meditating and preaching on *Acts* for the past 30 years. In this volume, he offers the reader forty-one keys from the entire book of Acts to unlock spiritual growth in everyday life.

Open Before Christmas: Devotional Thoughts For The Holiday Season
Will Vaus

Vaus seeks to deepen the reader's knowledge of Advent and Christmas leading up to Epiphany. Readers are provided with devotional thoughts for each day that help them to experience this part of the Church Year perhaps in a more spiritually enriching way than ever before.

"Seasoned with inspiring, touching, and sometimes humorous illustrations .... I found his writing immediately engaging and, the more I read, the more I liked it."
　　　　The Rev. David Beckmann, Founder of The C.S. Lewis Society of Chattanooga

Called to Serve: Life as a Firefighter-Deacon
Deacon Anthony R. Surozenski

Called to Serve is the story of one man's dream to be a firefighter. But dreams have a way of taking detours – so Tony Surozenski became a teacher and eventually a volunteer firefighter. And when God enters the picture, Tony is faced with a choice. Will he give up firefighting to follow another call? After many years, Tony's two callings are finally united – in service as a fire chaplain at Ground Zero after the 9-11 attacks and in other ways he could not have imagined. Tony is Chief Chaplain's aid for the Massachusetts Corp of Fire Chaplains and Director for the Office of the Diaconate of the Diocese of Worchester, Massachusetts.

Harry Potter

The Order of Harry Potter: The Literary Skill of the Hogwarts Epic
Colin Manlove

Colin Manlove, a popular conference speaker and author of over a dozen books, has earned an international reputation as an expert on fantasy and children's literature. His book, *From Alice to Harry Potter*, is a survey of 400 English fantasy books. In *The Order of Harry Potter*, he compares and contrasts *Harry Potter* with works by "Inklings" writers J.R.R. Tolkien, C.S. Lewis and Charles Williams; he also examines Rowling's treatment of the topic of imagination; her skill in organization and the use of language; and the book's underlying motifs and themes.

Harry Potter & Imagination: The Way Between Two Worlds
Travis Prinzi

Imaginative literature places a reader between two worlds: the story world and the world of daily life, and challenges the reader to imagine and to act for a better world. Starting with discussion of Harry Potter's more important themes, *Harry Potter & Imagination* takes readers on a journey through the transformative power of those themes for both the individual and for culture by placing Rowling's series in its literary, historical, and cultural contexts.

Repotting Harry Potter: A Professor's Guide for the Serious Re-Reader
Rowling Revisited: Return Trips to Harry, Fantastic Beasts, Quidditch, & Beedle the Bard
James W. Thomas

In *Repotting Harry Potter* and his sequel book *Rowling Revisited*, Dr. James W. Thomas points out the humor, puns, foreshadowing and literary parallels in the Potter books. In *Rowling Revisited*, readers will especially find useful three extensive appendixes – "Fantastic Beasts and the Pages Where You'll Find Them," "Quidditch Through the Pages," and "The Books in the Potter Books." Dr. Thomas makes re-reading the Potter books even more rewarding and enjoyable.

The Deathly Hallows Lectures:
The Hogwarts Professor Explains Harry's Final Adventure
John Granger

In *The Deathly Hallows Lectures*, John Granger reveals the finale's brilliant details, themes, and meanings. *Harry Potter* fans will be surprised by and delighted with Granger's explanations of the three dimensions of meaning in *Deathly Hallows*. Ms. Rowling has said that alchemy sets the "parameters of magic" in the series; after reading the chapter-length explanation of *Deathly Hallows* as the final stage of the alchemical Great Work, the serious reader will understand how important literary alchemy is in understanding Rowling's artistry and accomplishment.

Sociology and Harry Potter: 22 Enchanting Essays on the Wizarding World
Jenn Simms, editor

Modeled on an Introduction to Sociology textbook. this books is not simply about the series, but also used the series to facilitate reader's understanding of the discipline of sociology and a development of a sociological approach to viewing social reality. It is a case of high quality academic scholarship written in a form and on a topic accessible to non-academics. As such, it is written to appeal to Harry Potter fans and the general reading public. Contributors include professional sociologists from eight countries.

Harry Potter, Still Recruiting:
An Inner Look at Harry Potter Fandom
Valerie Frankel, editor

The Harry Potter phenomenon has created a new world: one of Quidditch in the park, lightning earrings, endless parodies, a new genre of music, and fan conferences of epic proportions. This book attempts to document everything - exploring costuming, crafting, gaming, and more, with essays and interviews straight from the multitude of creators. From children to adults, fans are delighting the world with an explosion of captivating activities and experiences, all based on Rowling's delightful series.

Hog's Head Conversations: Essays on Harry Potter
Travis Prinzi, editor

Ten fascinating essays on Harry Potter are divided into five sections: Conversations on 1) Literary Value, 2) Eternal Truth, 3) Imagination, 4) Literary Criticism, and 5) Characters. Contributors include the following popular Potter writers and speakers: John Granger, James W. Thomas, Colin Manlove, and Travis Prinzi.

Fiction

The Iona Conspiracy (from The Remnant Chronicles book series)
Gary Gregg

Readers find themselves on a modern adventure through ancient Celtic myth and legend as thirteen year old Jacob uncovers his destiny within "the remnant" of the Sporrai Order. As the Iona Academy comes under the control of educational reformers and ideological scientists, Jacob finds himself on a dangerous mission to the sacred Scottish island of Iona and discovers how his life is wrapped up with the fate of the long lost cover of *The Book of Kells*. From its connections to Arthurian legend to references to real-life people, places, and historical mysteries, *Iona* is an adventure that speaks to eternal truths as well as the challenges of the modern world. A young adult novel, *Iona* can be enjoyed by the entire family.

Poets and Poetry

Remembering Roy Campbell: The Memoirs of his Daughters, Anna and Tess
Introduction by Judith Lütge Coullie, editor
Preface by Joseph Pearce

Anna and Teresa Campbell were the daughters of the handsome young South African poet and writer, Roy Campbell (1901-1957), and his beautiful English wife, Mary Garman. In their frank and moving memoirs, Anna and Tess recall the extraordinary, and often very difficult, lives they shared with their exceptional parents. The book includes over 50 photos, 344 footnotes, a timeline of Campbell's life, and a complete index.

In the Eye of the Beholder: How to See the World Like a Romantic Poet
Louis Markos

Born out of the French Revolution and its radical faith that a nation could be shaped and altered by the dreams and visions of its people, British Romantic Poetry was founded on a belief that the objects and realities of our world, whether natural or human, are not fixed in stone but can be molded and transformed by the visionary eye of the poet. Unlike many of the books written on Romanticism, which devote many pages to the poets and few pages to their poetry, the focus here is firmly on the poems themselves. The author thereby draws the reader intimately into the life of these poems. A separate bibliographical essay is provided for readers listing accessible biographies of each poet and critical studies of their work.

The Cat on the Catamaran: A Christmas Tale
John Martin

Here is a modern-day parable of a modern-day cat with modern-day attitudes. Riverboat Dan is a "cool" cat on a perpetual vacation from responsibility. He's *The Cat on the Catamaran* – sailing down the river of life. Dan keeps his guilty conscience from interfering with his fun until he runs into trouble. But will he have the courage to believe that it's never too late to change course? (For ages 10 to adult)

"*This book is a joy, and as companionable as a good-natured cat.*"
   Walter Hooper, author of *C. S. Lewis: Companion and Guide*

The Half Blood Poems
Inspired by the Stories of J.K. Rowling
Christine Lowther

Like Harry Potter, Christine's poetry can soar above the tragic to discover the heroic and beautiful in such poems as "Neville, Unlikely Rebel," "For Our Wide-Armed Mothers," and "A Boy's Hands." There are 71 poems divided into seven chapters that correspond to the seven books. Fans of Harry Potter will experience once again many of the emotions they felt reading the books – emotions presented most effectively through a poet's words.

Pop Culture

To Love Another Person: A Spiritual Journey Through Les Miserables
John Morrison

The powerful story of Jean Valjean's redemption is beloved by readers and theatergoers everywhere. In this companion and guide to Victor Hugo's masterpiece, author John Morrison unfolds the spiritual depth and breadth of this classic novel and broadway musical.

Through Common Things: Philosophical Reflections on Popular Culture
Adam Barkman

"Barkman presents us with an amazingly wide-ranging collection of philosophical reflections grounded in the everyday things of popular culture – past and present, eastern and western, factual and fictional. Throughout his encounters with often surprising subject-matter (the value of darkness?), he writes clearly and concisely, moving seamlessly between Aristotle and anime, Lord Buddha and Lord Voldemort.... This is an informative and entertaining book to read!"
　　　　　Doug Bloomberg, Professor of Philosophy, Institute for Christian Studies

Above All Things: Essays on Christian Ethics and Popular Culture
Adam Barkman

"Whether discussing Winnie the Pooh or The Walking Dead, this book digs up buried philosophical treasure. Those who don't normally think of themselves as philosophically inclined will be surprised and delighted as Barkman rescues philosophy from dry classroom abstractions and reveals how it fills the glorious messiness of everyday life."
　　　　　Dr. Kevin Flatt, Assistant Professor of History, Redeemer University College

Spotlight:
A Close-up Look at the Artistry and Meaning of Stephenie Meyer's Twilight Novels
John Granger

Stephenie Meyer's *Twilight* saga has taken the world by storm. But is there more to *Twilight* than a love story for teen girls crossed with a cheesy vampire-werewolf drama? *Spotlight* reveals the literary backdrop, themes, artistry, and meaning of the four Bella Swan adventures. *Spotlight* is the perfect gift for serious *Twilight* readers.

Virtuous Worlds: The Video Gamer's Guide to Spiritual Truth
John Stanifer

Popular titles like *Halo 3* and *The Legend of Zelda: Twilight Princess* fly off shelves at a mind-blowing rate. John Stanifer, an avid gamer, shows readers specific parallels between Christian faith and the content of their favorite games. Written with wry humor (including a heckler who frequently pokes fun at the author) this book will appeal to gamers and non-gamers alike. Those unfamiliar with video games may be pleasantly surprised to find that many elements in those "virtual worlds" also qualify them as "virtuous worlds."

www.ingramcontent.com/pod-product-compliance
Lightning Source LLC
Chambersburg PA
CBHW020349080526
44584CB00014B/953